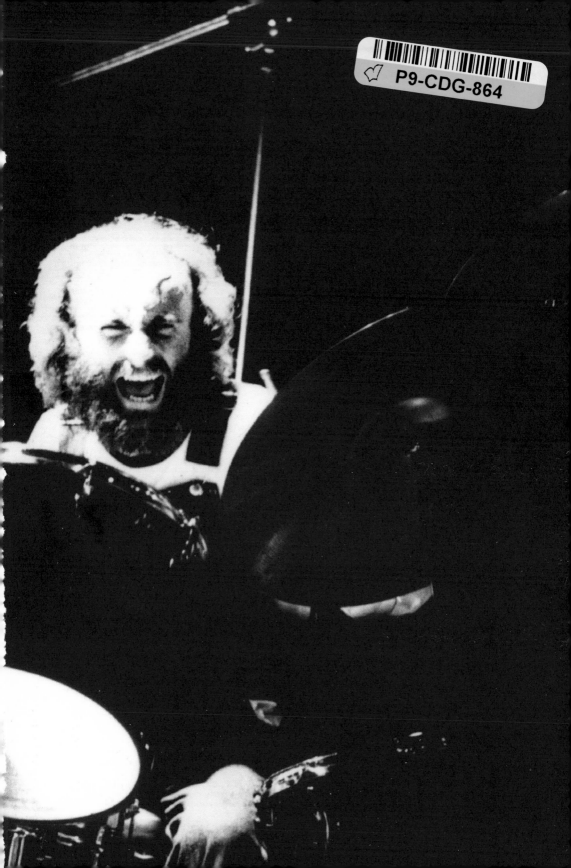

Not Dead Yet

Not Dead Yet

The Memoir

Phil Collins

Crown Archetype
New York

Library of Congress Cataloging-in-Publication data is available upon request.

ISBN 978-1-101-90747-4
eBook ISBN 978-1-101-90749-8

PRINTED IN THE UNITED STATES OF AMERICA

Frontispiece: Aaron Rapoport/Corbis Premium Historical/Getty Images
Jacket design by Christopher Brand
Jacket photograph by Lorenzo Agius
Endpapers: Genesis Archive

10 9 8 7 6 5 4 3 2 1

First U.S. Edition

What you are about to read is my life, as seen through my eyes. It might not comply with the memories of others involved, but it's the way I remember it.

I've held a lifelong belief that we all have our "camera shutter" moments, when we will all remember a scene differently, or we don't remember a scene at all. Sometimes that memory can shape a person's life, yet other people involved don't even recollect it.

PC

CONTENTS

Not Dead Yet

PROLOGUE

Or: Greatest hits and broken bits

CAN'T HEAR a thing.

Much as I try to shake free the blockage, my right ear is unyielding. I attempt a little rummage with a cotton swab. I know this is never advised—the eardrum is sensitive, especially if it's been subjected to a lifetime of drumming.

But I'm desperate. My right ear is kaput. And it's my *good* ear, my left having been dicky for a decade. Is this it? Has music, at last, done me in? Am I finally deaf?

Picture the scene (and readers of a nervous disposition may wish to look away now): I'm in the shower. It's March 2016 and I'm at home in Miami. This is the morning of a very special gig—my first time onstage in years and, more importantly still, my first proper public performance with one of my sons, fourteen-year-old Nicholas.

The kid will be drumming, the old man will be singing. That's the plan anyway.

To rewind a little: 2014 saw the launch of Little Dreams USA, the American wing of the charity that my ex-wife Orianne and I founded in Switzerland in 2000. Little Dreams helps children with tuition, coaching and guidance in the fields of music, the arts and sport.

To get things rolling in the U.S., and to raise some cash, we had long planned a gala concert for December 2014. But in the interim I'd endured a pile-up of health issues. Come the day of the show, I wasn't physically up to singing.

I had to call Orianne, mother of Nic and his brother Mathew, who'd just turned ten, and tell her that my voice was gone and that I couldn't perform. I didn't tell her that my confidence was gone, too: there's only so much bad news you can put in one phone call to your ex-wife. Particularly, maybe, when she's your third ex-wife.

Sixteen months later, I have some making up to do. But 2016 feels like not only a new year but a new me—I'm ready for this gig. I'm not ready to play a full show, though, so we need a cast of supporting artists.

But even with that musical help, I realize that this show is mostly going to be down to . . . me. This is a scenario familiar from forty years of back-to-back touring and three decades of one-after-the-other Genesis and solo albums: I'm being written back into a script that's not entirely of my own making. But I can't bail again. Not if I want to live to see my sixty-sixth birthday.

Some long-standing musician compadres join me for rehearsals in Miami, as does Nic. He knows we're going to do "In the Air Tonight," but once it's clear just how good a drummer he's become, I throw some more songs into the mix: "Take Me Home," "Easy Lover" and "Against All Odds."

The rehearsals are great; Nic has really done his homework. More than that—he's better than I was at his age. As with all my children, I'm bursting with paternal pride.

Reassuringly for me, too, this time my voice feels and sounds strong. At one point guitarist Daryl Stuermer, a wingman of many years' standing, says, "Can I have some vocals in the monitor?" That's a good sign—nobody wants the singer in the monitor when he's sounding crap.

The following morning, the day of the gala concert, I'm in the shower. That's when the ear goes. And if I can't hear, I certainly can't sing.

I call the secretary of one of the many Miami medical experts that I by now have on speed-dial. An hour later I'm at a surgery, a hearing specialist applying his mining-grade suction apparatus to both ears. Instant relief. Not deaf yet.

Onstage that night at the Jackie Gleason Theater we play "Another Day in Paradise," "Against All Odds," "In the Air Tonight," "Easy Lover" and "Take Me Home." Nic, whose appearance onstage after the opening number gets a big whoop from the crowd, handles all of this brilliantly.

It's a wild success, way better—and way more fun—than I thought it would be. Post-show, I end up alone in the dressing room. I sit there, soaking it all in, remembering the applause, thinking, "I've missed that." And, "Yeah, Nic *is* really good. Really, really good."

The feeling of a gig well done is not a sensation I ever expected to have again. When I retired from solo touring in 2005, from Genesis in 2007 and from my recording career in 2010, I was convinced that was it. By then I'd been at it—playing, writing, performing, entertaining—for half a century. Music had brought me more than I could ever have imagined, but it had also taken more from me than I could ever have feared. I was done.

And yet, here in Miami in March 2016, I find it doing the opposite of what it's done for years. Instead of separating me from my kids, from Simon, Nic and Matt and their sisters Joely and Lily, music is connecting me with them.

If ever anything is going to blow off the cobwebs, it's playing with your children. A billion-dollar-payday offer to re-form Genesis wouldn't get me back on the road. A chance to perform with my boy might.

But before we go forward, we have to go back. How did I get here, and *why* did I get here?

This book is my truth about things. The stuff that happened, the stuff that didn't happen. There are no scores settled, but there are some wrongs righted.

When I went back there, looking at my past, for sure there were surprises. How much I'd worked, for one thing. If you can remember the seventies, you clearly weren't on as many Genesis tours as me, Tony Banks, Peter Gabriel, Steve Hackett and Mike Rutherford. And if you can remember the eighties, I'm sorry about me and Live Aid.

It's 2016 and we've lost many of my peers, so I've had cause to reflect on my mortality, my frailties. But also, courtesy of my children, I've had to think about my future.

Not deaf yet. Not dead yet.

That said, these aren't new sensations. I was hit by death when my dad passed away just at the point when his hippie son's decision to reject a life in insurance for a life in music started to bear fruit. I was further blindsided when, within two years of each other, Keith Moon and John Bonham died, both aged thirty-two. I worshipped them. I thought at the time, "These guys are supposed to be around forever. They're indestructible. They're drummers."

MY NAME IS Phil Collins and I'm a drummer, and I know I'm not indestructible. This is my story.

1

NOT DROWNING BUT WAVING

*Or: my beginnings, my childhood and how my
relationship with my dad was a bit tidal*

WE THINK MUMS and dads know it all. But in fact they're making it up as they go along. Every day, busking it, winging it, putting on a brave—sometimes false—face. It's something I suspect throughout my childhood, yet it's only confirmed in adulthood, and only with a little help from the Other Side.

One gray autumn evening in 1977, I go to see a medium. She lives in Victoria, central London, round the insalubrious back of Buckingham Palace, in a flat near the top of a tower block. It's no gypsy caravan, but I suppose it does mean she's nearer the heavens.

I don't have a particular affinity for spirits—that will come much, much later, and be less an affinity than an addiction—but my wife, Andy, is somewhat that way inclined. My mum, too, is no stranger to the Ouija board. At our family home on London's suburban western edges, my mum, nana and auntie, along with my so-called uncles Reg and Len, enjoyed many a happy late-fifties and early-sixties evening summoning the dearly departed from beyond the veil. Better that than the meager monochrome offerings flickering from the newfangled television set.

The reason for my and Andy's visit to this high-rise Madame Arcati: a naughty dog. Ben, our beautiful boxer, has a habit of dragging from under our bed a pile of electric blankets. We're holding on to these for our kids—Joely, five, and Simon, one—for when they stop wetting the bed and need a bit of extra warmth. It has not dawned on me that the folded electric blankets promise more than a toasty bed—bent filaments can break and catch fire. Maybe Ben knows this.

Andy comes to the conclusion that there's a supernatural element to Ben's nightly ritual. He's probably not clairvoyant but there's clearly something we humans don't know.

At this time I'm manically busy, touring with Genesis—we've released our album *Wind & Wuthering* and I have only recently taken over singing duties from Peter Gabriel. I am, accordingly, often an absent husband and father, so I feel perennially on the back foot when it comes to matters domestic and familial. I duly offer no opposition to this unorthodox course of action.

So off to a medium we go. Into bustling Victoria, up in the tower-block elevator, a ring on the doorbell, small talk with the husband, who's watching *Coronation Street*. It couldn't be any less spiritual. Finally he pulls himself away from the TV and gives me a nod: "She'll see you now . . ."

She's an ordinary-looking housewife, perched behind a small table. No sign of any other-worldly virtues. In fact she appears totally normal, in a matter-of-fact way. This completely throws and somewhat disappoints me, and my skepticism now comes with a topspin of confusion, and just a shade of grumpiness.

As Andy's I Ching readings have informed her that it's the spirits on my side of the family that are the dog-botherers, I draw the short straw and enter the chamber of the supernatural. Through gritted teeth I tell the medium about Ben's nightly antics. She nods gravely, closes her eyes, waits for a meaningful length of time, then finally replies, "It's your dad."

"Pardon?"

"Yes, it's your dad and he wants you to have a few things: his watch, his wallet, the family cricket bat. Do you want me to ask his spirit to speak through me? Then you could hear his voice. But sometimes the spirits don't want to leave and that becomes a bit awkward."

I splutter a no. Communication with my father wasn't at its best when he was alive. Talking to him now, nearly five years after his death at Christmas 1972, via a middle-aged housewife in a disconcertingly drab domestic setting in a tower block in the heart of London, would just be weird.

"Well, he says to give your mum some flowers, and to tell her he's sorry."

Of course, being a fairly rational twenty-six-year-old who likes things to be down-to-earth and regimented—I am a drummer, after all—I should have discounted this as mumbo-jumbo con-artistry. But I agree that our dog habitually dragging electric blankets from beneath our bed is behavior possibly not of the mortal plain. On top of that, Madame Arcati has said some things about my dad that she couldn't possibly have known, not least that stuff about the cricket bat. That cricket bat has been part of the Collins clan's meager sports equipment for as long as I can remember. Outside the family, no one would know about it. I wouldn't say I'm convinced, but I am intrigued. Andy and I depart the anteroom of the afterlife and re-enter the real world. Back on terra firma I tell her the news. She replies with a look understood on both sides of the veil: "I told you so."

The next day I phone my mum and relate the previous evening's events. She is blithely spirited, and unsurprised by both the message and the medium.

"I bet he wants to give me flowers," she says, half laughing, half harrumphing.

This is when she tells me everything. My dad, Greville Philip Austin Collins, was not a faithful husband to my mum, June Winifred Collins (née Strange). Having been recruited at the age of nineteen, he was a lifelong employee, like his father before him, of the London Assurance Company in the City of London. "Grev" had used his quotidian, bowler-hatted, nine-to-five suburban commuter's existence to maintain a secret life with an office girlfriend.

Dad was not a particularly obvious heart-throb or lady's man. He was a little tubby round the middle, and his RAF mustache topped off his patchy head of hair. I got all my looks from my mum, clearly.

But it seems that behind that mild-mannered insurance-man exterior lurked something more Lothario-shaped. Mum tells me about a particular incident. Alma Cole was a lovely lady who worked with my mum in the toyshop she managed on behalf of a family friend. Alma was from the north of England and there was always a conspiratorial tone to whatever she said.

She and my mum were close, and one day a slightly miffed Alma sniffed, "I saw you with Grev in the car on Saturday and you didn't wave back to me."

"I wasn't in the car with him on Saturday!" The passenger, patently, was Dad's lady friend, being taken for a romantic spin in our black Austin A35.

Now, nearly five years after Dad's passing, while I find it wonderful that my mum is confiding in me in this manner, hearing these revelations makes me simultaneously mad and sad. I now know that my parents' marriage didn't so much dissolve as fizzle out, partly due to my dad being, shall we say, distracted elsewhere. His infidelity was very much news to me.

But why wouldn't it be? I was a very young boy back then and, to me, my parents seemed deliriously happy. Life at home had appeared normal and quite calm. Straightforward, simple. To my mind, Mum and Dad were happily in love for all their long married life.

But I am very much the baby of the family, almost seven years younger than my sister, Carole, and nine years younger than my brother, Clive. Certain, grown-up aspects of home life would have gone straight over my head. Now, when I consider the facts before me this evening in 1977, I think I can divine an undercurrent of unrest in the house, something to which I was completely oblivious at the time. That said, perhaps I felt it in my water: I was a chronic bed-wetter to an embarrassingly old age.

When I later relay this earth-shattering news to Clive, he gives it to me straight. All those sudden long walks I was taken on by my siblings? Those lazy, hazy strolls past the post-war prefab housing on Hounslow Heath with my brother and sister? Not the cheerfully nondescript norm of a simple late-fifties and early-sixties suburban English childhood. In fact I was being unwittingly complicit in the papering over of cracks.

My father acting a little fast and loose with his marriage vows is something I still have trouble coming to terms with. His disregard for my mum's feelings is beyond me. And before anyone steps forward to state, "That's a bit rich coming from you, Collins," let the record show: I hear what you're saying.

I am disappointed that I have been married three times. I'm even more disappointed that I have been divorced three times. I am considerably less bothered by the fact that these resulted in settlements with my ex-wives to the order of £42 million. Nor am I fussed that those sums were widely reported and are widely known. In this day and age, nothing is private anymore. The internet has seen to that. Additionally, while three divorces might seem to suggest a casual attitude toward the whole *idea* of marriage, this couldn't be further from the truth. I'm a romantic who believes, hopes, that the union of marriage is something to cherish and last.

Yet certainly that trio of divorces demonstrates a failure to coexist happily and to understand my partners. It suggests a failure to become, and to stay, a family. It shows failure, full stop. Over the decades I've done my diligent best to make every aspect of my life, personal and professional, work like clockwork—although too often, I have to acknowledge that my "best" just hasn't been good enough.

Still, I know what "normal" is—it's in my DNA; I grew up with it, or at least the semblance thereof, in the London suburbs—and that's what I strove for while trying to make a living playing music.

I have endeavored to be honest with all my children about my personal history. It involves them. It affects them. They live with the consequences of my actions, inactions and reactions every day of their lives. I try to be as straight and forthright as it's possible to be. I will do the same throughout this story, even in the parts where I don't exactly come out smelling of roses. As a drummer I'm used to giving it some stick. I've had to become used to taking some stick, too.

However, to return to my mum: her stoicism, strength and humor in the face of my dad's straying (to use that very English word) says a lot about a wartime generation who would go through thick and thin to maintain their marriage commitments. It's something we all could learn from, myself very much included.

All that said: when I consider my childhood from the vantage point of my advanced age, perhaps close-to-the-bone emotional upset and turmoil seeped into my young self, without my even knowing it.

I WAS BORN in Putney Maternity Hospital, southwest London, on January 30, 1951, a belated—and by all accounts surprise—third child to June and Grev Collins. Apparently Mum initially entered West Middlesex Hospital to have me, but they weren't very nice to her, so she crossed her legs, left and headed to Putney.

I was the first "London" child, as both Carole and Clive had been born in Weston-super-Mare after the entire family had been relocated there by London Assurance prior to the Blitz. Carole was not best pleased by my birth. She'd wanted a girl. Clive, though, was over the moon—finally, a little brother to play football with, wrestle with and, when all that got a bit boring, to pin down and torture with his smelly socks.

With Mum and Dad aged thirty-seven and forty-five respectively, my arrival made them, for the times, old parents. This didn't bother my mum in the slightest. She remained a generous and loving woman her entire life, without a bad word for anybody until the day she died on her birthday in 2011, aged ninety-eight. That said, she did once call a London policeman a "dickhead" when he chastised her for driving in a bus lane.

Dad, born in 1907, came from then-fashionable Isleworth, a riverside neighborhood on London's western edges. His family home was big, dark, musty, quite imposing, not a little scary. Ditto his relatives. I have no recollection of my paternal grandfather, a time-served London Assurance man just like his son would become. But I do have vivid memories of Grandma. She was warm, embracing and very patient with me, but seemed stuck in the Victorian period, and as if to prove it was permanently clad in long black dresses. Maybe she was still mourning Prince Albert, too.

She and I were very close. I spent a lot of time in her constantly damp below-stairs rooms, watching her paint watercolors of boats and the river, an enthusiasm I've inherited.

Dad's sister, Auntie Joey, was a formidable woman, armed with a cigarette holder and a rough throaty voice, a little like the baddie in Disney's *The Rescuers*: "Dahling, *doooo* come in . . ." Her husband, Uncle Johnny, was also a case. He had a monocle and always wore heavy tweed suits, another Collins from the land that the twentieth century forgot.

Family history has it that a couple of Dad's cousins had been incarcerated by the Japanese in the notorious Changi Prison in Singapore. Great store was put by them—they were war heroes, men who survived the pitiless Far East campaign. Another cousin was apparently the chap who first brought launderettes to England. In Dad's family's eyes, they were all, each of them, "somebody." Or, in other words, toffs. H. G. Wells was said to be a regular caller on the Collins household.

Clearly Dad's family formed his attitudes, not to mention his working life—although after he died I discovered that he had tried to dodge conscription into London Assurance by running away to become a merchant seaman. But the ocean-going rebellion was short-lived and he was told to snap out of it, pull himself together and fall in line under the insurance-salesman yoke imposed by his own father. Conformity was the order of the day. With this in mind, it could be suggested that Dad was a little bit jealous of the freedom the sixties offered Clive, Carole and myself in our chosen fields: cartoonist, ice skater, musician. Call them proper jobs? Dad didn't.

There's little proof that Grev Collins ever got used to the twentieth century. When North Sea gas came on stream and all the boilers in the U.K. were converted, Dad tried to bribe the Gas Board to leave us out of the conversions, convinced that somewhere there was a gasholder that would provide fuel just for the Collins family.

For some reason, Dad loved washing-up, and he insisted on doing this on Sundays after the family lunch. He preferred to do this alone as it got him out of socializing at the table. All would be well until a crash exploded from the kitchen. All talk would cease, and Mum would go to the French windows and close the curtains. Within a few moments of the crash, Dad could be heard swearing hard, and then would come the sound of crockery being swept into a pan. The back door would be loudly hauled open and the crockery scattered noisily into the garden, whereupon Dad would kick it around outside the window, accompanied by more loud swearing.

"Your father's killing the plates," Mum would wearily explain as us silent children found something profoundly interesting to stare at on the tablecloth. Just your traditional British family Sunday lunch.

Dad wasn't ignorant of home improvement, but he had no real interest in it. So far as he was concerned, if things were working OK, then everything was fine. This especially applied to electricity. In the early fifties, the plugs were brown Bakelite and the wires had a woven cord covering. They were somewhat unreliable, and in the back room, where the radio was kept, the main plug at the skirting board would often feed five or six other plugs. Electricians would refer to it as a "Christmas tree." Ours was habitually fizzing, which isn't ever a sound you want to hear where domestic electricity is concerned, and, as the eldest, Clive was always the one chosen to place a further plug into the already overloaded socket. Carole and I would watch with mischievous fascination as he invariably received a mild shock that ran up his arm like a violent tickle.

"That means there's power there. No problem with that," Dad would comment before settling down with his pipe to listen to the radio or watch TV, oblivious to poor Clive and his smoking arm.

Prior to my arrival the family didn't have a car, as Dad didn't pass his driving test until 1952, one year after I was born. It was only his seventh attempt. If the car didn't "behave" itself, Dad would swear at it, believing the malfunctioning motor was part of a plot against him. The iconic scene from *Fawlty Towers* with John Cleese's Basil Fawlty apoplectically thrashing his disloyal Austin 1100 Countryman is an accurate glimpse into our family life.

It was around this time that, armed with his first car, Dad decided to take Carole and me out for a spin in Richmond Park. He also thought he'd use this opportunity to carry out some random safety checks on his new vehicle. I was standing in the back of the car, and all seemed to be normal. Suddenly, without announcement, Dad tested the brakes. I flew forward over the seats at some speed. Luckily the dashboard and my face broke my fall. I still have the scars on each side of my mouth.

Dad was so rutted in the past that, when decimalization was introduced in 1971, he declared that it would be the death of him. The nation's new coinage was a new threat. Taking the long view, I have no reason to doubt that the demise of the shilling did actually help to kill him with worry.

Mum was another time-served Londoner. She grew up in North End Road, Fulham, one of three sisters who were seamstresses. Her brother, Charles, was a Spitfire pilot who had been shot down and killed in the war. One of her sisters, Gladys, lived in Australia and we always exchanged audio tapes at Christmas. She, too, died before I could meet her. Mum's other sister, Auntie Florrie, was lovely, and as a youngster I'd visit her once a week at her flat in Dolphin Square in Pimlico. My maternal grandmother, Nana to me, was a sweetheart, another strong, formative female influence on my young self.

In the early thirties, when Mum was in her late teens, she danced with Randolph Sutton, the music-hall star of "On Mother Kelly's Doorstep" fame, before finding a job in a wine store. Dad's family would always make it clear that he had married beneath him by wedding a shop girl. But after they met on a boat trip at St. Margarets on the Thames, it was love at first sight. They were married within six months, on August 19, 1934. Mum was twenty, Dad twenty-eight.

By the time I came along, just over sixteen years later, the Collins family were living in Whitton in the borough of Richmond-upon-Thames. Then came a large, three-floored Edwardian house at 34 St. Leonards Road in East Sheen, another corner of southwest London.

As Mum was working full-time at the toyshop, Nana looked after me while Clive and Carole were at school. Nana adored me and we formed a wonderfully close bond. On our pram perambulations she'd push me along the Upper Richmond Road, where she'd routinely buy me a penny bun from the baker's. The fact that I have vivid memories of this daily treat speaks volumes about my closeness to my nana.

Dad clearly wasn't one for progress or upheaval, on the surface at least, so much so that when Mum asked if we could move from St. Leonards Road to a slightly bigger, slightly better, slightly less damp house, Dad replied thus: "You can move if you want. But you'll have to find the house for the same money we sell this place for, I'll leave for work in the morning from this place, and I'll come back the same day to the new place, and everything will be moved in." And so it came to pass that Mum, bless her, managed to do that.

Which is how, aged four, I find myself in 453 Hanworth Road, Hounslow—the house that my resourceful mum found and moved us into in the course of one day.

As is the norm, the house you live in when young seems enormous. Visiting it years later can be a shock. How did we all fit in there? Mum and Dad have the master bedroom, obviously, with a small room next door for Carole. Clive and I are at the back of the house, in bunk beds. Our room is so poky we have to go outside to change our mind. By the time I am a teen, there is barely room to conceal under my bed the collection of girlie mags that have somehow come into my possession. We share those quarters throughout my childhood until 1964 when, aged twenty-two, Clive leaves home.

Being born in the early fifties means growing up in a London still recovering from Hitler's hammering. Yet I have no memories of bombsites or devastation of any kind in our neighborhood.

The only time I remember seeing anything like the aftermath of bombing was when the family ventured into the City for Dad's office shows. London Assurance put on plays with their dramatic society, and the family dutifully made the long trip from Hounslow, via Cripplegate, to London's financial district. My memories of those journeys are studded with images of flattened wasteland around the old London Wall, like the scenes in the 1947 Ealing comedy *Hue and Cry*, complete with street urchins playing among the rubble.

In fact the London of my childhood was just like that of those Ealing films, or of my comedy hero, Tony Hancock, inhabitant of the fictional London suburban address of 23 Railway Cuttings, East Cheam. No traffic to speak of, even in central London, and certainly no jams or parking problems—I have home-movie footage taken by Reg and Len of the Great West Road, and you can count the cars that pass by. Droves of bowler-hatted gents trudging over Waterloo Bridge. Teeming football crowds, the supporters flat-capped to a man. Holidays by the seaside—in our family's case, Bognor Regis or Selsey Bill in West Sussex—with the menfolk getting into the beachside swing by perhaps slightly loosening their shirts and ties. At home, the Saturday 4:45 p.m. family ritual of sitting around the telly, tea and toast and dripping to hand, listening to the football scores come in. Glimpsing the wider world via Disney's 1955 film *Davy Crockett: King of the Wild Frontier*, a revelatory moment that launched a lifelong interest in the Alamo.

It's an idyll, of sorts, one that's very much of a time and a place. My time, my place, my tightly defined patch.

Hounslow is in the outer reaches of Middlesex, where capital city meets Home Counties. The westernmost extreme, the last stop, on the Underground's Piccadilly Line. Nowhere near the hub of anything. A 45-minute train journey to the West End. London, but not London. Not quite this, not quite that.

How do I feel growing up at the end of the line? Well, everything is a walk, and then a bus, and then another little bit of a walk, and then a train. Everything is an effort. So you make your own fun. For some kids, unfortunately, their fun is no fun for me.

At Nelson Infants School I seem to be habitually bullied by Kenny Broder, a pupil at St. Edmund's Primary, which is unhelpfully situated right across the road. Like me he's only ten, but he has the face of a boxer, with high cheekbones and a nose that's already seen some action. I dread Broder emerging from his school gates at the same time as I exit mine. He'll eyeball me the whole journey home, silently threatening violence. It seems to me like I'm always picked on—and, it seems to me, always for no reason. Is there a target on my forehead, a "kick me" sign on the back of my shorts?

Even my debut experience with the opposite sex is warped by the prism of schoolboy violence. I take Linda, my first girlfriend, to a funfair on Hounslow Heath, my pockets bulging with the hard-saved coppers that will buy us passage on the helter-skelter of love and/or the dodgems, whichever has the shorter queue. No sooner have we arrived than a chill runs up my neck. "Oh God," I think, "there's Broder and his gang."

Thinking I'll be safer on higher ground, I mount the carousel with Linda. But as the galloping horses rotate, each time I pass the gang are giving me the hard stare, and each time they seem to swell in numbers. As sure as eggs is broken legs, I know I'm in for a kicking. Right enough, as I dismount, Broder swaggers over and wallops me. This cowboy tries not to cry. I go home from the funfair with a blackening eye. Mum says, "What happened to you?"

"I got hit."

"Why, what did you do?"

Like it was my fault.

Still, aged twelve, I manage to break my fight virginity in the park beside my mum's toyshop. We generally congregate here, near a hefty horse trough from days gone by and a slip road where the 657 trolley buses turn around. Because this, remember, is the end of the line.

The park, then, is our territory. I don't belong to a proper gang; we're just a group of young would-be toughs dedicated to guarding our turf. Especially if there are some bigger local lads around to provide back-up.

One day the park is invaded by another group of kids. Some vicious words are exchanged: "'Oo you screwing, moosh?" "'Oo you calling moosh?" It's like the Sharks and the Jets, with less blaring jazz. The baiting goes on, and before long I'm rolling and punching and pulling at another lad. After a bit we just stop. We're not getting anywhere. A score draw. A nose may have bled.

We both feel we've stopped with honor. But then the older lads arrive and insist on pressing home our advantage. They prize out of me the location of the infiltrators. Big Fat Dave—not usually called this to his face, especially by me—sets off to "sort him out." He's oblivious to my cries of "Stop, we agreed it was a draw!" I feel terrible because, from a distance, I see Big Fat Dave jumping up and down on my adversary's bike, parked opposite, just outside the sweet shop. Oh well, at least they won't be messing with Hounslow for a while.

Out here in the suburban sticks you find enjoyment where and how you can. On the downside, this means common-or-garden inter-schoolboy argy-bargy, violence wrought by boredom. On the upside, my mum runs a toyshop, which means I have the pick of the new toys when they arrive. No freebies, just great access. My interest lies in making model airplanes, so when each new Airfix kit comes in, I'm all over them like a Lancaster over the Ruhr.

The environs of the local pub, the Duke of Wellington, soon become a haunt, and I befriend the son of the landlord. Charles Salmon is a couple of years younger than me, but we become fast friends. In our adolescent years we develop shared bad habits, liberating alcoholic drinks from the pub's on-site off-license and, when Charles's big sister Teddy is behind the counter, pilfering cigarettes by the fistful. We repair to his garden shed and smoke till we're sick. I puff my way through cigars, cigarillos, French cigarettes, everything. By the time I'm fifteen I'm smoking a pipe like my dad.

I also become good friends with local lads Arthur Wild and his younger brother Jack. The lives of Jack and me will later entwine: as child actors, we share a West End stage, him playing Charley Bates, best mate to my Artful Dodger in the first staging of *Oliver!* the musical. He will, however, trump me by going on to play The Dodger in Carol Reed's Oscar-winning 1968 film.

So this is my life, here at the end of the line. I don't know what happens even a short way farther up the road. Hounslow ends and then . . . London? It seems another world. The City proper, where Dad works, doesn't feature in my mind at all.

As with any young boy, football looms large in my life. In the early sixties I'm an ardent fan of Tottenham Hotspur, worshipping goal-scoring machine Jimmy Greaves. I can still name the team, such is my affection. But Spurs are a north London club, and north London might as well be Mars. I'd never dare venture so far out of my safety zone.

Brentford FC are the closest big club to Hounslow, so I attend their matches regularly. I even sit in on training sessions, getting known around the ground. Sometimes I go to see Hounslow FC play, but that's very low-key. So low-key that one match day the other team simply don't turn up.

My horizons are broadened somewhat by the Thames. My dad might not display much in the way of passion, but what enthusiasm he does have is focused on matters riverine.

Grev and June Collins are both keen boat folk, and help to run the newly formed Converted Cruiser Club. They're part of a wide, river-loving social circle, which includes Reg and Len Tungay, the so-called uncles mentioned earlier. The brothers have their own boat, *Sadie*. She's another war veteran, a member of the Dunkirk flotilla, and is a craft big enough for us to sleep on, something I do on many a happy occasion.

Most weekends, and many a Thursday (the designated meeting night for club members), are spent in the company of others with boats: hanging out at a temporary clubhouse, or a mooring somewhere, rowing around for pleasure, the proverbial messing about on the river. Or, most of the time, just *talking* about messing about on the river. Soon I share Dad's love for the life aquatic.

There is an annual event, held at Platt's Ait in Hampton, where the club members gather for a weekend with their beloved boats and have rowing races, tug-of-wars and a knot-tying competition. I handle a rope and row a dinghy from a very young age, and am never scared of the water. For a little chap like me this is heady stuff, fostering a great feeling of bonhomie. In today's world it might sound a bit dull, but not in my youth. I even feel it a point of honor that I attend Nelson Infants. As a sidebar to the water and its influence on our family: my dad never learnt to swim. His dad instilled in him a fear of ever being more than waist-high in water. Anything more, and he'd drown. He believed him. And this is the man who tried to run away and join the merchant navy.

One way or another, the Thames plays a big part in my early years. Most weekends, even from a very young age, I'll take out a rowboat and potter between bridges. At this time the Converted Cruiser Club lacks its own clubhouse, so for meetings and socials we use Dick Waite's Boatyard on the riverbank at St. Margarets, where Dad moors his small motorboat, *Teuke*. Eventually Pete Townshend buys the place and converts it into his Meher Baba Oceanic recording studio. I have an old photograph of me in my mum's arms on the very spot, so I made him a copy. Pete, ever the gent, wrote me a lovely, tear-stained letter, thanking me. The photo hung in the studio for many years.

By the late fifties the club is renting a plot on Eel Pie Island for a penny a year. I spend a good deal of my early years first helping build the permanent clubhouse, then joining in the shows and pantomimes put on by the members. I can lay genuine claim to have played this famous venue in the middle of the Thames—the sixties seat of the British blues explosion—long before The Rolling Stones, Rod Stewart and The Who.

Apart from that, I'm still just messing about on the river. But these regular boat-club revues do, eventually, give me the opportunity to play drums publicly for the first time. Footage exists of a ten-year-old me performing as a member of the Derek Altman All-Stars, led by the squeezebox-playing maestro. Carole and Clive are involved, too, performing comedy sketches. Mum also does her bit, singing "Who's Sorry Now?" with some feeling.

In fact, the whole family are part of the waterside troupe. Dad regularly wheels out his evergreen song about a farmer, deploying lots of rude noises to impersonate the animals. I entertain my youngest kids with this song even now: "*There was an old farmer who had an old sow . . .*" (insert various raspberry and fart sounds).

These occasions are the rare times Dad slips off the bowler, suit and tie and becomes a lovable rogue. Unfortunately, I don't have enough detailed memories of my dad, happy or otherwise. What images I have, I later put in a song, "All of My Life," on my 1989 album *...But Seriously*: Dad coming home from work, changing out of his suit, sitting down to dinner, and then an evening watching TV with just his pipe for company. Mum's gone out; I'm upstairs playing records.

Recalling that scenario now, I'm overwhelmed with sadness. There are so many things I could have asked my dad; if only I'd known I'd be just twenty-one when he died. Simply, there wasn't much intimacy or dialogue between us. Maybe I've blotted out the memories. Maybe they don't exist.

Something I do recall vividly is my bed-wetting, and sleeping with a rubber sheet under the cotton one. If I do "have an accident," the rubber sheet simply prevents the wetness from spreading, leaving me to sleep in a small pool of trapped wee. What do you do in this situation? You go and sleep with your mum and dad and then wet *their* bed. This must truly endear me to my father. We have no shower in our small semi-detached house, and early-morning baths are not normally taken, so I fear that for a good few years Dad goes to work every day with a slight hint of urine about him.

Perhaps inevitably, no matter how much he loves the river, Dad can't help but revert to the occasionally insensitive action. I have cinematic proof. A home movie shot by Reg Tungay shows me and Dad by the water's edge on Eel Pie Island. I'm about six. There's a fifteen-foot drop below me into the Thames.

I know now, as I knew well then: this is a very dangerous river. There are fantastically strong undercurrents, and many tidal ebbs and flows. Quite frequently bodies are washed up by the sluice gates at the half-tide bridge at St. Margarets. As all good members of the Converted Cruiser Club are aware, you don't take risks with the Thames.

In this old cine camera footage, you see my dad abruptly turn and walk away. He clearly says nothing to me, offers no warning or concern. He just leaves me teetering on the edge. It's an ugly drop onto the water-lashed, stony foreshore. If I fall, I would badly hurt myself, if not be swept away. But Dad just abandons me there, without so much as a backward glance.

I'm not saying he didn't care, but I believe he sometimes just didn't think. Maybe as he left me hanging on the edge of the Thames, his mind, his emotions, were elsewhere. He was making it up every day.

In adulthood I'd do that, too. Partly in a positive, creative way— I'm a songwriter and performer, and making things up is at the heart of the job description. But also, partly, I concede, in a negative way. As I toured the world incessantly for almost four decades, in Genesis and as a solo artist, I was constantly shoring up a fiction: that I could maintain a solid family existence of my own while maintaining a career in music.

Us mums and dads, we don't know it all. Far from it.

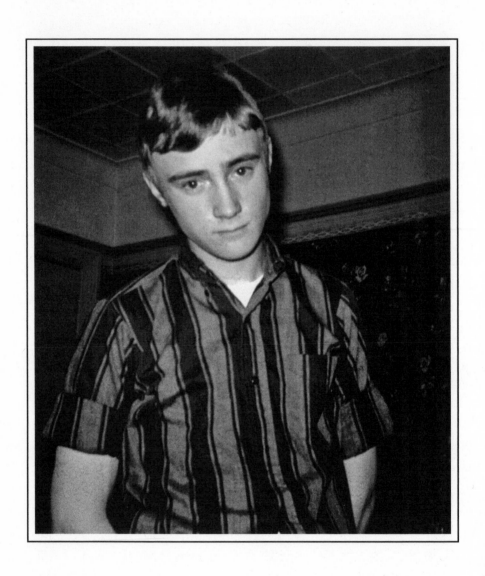

2

TRAVELING TO THE BEAT
OF A DIFFERENT DRUM

Or: a starry-eyed sixties youngster's adventures
hitting the stage and hitting the drums

I
T'S ALL Santa's fault.

Yes, I'm blaming the big red beardy fellow in a bid to explain the roots of a lifelong passion, an instinctive habit that will have me hitting things with varying degrees of relish until the fateful time, some half a century later, when first the flesh and then the spirit start to fail me.

As if I'm not making enough racket as a typically tyrannical toddler, aged three I receive an infant's plastic drum for Christmas. The family Collins are staying, as we often do at this time of year, with Reg and Len Tungay. Armed with this new drum, it's immediately and noisily apparent to everyone around me that I take to it completely. Or it takes to me completely. Even at this early age, I have no doubt about the all-round brilliance of this new toy. I can now "communicate" by bashing things to my heart's content.

The Tungay brothers, frequent visitors to 453 Hanworth Road, especially for Sunday lunch—a weekly opportunity for Mum to assiduously boil all the greens until they're grays—notice my enthusiasm for matters percussive and rhythmic. They're perhaps less mindful of my dad's views on the subject.

When I'm five years old, Reg and Len fashion for me a home-made set-up. Two lengths of wood are screwed into a crosspiece. Each end has a hole drilled in it, into which is pushed a pole. These four poles are topped off with two biscuit tins, a triangle and a cheap plastic tambourine. It's collapsible and fits neatly into a brown suitcase.

To call this a drum "kit" is pushing it. It's more Heath Robinson than Buddy Rich. But I'm in heaven, and this crash-bang-wallop apparatus will serve as both my musical tools and my best friend for several noisy years to come.

I practice wherever, whenever, but usually in the living room when everyone's watching TV. I'll set up in the corner and play along to that late-fifties obligatory viewing experience, the variety show *Sunday Night at the London Palladium*. Mum, Dad, Reg, Len, Clive and Carole sit patiently through my unschooled clatter, trying to watch the latest routines from funnymen Norman Vaughan and Bruce Forsyth, and from whichever pre-rock'n'roll musical turn is guesting that week.

I hammer along with The Harmonics and their massed mouth organs. I supply a boom-*tish* for the comedians' punchlines. I accompany all the Jack Parnell Orchestra's intro and outro music. It doesn't even have to be an act. I'll play to anything, with anyone. I'm a versatile jobbing drummer, even then.

As I approach adolescence my commitment only hardens. Piece by piece I assemble a semi-decent kit. Snare drum is followed by cymbal is followed by bass drum bought from the guy across the road. This tides me over until I'm twelve. Now, on the cusp of my teenage years, Mum says she'll go halves with me on the purchase of a proper kit.

It is 1963, and the sixties are in full flow. The Beatles have landed and the future can begin. Their first single, "Love Me Do," came out the previous October and already Beatlemania has me firmly in its grasp. I make the ultimate sacrifice: I will sell my brother's toy train set to raise my half of the bargain I've made with Mum. It doesn't occur to me that perhaps I should have asked his permission.

Flush with £50, Mum and I go to Albert's Music Shop in Twickenham and purchase a four-piece Stratford kit in white pearl. I am sitting at that kit in the photograph of a thirteen-year-old me on the cover of my 2010 album, *Going Back*.

I feel my drumming game is stepping up, not least because I play whenever possible. I'm sure I must have put in my 10,000 hours before I'm even a teenager, as my neighbors at 451 and 455 Hanworth Road would confirm. When I'm home I drum to the exclusion of pretty much all else, a fact to which the teachers who marked my homework at first Nelson Infants and then Chiswick County Grammar would probably attest.

But I'm no drumming dummy: I do pass my 11-plus exams. That enables me to bypass the then rather bog-standard comprehensive school structure and enter the grammar-school system.

I will admit, though, that for all the time I spend in my bedroom, not much of it is taken up with studying. The Stratford dominates the space and I sit there, endlessly, drumming and drumming and drumming, positioned in front of the mirror. This is part vanity, for sure, but it's also part learning. I've watched Ringo Starr with ardent fascination, and if I can't sound like him, maybe I can try to look like him when he plays. Then, when in early 1964 The Rolling Stones hit number 3 with their third single, "Not Fade Away," fickle youth that I am, I move on to copying Charlie Watts.

But for all my zeal for the drums, I am also developing another interest: acting.

The seeds were sown at those boat-club pantomimes, performed at the Isleworth Scout Hall, when I knocked 'em dead as Humpty Dumpty and Buttons. It was at one of these stellar performances that Dad, dressed as Sir Francis Drake, wandered out to take a breath of fresh air. Next door was an ancient church with a number of open tombs courtesy of Adolf's bombs. Pipe-puffing Dad, shrouded in midnight river mist, looked like a ghost risen from the grave. This apparition was caught in the headlight glare of a passing motorist. Braking sharply and turning on a sixpence, he reported it to the local police. They in turn reported it to the local paper. Cue the headline in that week's *Richmond and Twickenham Times*: "Ghost of Sir Francis Drake seen in Isleworth."

It's around this time that I also have an unfortunate but mercifully brief outbreak of childhood modeling. Alongside half a dozen other adolescent boys, all of us gazing thoughtfully into the middle distance, I star in advertisements and knitting patterns. Possessed of a flicky blond fringe and a cherubic smile, I wear a mean pair of pajamas and am a very good sporter of woolly sweaters.

Still reeling from witnessing my Shakespearean Humpty Dumpty and impressed by my proto-Zoolander modeling brilliance, my eager mum coerces me into spending my Saturday mornings taking elocution lessons in a dour basement in Jocelyn Road, Richmond, taught by a lady named Hilda Rowland. There is lino on the floor, ballet mirrors on the wall and the slight odor of female hormones in the air. Mrs. Rowland has a special friend named Barbara Speake, who founded her titular dance school in Acton in 1945. My mum becomes friends with Miss Speake. At a loose end, having stopped managing the toyshop, Mum starts working with her, launching the school's theatrical agency from our house. June Collins supplies all-singing, all-dancing children to London's West End, and to the blossoming commercial TV and film world.

In these, the early days of advertising on TV, there is always a need for children. The Milky Bar Kid is the choicest role to land. Casting this and many other commercials gives my mum a daily challenge as she decides which child she represents would best fit the bill. She throws herself into this completely, which is how, in 1964, she hears about auditions for *Oliver!* The hit Lionel Bart musical adaptation of Charles Dickens' *Oliver Twist* is now in the fourth year of its blockbuster ten-year run. I go for the part of The Artful Dodger, a role future Monkee Davy Jones has already played and would do so again in the Broadway transfer.

After multiple auditions, and recall after recall, much to the surprise and excitement of my thirteen-year-old self, I'm chosen for the part. I'm cock-a-hoop. As far as I'm concerned, street-smart, wise-cracking Dodger is the best kids' role in the show. Oliver, that simpering goody two-shoes? No chance.

I make an appointment to see my headmaster at Chiswick County Grammar to give him the good news. Mr. Hands terrifies the entire pupil body. He is a stern educationalist of the old school, always sweeping into assembly, his robe flowing like bat wings, mortar board firmly planted on his head, cheeks ruddy and ready for a day's stiff learning.

To go to his office means one of only two things. You're either due a caning, or you have something to impart that had better be highly important. To give Mr. Hands his due, he does seem pleased that I have landed a major part in an important and critically acclaimed London theater production. But it is also his somber duty to inform me that if I accept the part he will have no option but to remove me from the school.

The rules governing under-fifteens working in the West End at this time are strict. The maximum you can perform anywhere is for nine months. This comprises three three-month contracts, during which period children must have three weeks off per contract. Mr. Hands cannot allow such term-time laxity. I will much later discover, via Reg and Len, that he followed my career with great interest and not a little pride. This comes as a shock, as he always appeared so witheringly uninterested in matters of entertainment. On the subject of whether Mr. Hands was more a Genesis man or a Phil Collins man, the jury is still out.

I tell Mum and Dad about his stage-or-school ultimatum, and their response is swift and simple: stage school. They will withdraw me from Chiswick County Grammar and install me in Barbara Speake's newly instituted acting school. Such has been Mum's success running the Barbara Speake Theatrical Agency that she and Miss Speake have turned the dancing school into a fully fledged establishment to teach the performing arts.

In many ways, this will prove a win-win for me. For one thing, I can act as much as I like. For another, at the Barbara Speake Stage School girls outnumber boys by some considerable margin. In the newly formed "student class" there's me, one other boy, named Philip Gadd, and a dozen girls.

In fact, it's a win-win-win. With the priority being firmly on improving performance, taking auditions and winning parts, my formal education as good as ceases at this point. As a not-atypical adolescent boy, to me this is heaven. It's only later that I will wish I'd had a little bit more traditional learning and a bit less ballet. However, I would have liked to have studied tap dancing. It's something that all the great early drummers, legends such as Buddy Rich, knew how to do. Likewise, great dancers like Fred Astaire were also great drummers. The two skills are close rhythmic cousins, and I wish I'd been more interested. Who wouldn't have loved a bit of tap at Live Aid?

When I enroll at stage school I am thirteen. My teenage years start with a bang, in every sense. I'm a drummer, which is hip at school. I'm in a big West End show, which is the envy of my acting peers. And I am one of only two boys in a class literally teeming with girls—girls of an extrovert, artistic bent.

I hesitate to say that I squired my way through the entire pupil body in my four years at drama school, but I suspect there are probably only one or two girls who escaped my attention. I've never been so cool. I'll never be so cool again.

History suggests that I am fourteen when I first have sex. I say "suggests" because it is over so quickly that it might not, in the intercourse scheme of things, count. But as a horny teen in a close-knit suburban neighborhood, your options are limited. By the time you're in a situation where *it* might happen, you'll already be in trouble and out of the starting gate. So it comes to pass that Cheryl—like me, fourteen, and also, like me, a wannabe Mod—and I get down and dirty in an allotment. I didn't intend it to be outside in the mud, in the midst of small plots of potatoes and carrots, but I didn't have much choice.

I had, of course, had a lot of experience of sex as a solo artist. I am embarrassed now to even *think* about this, as it must have been so blatantly obvious to the other family members. Without going into any more detail than needed, I will say that I would often retire to the toilet at 453 Hanworth Road with my big collection of *Parade* girlie magazines. I'm pretty sure everyone must have known what was going on. The paper rustling, if not the other noises, would have been a giveaway.

Resuming normal service: at Barbara Speake's I meet two girls who will play significant and ongoing roles in my life, personal and professional, for a long time hereafter. Over the span of my teenage years either I'm going out with Lavinia Lang or I'm going out with Andrea Bertorelli. The three of us seem to date on heavy rotation, and that back-and-forth will reverberate down the decades.

That first year of my teens is a significant one. In early 1964 I'm told by my acting agent—my mum—to make my way to the Scala Theatre in Charlotte Street in central London. As I travel in on the Piccadilly Line that afternoon, I have no idea what the job is. I guess that's part of the plan, as none of the hordes of teens assembling inside the theater seem to know what's going on. If you want a genuine audience response, you corral a bunch of kids in front of a stage that's empty save for some musical instruments and don't tell them who's about to appear.

That said, I am privy to some insider's intel: I would recognize Ringo Starr's Ludwig drum kit anywhere. But I wouldn't have guessed that The Beatles were making a film.

Suddenly, a commotion in the wings. As if by magic, the stage is busy with Ringo, John Lennon, Paul McCartney and George Harrison, togged out in their fabulous gray mohair suits with the black collars. The Scala Theatre erupts.

This is a performance scene in the film that will become the finale of the Fab Four's debut cinematic feature, *A Hard Day's Night*. When they're shooting us kids in the audience, there are stand-ins onstage. But when John, Paul, George and Ringo are playing, they're only about thirty feet away from me. As a fully-paid-up member of The Beatles fan club, I can't believe my luck. Not only am I out front and center at an intimate gig (of sorts), I am being immortalized on celluloid alongside my first musical heroes.

If only. Master Philip Collins is conspicuous by his absence from the film released in cinemas that summer. My performance that day ends up on the cutting-room floor. Was I not screaming enough?

Fast-forward to the early nineties. The film's producer, Walter Shenson, visits me at Genesis' recording studio, The Farm, in Surrey. It's the thirtieth anniversary of *A Hard Day's Night* and he asks me to record the narration on a "making of . . ." documentary being released on DVD. He sends me the out-takes of "my" scenes.

I freeze-frame several times, intent on finding thirteen-year-old me. Because I know I was there: I'd received my £15 fee and cashed the check; this was not a sadly deluded Fab Four fan's dream. By repeated viewing and peering intently, I find someone I'm convinced is me. I remember the tie I was wearing (red and diamond-studded; thank God the film was in black and white) and a pink tab shirt. The same shirt, incidentally, I'm seen to be wearing on the *Going Back* sleeve. I'm convinced enough for them to put a circle round me on the finished DVD. Here's this young lad just sitting there, transfixed, in among all these kids who are standing up, screaming and quite possibly wetting themselves with excitement.

That's probably the reason I'm not in the film: because I'm not displaying enough Beatlemania. You can imagine the director, Richard Lester, shouting to the editor: "Get rid of that frame, that daft kid's sitting down!" But it's not like I was trying to be cool. I was just utterly flabbergasted to be listening to—watching—experiencing— The Beatles. *I wanted to see this.* I didn't want to scream through it.

This was "Tell Me Why," "She Loves You," "All My Loving," the songs that were firing my fast-forming musical synapses. This, I knew, was the future, my future, and I wanted to enjoy it. Forget bloody acting. That may have been the reason I was there in the first place, but in the scheme of things, I was wholly uninterested.

Later in life I tell this story individually to Paul, George and Ringo (I never met John). The time I presented Paul with an American Music Award at London's Talk of the Town supper club, he said, "Were you really in *A Hard Day's Night*?" Yes, I was. I might not have made it to the final cut, but I was. Little did I know that ending up on the cutting-room floor would become something of a theme for me. Fortunately you can't be edited from a West End show. Well, you can, and I will be, but not for a while at least.

The show timings for *Oliver!* are such that I have to travel to the West End straight from stage school each day. Still, I usually arrive in Soho around 4 p.m. with time to kill. Often I slide into one of the little cinemas scattered all over central London that show cartoons on an hourly rotation. I think they're intended for commuters with some spare minutes before the next train. Unknown to me they have another use. In a Britain where homosexuality is still illegal, men use them as discreet(ish) pick-up joints. One time a guy sidles up during a Loony Tunes 'toon and places a tentative hand on my schoolboy knee. I snarl a "fuck off," and he exits faster than the Road Runner.

Over the coming months I become quite used to this murky side of the West End, and these overtures become almost boringly ritual. My afternoons and evenings develop a happy routine: train from Hounslow, cinema, a mooch around the Soho coffee bars and record shops, and a quick burger in Wimpy. Then I head for the stage door of the New Theatre on St. Martin's Lane, not far from Trafalgar Square.

I hit the ground running in *Oliver!*, because I have to: this is a huge, ongoing and usually sold-out show. There's no time for first-night nerves, even for a thirteen-year-old.

On top of that, this is a big part. The entrance of The Artful Dodger is the moment when the show lifts. This tale of Victorian workhouses and grinding poverty is pretty much doom and despair till the chirpy, light-fingered urchin comes on and sings "Consider Yourself." Then the Dickensian East End of Lionel Bart's picaresque, exuberant imagination bursts into glorious life. Consider, too, that the Dodger also sings wonderful, now-timeless songs like "I'd Do Anything" and "Be Back Soon" with his gang. They're my first lead vocals, and I relish performing them eight times a week, night after night (with matinees on Wednesdays and Saturdays).

There are fringe benefits, too. While I'm treading the boards at the New Theatre, my girlfriend Lavinia is appearing in *The Prime of Miss Jean Brodie* at Wyndham's Theatre just yards away. Their stage door backs onto ours. Our intervals don't usually align, but before the shows go up, there's usually enough time to nip out and meet the love of your teenage life for a quick snog and a cuddle.

I pass my fourteenth birthday while on *Oliver!*, and change is afoot. One night I'm in the middle of "Consider Yourself," belting it out with the requisite cheery, cheeky gusto. Then, from the back of my usually golden throat, a squawk and a croak and my singing voice suddenly gives out. I struggle on manfully, but at the interval I rush to the stage manager. I can't understand what's happened to my voice. I don't have a cold, I've never had any problems singing before, not even an off night, and it can't be the fags. Courtesy of petty larceny from the off-license in Charles Salmon's dad's pub, I'm a pro-smoker of several years' standing.

The stage manager, experienced West End wrangler of many a child actor that he is, gives me the lowdown: my voice is breaking.

Forget any heartening sense that I'm becoming a man, my son. Right here, right now, in the wings, huddled behind the safety curtain, I'm devastated. I know what this means.

I soldier through the second half, but my voice is shot. The entire theater knows it; from beyond the stage-lights, I can sense a shuffling in the stalls. It's a terrible feeling. I hate letting down an audience, a pathological worry that I will carry with me forever. I can count on one hand the number of shows I canceled with Genesis or on my solo tours. Over the course of my career I will do whatever I can to ensure the show goes on—even if that means dodgy doctors, dubious injections, catastrophic deafness and sustaining injuries that will require major, invasive, flesh-ripping, bone-bolting surgery.

Yet that, there and then, is the end of my time playing The Artful Dodger, the best part for a kid in all London. With sentiment-free efficiency, I'm immediately off the show and cast out of the West End and back to the end of the line.

For a hormonal teenage lad ragingly obsessed with all that an increasingly swinging mid-sixties London has to offer, *Oliver!* has been a trip both on- and offstage. During my seven months' happily indentured West End service I get to know the house musicians at the New Theatre. The bandleader is a drummer, and fortuitously he and I take the same train home. We chat. Well, I chat, pumping him for information about the life of a musician, and he patiently replies. I soon see that being a jobbing player, in show bands, in the orchestra pit, in clubs—that's a great career. I'll have that.

At this point I am an entirely self-taught musician. But I realize I need to sharpen up my act if I'm to have any hope of becoming a professional.

I start taking piano lessons with my Great-Auntie Daisy at her musty Edwardian house in Netheravon Road, Chiswick. She's charming, patient and helpful and, to the surprise of both of us, it comes to me easily. Once I hear something, I never have to look at the page again. I have what they call "big ears," which is great for learning songs, less good for learning to read music. This frustrates Auntie Daisy, but she doesn't hold it against me. On her death, I inherit her 1820 straight-strung Collard & Collard. I will record all of *Face Value*, my first solo album, using that piano.

I never do learn to read music, and still can't to this day. If I had, things might have been very different. When I form the Phil Collins Big Band in 1996, to communicate with the brilliant, seasoned jazz players in that combo I have to invent my own phonetic way of doing the charts. They'd certainly be forgiven for thinking, "How can this untutored clown hope to work with the likes of Tony Bennett and Quincy Jones?"

But at the same time, not being able to read music is absolutely liberating for me. It gives me a wider musical vocabulary. There are learned, technically accomplished players who sound regimented, taught and clinical. Maybe a more traditionally schooled player couldn't have come up with an unorthodox song like "In the Air Tonight." If you don't know the rules, you don't know what rules you're breaking.

Nine years after taking receipt of my first kit from Uncle Reg and Uncle Len, I finally decide to take some drum lessons. When I start attending Barbara Speake's, my route to school from Acton Town station up Churchfield Road takes me past a drum shop owned by Maurice Plaquet. This place is a mecca for players from all over London, while Maurice himself is an in-demand session guy, quite a big name in the drummers' world of which I am desperate to be a part. He's too big a fish to school me, so I approach one of his lieutenants, Lloyd Ryan, who teaches out of Maurice's basement.

Lloyd is a flash young guy. He tries to teach me to read music, but again my ears get in the way. Five years hence, in 1971, I'll go back to him for a few top-up lessons after joining Genesis. We're already doing gigs but I figure I'll have another crack at trying to read music. Lloyd attends one of the band's now-famous (among hardcore fans, at least) lunchtime shows at the Lyceum Theatre, just off the Strand.

Onstage I have a Dexion frame supporting hanging bits and bobs: percussion, bells, whistles. A sophisticated but cheap array of noisy stuff. At my next lesson I notice that Lloyd now has the exact same set-up. This is the tail wagging the dog. I don't go to him again.

At the end of the sixties, during another brief West End acting run (back in *Oliver!*, but in a more grown-up role this time, that of cowardly bully Noah Claypole), I take some lessons with a lovely man named Frank King. He teaches in historic drummers' shop Chas E. Foote's, located just opposite the stage door of my then day job in the Piccadilly Theatre. As far as my formal musical education is concerned, that's about it. My lifetime tally of drum lessons has been approximately thirty.

For my teenage self it's more useful to learn on the hoof, in the raw and in the moment, by taking advantage of the hip-and-happening environment that I come to view as very much my playground. As a wannabe drummer in mid-sixties London, I couldn't have picked a better time and place in which to learn my craft. Music is everything and everywhere. By a little doggedness, a lot of luck and a liberal demonstration of enthusiasm, I find myself at the heart of the first great British pop cultural explosion.

The money I'm earning as an occasional actor—I was paid £15 a week for my second stint on *Oliver!*—is entirely spent on my all-consuming hobby. I become an avid collector of records and purchaser of gig tickets. After breaking my 45-buying duck with Joe Brown's "It Only Took a Minute," I swiftly move on to collecting anything bearing the imprimatur of Northern Songs, the publishing company founded by Brian Epstein and The Beatles: "Do You Want to Know a Secret?" by Billy J. Kramer, The Swinging Blue Jeans' "Hippy Hippy Shake" and loads more. My ears burning at the torrent of fantastic music that's suddenly pouring out of the radio, clubs, pubs and bedrooms the length and breadth of the country, I tune in religiously to Sunday afternoon's *Pick of the Pops*, Alan Freeman's hit-parade show, and Brian Matthews' *Saturday Club*, both broadcast on the BBC Light Programme.

With changing tunes comes changing fashion. It's 1966, and I go shopping at I Was Lord Kitchener's Valet at Foubert's Place, off

Carnaby Street, very much the boutique *du jour*. I'm seeking out the military gear that key faces on the scene are wearing, notably two musicians in a new band with which I've become obsessed. Eric Clapton and Ginger Baker are, respectively, cool-as-they-come lead guitarist and mad-as-a-hatter drummer in Cream, a trio history will recognize as rock's first supergroup.

My introduction to Cream comes, ironically enough, in dear old Hounslow. One night in 1966 I'm waiting for the last bus at Hounslow bus station, and I can hear the sound of a blistering blues band punching through the walls of a local club called The Attic. I'm fifteen, and I'm hearing Cream playing songs that will appear on their debut album, *Fresh Cream*, which is released at the end of that year. I never imagine that in time I will become a great friend, sideman, producer and party companion with their already incendiary guitarist.

Yes, of course, 1966 is the year that England wins the World Cup. But for me it's a banner year for another reason: I form my first band with some fellow Barbara Speake pupils. The Real Thing are me on drums, Philip Gadd on guitar, his brother Martin on bass and Peter Newton on lead vocals. On backing vocals we have both the key girls in my life, Lavinia and Andy.

We are drama-school kids, used to slacking off in class and listening to the latest platters by The Beatles and The Byrds while we study, and we go for this with some gusto. Albeit within limits—we don't travel or gig much farther than Acton. Even East Acton is out of bounds. It's lethal for us drama-school kids, as it's the location of Faraday School, which is full to the brim with hard nuts who like nothing better than duffing up a boy who's known to wear tights. Poor Peter, who's black, lives near East Acton station, which is in the danger zone. His skin color means he gets beaten up with extra regularity and extra relish.

Undaunted (mostly), The Real Thing absorb soul music and Motown, and perform cover versions of everything we can find. Essentially we're ripping off the set-list of The Action. They're a group of sharp-dressed Mods from Kentish Town, northwest London, whose slink-hipped 1965 debut single, "Land of a Thousand Dances," was produced by George Martin. Peter and I consider ourselves their biggest fans. I'm still a fan come 1969, when they rename themselves Mighty Baby. In 2000, Mod guru Rob Bailey gives me the phone number of The Action's Roger Powell, probably my biggest drumming influence. I call him and we become the greatest of friends. Due to our friendship, I have the good fortune of joining the reunited Action for a show at the 100 Club on London's Oxford Street. Playing beside my hero Roger, I finally get to meet the entire band forty years after stalking them at the Marquee. I'm not exaggerating when I later tell *The Guardian* that for me it was like playing with The Beatles.

Throughout '66 and '67, Peter and I try to see every Action gig we can at London's best venue, the Marquee. We'll report back to our Real Thing band mates and try to play whatever we've heard: "You Don't Know Like I Know" by Stax's "Double Dynamite" duo Sam & Dave, "Do I Love You" by all-female American soul outfit The Ronettes, "Heatwave" by Martha Reeves & The Vandellas. The words of the songs that we can't follow, we make up. The kids at the school, our usual audience, don't know any better. As if that wasn't enough excitement, in 1967 Tottenham Hotspur win the FA Cup.

We try to emulate The Action in every way. Roger has this fantastic blue nylon jacket. Fanboy and clothes-horse that I am, after some scouring of Carnaby Street's key Mod outlets, I manage to find one just like it. I enjoy it for a couple of weeks, and then my mum washes it. Somehow it gets both shrunk and shredded. It's ruined. For a young Mod, this is a dagger through the heart.

I recover fast. Here at the heart of the sixties, change is the only constant. Week in, week out, I buy all the music papers—*New Musical Express, Record Mirror, Melody Maker*. I pore over every page, notably the gig adverts in the back: I need to know who's playing where and with whom. I even collect these adverts in scrapbooks, which also feature my own handwritten reviews of the shows. Living at the end of the line, what else is an eager, music-obsessed schoolboy to do? In distant adulthood I will show my Action scrapbook to Roger and the surviving members. They are touched to the point of tears. I may have got a little moist around the eyes myself. I will also fund the writing of a book telling their story, *In the Lap of the Mods*, just so I can have a copy myself.

I start frequenting the Marquee, at least once or twice a week, heading for Soho straight from school. I'm usually first in line. Soon the manager, John Gee, is letting me in for free, in return for sweeping up, putting out the chairs and putting up with his harmless advances (and those of his similarly inclined assistant manager, Jack Barrie). "Oh, Philip," he'll sigh, "how old are you again?" They become, over time, great friends to me.

At this stage in the Wardour Street institution's many incarnations, the Marquee has no proper bar. You can only buy Coca-Cola, and that from a small stall at the back. The priority is space for the gigs—1,200 people can be crammed in. This is, I've no doubt, way above fire regulations, but no one cares about such safety concerns, just as they don't care about car seat belts, cigarettes causing cancer and 100,000 men and boys packed on football terraces with no seating or crush barriers. Simpler times. If you survived them.

Presently the Marquee installs a proper bar, which cuts the capacity nearly in half, but not the excitement. These are the days when someone will join a band in the afternoon and be playing with them that night. Jeff Beck joins The Yardbirds one afternoon, Jimmy Page another. I'm in the crowd for both their debuts.

I'm a Yardbirds fan, and when they become The New Yardbirds, I'm also a fan of their drummer, John Bonham. Alongside Roger from The Action, he's my drumming hero. I go to see Tim Rose—I have a soft spot for the American singer-songwriter, and I love his cover of Bonnie Dobson's "Morning Dew"—because Bonham is his hired drummer for the tour. My oldest friend Ronnie Caryl and I still talk about that show at the Marquee—"My God, what was he doing with his foot?" Bonham was incredible.

Being a serious regular, and a serious fan, I am often in the right place at the right time: by following Bonham's progress, at the Marquee I see the first London show by The New Yardbirds, soon to be renamed Led Zeppelin. I witness some floor-shaking, maximum R&B Who shows. I experience Yes in their earliest days, around 1968, when they were good. As with my future friendship with Clapton, I never could have conceived that I would become a close collaborator with teenage heroes such as Robert Plant and Pete Townshend, or that Yes's Bill Bruford would one day help me become a reluctant frontman by taking over the drums in Genesis.

In my mid-teens in mid-sixties London, that present from Santa Claus to the three-year-old me is the gift that keeps on giving. That first child's drum put me on a path that has taken me to the epicenter of a revolution. The drums will continue propelling me, onward, upward, sometimes even sideways. But right now they've kick-started something that's thrumming deep inside my head with increasing agitation.

At this stage I am still a kid. A schoolboy. And a schoolboy who lives way out west, in the increasingly claustrophobic sticks. This starts to get on my pip when it begins interfering with my gig-going. The Marquee evening performance schedule usually goes like this: support band, headliner, support band again, headliner again. I can usually see the first three, but have to leave before the final headliner's set so I can catch the train that gets me home in time for my curfew of 10:30 p.m. Then, on January 24, 1967, Jimi Hendrix plays the Marquee for the first time. The first of the tyro American guitarist's four legendary shows there, this will go down in the annals of rock history as one of the epochal rock shows of the sixties. He is one of the first acts to do one long set instead of two.

As is increasingly usual, I'm first in line to get in, nab a front-row seat . . . but then in frustration have to leave before Hendrix comes on. The last train to the end of the line is calling.

The sooner I can get out of there, the better.

3

"DRUMMER SEEKS BAND; HAS OWN STICKS"

Or: trying to catch a break in swinging London. How hard can it be?

I GOTTA GET OUT of this place. But how? It certainly won't be via *London Assurance*, despite my dad's strenuous efforts to persuade me to carry on the family tradition. I am a time-serving child of the sixties and the nine-to-five is very much not for me, daddy-o.

So via what route do I escape, and by what means? Music is my passion, and London is the global center of the whole scene. Stuck here at the end of the Piccadilly Line, my skill on the drums improving with every practice, it feels like I am so near yet so far. I need an exit strategy, and ideally I need someone to come with me. Luckily, I know just the fellow.

In early 1966, aged fifteen, word reaches me of a kid who's apparently as much a whiz on the guitar as I am on the drums. He's from Hanworth, straight down the road from Hounslow, and he attends a rival performing-arts establishment, the Corona Academy. The inter-drama-school rumor mill has made each of us aware of the other, with each of us considered "cool" by the cliques at our respective song'n'dance alma maters.

I find out where this alleged guitar-slinging hepcat lives, and one summer morning I briskly walk the couple of miles to his house. I knock on the door of his semi-detached, and his mum answers.

"Is Ronnie there, please?"

"Ronnie! There's a boy with a blond fringe and a pink shirt at the door for you!"

A thunder of feet on the stairs and there, looking at me quizzically, is this kid, a little younger than me, with dark curly hair and an interesting mouthful of teeth.

"Yeah?"

"Hi, I'm Phil Collins, do you want to join a supergroup?"

"Well, who else is in it?" comes Ronnie Caryl's reply. I'm instantly impressed. He's not querying the very idea of a supergroup being formed by a couple of adolescents in boring, mid-sixties Middlesex. Conceptually, he's already on board. I like that attitude.

"Just you and me," I reply confidently.

Within a few days, Ronnie and I have started playing in my front room at 453 Hanworth Road, messing around, trying to re-create our fave raves of the day: Cream's "Cat's Squirrel," "Spoonful" and "NSU," Jimi Hendrix's "Hey Joe"—you name it, we're mangling it.

Actually, if I do say so myself, we're pretty quickly pretty decent. I have a tape of Ronnie and I playing for hours on end, and it still sounds rather impressive. Despite the fact that there are only two of us, we're both good players and the combination is full and bluesy.

In due course we add a bass player, a friend of a friend called Anthony Holmes. But it soon becomes clear that while he *owns* a bass, he can't actually play it. This doesn't deter Anthony, though. He just plays very quietly so it's hard to tell whether he can or can't. With our performances confined to my parents' front room, this isn't much of a problem, nor is our lack of a band name. Soon we've learnt almost the entire track listing of *Fresh Cream*. We've also picked up on John Mayall and an impressive collection of old blues tunes. If we're not quite a supergroup, we're certainly a tasty trio.

That said, Lonnie Donegan thinks we're rubbish. The "king of skiffle" becomes the first pop star I ever meet when he comes round to our house one Sunday afternoon to visit my sister Carole—now that she's a professional ice skater, they've met on the road somewhere. I think they're seeing each other, or at least he'd like them to be. He has a listen to one of our practice sessions, sitting on a chair in an extraordinarily long fur coat. He seems a little out of place in this very suburban setting, as does his coat. But when you're the king of skiffle you can do, and wear, what you like, I suppose.

Donegan proceeds to tear us apart. His critique of Anthony is particularly brutal. He asks our hapless bassist: "Can't you sing either?" This does nothing for his confidence but confirms what Ronnie and I already know. Anthony likes the *idea* of being in a band and not much more.

Then Donegan mentions that he might be looking for a drummer, and for a second I see a glittering future ahead of me, helping to prolong a musical revolution that is already, if truth be told, past its skiffle-by date. Unfortunately I fear that in truth Donegan has no intention of hiring Carole Collins' fifteen-year-old brother, if only because I'm too young for the hurly-burly of his frenetic gigging schedule. He does, however, think I'm good enough to offer to shop around for a band that might hire me. But despite his enthusiasm, nothing presents itself.

Shortly thereafter Anthony hangs up his bass forever, but Ronnie and I plow on undaunted. Best pals till we die, our relationship is honest to the point of combustibility. We are no strangers to the horrendous argument, usually after we've had a beer or two. Sometime in the late sixties, Ronnie will find himself minus one tooth, courtesy of my fist. It's not something of which I am proud, nor something I ever do to anyone ever again.

As musical comrades and brothers-in-bands, Ronnie and I will go on to have many adventures together over the ensuing fifty years. At one end of the time spectrum, both of us will try out for Genesis. Further down the line, when I'm making my sixth solo album, 1996's *Dance into the Light*, I am conscious I need a second guitar player to accompany the long-serving Daryl Stuermer. I invite my oldest friend to come to rehearsals in Switzerland.

My band at this time are top-drawer Los Angeles players, shiny with excellent chops and an acceptable level of smoothness. Ronnie at this time is as he always was: an all-drinking, all-smoking, occasionally farting rough diamond. The culture clash is as swift as it is inevitable. The LA contingent embark on a silent mutiny; on a short journey in my car back to their hotel, I'm told Ronnie "doesn't fit in." I retort, "Either Ronnie's in the band, or you're not." Such is my love and appreciation of his skills and musicality, to say nothing of his much-needed humor.

Within a few weeks Ronnie is fully integrated and harmony reigns, as I trusted it would. I tell my oldest friend, "As long as I'm working, you're working." Whenever I need a guitarist, he's my go-to guy. Same as it ever was. Such are the soul-solid bonds that are forged in the furnace of first musical loves. Those bonds will support me throughout my sixties musical finishing school, from bedroom practice sessions to pubs, clubs, holiday-camp gigs and beyond.

Come 1967, The Real Thing are less of a sure thing. The wild enthusiasm we had for our first school combo has morphed into the serious business of becoming professional dancers or actors, albeit less so for me than for my erstwhile band mates. But being a cock-sure sixteen-year-old I'm sure a clear path will open up ahead of me. To be honest, I'm not yet convinced this still-new pop group "thing" will last that long. If it does, it certainly won't involve me. But I'll ride it until it burns itself out; then I'll do some recording sessions for other people. Following a successful run of session work I'll plug into a show band/big band/jazz world. I'm already ears-deep in Buddy Rich, Count Basie and John Coltrane, so this feels like a natural progression. I will then spend the twilight of my life playing in the orchestra pit for one of the top London theater shows. Those players I met doing *Oliver!* all seemed happy enough.

Again, this seems a logical course to take. But it will mean learning to read music. I'll get round to that sometime soon.

Ah, the naivete of youth. It's '67 and I have my sixteen-year-old mind blown by The Byrds' *Younger Than Yesterday* and The Beatles' *Sgt. Pepper's Lonely Hearts Club Band*. These albums, cornerstone moments in the history of rock, are cornerstones of my young life, too. They come out within five months of each other, and everything changes. I start collecting Technicolor dream posters, paint my bedroom black—by now it is solely mine, Clive having left home to get married to a lovely lady, Marilyn, and to concentrate on being a professional cartoonist—and cover one wall in aluminum foil. The freak flag is flying high at 453 Hanworth Road. Getting itchy feet and an itchy attitude, I will gladly sign up for the psychedelic revolution, if they'll have me. Unfortunately I have a prior engagement with a cow on a farm in Guildford, Surrey.

With some experience under my belt, and now that I'm a senior student at Barbara Speake's, I'm receiving quite a few acting offers. Most of them I decline, much to my mum's frustration. But I decide to take a cinema job I'm offered by the Children's Film Foundation, wholesome purveyors of wholesome films for the Saturday morning picture clubs. These have exploded in popularity by the mid-sixties, not least as places parents can safely leave their children while they do their shopping. So what if the little movie is called *Calamity the Cow* and is unlikely to feature much in the way of groovy psychedelia? It means I'll be seen on the big screen by kids up and down the country. It also means I'll earn some money to buy more records, gig tickets and cod-military clobber. Plus, I have the biggest part—other than the cow, obviously.

The filming location is in Guildford, which funnily enough will become my stomping ground some years later, when Eric Clapton and I are country neighbors. But in '67 all Guildford represents to me is a place that seems miles away from Hounslow, and that's the setting for a pig farm so noxious I can smell it to this day.

That balmy Summer of Love it is quickly apparent that I have made an error of judgment in accepting the lead part in this film. As this is a CFF production, intended for Saturday morning entertainment, we have to play things young. Very young. Enid Blyton young. The plot can be summed up as: boy finds cow, boy loses cow, boy finds cow. I should be tuning in, turning on and dropping out. Instead I'm getting cozy with cattle.

To a too-cool-for-school sixteen-year-old drummer and *Sgt. Pepper's* "head," this is mortifying. It's a sensation that doesn't bring out the best in my behavior. Still carrying something of a wide-boy Artful Dodger accent, I decide to play my part with some cocky East End swagger. This doesn't thrill the director. Complicating matters is the fact that the director is also the writer. Not unsurprisingly, he feels proprietorial over his script, and isn't so keen on having his "vision" messed with by a snotty-nosed teenager with his head in Haight-Ashbury and his tongue lolling somewhere within the sound of Bow Bells.

"Ah, Philip," he sighs in his broad Australian accent, exasperated at yet another overly cockney take, "could you perhaps say it like *this* instead . . ."

In the end he becomes tired of me and writes me out: midway through the action, the leading boy mysteriously disappears on his bike.

"Oh, Michael, do you really have to go on that bicycle holiday?"

"Yes, I'm afraid I do . . ." I reply lamely. Exit, pursued by a cow.

No plausible reason for my departure is given to the audience; I simply vanish from the screen. Accordingly I'm discharged from filming halfway through, but still have to come back in time to film the nail-biting climax to *Calamity the Cow* (spoiler alert: cow wins first prize in county show). Disgruntlement is compounded by embarrassment and amplified by frustration. I sigh to myself: *I've had enough of this.*

Except I've not, not quite. In early 1968 Mum gets me a job on another film. It's also a kids' movie, but this one is a serious production: an adaptation of a book written by James Bond creator Ian Fleming; scripted by children's author Roald Dahl; songs by Disney's Oscar-winning writers the Sherman Brothers (they did *The Jungle Book* and *Mary Poppins*); and directed by Ken Hughes, who'd just worked on a Bond film, 1967's *Casino Royale*. I don't have any kind of speaking part—it's extras work, as on *A Hard Day's Night*—but it means being out of school for a week, and it means filming at the famous Pinewood Studios.

All things considered, for a seventeen-year-old chafing against the limitations of his childhood, *Chitty Chitty Bang Bang* is a great gig. On paper at least.

At Pinewood there are hundreds of kids who've been sent on this casting call, all from different stage schools. There are chaperones and tutors everywhere, and everyone is trying to artfully dodge them as best they can. In your time out of class, you're intent on doing as little schoolwork as possible.

I don't remember meeting any of the cast. We were only extras, so no mingling with the stars—not Dick Van Dyke, not Benny Hill, not James Robertson Justice. I do remember having some kind of cyst on my forehead, which is dressed, on doctor's orders, with a bandage. Us kids, captives of the terrifying Child Catcher, are meant to look beaten, bedraggled and dirty. But in the cutting room my pristine, medically applied bandage catches the eye of director Hughes and he snips me out of the film. Exit stage right, Collins, again.

This is a further nail in the coffin of my enthusiasm for acting. And quite frankly, I couldn't give a fuck. We are now in 1968, another massive moment for music, and something has to give.

In the year of The Beatles' *White Album*, The Zombies' *Odessey and Oracle*, The Rolling Stones' *Beggars Banquet*, The Kinks' *Village Green Preservation Society*, Van Morrison's *Astral Weeks*, Pink Floyd's *A Saucerful of Secrets* and Cream's *Wheels of Fire*, I leave school. I have GCEs in art, English language and religious knowledge. I just get by. Even if I was, God forbid, set on a career as an insurance salesman in the City, with those scant qualifications I would struggle.

Such were the benefits of an education at Barbara Speake's. In my whole time there my head wasn't present, or I wasn't present, or both. What early enthusiasm I had for the place was mostly predicated on the chance to escape Chiswick Grammar, and the prospect of all those girls. The object of the school was to morph you into a young adult theatrical star. For me, that was never going to happen, so I couldn't wait to get out of it. For sure, the acting opportunities it helped to present did push me out on a stage in front of people, but it never felt like a glittering start to any sort of career.

But through financial necessity I give the acting one more shot, appearing at the Piccadilly Theatre in 1969 in that previously mentioned latest staging of *Oliver!* (Barry Humphries is Fagin). Carol Reed's film adaptation came out the previous year and there's renewed excitement around the production. On top of that I am, at this point, that rather pitiable figure: the jobbing drummer without a job as a drummer. Acting will, again, have to put a bob or two in my pocket.

A twenty-two-year-old Cameron Mackintosh is the show's assistant stage manager at this time. These days he's perhaps the most powerful man in theater, an impresario with a £1 billion empire, the man behind *Les Misérables* and *Miss Saigon* and many more. But at the tail end of the sixties, at the Piccadilly Theatre, I'm higher than him in the pecking order. I tell him this years later, at Buckingham Palace. Sir Cameron, Sir Terry Wogan, Sir George Martin, Dame Vera Lynn and I have been chosen to meet the Queen and Prince Philip on their way to a celebration of British music that also features Jeff Beck, Jimmy Page, Eric Clapton and Brian May.

As we stand in line waiting to bow and scrape before their royal majesties, I whisper out of the side of my mouth, "You realize, Sir Cameron, that we worked in *Oliver!* at the same time?"

"No!"

"Yeah! So, what have you been up to since then?"

BACK IN 1968 my sights are firmly set on music. I tell Mum I want to give up acting and make a living as a drummer. She tells Dad. Within the hushed walls of London Assurance it has been a matter of fatherly pride that Greville Collins' youngest son is a star of stage and screen. But playing with one of those *pop groups*? In short order I'm sure to be a long-haired destitute, raping and pillaging my way across the world, the father of a fistful of illegitimate children, or worse.

Dad sends me to Coventry for a few weeks. He simply stops talking to me, just to demonstrate his anger.

I don't care, and I don't wobble. I have my head stuck in the back pages of *Melody Maker*, or down the front of Lavinia's cheesecloth shirt, or sometimes both at the same time.

I embark on the life of the jobbing drummer. Or, rather, I set about trying to establish myself as the kind of person who might be viewed as a jobbing drummer.

Some of my earliest professional engagements are courtesy of Ronnie. His parents are in *real show business*. His dad, also called Ronnie, is pianist and leader with a little band, the adventurously named The Ronnie Caryl Orchestra. His mum, Celia, is the singer, and they regularly play the Stork Club and the Pigalle, both in London's West End. When I have some time and no money, I join them.

The Caryls also have a nice routine playing cruises and the holiday camps run by Butlin's and Pontin's. In the sixties, before the seventies package-holiday boom and long before the cheap-flight revolution, a holiday-camp vacation is a staple of British life. For teenagers everywhere it's also a sexual rite of passage, the absent parents and the rows of chalets offering possibilities galore.

One Christmas the Caryls ask me to join a band they've put together to play at Pontin's in Paignton, Devon. I try my best to fit in. I learn to Brylcreem my hair and tie a bow tie, wear the band jacket, and I find my feet playing waltzes, rhumbas, two-steps, a bit of rock'n'roll. Our repertoire is all kinds of standards and all kinds of genres.

Mrs. Caryl is a lovely lady with a great voice and a charming manner with a roomful of patrons. Mr. Caryl is a polished, mustachioed bandleader, armed with all the tricks of the trade. He can bollock you while he smiles at the audience, something he does to me countless times. With a wink to the punters enjoying their chicken-in-a-basket, mid-set he'll lead the band offstage so they can slake their thirst at the bar, leaving me to single-handedly entertain the crowd with the meager show of drum trickery I have at my disposal.

"Do you want a drum solo, Phil?"

"No!"

"It's all yours . . ."

At such moments the stage is mine for what seems like an eternity. As the band merrily raise their pint glasses in my honor, I'm frantically gesticulating to get them back to help me out of my misery. And gesticulating is a challenge when you're holding the beat and two drumsticks.

The solo stage, it's obvious, is far from my comfort zone.

Talk about learning your trade: this is an apprenticeship in the boozy raw. But then, after the final set of the evening, Ronnie and I excitedly roam the holiday camp, playing with some relish the "we're in a band" card to all the girls we can find. Then, on a good night, we might repair to a chalet with a couple of suitably impressed fellow teenage babes.

There are more rites of passage in another regular gig I have around this time. Through another friend of a friend, I hear of a band in need of a drummer. The Charge are a semi-professional R&B combo who play American soul music, led by an extremely unlikely frontman in the shape of a singing Scottish bass player called George. I'm the best player by some distance, but the least experienced in the ways of gigging at the sharp end.

The Charge have a lucrative if perilous line in gigs at American army bases in Norfolk and Cambridgeshire. We drive all over those counties, crammed into a battered Ford Transit, playing the Motown, Stax and James Brown hits of the day, the faster the better. As the evening wears on the GIs become more excited, more enthused and more pissed (in both the British and American senses of the term). If you're the entertainment it's better to stay onstage, because it's safer onstage. It's U.S. army regulation that a fight will break out at some point, so the longer you can keep playing and keep them distracted, the less likely you are to be dragged into the fray. The Charge play James Brown's locomotive version of "Night Train" with suitable vigor.

Aged seventeen and not long out of school, I am fast developing some kind of staying power onstage. I also develop some leaving power, which comes in useful when The Charge's keyboard player introduces me to a chap of his acquaintance named Trevor. He too plays keyboards—among other things, most notably perhaps "the pink oboe," as Peter Cook put it. This Trevor frequents a Soho amusement arcade, a gay pick-up joint with added slot machines. He tells me that The Shevelles, a very popular gigging band in the fashionable London clubs, are looking for a drummer. Dennis Elliott is leaving them, and will in fact end up as the drummer in Foreigner.

At this point I'll explore any, and every, opportunity. In The Charge I'm a professional musician in a semi-professional band. The other guys have day jobs; this *is* my day job. So the meager income—perhaps a fiver a week—has to be supplemented by my mum. She helps with the odd backhander so I can keep myself in gig tickets and take out girlfriends. Unlike my vow-of-silence dad, she's very supportive. Still, my lack of a reliable source of income points to an uncomfortable reality: I'm stuck in a twilight zone between childhood and adulthood, between unemployed school leaver who still lives with his parents and occasionally busy drummer.

Not yet knowing the decadent side of Trevor, I decide to give him a go. He takes me to the Cromwellian Cocktail Bar & Discotheque in Kensington. Upstairs there's a casino and bar, but the basement is a swinging sixties in-spot for the in-crowd. Up-and-coming musos fill the small stage—Elton John, when he's plain Reg Dwight, gigs there with Bluesology—while visiting players will readily hop up for a jam. It's also another gay pick-up joint, and I'm about to be firmly inducted into London's sleazier side in one alarming evening.

As I'm sitting there in the buzzy gloom, waiting to jam with The Shevelles, The Animals' Eric Burdon clambers up for a spot on the mic. I'm still reeling from the thrill of hearing the charismatic voice of "House of the Rising Sun" when a lanky dandy I immediately recognize as Long John Baldry slides up to our table.

"Hello, Trevor," he purrs, taking a long, slow look at me, "who's this?" A few minutes later, over wanders Chris Curtis, drummer with The Searchers. He says the same thing, and I begin to wonder if I'm really here for an audition of the musical kind.

Sure enough, The Shevelles come offstage and pack up. No audition. Trevor tries to sweeten the disappointment by inviting me back to his flat in Kensington. I'm dubious, but it is late, and it is a long way to the end of the line.

I go back to his place. One thing leads to another—that is, innocence develops into awkwardness. Because he has a flatmate, I have no option but to share Trevor's bed. Terrified, I try to sleep, fitfully and fully dressed on top of the blankets. Presently, the fidgeting begins, and soon a hand is creeping over.

I'm out of there quicker than you can say "paradiddle."

At this time I'm always open to an offer. I play the odd gig with The Cliff Charles Blues Band, who are pretty good but not about to set the world on fire, and I have a brief stint in a group called The Freehold. Another jobbing band with no real fixed talent.

The Freehold base ourselves in a small, seedy hotel in Russell Square in Bloomsbury. This is a bit of a muso hang, full of interesting permanent boarders such as the road crews for Jimi Hendrix and The Nice. Jimmy Savile also maintains a room here. A well-known face on TV and radio—he'd presented the very first episode of *Top of the Pops* in 1964—he's rarely unaccompanied at the hotel. A stream of girls seem to ebb and flow around his room.

This hotel is also the place where I run into Tony Stratton-Smith for the first time. A decade earlier, in his former life as a sports journalist, he'd flown with Manchester United to play a European Cup fixture in Belgrade. The morning after the match he missed his alarm call and the flight. The plane crashed after a refueling stop at Munich airport, killing twenty-three of the forty-four people on board, and from that day onward Strat would always take the flight after the one that was booked for him.

He and I quickly become good friends, despite him insisting on calling me "Peelip." Strat is a great and generous man, and becomes instrumental in my future, and the future of Genesis.

My time in The Freehold draws to an end almost as soon as it's begun, mainly out of boredom on my part. I press on, chasing that elusive big break. Ronnie and I attend an audition for a band to back a British Four Tops–type outfit. We both get the gig, me on drums, Ronnie on bass, joining a keyboard player called Brian Chatton and a guitarist named "Flash" Gordon Smith.

The four of us call ourselves Hickory, while the vocal group are dubbed The Gladiators. It soon becomes apparent that the players are better than the singers, so us players decide to hive off and make a go of it on our own.

Via a lot of graft and some luck, it looks like I am finally in a real band with real prospects. Suitably inspired, I embark on something I have studiously avoided until now: trying to write a song.

One day at home in Hounslow I start messing about on the piano in the back room. I hover around D minor—which, as any Spinal Tap fan knows, is the saddest chord of all—and pick through some lyrical ideas. I am wracked with imaginary heartbreak at the prospect of losing Lavinia.

Soon I think I have something. *"Can't you see it's no ordinary love that I feel for you deep inside? / It's been building up inside of me and it's something that I just can't hide / Why did you leave me lying there, crying there, dying there . . ."*

This is "Lying, Crying, Dying," and it is the first song seventeen-year-old Peelip Collins has ever written. I'm pretty pleased with my creation, so much so that I make another leap: I decide I want to sing it, too.

Hickory book a recording session at Regent Sound, a cheap basement studio in Denmark Street. We record four tracks, including my ink-still-wet-on-the-page composition.

Back in west London, I visit Bruce Rowland. He's the son of my old elocution teacher, Hilda; a year from now he'll play with Joe Cocker at the era-defining Woodstock festival and thereafter become the drummer with Fairport Convention. I will buy his Gretsch drums, a kit I have to this day.

As he's a drummer, a few years older than me and clearly destined for great things, I regularly visit Bruce for words of wisdom and encouragement. He plays me "Loving You Is Sweeter Than Ever" by The Four Tops, instructing me to "listen to the groove. *Beautiful.* Just beautiful." He introduces me to The Grateful Dead's double live album *Live Dead*, which features two drummers, something else that will come to play a role in my life some years later.

Cautiously, I play Bruce a tape of Hickory's recording of "Lying, Crying, Dying." To my huge relief he announces that he loves it. More than that, he loves my voice. "You should sing, not drum," says Bruce. No one has previously commended me on my singing voice, probably because hardly anyone has heard it post my *Oliver!* days. This is a lovely aside, but that's all I view it as. I'm a drummer, not a singer.

And I am, temporarily, a songwriter. Not that I know it at the time, but with my very first song I've shown my hand: I've demonstrated that I have a talent for writing sad songs, and that I enjoy dwelling on matters melancholy. The lyrics are fairly average but they're straight from the heart.

Through another friend of another friend, we come into the orbit of a pop group called Brotherhood of Man. With a different line-up they will win the 1976 Eurovision Song Contest with "Save Your Kisses for Me." However, in 1969 John Goodison is a member and writer. At his encouragement, we go into a studio owned by CBS Records, and record a nondescript pop ditty, "Green Light." It's our first experience in a proper studio, and we're recording a single. It looks like I've finally hit the big time.

If only. "Green Light" hits a brick wall but, undaunted, Hickory continue gigging around London, playing dodgy clubs and performing mostly covers like Joe Cocker's "Do I Still Figure in Your Life," "I Can't Let Maggie Go" by Honeybus and Tim Hardin's "Hang On to a Dream" and "Reason to Believe."

Hickory rehearse on Eel Pie Island, in the ballroom of the hotel, near the Converted Cruiser Club's premises. Just as Mum's friendship with the hotel's owner facilitated this choice berth for the club, so it gives our band access to the best sprung dance floor in all of England. We can't dance, but we do rehearse a lot.

One day two distinguished, rather spiffily dressed older gents come to see the four of us. Songwriters Ken Howard and Alan Blaikley are Hampstead-dwelling habitués of the swinging London scene. These movers, shakers and ravers have written all the key songs for The Herd, featuring a young Peter Frampton, and for Dave Dee, Dozy, Beaky, Mick and Tich. Hits, lots of hits—"The Legend of Xanadu," "Bend It" and many more. They're regulars at a club on Soho's Wardour Street, La Chasse. It's a musicians' drinking haunt, popular because it's a few doors down from the Marquee. All the guys from the bands gather there, crowded into a modest, living-room-sized space in front of the bar—or, in the case of Keith Moon, behind the bar.

When he isn't drumming with The Who, Moonie seems to like playing barman in La Chasse. I buy a round from him one night, and he gives me back more money than I'd handed over. Another reason to love him.

Brian Chatton, Hickory's keyboard player, a very good-looking chap from Bolton, lives in the West End and is a regular in La Chasse.

Always possessed of an eye for fresh talent, Howard and Blaikley gravitate toward him.

One night over their gin and tonics, Howard and Blaikley mention to Brian that they're writing a concept album. *Ark 2* concerns the evacuation of a dying Earth, which is a very current topic here at the twilight of the sixties: men are flying to the moon; the space race is in full flight; a lot of people are very high. This rocket-powered pair have the songs; they just need the musicians to perform them. Brian does the decent thing and invites them to come see his band.

Now, here they are on Eel Pie Island, watching Hickory go through our paces. We're nervous to be auditioning for such well-connected chaps. Prior to now, my early optimism at the band's prospects has quickly slid into pessimism—"Lying, Crying, Dying" was never anything more than a demo and, again, we seem to be going nowhere. But here are two Svengali figures with the potential to fly us to the moon.

Howard and Blaikley like what they hear and, with little fanfare it seems, Hickory have bagged the job of being the interstellar vehicle for their space-age song suite. We agree to climb aboard even before we've heard any of the songs.

Ronnie, Brian, Flash and I travel to a beautiful corner of old Hampstead to hear the demos of *Ark 2*. Howard and Blaikley's home is quite the sixties luxury dwelling, an immaculate bachelor-pad townhouse with a rolling roof garden. It will prove the perfect vantage point from which to stare at the moon on the night of July 20/21, 1969, the night Neil Armstrong makes his small step/giant leap.

Their demos are, to say the least, rough, a fact not helped by Howard and Blaikley's rather poor singing voices. The material sounds florid and camp in a "rock musical" way. It only adds to my rapidly growing skepticism—to my mind, the whole "concept" is a bit schoolboy. Next to The Who's magisterial *Tommy*, released that May, *Ark 2* risks looking a bit, well, daft.

But we are a no-hope band who've suddenly been thrown a lifeline by two guys with several number 1 singles under the belts of their chinoiserie robes. With Brian and Flash at the vocal helm—they're both great singers—and Ronnie and I providing a finely tuned musical engine, Hickory are confident we can give this project lift-off.

We record at De Lane Lea Studios in Holborn under the watchful eyes of producers Howard and Blaikley. Arranger Harold Geller is second in command and has worked with the duo many times. Brian and Flash sing most of the songs, although I land one of the Planets Suite, a music-hall-style interlude called "Jupiter: Bringer of Jollity," and am front and center on "Space Child." Howard and Blaikley change our name to Flaming Youth, which is a phrase taken from a speech by Franklin D. Roosevelt. "The temper of our youth has become more restless, more critical, more challenging. Flaming youth has become a flaming question," the thirty-second President of the United States told the Baltimore Young Democratic Club in 1936.

Ark 2 is unveiled with a publicity-stunt launch at London's Planetarium. The sixties scenesters come in two-by-two. By now I'm squirming at all this ultra-fab cod-psychedelia; it's both pretentious and cartoonish. As a headstrong eighteen-year-old, I also bristle at Howard and Blaikley's tendency to treat us as their creation, a prefab-four entirely of their making.

But to our pleasant surprise the record gets good reviews. In *Melody Maker* it's even October 1969's Album of the Month ("adult music beautifully played with nice tight harmonies"), beating the month's other notable release, *Led Zeppelin II*. It won't be the last time I'm blamed for spoiling things for Led Zeppelin.

It even does well internationally. Well, the Dutch like it, so much so that Flaming Youth travel to Amsterdam to record a five-song performance. It's my first time abroad, my first time performing on-screen, but not my first time actually playing in front of cameras—the whole thing is mimed.

In Amsterdam, Howard and Blaikley take us round their favorite haunts. These bring their own surprises, including my first encounter with a transvestite. I thought London was swinging; it has nothing on Holland's party capital. Despite my concerns about the music we're being forced to play, I can't deny that *Ark 2* is propelling me into interesting new worlds.

Yet despite the good notices, and the enthusiasm from the Netherlands, *Ark 2* doesn't make much difference to the fortunes of Flaming Youth. We rehearse till we're blue in the face, finessing a new direction suggestive of Yes-type arranged pop. But we're also a good solid rock band, at our best onstage. However, we're performing less and less, and what shows we do play are gigs of two halves: one half consists of smart arrangements of interesting things—The Vanilla Fudge version of "You Keep Me Hangin' On," "With a Little Help from My Friends" à la Joe Cocker, and one of my favorite Beatles songs, "I'm Only Sleeping," plus some of our own material—and the other half is *Ark 2*. Live, the album is not so much rocket-powered as a damp squib. The audiences are as puzzled as we are. The future viability of Flaming Youth has become the flaming question.

I can see the end is coming, so I start putting my nose about, seeing what else is out there. I'll take Ronnie with me if I can find the right thing for both of us. But, equally, I'll go it alone if I find the right drummer-only opening. So far my professional musical career, such as it is, has involved a lot of me saying yes to any and all opportunities, only to be frustrated at the outcomes. It's time to get a bit more pushily proactive.

I become a professional auditioner, forever scouring the "musicians wanted" notices in the back pages of *Melody Maker*. If the ad is in there, the act has some integrity. I try out fruitlessly for Vinegar Joe, future home of Robert Palmer and Elkie Brooks. I fail to impress Manfred Mann Chapter Three, serial bandleader Mann's jazz-rock experimentalists. I even give it a go with The Bunch, a working but nondescript band based in Bournemouth.

Well, in the case of the latter, I don't quite give it a go: when I find out over the phone that they're based on the English south coast, I tell them I can't come because my mum doesn't like me to travel. Lord knows what they thought of me. "London ponce" or "mummy's boy," probably. I couldn't think of a better excuse. It didn't occur to me that I'd just been to Holland. In truth, I didn't fancy the long train journey with my drums.

There's a sense of jittery urgency about me, but also a sense of not knowing which way to turn. I've been first in line, I've been down the front at the Marquee, I've seen all the top acts of the day. I've been that close to all these incendiary new talents—The Who, Hendrix, Page, Plant, Bonham, Beck—and often at the beginnings of their careers. I've touched the hems of their bell-bottoms. So near yet so far.

I've put myself about and stuck my neck out. When Yes play at the Marquee in front of fifty hardy souls, I go backstage during the intermission because I've heard Bill Bruford is about to go back to Leeds University. Frontman Jon Anderson gives me his number, but I never bother to call. I don't know why, but I often wonder: how would my life have been if I'd said yes to the Yes audition?

As the seventies dawn, and with it the end of my first year of adulthood, I'm foraging for food, money and a future. I've been in a few bands, none of which have come to anything. I'm hungry, but I'm still stuck in Hounslow and all that goes with living at the end of the line. Underlining the emptiness of my existence is the fact that I'm by now home alone.

While my life has been inching along, there have been major changes at 453 Hanworth Road. Not to put too fine a point on it, but everyone's buggered off and the Collins family has disintegrated. Clive and Carole have their own grown-up lives, and my parents' relationship has ground to a halt. Mum has been spending increasing amounts of time at Barbara Speake's house, closer to work. Dad is looking forward to retiring, and the moment when he can finally grow a beard. He is a frequent visitor to Weston-super-Mare, and is spending long weekends there. It's a place he grew to love during the war, when the family were relocated by London Assurance and he was stationed there as part of the local detachment of Dad's Army, the Home Guard.

So, while I technically have a place to stay, my soul has no fixed abode.

I gotta get out of this place. But how?

Then a Beatle throws me a bone.

4

THE BALLAD OF *ALL THINGS MUST PASS*

Or: (don't) meet The Beatles

WHEN OPPORTUNITY KNOCKS, I'm just climbing out of the bath in the house I grew up in. It's a quiet Thursday afternoon, I'm living alone most of the time in the otherwise deserted Collins family home, and the most I have to look forward to is *Top of the Pops* on the telly and beans on toast for tea. I might watch TV and eat my dinner in my underpants. Because I can. It is May 1970, I am nineteen, and the swinging sixties have very much ended. Roll on the soggy seventies.

Still, I remain a minor star in Ken Howard and Alan Blaikley's orbit. They're friendly with a guy called Martin, another acquaintance from La Chasse, who happens to be Ringo Starr's chauffeur. One night at the club Martin asks Blaikley if he knows any good percussionists. "Sure," says Blaikley, "I'll find someone."

Blaikley calls me as I'm still dripping from the bath. "What are you doing tonight?"

"Well, *Top of the Pops* is on . . ." I reply, hedging my bets. Right now, seeing bands promoting their singles on the televised weekly chart rundown is the closest I'm getting to live performance.

"Forget that. Do you want to go to Abbey Road for a session?"

He offers no details of the artist hosting the session, but at just the mention of Abbey Road, I'm suddenly not so uninterested. *Doesn't matter who it is. I can see where The Beatles recorded . . .* McCartney announced that he was leaving the band only a few weeks previously, and his first solo album, *McCartney*, has just come out. The end of the Fab Four is all anyone is talking about. *Let It Be*, The Beatles' swan song, is barely in the shops and already there is feverish discussion in the music press of the first post-Beatles solo album.

But thinking on my feet while dripping in my towel, my mind isn't going there. At this point in my stop-start, still stubbornly embryonic music career, this is a chance to demonstrate my drumming chops to an artist good enough to be booked into Abbey Road. I'm a jobbing drummer without a job, and this is a job.

"What time do you want me there?"

I get dressed for the occasion, which means a T-shirt over jeans. I am a nineteen-year-old long-hair, and this is my look. I call a cab, jump in and am extraordinarily pleased to be able to utter the immortal line: "Abbey Road, please, driver."

When I arrive, Martin the chauffeur is standing on the steps of the studio in St. John's Wood, northwest London. "Come in, come in, we've been waiting for you."

"Really? *Me?*" I wonder. "And who's this 'we' he's referring to?"

He takes me in and we make small talk. "They've been here four weeks," he says. "They've spent *a thousand pounds*. And they haven't recorded anything."

I'm thinking, "Wow, this must be serious."

I walk into Abbey Road Studio Two, and into a scene that is now famous. The cast of this mystery session are in the middle of a photo shoot, meaning everyone involved is lined up: George Harrison with his long hair (I'm feeling good about my hair at this moment); Ringo Starr; producer Phil Spector; legendary Beatles road manager Mal Evans; a couple of members of Badfinger; artist-turned-bassist Klaus Voormann; Hammond virtuoso Billy Preston; stellar pedal steel guitar player Peter Drake; and Beatles engineers Ken Scott and Phil McDonald.

Later I will memorize the personnel on these sessions, and realize that there's no Ginger Baker at this point. I also learn later that Eric Clapton probably left as I was arriving.

The penny drops: George is in the process of making that first post-Beatles solo album, and I am suddenly in the middle of it. Well, on the edge of it.

Everyone stops talking as I come in. I'm on the receiving end of a collective quizzical frown: *Who's this kid?*

Chauffeur Martin pipes up: "The percussionist's here."

I don't really know my expected role in the proceedings, but "percussionist" sounds OK to me, even if I don't really consider myself exactly that. Anyway, there's no time to quibble, because now George is actually speaking to me: "Sorry, man," he drawls in that familiar Scouse burr, "you haven't been here long enough to be in the photograph." I laugh nervously, a little embarrassed.

Am I quaking in my bell-bottom jeans? Let's just say I'm confident but I'm not cocky. I know I have a job ahead of me, firstly impressing this gang, and secondly playing percussion well—a skill that has nothing to do with playing the drums well. Percussion can mean a lot of different things, encompassing as it does congas, bongos, tambourine and more. It's not just a question of hitting something different; they each have an art to them. I already know that, but I'll soon find out the finer points.

The vibe is . . . *relaxed*. No highly trained EMI boffins in white lab-coats, yet no sign of anything being smoked either. I later read about how George had set up an incense area, but I don't smell anything unusual.

The photo shoot completed, everyone resumes their positions. I'm led upstairs to the control room, the very same one in which George Martin sat during the landmark *Our World* broadcast in 1967, when The Beatles performed "All You Need Is Love" to 400 million viewers. Sitting in the same producer's chair is Spector. We're introduced, and he's polite if hardly chatty. The shades stay on. At least there's no gun. Not that I can see anyway.

Back down the stairs and Mal Evans, with his big glasses and his early mop-top fringe haircut—even The Beatles' roadies were heroes—shows me to my spot. "Here's your congas, kid, next to Ringo's drums."

I'm looking at those drums. *I want to touch those drums.* Feel those drums. If I thought I could have got away with resting my cheek on the skins, I would have. *How does Ringo mic his kit? Ooh, towel over the snare—that's interesting.*

To me, Ringo's a great drummer. In this period he'd been taking a lot of flak. But I always thought, and still do, that that stuff he played was magical. It wasn't luck. He had an incredible feel. And he knows this. Years later, when I properly meet him, I'll tell him that I'm a supporter. Back then though, Buddy Rich was dissing him, and even Lennon was putting him down.

That was great, eh? The world hearing that you're not even the best drummer in The Beatles. I remember reading an interview in *Modern Drummer*—I used to get it religiously—where Ringo said how people would refer to "Ringo's funny little drum fills." He'd get annoyed at that, quite rightly. "They aren't funny little drum fills. They're quite serious," he'd say. You listen to "A Day in the Life," and it's really fantastic, complicated, unusual, unorthodox. Not nearly as simple as he makes it appear. So I've got my Ringo hat and I will gladly put it on when needed.

Anyway, Abbey Road, a Thursday evening in late spring/early summer 1970. I've got my congas, and Ringo's on my right, and Billy Preston's on my left. And somewhere over there are George and Klaus. We're going to record a song called "Art of Dying."

"Well, shall we play Phil the song first?" No one says that. Not George, not Ringo, not Spector. Something else no one says: "Here's the sheet music, Phil. That's how it goes, and that's where you come in." George doesn't come over and do that. He doesn't hand me anything. He's over there, doing his thing, getting his head together, whatever.

Instead, all I hear is: "One, two, three, four!"

After an initial, fairly tentative take, I make a mistake. Unfortunately, it won't be my last. I don't really smoke cigarettes anymore but I'm that nervous, and that keen to fit in, that I say to Billy Preston, "Could I have a fag?"

"Sure, kid."

Soon I'm chain-smoking. I take a couple from Billy and ponce a couple from Ringo. I don't feel so good, and not just because I'm quickly puffing my way through the best part of a packet. I sense I'm really getting on everybody's nerves. Years later I was due to present a gong to Ringo at the Mojo Awards, and I had a packet of Marlboros ready for him. Unfortunately I fell sick and couldn't make the ceremony. So I still owe Ringo those fags.

Before long Billy is yelling at me. "Fuck, man, buy a pack of cigarettes!" Well, that's what his look says. It's the only really awkward moment during the whole thing. At least, I thought it was.

The evening wears on. We're playing and playing, and I'm puffing and puffing (and poncing and poncing). I have headphones on, and hear Spector's instructions: "OK, let's hear the guitars, bass and drums only . . . Now the bass, keyboards and drums only . . ."

Presumably this is how he made those wonderful records. And every time he says "drums," I play. I prefer to err on the side of caution than risk having the famously combustible (not to mention trigger-happy) Spector shout at me: "Why aren't you playing, man?" So I play, and keep playing. Because I'm not a percussionist, and because of the anxiety, I probably over-play. So I'm *giving it*. After an hour my hands are in some state. Red raw, blistered. I'd have similar session experiences much later, with Elton John's preferred percussionist Ray Cooper, a great player who can really push it, then push it some more. There was blood on the walls. No wonder Elton loves him.

A dozen takes, and I've still not been asked to play something particular. So I've just played what I thought was appropriate. I keep playing, and playing, and playing. All this time I'm not getting any feedback from Spector, which is a little bit disconcerting. But I'm just trying to fit in, look cool, not drop the ball, or the beat.

At one point Chauffeur Martin comes over. "Everything all right, Phil?"

"Yeah, yeah, great . . . Got a cigarette?"

Finally, after running countless times through "Art of Dying," I hear the fateful words from Spector. "OK, guys. Congas—can you play this time?" I don't even have a name. Worse, he's not even heard me. Not once.

I'm standing there, looking at my bleeding hands, probably a bit dizzy with all the cigs, and I'm thinking, "Spector, you *bastard*. My hands are completely shot, and you haven't even been listening to me."

Billy and Ringo, positioned each side of me, laugh. I can see they feel for me. They know how hard I've been working, and they must understand how nervous this teenage kid is. How nervous he must have been all evening. To be so enthusiastic, and then to be so cruelly shot down.

But at least that breaks the ice, and we play it a few more times. And then everyone disappears. Just like that. I go out and I call Lavinia from the pay phone in the foyer. "You'll never guess where I am? Abbey Road! With The Beatles!" What I'm really saying is: "I can't believe my fucking luck. You're really going to want to get frisky with me after this!" Sore hands? What sore hands?

I saunter back into the empty studio. It's like the *Mary Celeste* in here. George, Ringo, Billy, Klaus, Mal—gone. Clearly there's a party going on somewhere, and clearly I'm not invited. Then Chauffeur Martin appears. "Oh, I think that's it for the night. I think they're going to watch the football," he says, indicating the lure of an England match on the telly.

I manage a saddened bleat: "I didn't get to say goodbye to anyone . . ." No opportunity to say, "Thanks, Ringo. Thank you, George, here's my number. Billy, if you're ever in town . . ." Nothing like that. It's only Chauffeur Martin, saying to me, "Do you need a cab somewhere?"

It's dark when I leave. I make the long journey home, remembering every note of the session clearly. My hands are still throbbing and bloody, but I am a nineteen-year-old wannabe musician and I have recorded at Abbey Road. *With The Beatles*. OK, with half of them. But still.

A few weeks later, I get the check in the mail. It's from EMI, it's for £15 and it's for services to Mr. George Harrison, on the making of the album *All Things Must Pass*. I would have kept the check as a souvenir had I not needed the money so badly.

The next step is to pre-order the record. I go to my local record store in Hounslow, Memory Discs. "I want to order the George Harrison album, *All Things Must Pass*. I'm on it, you know?" I don't say that. I don't *think* I said it. But I wouldn't have put it past me.

Then, after an interminable wait, late that November, the phone rings. "Hello, Mr. Collins? It's Memory Discs. Your record's in." Yeah, it is *my* record. And it's in the shops, at last.

I could walk there, but this is urgent. So I get the bus—110, 111, 120, doesn't matter, all of them pass the record shop. I buy the record, and it's beautiful. That lovely, triple-album, box-set packaging. I come out of the shop, and I'm turning it in my hands, thinking, "Inside here . . . is me . . . on a Beatle's album."

Standing on the pavement I open it up. I race through the credits. Klaus Voormann . . . Ginger Baker . . . Billy Preston . . . Ringo Starr . . . They're all present and correct, the cats I saw in the studio that night, and more besides, from Eric to Ginger to future Yes drummer Alan White and Stones saxophonist Bobby Keys. Everyone is there. Everyone but me. Must be some mistake. *My name's not there*. They've left me off.

This is a crushing disappointment. I'm devastated. Then I perk up. Oh well, never mind, I'll go home and have a listen. If I can't see myself on the sleeve, at least I'll hear myself in the grooves. But as soon as the needle hits the record and the song starts, I know I'm not on "Art of Dying." They've not even used the arrangement I worked on. *Oh my God*. What's going on?

At this time, the concept of recording different versions of songs is unknown to me. Yes, I'd made *Ark 2* with Flaming Youth. But that aside, I'm a young shaver who's barely been in any recording studios, far less the most famous recording studio in the world, with the most famous American producer in the world, with *two Beatles*. I didn't know that multiple arrangements are meat and potatoes to Phil Spector. "We're gonna have to abort last week's session, I gotta new idea . . ."

I've gone from soaring high to crashing low.

It's not like I've been thinking, "I'm going to hear from George Harrison daily. When he goes on the road as a solo artist, I'm going to be his drummer. Or, at least, his bloke on the congas." But at least *All Things Must Pass* would be on my CV, surely?

That kind of experience, that kind of validation, is hugely important to me. Forget *Oliver!*, or the fact that I was on the books at an agency as a serious child actor. I coulda been a contender, but acting didn't interest me. All I want to be is a drummer, and I duly have my life mapped out in my head: pop for as long as it lasts, then The Ray McVay Show Band every Friday and Saturday at the Lyceum. Maybe some recording sessions, if I learn to read music, then the orchestra pit.

Then: I get the call to play with a Beatle on his first post-Beatles solo album. Forget the pit, and the pendulum of show-band gigs and tea-dance bookings. I was going to be a proper drummer!

Then: the Beatle dumps me off his album, and nobody tells me. First they cut me from *A Hard Day's Night*, and now this. What have I ever done to the Fab Four?

The Ballad of *All Things Must Pass*: I wrote a story to myself to account for the events surrounding that fateful day at Abbey Road. Several stories. After all, I had thirty years to pick at the scab of that bruising and literally bloody encounter and come up with reasons for my rejection. Thirty years to explain away the fact that the leading musicians of my teenage days saw fit to give me the run-around, then dump me.

So, I told myself, here's what happened: *they had decided to go in another direction with the production of the song.* Of course they had. It was Phil Spector. Notorious for it. He was a mad genius, and would one day get very much madder still.

Or: *George had a new vision for the song.* Bet he did. This was his big, post-Beatles statement record—triple album, twenty-eight tracks, a whole load of ideas. *Naturally* he was going to change his mind about how he wanted "Art of Dying" to sound.

Plus, he was George Harrison, of The Beatles. The Quiet One. He was called that for a reason. No wonder he didn't tell me.

ONE DAY IN 1982 I'm working at The Farm with Gary Brooker from Procol Harum on his *Lead Me to the Water* album. Gary asks, "Should we get Eric or George to play guitar?" Gary has spent the last couple of years in Clapton's touring band, and he knows Harrison—he performed on *All Things Must Pass* as well, but at least his piano playing made the cut.

So, because he can, Gary asks both to play guitar, and both agree. When George arrives I introduce myself. "Yeah, George, we've actually met before . . ." I begin, then tell him about that May evening in Abbey Road twelve years previously.

"Really, Phil? I don't remember that at all."

Brilliant. A Beatle ruined my life and can recall nothing whatsoever about it. If I was feeling bad before . . .

At least George puts my mind at ease over another matter. Rumors had been circulating that I was going to join his old mate McCartney in Wings. There was no truth in the whispers, though it sounded like an intriguing idea. George is quick to reassure me that it wasn't a gig I'd have wanted. Becoming the fifth drummer in Wings would have been "a fate worse than death."

Anyway: I still do not have closure. Throughout the eighties and nineties, when things are going pretty well, still nothing can rid me of this troublesome niggle. Was I really, actually, ditched from *All Things Must Pass* because I was not good enough?

In 1999, I'm at Formula One racing legend Jackie Stewart's sixtieth birthday party. I met Jackie in the gadabout eighties, and we get on famously. Jackie would take me clay-pigeon shooting, which was not really my kind of thing, and I'd get him tickets to see Genesis and invite his sons Paul and Mark to my gigs.

Cementing our friendship even further is the fact that, in 1996, I bought Jackie's house in Switzerland. So by the end of the nineties, when he's launching Stewart Grand Prix with son Paul, we're great pals. I've never been to a Grand Prix, but George and Eric are huge fans of motor-racing. So, my wife Orianne and I are invited to these lovely weekends—go to Hockenheim and meet Schumacher, Coulthard, Barrichello and all the other top Formula One drivers. The actual race day is almost a sideshow, because you never see anything at a Grand Prix. You're better off sitting in a caravan and watching it on TV. But the practice day and qualifying are great fun. High-speed hospitality at its finest.

So here we are at this party for Jackie's birthday, at his new U.K. residence near the Prime Minister's weekend retreat, Chequers, in Buckinghamshire. In attendance are lots of high rollers, royalty and racing drivers. I'm at a table with Princess Anne's kids, Zara and Peter. Also present and correct: George.

By this point I've met him a couple of times with Eric. I've come to know him as a lovely man, and my favorite Beatle. So I'm familiar enough to offer a cheery: "Hey, George, how you doing?" And again, I casually (I hope) ask him about *All Things Must Pass*. But still, no memory. Nothing, nada, zip.

Maybe, thirty years on, I should, finally, take George's solo masterpiece at its word. All things must pass, especially my rejection from one of the greatest albums ever.

The following year a music journalist approaches me at Hockenheim. Out of nowhere, he says, "Phil, you were on *All Things Must Pass*, weren't you?" Inside I'm shouting, "YES! Yes, I was!" Instead I try to play it cool to this stranger and say, "Well, it's a long story . . ."

Then he says, "You know George is remixing it? For a thirtieth-anniversary reissue? I know George, and since he's got all the master tapes out, I'll ask him if he can find you."

Suddenly, I'm excited. "Oh, that'd be great." Not just to find out what happened to it, but to have a copy of my session. "Yeah, that'd be great. 'Art of Dying' is the song. How long do you think it'll take?" Needy, *moi*?

Still, it's been so long, I'm not holding my breath. In my heart of hearts I don't think I'm going to hear any more about it. Then, on the Wednesday following, I receive a little package in the post. It's a tape, with a handwritten letter.

"Dear Phil. Could this be you? Love, George."

I think, "*This is it*. Somewhere on this tape . . ." It's almost like I'm holding the Holy Grail (of teenage conga sessions). "I didn't dream it. And it's not like George dug it up in that Tokyo record shop that's famous for stocking every Fab Four bootleg, ever." Because I've already looked in that shop and it wasn't there. "George himself has sent me this."

I don't listen to it immediately. I can't bring myself to. But eventually I step somberly into my home studio. I close the door, pull up a chair, insert the tape and press play. Lo and behold, bit of hiss, and the drums start.

Ba-da-dad doom!

Then the sound of the congas bursts out of the speakers. To trained ears the shortcomings of the wincingly arrhythmic clatter are immediately apparent. *Christ almighty!* Turn it off!

A hyperactive toddler had been let loose. Well, you can tell the player had some semblance of talent—it's not completely all over the place. But it's all over the place enough for someone in charge to say, "Get rid of that kid!"

I'm shell-shocked. I don't remember it being this bad. My playing is too busy, too hyper, too amateur. And clearly not what was required by Messrs Harrison and Spector.

The track peters out as people stop playing. Then I hear this distinctive voice. It's Harrison speaking to Spector. "Phil? Phil? Do you think we can try it one more time, but without the conga player?"

I rewind it four or five times until I'm sure I heard it correctly—Harrison shouting to Spector, confining me to the dustbin, my worst fears realized.

Phil? Phil? Do you think we can try it one more time, but without the conga player?

Suddenly, finally, the truth. All these years I thought—hoped—they'd gone in a different musical direction with the track. I'd consoled myself, soothed my disappointment of thirty years' standing, with that thought. And now I realize: I was fired. They didn't disappear to watch football, or do drugs. They were getting rid of me. Someone had said, "Lose the kid conga player. We're disappearing." As one would if you don't know what to say, especially if you're a bunch of big rock stars. You disappear and leave it to Chauffeur Martin to do the dirty work and ditch the nineteen-year-old.

A few days later I'm sitting in my youngest son Mathew's bedroom at home. The phone rings. It's Jackie Stewart. "Hey, Phil, how are you?" A little bit of small talk. "Thought I'd see you at the John Lennon tribute concert the other night at the Royal Albert Hall . . ."

"Was there a concert?" I reply, trying to sound casual. "I didn't know."

"Yeah, it was a great evening. A lot of drummers there."

"Really?"

"Yep. And a lot of conga players."

I'm confused. Since when is Sir Jackie Stewart, racing legend and champion clay-pigeon shooter, interested in conga players? Then he says, "I've got a friend of yours here, wants to talk to you." He passes the phone over and George Harrison starts speaking.

"Hi, Phil. D'you get the tape?"

Finally, thirty years of hurt tumbles out. "You bastard, George."

"Eh? Why?"

"Well, for thirty years I had my own version of what happened that night, and why I was chopped from *All Things Must Pass*. And now I realize that I was so lame that you and Phil fucking Spector fired me."

Harrison laughs. "*No, no, no!* We just made that tape the other day."

"Eh? What do you mean?"

"Ray Cooper was in, helping me remix the album. I told him to play congas badly over 'Art of Dying' so we could record a special take just for you!"

I'll say it again: you bastard, George. Thirty years of roller-coaster emotion, and now here's another lurch. That wasn't me. It was Cooper, monkeying around with Harrison.

Eventually I see the funny side, especially when George confirms that—to the best of his memory—I wasn't fired.

Did George ever tell me what happened to my actual take? No, he did not. He couldn't remember. He had no recollection of those sessions. I believe it, but I find it hard to understand. How can you not remember making *All Things Must Pass*? There's so much to remember, and yet he seemed to have forgotten most of it. Maybe if you're a Beatle there's too much to remember, so it's easier to some-times forget.

In the booklet accompanying that thirtieth-anniversary edition, released in March 2001, seven months before he died, there are new sleeve notes written by George himself. And there I am, finally: "I don't remember it, but apparently a teenage Phil Collins was there . . ."

George, bless him, sent me a copy of the remixed reissue of the album. It's brilliant, although of course it would be immeasurably improved by the inclusion of "my" version of "Art of Dying."

I still have that comedy congas tape. It's one of my treasures. Here's to you, George—you lovely bastard.

5

THE GENESIS OF GENESIS

Or: the beginnings of my beginnings

S PRING IS BLOSSOMING into summer 1970, and I can describe my mood as both blooming and withering. On the plus
side, I've just been in Abbey Road with two Beatles and have the raw
and blistered fingers and palms to prove it. As far as I'm concerned
at this stage, I am a member of the all-star recording cast of *All
Things Must Pass*. Knackered hands notwithstanding, that's surely
as good as things can get for a nineteen-year-old drummer with jittery ambition in his sticks.

On the negative side, Flaming Youth are, at best, smoldering. *Ark
2* had set the controls for the heart of the sun, but had thumped
back to Earth. I know I'm a good player, but I don't imagine for one
second that George Harrison is about to ask me to join his touring
line-up. I need a full-time gig, or a better gig, or preferably both.

Every Thursday I hotfoot it to my local newsagent and pick up
that week's music papers—all of them. Like any football fan, I start
reading from the back. I pore through the job ads, dismissing the ones
that don't fit: "Skiffle quartet seeks percussionist. Must have own
washboard and teeth"; "Country band needs quiet drummer with
cowboy hat." I also study the concert listings, to see which groups
are busiest with bookings. I'm keen to avoid another rehearsal-room

band like the one Flaming Youth have become. I want to get out and play to people other than ourselves.

Finally, one ad catches my eye because it has a box around it, which is always a good sign (they've paid a bit more for that box—they must be serious): "Tony Stratton-Smith is looking for 12-string guitarist plus drummer sensitive to acoustic music." Only one of those words applies to me, although on a good day I like to think I'm "sensitive" to my girlfriend's needs. Acoustic music, though? That'll be a bit of a stretch. Ultimately, I decide, "Fuck it, I'm a drummer, I'll go anyway."

One of the reasons for my interest is mention of Stratton-Smith. I know him from hanging about at the Russell Hotel with The Freehold. Since then he's had some success managing The Koobas, a beat group from Liverpool, and Hertfordshire rock band The Creation—their singles "Making Time" and "Painter Man" were both big hits. I also know he's started his own record label, Charisma.

I'm no particular fan of The Creation, The Koobas even less, but I like and respect Strat, and he likes me. His involvement suggests this band might be something more than run-of-the-mill. The next evening I track down Strat at the Marquee, one of his preferred watering holes. I buy him a drink, remind him of my credentials ("You must remember The Freehold? No?") and attempt to fast-track myself into this band.

"No, no, no, dear boy," tuts Strat, "these are fussy chaps. You're going to have to call them. And you're going to have to audition."

These "fussy chaps," he tells me, are Genesis. I don't know much about them except that they're constantly appearing in the back pages of *Melody Maker*—this is a busy gigging band.

I phone my old mate Ronnie Caryl. I'm thinking that if we present ourselves at this audition as a package, we'll stand a better chance of getting the gig. He's not hugely experienced on the 12-string, but he's a great player and is bound to be able to rustle up the appropriate chops. Ronnie, as keen as me on an escape route from Flaming Youth, agrees.

I phone the number Strat has given me and speak to the singer with Genesis, who appears to be in charge of the auditions. He's a soft-voiced, nervous-sounding, well-spoken chap who goes by the name of Peter Gabriel. I present my and Ronnie's credentials, such as they are, amping up our sensitivity to acoustic music, and he tells us, with great politeness and civility, to come down to his parents' home in Chobham, Surrey, a week from now.

So we decide to go for it, and we go for it in Ronnie's battered car, cramming into an ageing Morris Minor his guitars and the Gretsch drum kit that I bought from Bruce Rowland. We drive southwest out of London, headed for Surrey. We pass trees, lots of trees. I've seen a tree before—I'm far from worldly-wise, but I'm not that much of a plank—but this is my first inkling that I am traveling into uncharted territory. I realize I'm a city boy, and that this is very much the leafy Home Counties. Our next thought: "Wow, they've got some money round here."

After some furrowed-brow map-reading and a couple of wrong turns up country lanes, we arrive at the address we've been given. Ronnie noses the Morris Minor up an appropriately crunchy gravel drive and we pull up outside an oversized, beautiful country pile. Our guitars and drums seem to spew out of the car, instantly making the whole scene look a lot less tidy. I'm suddenly self-conscious of my apparel. My lived-in flares and T-shirt look a little downmarket for this gig. I ring the bell, and after what seems an age a distinguished-looking, middle-aged woman opens the door. Somehow Mrs. Gabriel works out that we're not here to sell *Encyclopædia Britannica* or join her bridge circle. We must be here to try out for her son's pop group.

"Oh, do come in," she says, smiling. "You're a little early. Please feel free to have a swim while you're waiting."

I think, "Wow, trees *and* a swimming pool." Things are looking up. If only I'd thought to bring my swimming trunks to this rock'n'roll audition. But trunks or not, I decide to take the plunge. If I've learnt anything over the last couple of years, it's to grab any and every opportunity. Who knows if I'll ever again get the offer of a dip in a private heated pool in the countryside. I nonchalantly slip off my jeans, leaving me in just my graying Y-fronts, and jump in. The pool is lovely. This is first-class luxury.

We've arrived a couple of drummers early and, as I'm splashing about, I hear my rivals go through their paces. The standard is decent and I quickly appreciate what I'm up against. I keep my head down in the water a bit longer, calming my nerves. I later discover that Peter's father works at ATV television. Or, perhaps, owns it.

Fresh from my swim, I heave my Gretsch into the garden and, following Mrs. Gabriel's directions, go through to the back terrace, trying not to knock over any of the ceramics or statuary. The first person I see is a tall, distinguished-looking fellow in carpet slippers and what looks like a Noël Coward smoking jacket.

The only thing missing is a Sobranie being inhaled through a cigarette holder. He's youthful-looking, but wonderfully casual, the kind of guy you want to be when you grow up. But if this is Peter Gabriel's dad, how young is Gabriel?

Turns out it's not his dad, it's his band mate. Mike Rutherford, nineteen, is the bassist/guitarist with Genesis. Like my dad, his dad has a lot of experience of boats. Except his dad is a Royal Navy admiral.

A grand piano has been hauled onto the terrace, and hovering in the shadows, about to play it, is another chap. He introduces himself as Tony Banks, Genesis' twenty-year-old keyboard player. My first impressions? I don't really have any. Tony is reserved to the point of invisibility, another politely spoken young man who won't say boo to a goose—unless, I soon find out, that goose plays the wrong chord.

Finally I meet Peter Gabriel. He's twenty and cut from the same fine cloth as his band mates. His demeanor can be summed up as hesitant, one hand clutching the other arm at the elbow, almost shy, very embarrassed, don't-look-at-me-I'm-not-here. He's in charge—well, his parents are, it being their house—but doesn't want to be seen to be in charge.

"Um," he begins, "maybe we should go indoors and listen to the album in the living room?" These three, I later learn, are old school friends. Their alma mater is Charterhouse in Surrey, a grand and exclusive—not to mention expensive—400-year-old Church of England private boarding school of significant educational repute. It's a boys-only establishment that, by definition, prizes tradition, heritage, discipline, sporting and academic achievement, and much arcane phraseology and terminology. Former pupils like Mike, Peter and Tony are known as Old Carthusians. Charterhouse also lays claim to having helped invent football.

In short, it's posh with a capital *p*, and not much like the Barbara Speake Stage School at all.

Peter and Tony met when they arrived at Charterhouse in 1963, with Mike enrolling a year later. Genesis formed in 1967 out of two school bands, with fellow pupils Anthony Phillips on guitar and Chris Stewart on drums. That year, Jonathan King—an Old Carthusian who'd had some success in the music industry—became the five-piece's "manager," and secured them a record deal with Decca.

Taking the name Genesis (a suggestion of King's), they released their first single, "The Silent Sun," in February 1968. That summer Chris Stewart left, and was replaced on drums by another Charterhouse boy, John Silver. In August, Genesis took ten days out of their school summer holidays to record their debut album, *From Genesis to Revelation*. It was released in March 1969. Tony Banks would later suggest that "after a year or so" the LP had sold "649 copies."

The summer of '69, having all left school, Genesis regrouped to consider a second album. Before they could do that, though, they lost another drummer, Silver being replaced by John Mayhew. He was an occasional carpenter who'd been looking for a drumming gig when Mike came across his number. Genesis played their first show in September 1969, at a teenager's birthday party. Now devoting themselves full-time to the band, they began to rehearse and perform wherever and whenever. Little wonder I kept seeing their name in the pages of *Melody Maker*. In spring 1970, midway through a six-week residency at Upstairs at Ronnie's, in Ronnie Scott's Jazz Club in Soho, Tony Stratton-Smith came to see them. He promptly signed them to a management and record deal with Charisma.

In June, Genesis began recording what would become their second album, *Trespass*, at Soho's Trident Studios with producer John Anthony. But in July, before the album was released, Ant Phillips announced that he was leaving. He was ill through overwork, and also falling prey to stage-fright.

This hit Mike, Tony and Peter hard. Ant was a founder member, an old friend and a great musician. As Mike would later say, "That was the closest we came to busting up. For some reason we felt so close that if one left, we thought we couldn't carry on. Of all the changes we've been through, surviving Ant leaving was the hardest."

But they decided to plow on with a new guitarist, with Tony's proviso that they also take the opportunity to replace Mayhew with—to be brutally frank—a better drummer. Losing drummers was clearly becoming a habit with these guys. At least they weren't spontaneously combusting. As far as I could tell anyway.

Cue that *Melody Maker* advert in July 1970—by which time Tony, Mike and Peter have been through a lot in their seven years of friendship and music-making. They have certain methods, and certain expectations, and certainly certain ways of relating to each other.

It will take me awhile to understand these dynamics. Tony and Peter, for example, are the best of friends, and the worst of enemies. Tony is prone to losing his temper, but this only makes itself apparent later, with Peter and Tony taking it in turns to storm out of studios in a huff. Mike keeps a delicate balance between the two. But all three of them are what they are: ex–public school boys, with all the privilege and baggage that comes with that kind of background. Immaculately bred as officers and gentlemen for a bygone age— perhaps less obvious fodder for a rock group emerging from the tumult of the swinging sixties.

Equally, I don't know at the time how close they've come to splitting, and therefore how much is riding on these auditions. Nor am I aware that Genesis' finely balanced creative symmetry has had the legs kicked from under it. Previously Genesis had the benefit of two pairs of writers, Mike and Ant, and Tony and Peter. And then there were three.

So the atmosphere today chez Gabriel is fragile, and tense. Also frightfully reserved, highly strung, not a little rarefied and terribly uptight. In sum, then, nothing at all like me or my background. What could possibly go right?

But there's one thing we all do have in common: we're all good musicians.

Right now, though, Ronnie and I are oblivious to these subtleties and undercurrents. We're sitting, alongside the handful of other disorientated hopefuls, in a giant living room made all the more cavernous by the absence of the grand piano. Now sitting on the terrace, by the swimming pool, it lurks under a giant umbrella. It's a still-life, like Dalí by way of Storm Thorgerson, an image in search of the sleeve of a seventies prog-rock album.

Peter appears, brandishing the as-yet-unreleased *Trespass*. He plays three tracks: "Stagnation," "Looking for Someone," "The Knife." Truth be told, I don't quite know what to make of it. I don't think much of the drumming—it's a little clumsy, and there's not much groove. There are some soft harmonies that remind me of Crosby, Stills & Nash. But the whole record seems like a . . . blancmange. You could put your finger in it and it would somehow reseal.

Ronnie goes off to give it a shot on the 12-string with Mike. Then, once Mike reappears, I finally get my turn. We move on to the terrace. Based on that quick, one-off exposure to the tracks from *Trespass*—an album with only six tracks, each averaging seven minutes—I'm trying to get a feel for Genesis. Now, as Tony starts on piano, Mike on guitar and Peter on his bass drum (he reckons himself a drummer, which will prove perilous in the months and years ahead), I have to join in with whatever I feel appropriate at the required moments.

We do three or four songs, including *Trespass*'s epic closer "The Knife," and some acoustic bits, to see how sensitive I really am to acoustic music.

I'm the last drummer that day and I'm trying to divine how well—or otherwise—I have done. To no avail. These are tightly wound English public schoolboys, and reserve and politesse are their key fighting skills. They will, they say gravely, "let me know."

Ronnie and I gather up our guitars and drums, load up the Morris Minor and start heading back to London, back to the real world.

"Yeah, I think you blew that," offers Ronnie helpfully. "I think I did well, but you definitely blew it."

"Really?" I reply. "No, I thought I did all right." We're arguing again already.

But as we approach the outskirts of London I start to feel less sure about how well I did. I couldn't read those guys. Neither Peter nor Mike nor Tony said, "That was really great!" No one was going to speak up; it's not in their make-up. They'd have a serious conversation about it afterward. In their own good time, without being rushed by anyone—and certainly not an eager jobbing drummer from Hounslow—Genesis would reach a decision.

I later learn that Peter knew the moment I sat down that I was the guy; seemingly the assured way I set up my kit was telling. Mike was less convinced. Tony felt quietly confident. History does not record the opinion of Mrs. Gabriel.

On August 8, 1970, the phone rings on the red leatherette and white wrought-iron telephone seat at 453 Hanworth Road. A voice I'll get used to hearing over the next few years says down a crackly telephone line, "Er, um, ah, hello, Phil? It's Peter Gabriel here. From Genesis. You've got the gig, if you want it."

"Yeah, Peter, thanks a lot."

I try to play it cool, but inside I'm jumping. I've finally found a band; or a band has found me. At last I'm going to play drums in front of people. It doesn't get much better than that.

First things first: I call Ronnie.

"Seems like I got the job with Genesis."

"Oh yeah. Did they say anything about me?"

"Ah, no . . ."

"Fuck! Ah, well, I think I was a bit too bluesy for them anyway . . ."

Ronnie's disappointment is understandable, and will also be long-running. He will come dutifully to support his old mate at all of Genesis' London shows, but equally dutifully he will always slag us off. It becomes a predictable part of the post-show: drink, rant, criticism, expression of lifelong friendship.

A few days after the phone call, Genesis and their new, fifth drummer meet at Strat's Charisma office in Soho. Already I feel like I've stepped up a gear or three. A band meeting, in Soho, in the office of our manager, who also looks after Van Der Graaf Generator and Lindisfarne. Having been on the outside looking in for so long, now I'm smack in the heart of things. I'm in a band, which is on a record label, in the music industry. They even have a tour van. Well, access to a tour van. A rented tour van.

All goes well at the meeting. The bit about Genesis being on a weekly wage of £10 is especially welcome, doubling as it does the income level I'm used to. Then Tony, Mike and Peter drop a bombshell: "We're taking two weeks' holiday to regroup." My mouth drops. I have nothing from which to regroup. I just want to group. More pertinently, what am I going to do for money?

And so my rock'n'roll dream splutters before it's even begun. I have no option but to embrace the idea of a frankly hideous thought: a day job.

At this point in time I can once again count Lavinia as my girl-friend. She's decided that this week she fancies me, even though that might change by Saturday. Her folks are, as ever, lovely to me, even trying to talk her into some kind of loose commitment. I could handle a loose commitment.

In dire need of money, not least to take Lavinia out, I feel like I have no option but to exploit our latest bout of "going steady": I ask her dad if he has any work. Fred Lang is a builder and jack-of-all-trades who is currently engaged in a large exterior decorating job in Wembley. Grateful but not a little mortified, I exchange drumsticks for paintbrush. Rock'n'roll and my role in its future will have to wait just a bit longer.

The job entails repainting all the windows and wooden areas on the outside of this poor unsuspecting couple's house. The actual painting is the easiest part. It's the preparation—stripping off the old paint and treating the bare wood—that kills you. As the old paint is usually lead-based, it's quite possibly literally killing you.

Excitable and frustrated teenager that I am, and a musician desperate to leave the starting blocks, I have zero patience with methodical stuff like stripping old paint, especially outdoors in a cold, damp English summer. The painstaking finesse I will later apply to my demos, and even my model trains, does not happen here. This is unfortunate, as finesse is exactly what's required of this job. But somehow I manage to pull the wool over Fred's eyes and pretend that this preparation has been carried out perfectly, thus enabling me to execute the final stage of painting.

With regard to slopping on the paint, I'm pretty talented. Over the padlock on the garden shed, over the locks on the doors, over the window frames—on it goes, slap-dash and willy-nilly. Sure, the straight lines round the windows leave a little to be desired. But by the time the shortcomings in my handiwork are revealed, I'll be miles away. It doesn't occur to me that messing up at my girlfriend's dad's place of work is perhaps not the best idea a hopeful young suitor ever had.

After the longest two weeks in history, Peter, Mike and Tony return from holiday. As they all live in the Surrey environs and I'm in distant west London, Mike invites me to stay at his mum and dad's house in Farnham. It's another grand home, although with a very warm, homely ambience. I gladly say farewell to London and move in with Mike, while also resolving to never again pick up a paint-brush for as long as I live.

The rest of my life finally begins with the new line-up of Genesis' first rehearsals in September 1970, in the pigeon-shit-encrusted environs of the Maltings, an old, barn-like complex in Farnham. We set up our gear and start playing with what I can describe as hazy enthusiasm: various public-school friends of Peter, Tony and Mike's drop in, I discover exotic new foodstuffs like Marmite and tahini, and the whole affair is often shrouded in the sweet smell of grass.

A constant presence is Richard MacPhail. He'd been singer in The Anon, one of the pre-Genesis bands at Charterhouse. He's the road manager and sound engineer, and a big spliff-head. Maybe he has to be, as he sleeps in the Maltings, sharing a berth with the pigeons and their guano, and guarding the gear. He introduces me to the pleasure of the stoned headphone experience. Crosby, Stills & Nash's *Déjà Vu* is not long out, and Richard brings round the LP, builds a giant joint and instructs Mike and me to immerse ourselves

Dad on the left, his dad on the right. This is the only photo I have of my grandfather. He was much loved by all. He and Grandma were cousins who met and fell in love. They were both very gentle people. However, when Grandpa insisted Dad reject the "silly idea" of running away to sea, Dad did as instructed. He had great respect for his father's opinion, though rumor has it he never forgave him for dragging him back.

Nana and baba Philip Collins. My earliest memories are of both of us doing things together: buying penny buns or standing outside the East Sheen house in the rain because she'd forgotten her key. We'd have to wait for Dad to come home from work to let us in.

My beautiful mum with her "Diana" smile. There is something about that smile; she seems so happy and radiant.

Pipe-smoking Dad: This is how I will always remember him. PS: I think the pipe has gone out.

Dad, little PC and Grandma on the banks of the river at St. Margarets, Twickenham, directly opposite Dick Waite's Boathouse. I sometimes give my dad a hard time for not leaving me enough memories of us together. He died when I was young, only twenty-one, which didn't help. It came completely out of the blue, and I guess I was angry about this uncontrollable turn of events. We had a lot of unfinished business.

Dick Waite's Boathouse in St. Margaret's, around 1954. This spot would eventually become Pete Townshend's Meher Baba Oceanic Studio. I'm the baby in Mum's arms, with sister Carole on the left just beside us. This is the photo I sent Pete that hung in the studio for years. Uncle Len Tungay stands far right, next to the river where Mum's ashes were later spread.

A family Christmas: Dad, Uncle Reg, Uncle Len, me, Mum, Carole and Clive at a Brighton hotel. Although we had many Christmases at Reg's and Len's houses, Christmas dinner was sometimes spent at this nice establishment.

Me as the Artful Dodger in 1964, at the New Theatre, St. Martin's Lane, in London's "glittering" West End. I can still remember everyone's names (left to right): Standing, Michael Harfleet (we're still in touch), Ralph Ryan, Arthur Wild, me, Jack Wild, Beryl Corsan, Jimmy Thomas and Chris Cooper.

Ronnie Caryl and I, mid-sixties, in a photo booth somewhere. I remember the Afghan coat very well—I wore it everywhere, and it got so dirty it could actually walk on its own.

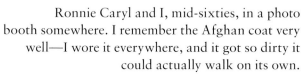

This was a publicity photo for Flaming Youth that turned up as I worked on the book. Our managers Ken Howard and Alan Blaikley dressed us up as a band, but it was never our intention to be (literally) stitched up like that. Top row: Flash Gordon, Brian Chatton, Ronnie Caryl. Seated: me.

At the Gorham Hotel in New York, circa 1973, looking for something to listen to. The only reason I wore those underpants was because they went with the wallpaper. This is my David Niven look (younger readers, look him up). I don't ever remember just having a mustache, but clearly I did.

Ronnie (far left) and I at the Reading Festival, in 1972 or '73, on Genesis duty. My fashion sense only got better, trust me. Even here Ronnie and I look like we're about to do battle, but I love him and always will.

Peter Gabriel and I, waiting for something to happen at the Una Billings School of Dance in Shepherd's Bush, West London. We were writing *Selling England by the Pound*. I'm sitting on Peter's bass drum, which was probably the best thing to do with it.

Photographer Armando Gallo was an early believer in Genesis and continues to be a friend to this day. I think he took this photo in Woolwich, London, around the time we were rehearsing there. I can't believe we were as bored as we look, but you never know.

Me, Andrea and a very young Joely at Headley Grange, circa 1974.

Happy Dad: One of my favorite photos of me and Joely, age four. I adopted Joely when I got back together with Andy in 1974. To me she was, and always will be, my daughter.

PC as Monty Python's Gumby, Nurse Joely and Cowboy Simon on our way to Eric Clapton's New Year's Eve fancy dress party at Hurtwood Edge around 1980. (Everyone was in fancy dress as instructed, but Eric had refused, so I was given responsibility for taking him upstairs and dressing him up. I took a nice frock of Patti's and a bath sponge for a wig. Despite his resistance, we went downstairs and he was a hit.)

Simon was my first son, and we are very close. Getting him to eat was not always easy, though! I think this was taken on tour in Paris in 1978, near the end of mine and Andy's marriage.

The legendary head of Atlantic Records, Ahmet Ertegun—what a great man he was. A huge musical brain, a big heart and great jokes. If he spoke, you listened. For as long as he was alive, he supported me. He used to call me the son he never had.

With Miles Davis at a small private party after the Grammys in 1986. He's telling me how much he loves "Separate Lives"—I didn't have the heart to tell him I didn't write it. Miles was a living legend, and here he was, talking to me.

Tony Smith and Genesis backstage at Milton Keynes in 1982. Tony was celebrating ten years of managing us. A fearsome beard, wouldn't you agree? Left to right: Steve, Peter, TS, Mike, PC, Tony and Daryl. Also present: my kids Simon and Joely, Kate Rutherford and Ben Banks (on far right).

By the pool at Sir George Martin's AIR studios in Montserrat. I was producing what would become Eric's *Behind the Sun* album. Sting arrived, as he was there on holiday, and Stephen Bishop turned up, as he knew we were all there.

in the sonic majestic harmonies of "Carry On." It's not quite kicking open the doors of perception, but I am knocking gently.

I enjoy living at Mike's parents' house. There are boiled eggs for breakfast and always a dish cooking on the Aga. For some reason, too, there's often talk between Mike and Tony about something called "kedgeree." I haven't a clue what it is.

Do I feel like a bit of an oik? For sure, a bit. But I know already that I can bring something to Genesis. Something that's needed. Not just in the way of musical skills, although I am aware that with my drumming I can make that blancmange as hard as we need.

Peter, Mike and Tony's background is a world away from mine. Our schooling, class, family—on paper, we couldn't be farther apart. For all of early Genesis' gigging and recording experience, they've been somewhat cloistered. I've been schooled in the rough and tumble of the life of a gigging performer and musician. I've been on the stage in London's West End, a regular down the front at the Marquee, the drummer for an almost comically diverse array of groups, bands and combos. I have ducked and dived through swinging sixties Soho, and I have the energy, momentum and enthusiasm to prove it. I can apply all of that to the rather more conservative, rather less worldly Genesis.

I'm also quick with a joke, a mood-lightening attribute that will come in very handy when Peter, Mike and Tony revert to school playground bickering. When they start arguing about who stole whose protractor, I can always step in with some distracting bonhomie. My personality, and my ability to break the ice, is exactly what these buttoned-up public schoolboys need, even if they don't know it. English reserve will only take you so far. In the same way that my very limited experience as a songwriter means I will end up being the band's musical arranger in these early days, I can also rearrange the mood.

All things considered, for me this is the perfect job. Genesis are a busy, gigging, well-regarded band with a record deal. On top of that, I like these guys. They're interesting. No twelve-bar blues here. We're different, but we have lots in common. I can make this work. I can definitely squeeze into these trousers.

6

FROM BLUE BOAR
TO FOX'S HEAD

Or: Genesis on the road and in the fancy-dress box

R EHEARSING AT THE Maltings, our chemistry is quickly apparent. It's a friendly old barn, and we feel comfortable playing, jamming and composing in it. A truer test of this experimental line-up will come with performing. Or, to be precise, traveling to the performing. How will the combustible elements of the "new" Genesis combine in the more controlled environment of a tiny, wheezing, British-made family car?

Our ambitions being considerably larger than rural Surrey, the latter months of 1970 find us gigging up and down the country in Peter's Hillman Imp or Mike's Mini Traveller. But even then, old school habits die hard, and a pecking order is soon apparent. Unsurprisingly, I come last.

Being the driver puts you in pole position. It means you're in control, and it means you can claim all the Green Shield stamps when you fill up with petrol. Peter and Mike will take proud ownership of a 24-piece dinner service long before I even catch sight of so much as a saucer.

When Peter is driving, Tony usually wins the argument about who's sitting in the passenger seat. The rest of us cram into the back, fighting for room with an assortment of electric and acoustic guitars.

For a while, "the rest of us" means three of us, as there's another guitarist, Mick Barnard. After the audition that Ronnie failed, we carried on as a four-piece, with no guitarist, Tony manfully trying to play all the guitar parts on a Hohner electric piano through a fuzz-box. Then we found Mick. He's a nice guy, and a good guitarist, but he doesn't last. My abiding memory of Mick's brief time in Genesis is not his playing, or anything musical, but us always dropping him off after gigs at Toddington Services on the M1 near Dunstable in Bedfordshire. How he gets home from there I've no idea.

So the search for a guitar player continues. Scouring *Melody Maker* one week, we read Steve Hackett's advert. "A Able Accordionist," it begins, which is a clever way of putting yourself top of the alphabetically arranged list, and Peter thinks it's interesting enough to follow up on. We invite Steve to Tony's new flat in Earls Court, to pitch his stuff to us. Arriving dressed entirely in black, something we will come to expect from him, he's quite an intense character. Clearly a big fan of King Crimson's Robert Fripp, Steve impresses everyone less with his technique than with his ideas. And now we are five.

These are exciting times—I'm still a couple of months shy of my twentieth birthday, I'm on ten quid a week (more than I can spend), and I find the romance of life on the road with a proper band utterly intoxicating.

That romance takes unusual forms, one of which is stopping at the Blue Boar services at Watford Gap on the M1. A lot of bands pull in there on the way back from gigs in the north. An early-hours' plate of beans on toast and an inter-band moan about the students at Leeds Uni are just the tonic for footsore rockers. And from here on in, you can see the light: up till this point it's been endless cat's eyes on the road. But from Watford Gap the motorway has overhead lamps to usher you south and homeward. In the absence of speed or any other pharmaceuticals, that's all the wake-up we're going to get.

When Peter drives, he talks. We'll be bombing up the M1 toward the Midlands and suddenly you'll tune into this high-pitched whining. It's not me, complaining from the back about my lack of Green Shield stamps. It's Peter, doing 80 mph in second gear. He's so wrapped up in what he's trying to say that he's forgotten to change gear. He finally shifts and the car relaxes.

At this time we have a couple of road crew, Gerard Selby, another Old Carthusian, and his nineteen-year-old brother Adrian. We later find out that Adrian has also been "managing" us for a year. Nobody thinks to tell us, and we didn't think to ask. Unfortunately, throughout this time he doesn't keep copies of any invoices, or any receipts for UV lights, drapes, batteries, cables and the like. Genesis have been earning a reasonable amount through gigs, but spending far more on actually doing them. Come the end of the tax year we're in trouble, and so is Adrian: he's fired.

Our audiences are mostly male, mostly hairy, mostly students. They favor fishing hats and long coats, accessorized with piles of LPs carried under fragrant armpits. Not the most practical of outfits for sweaty gigs in sticky venues. Fashion is not on our side, a status quo with which we will become well acquainted.

We take gigs whenever and wherever, with varying degrees of success. We support Atomic Rooster at a university show in London. I never went for Carl Palmer much as a drummer, but he's a nice guy, and while the band are playing I'm creeping around backstage, trying to find a good vantage point from which to watch the gig.

There's a Christmas tree of plugs jammed into a socket which, in the gloom, I manage to trip on and kick out. Bang goes all the stage power, and everything flops down: lights, sound, vibe. I scarper, fast, before the now rather sub-atomic headliners can spot me.

Mostly, though, the gigs are conducted in a fairly professional manner: get there, get on, get back. A few joints but no bawdy bacchanalia. The closest we get to that is at a show at London's City University, which happens to be Steve's first gig with Genesis. Our stage time is later than advertised so I pass the time by sinking a few Newcastle Browns. By the time we're onstage, I'm all over the place, literally. I do all the right fills but do them three inches to the right of each drum. Forget air-guitar, this is air-drums. Afterward I'm wincing: "What must this new guitarist think? First gig and the drummer's pissed." That is the first time I'm ever drunk playing, and it will be the last.

That's not to say I'm averse to having a few post-show, especially when there are other musicians to play with. Tony Stratton-Smith has the great idea of booking a tour with three of his strongest bands, playing nine concert halls up and down the country. The Charisma Package Tour kicks off at the Lyceum in London on January 24, 1971. For a very competitive six bob (30p in new money), you can catch Genesis ("now, without doubt, they have come of age"—*Sounds*), Lindisfarne ("their hallmark is strong, clear, straight-ahead songs"—*Melody Maker*) and, topping the bill, Van Der Graaf Generator ("as if heralding Armageddon, VDGG make great use of shock chords and pregnant pauses to highlight their brooding high-decibel tension"—*NME*).

The tour is a raging success, establishing all three bands as major, hall-filling acts. *NME* is on hand to describe the scenes in Newcastle: "Well over 500 people had to be left out in the cold while 2500 enthusiasts created scenes of almost unparallel [*sic*] hysteria in the sanctum of the City Hall." In Manchester, the Free Trade Hall "had crocodiles of long-haired youths surrounding it for the last remaining tickets."

It's great fun behind the scenes, too, with much Newcastle Brown-fueled merriment on the shared tour bus that transports us round the country. I fall in with Alan Hull and the Lindisfarne boys—hearty Geordies to a man—and enjoy a smoke or three with the road crews. But for Genesis as a whole, there is perhaps too much merriment: it is our first tour by bus, and it will be our last. Buses travel much slower than cars, and the journeys tend to drag out much more than they need to. London to Newcastle, 274 miles according to the AA handbook, is an interminable trek with a coach. So we decide to go our own way and thereafter revert to our own modes of transport—Peter's Hillman Imp and Mike's Mini Traveller.

In a sign of things to come, we divide the critics. *NME* reviews the tour's sixth show, at Manchester Free Trade Hall: "In the demonic, black-clad figure of Peter Gabriel, Genesis have a vocal performer who has the precocious magnetism of which contemporary pop heroes are hewn. A macabre entrepreneur, Peter introduces each selection with strange neo-fantasy monologues which at times border on the realms of insanity."

"Genesis, featuring their new but well-rehearsed guitarist Steve Hackett, played well," begins *Sounds*' review of the tour's penulti-mate stop, at Brighton Dome, "although they missed the encourage-ment they are normally given from the auditorium . . . Peter Gabriel was impressive as usual, although it was one of those nights when his funny little monologues fell on stony ground and were greeted by stony faces."

So, to recap: our frontman is a contemporary pop hero, a maca-bre entrepreneur but also a teller of funny little monologues that no one likes.

For some reason Genesis have made decent inroads in Belgium. After my trip to the Netherlands with Flaming Youth, all I need is some love from Luxembourg and I can confidently say I am big in Benelux.

So in March 1971 Genesis play their first foreign gig, in a little club in Charleroi called Ferme Cinq. We make the trip by cross-Channel ferry and, when we arrive, our excitement at now being an international touring band is undimmed when we see that the stage is made of beer crates. We have to arrange them carefully so they don't wobble and topple mid strange, neo-fantasy monologue. We somehow manage to stay upright, and we go down a storm. All of the half-a-dozen shows are the same: all packed, all incredible. Gen-esis have taken off, finally. In Belgium at any rate.

At home we're still playing places like Farx, a club within a pub in Potters Bar, and another Farx on the Uxbridge Road, Southall. The latter is one of the very few shows my dad attends, it being close to Barbara Speake's house, where my mum is living, and not far from Hounslow, where he's staying for a last few months before permanently exiting for Weston-super-Mare.

That said, my only recall of this is that of him actually attend-ing. No other details present themselves; I have no memory of Dad saying, "Good job, son." Perhaps he stuck it out just long enough to have a half-pint of bitter. I imagine he's still of the opinion that I'm not amounting to much. It's only a pub, and his youngest child ap-pears to be playing in a musical group with little musicality that he can understand. Round about this time it is not unknown for us to play tunes that have no lyrics yet, and songs that are patently incomplete, and/or for Peter to simply sing random syllables.

The audience don't seem to notice. Are they so transported by our wonderful music? Or are they pissed? It's probably as much to do with the fact that our used and abused PA is so knackered that no one's able to discern any lyrics anyway. Poor Dad. No wonder he hardly ever comes. No wonder he fears for his son's future.

Eventually, though, despite the relentless pressure of playing gigs, these wordless tunes (and some meaningless words), plus some rather foggy musical passages, coalesce into new songs. Finally we're ready to record my first album with the band, which means it's time for this "new boy" to become a fully blooded member of Genesis.

Ironically, this is also the moment my actual blood ties are stretched to breaking point. In June, Mum and Dad finally decide to sell 453 Hanworth Road. But here in summer 1971, a year on from my joining Genesis, band life rolls inexorably, distractingly on and we decamp to Luxford House in Crowborough, East Sussex. It's Strat's rented home, and also his suggestion: bands "getting it together in the country"—that is, writing some songs away from the hurly-burly of the city—is very much the in-thing. If it's all right for Traffic and Led Zeppelin, it's all right for Genesis.

The house is a beautiful Tudor pile, a picture-postcard mansion with a decent outbuilding that will do for the songwriting sessions. We eat great meals prepared by one of the roadies, we drink red wine by the barrel, we repair to the rolling lawns to play croquet. This old-fashioned, upper-crust, very English game informs the sleeve art for the album that is about to become *Nursery Cryme*. Personally I find the illustrations, by Paul Whitehead (he'd done *Trespass*, too), a bit naff. But I'm outvoted, and he will also create the art for our next album, *Foxtrot*.

When it comes to choosing rooms at Luxford House, once more the pecking order comes into play. Pete, Mike and Tony pick their sleeping arrangements first, and the new boys, Steve and I, get what's left.

Ultimately I'm not bothered, as there are more important things to think about—this will be the debut album by the new line-up of

Genesis. We write "The Fountain of Salmacis" and "The Return of the Giant Hogweed." I'm in my element, reveling in the creative freedom, the free flow of ideas, the scale of our ambition, the length of our songs. I feel emboldened and liberated, encouraged by the guys to contribute.

There's room for maneuver, too. Some writing sessions involve us gathering around Tony, sat at his Hammond organ, with Mike playing 12-string guitar and Peter improvising vocals. I'll improvise along with him. Similarly, Peter writes "Harold the Barrel" on piano and I stand beside him, singing harmony and chipping in with ideas. I can bang out a few piano chords, though my insecurity is shouting: "They've heard this all before!" One thing I learn from writing with the guys is to never accept the first melody idea that you sing. Dig deeper, and play around with it. Explore. If you listen to The Beatles' "She Loves You," it's a very simple chord sequence, but the melody that they put on top of that simplicity is beautifully crafted. I soak up all these tips and tricks from Peter, Mike and Tony, considerably more experienced writers to a man.

A natural progression from these writing sessions is that the drummer sings a song. Not a long one, and it's only the one song, but it's a song. The moment arrives when Steve comes up with a pastoral guitar piece, and I write the words. To acquaint the guys with the lyrics and melody, I open my mouth and go for it . . . a bit. I'm not sure about this—to me, my voice sounds soft and tentative. But the guys like it, and that's good enough for me. In the end "For Absent Friends," at one minute and forty-four seconds, is strictly speaking more an "interlude" than a "song." But it's my first Genesis lead vocal.

From that time, on every Genesis record, any voice you hear other than Peter's, on backgrounds and harmonies, is me. The other boys are frankly just not very good singers. But I'm happy to sing, in the background, from the comfort of my stool.

Nursery Cryme—recorded at Soho's Trident with John Anthony, who produced *Trespass*—comes out in November 1971. It reaches number 4 in Italy, making it the second European nation to embrace Genesis. We play the Italian capital's Palazzetto dello Sport, a venue built for the 1960 Olympics that can hold 3,500 seated Romans, 10,000 standing, and they love us.

This is the biggest place we've played, and we'll play it for many years to come. The Italian audiences are extraordinary. Not only do they love us passionately, but they really "get" it. They whoop and applaud even a change of mood, something at which Genesis are adept—we can go from up-tempo to a whispered nothing to pastoral interlude, with barely a swish of our hair. No wonder the Italians are so enthusiastic about us: we're an English band plumbing the operatic tradition.

It's a mutual love affair that will climax thirty years later, in 2007, when Genesis end the first leg of the *Turn It On Again* reunion tour with a free concert at Circo Massimo (Circus Maximus) in front of an estimated half a million people. As I'm passionate about Roman history, a venue where chariots once raced for the Emperor's entertainment is, to me, the epitome of maximus rock'n'roll.

But even in 1972 this Italian success is sensational, bigger than Belgium. Only eighteen months ago I was an end-of-the-line boy from Hounslow. And now this, international(ish) adoration. It doesn't matter that in Britain we're still not far from pub gigs, or gigs on beer crates, or both at once. Yes, back in the real world we're still gigging in a van, normally rented from a dodgy firm in Kensington. The quality of a rented van will determine whether we will actually make the gig in time. We have a habit of breaking down en route. Sometimes multiple times. On the way to Aberystwyth University, we break down three times on the way there, arrive too late to play, then break down twice on the way back.

These are days of merry, itinerant, sofa-surfing, wee-hours chaos. I'll occasionally pop back to 453 Hanworth Road, as it's still not sold, hopping out of the van sometime in the middle of the night. Or, if we have a gig the next day, I'll crash with one of the guys, usually Richard MacPhail. Some late-night/early-morning cornflakes, a small joint, sleep, more cornflakes, and we're off again.

We push on, and on. In October 1972, eleven months after the release of *Nursery Cryme*, comes *Foxtrot*. Genesis' fourth album, my second with the band, is recorded with co-producer Dave Hitchcock and engineer John Burns at Island Studios in Notting Hill—the place where, two years previously, Led Zeppelin recorded *IV* and Jethro Tull recorded *Aqualung*. Twelve years later I'll be back there, recording "Do They Know It's Christmas?" with Band Aid.

Foxtrot features "Supper's Ready," the 23-minute song suite that will, for much of the seventies, contribute to the public perception of the band. A lot of Genesis "heads" regard it as our magnum opus, and I'd go along with that. It's greater than the sum of its parts, though some of those parts are brilliant, notably "Apocalypse in 9/8 (Co-Starring the Delicious Talents of Gabble Ratchet)" and "As Sure As Eggs Is Eggs (Aching Men's Feet)."

This time, the writing for the album takes place a million miles from a country pile: prior to going into Island Studios, we bunker in the basement of the Una Billings School for Dance in Shepherd's Bush, west London. Where previously we could smell freshly cut grass, we're now high on the odor of ballet pumps. We set up our equipment in Una's basement, and start writing.

I am absent from Una Billings for a few hours one day, and when I return Tony, Mike and Steve have messed around with a riff in 9/8. I haven't a clue what is happening, and just start to play. At some points I play with the riff, at others I join Tony. I'm still immensely proud of the final recorded performance of the piece which became "Apocalypse in 9/8," which captures me making it up as I go along.

Most of all, though, credit must go to Tony, Mike and Peter for seeing that all those parts could fit and be more than just five songs strung together over twenty-three minutes.

Nonetheless, we are worried about "Supper's Ready" actually fitting on the album: the more music you have on a vinyl LP, the shallower the grooves, and the lower the volume will be. Twenty-three minutes is pushing the limit for one side of a 33-rpm long-player. Worse, if you have an eight-track cassette in your car—as most people do in 1972—it fades in and out three or four times. It's mad to think now of such physical limitations on music.

As a consequence, Genesis are literally pushing the boundaries of what bands can do on an album. The only other equally ambitious, similarly sized piece of music at this time is *Tubular Bells*. In the wake of its release seven months after *Foxtrot*, at our gigs we habitually play Mike Oldfield's groundbreaking debut over the PA system. It's there to vibe up the audience before we come onstage, and also to help us schedule our preparations. We'd know where we were by any particular section. "Oh, it's 'Bagpipe Guitars,' boys, time to get dressed!"

Performing "Supper's Ready" brings its own challenges. The first dozen or so times we do it, including its unveiling at Brunel University on November 10, 1972, the five of us are constantly trying to catch up with each other, such is the concentration needed to perform a long piece of music. However, from the off, it's a hit with our audiences, and we always breathe a sigh of relief when we reach the end. Especially if we reach the end at the same time. If only that were the only challenge with which we're wrestling onstage.

On September 19, 1972, the month before the release of *Foxtrot*, we're booked to play the National Stadium in Dublin. I view playing this 2,000-capacity boxing arena with some nervousness. It's our first time in Ireland, and I fear we're pushing our luck in a venue of this size and type.

But we roll onstage and get stuck into the set. Presently we come to the instrumental section of *Nursery Cryme*'s opening track, "The Musical Box," which is quite lengthy. Lengthy enough, in fact, to put on a dress.

Having taken himself offstage, Peter now re-emerges from the wings. I catch him out of the corner of my eye, gingerly feeling his way back to his microphone. Why's he taking so long? Normally he'd be back onstage with the "old man mask," a prop Peter had made that he pulled over his head, immediately making him a grizzly, balding codger. This was always worn during the finale of "The Musical Box."

As the stage lights catch him, the confusion lifts, only to be replaced by perplexity: Peter's wearing a frock (his wife Jill's, we later learn) and a fox's head. Jaws are dropping, on- and offstage. This is as much a surprise to Mike, Tony, Steve and me as it is to 2,000 Dubliners.

In the dressing room afterward, Peter isn't about to take on board any comments from the band committee with regards to his fantastic

Mrs. Fox outfit. Once he gets his paws dug in, he isn't budging. So, while there are no shouts of "Boy, that was fantastic!," nor is there arguing. There's just a collective shrug of: "OK . . ." Peter offers no explanation for his thinking, and I offer no protest. The music is still center stage, so I'm not really bothered. It's just Pete doing his thing. He'd always be getting up to something when we were digging into some long instrumental sections.

Prior to this there have been no hints that Peter was considering a new fancy-dress direction. Equally, moving forward, there is no flagging up of the flower mask he will wear for the "Willow Farm" section of "Supper's Ready," nor the triangular box head he wears for the next section, "Apocalypse in 9/8." We see none of it before the audience sees it. He will not entertain any ideas of a band decision. To his mind, such democracy on matters theatrical will only slow down the process and lead to debates over what color the dress should be and whether the flower is a hardy annual or a perennial.

This is what Peter Gabriel now does onstage with Genesis. After Dublin, Mrs. Fox appears at every show, at the same point in the set. We quickly become used to it, as well we should: a photograph of Peter in his new get-up goes straight on the cover of *Melody Maker*, and immediately puts a nought on Genesis' booking fee. We go from being a £35-a-night band to a £350-a-night band.

IT'S GETTING CLOSE to the end of 1972, and I have no idea that Dad is ill. He's moved lock, stock and barrel down to Weston and rarely comes up to London. But 453 Hanworth Road has finally been sold, it's the end of an era, and my life has to go on. I start renting a damp flat in Downs Avenue, Epsom, in a cheaply converted, dilapidated Georgian house. The walls are paper-thin; when it rains, it's as wet on the inside as it is outside.

In December 1972 we play our first two American shows. Our landfall in the new world is not incredibly auspicious. We arrive to discover that our U.S. manager, Ed Goodgold, also manager of Woodstock heroes Sha Na Na, has booked us a show at Brandeis University near Boston, Massachusetts. At lunchtime. So our first show on American soil is an unceremonious, crashing disappoint-ment. New England students are less keen on English rock bands than we'd assumed, and seem more interested in their studying or their sandwiches. This does not bode well for Genesis' fortunes in the United States of America.

Approaching New York for the first time, we're overwhelmed, the sheer enormity of the city bearing down on a band whose heads are already bowed after the letdown of Boston. But driving in over the George Washington Bridge at dusk, the Manhattan skyline is winking into life, illuminated by millions of lights. New York! We've seen it in the movies, and now we're here.

My senses reeling from the sight of steam billowing from sewer vents, the smell of pretzels cooking, the incessant honking of yellow cabs and the giddy views down the canyons of steel, that first visit to New York will stay with me no matter how many times I return.

We check into our hotel, The Gorham, an arty, slightly run-down place in Midtown near 5th Avenue. We do a little exploring, then we sleep. Next day we take some promotional photos in Cen-tral Park and outside legendary Greenwich Village venue The Bitter End. Then it's over to the Philharmonic Hall for our soundcheck and the discovery of a major problem: the different power system in the U.S. means that the motored instruments run on sixty cycles, not fifty cycles as in the U.K. This means the Mellotron (a new toy we've acquired from King Crimson) and the Hammond organ are out of tune with the guitars.

We devise a makeshift solution and, that night, muddle through our set. The audience doesn't seem to notice anything untoward, but, despite the five of us being telepathically in sync, for Genesis the show is a shambles. We come offstage, get into the lift up to the dressing room and the air is blue with rage. Even years later the men-tion of this first New York show rattles everyone's cages as all the horrific memories return.

But, all things considered, I fly back to the U.K. on something of a high. So Genesis' first trip to America wasn't entirely auspi-cious—at least I've been there, which is not something many people I know in 1972 can say.

Christmas is looming and I ring my dad to check that he's still coming back to London from Weston-super-Mare for the "family" festivities. I haven't seen him for many a month, and the plan is that the splintered Collins clan will reconvene at Barbara Speake's home in Ealing for something approaching a merry Christmas. He assures me he is.

Then, out of the blue, Clive receives a phone call: Dad's had a heart attack. The doctor assures Clive that Dad's OK to travel, so he drives down to Weston to collect him.

When he arrives at Clive's home in Leigh-on-Sea, Dad spends a restful night. But the next morning he takes a turn for the worse, and Clive takes him to hospital in nearby Southend, where he has yet another bad turn. It's Christmas Eve.

Dad dies on Christmas Day at 8 a.m.

Truthfully, I'm perhaps too preoccupied to feel distraught (that comes later), even when my brother recounts the sad state of my dad's living conditions: so much damp that it was visible all down the walls of the small cottage he was living in—a terribly unhealthy environment, especially for someone with heart problems. It's also likely he had diabetes, and when he'd arrived in hospital they were considering amputating both his legs. Mum and Clive both agreed that Dad would not have wanted to live had that happened to him.

Dad's funeral is on January 1, 1973. I'm in a daze. I remember the coffin entering the crematorium oven, and them playing "Jesu, Joy of Man's Desiring," one of his favorite Bach pieces. I don't remember crying. I may have done. But certainly the grief has increased as I've got older. With each of my five children, I'm far more aware of my role in their lives as a result of losing my father at such a young age. Christmas, too, always comes with more than a hint of sadness.

Dad never did grasp the idea of me wanting to play music for a living. He had little or no interest in music generally, especially in the kind that was being made in the sixties. In fact, pretty much the only musical memory I have of Dad is him singing, "*Hi-diddle-dee-dee, an actor's life for me . . .*" as he let go of my bicycle saddle for the first time when I was a small boy. I pedaled on, unaware I was flying solo.

I'm twenty-one. My adult life—my professional life—has begun, but my dad has died.

Everything feels muted, flattened. I find myself thinking something that will preoccupy me at various moments, in various shades, for years to come: did Dad, at the end, think his son had made the right decision? Was he impressed by my finally making a living, albeit via an unorthodox route? Was it a point of some fatherly satisfaction to Grev Collins that his youngest had made it across the Atlantic?

I'd like to think he would, ultimately, have been proud, but I've often wondered what would have been the tipping point. Maybe filling four nights at Wembley? Or: "My son, playing for the Prince of Wales—*marvelous*." The royal seal of approval would have bestowed the paternal seal of approval. That would have clinched it.

Postscript: During the writing of this book, I realized that Dad never had a marker put where his ashes were placed. I vowed to fix this, and Clive carried out some inquiries. My brother discovered that due to a mix-up between him and Mum, Dad's ashes were in fact never picked up. So Dad's earthly remains were left languishing in Southend Crematorium. To this day, no one knows where he is.

7

LAMB LIES DOWN, SINGER FLIES OFF

Or: cracking America and cracking up

LUCKILY, PERHAPS, I don't have too long to dwell on my dad's death. The *Foxtrot* tour resumes in Croydon, south London, on January 7, 1973, six days after his funeral. It continues through the rest of Europe, returns to the U.K. again and then moves to North America, where we play Carnegie Hall. We won't finish until we reach Paris and Brussels on May 7 and 8. A heavy bout of touring to deal with at a heavy time, with Peter's costumes becoming more outlandish as the tour progresses.

For "Watcher of the Skies" he wears fluorescent face paint, a cape and bat wings on his head. That's not the finale; that's the opening song in the set. The sense of drama is heightened by Tony playing a long, moody introduction on the Mellotron (now running on the correct cycles).

Peter's theatricality is now integrated into the live set. It is, as far as press and public are concerned, What Genesis Do. And in the early-seventies context it doesn't seem so crazy. Alice Cooper is doing weird things with snakes, Elton John is dressing like a duck and wearing glasses bigger than his head, The Who are making concept albums left, right and center. Ours, though, is a different kind of quirkiness, a strange English thing, which is perhaps one of the reasons it will do so well in the U.S.

In the words of the *Rolling Stone* review of that year's *Genesis Live*, released in July 1973: ". . . this album goes a long way toward capturing the gripping power and mysticism that has many fans acclaiming Genesis as 'the greatest live band ever.' Titles like 'Get 'Em Out by Friday' and 'The Return of the Giant Hogweed' tell much about this band's modus operandi: a strange, visionary moralism highly reminiscent of both Yes and Jethro Tull. Genesis predated both of those bands in audio-visual productions though, and their dues-paying days are well documented by the high degree to which they develop multiple themes on both lyrical and instrumental levels."

After the release of *Genesis Live* we barely pause before gathering at a lovely but slightly fading country house in Chessington, Surrey, to write the next album. I can't remember how we got there, but the owners were a nice couple and I know there were some attractive daughters involved. We set up our gear in their living room, so I can only assume the couple were absent.

It is in this oddly domestic setting that "The Battle of Epping Forest" and, more importantly, "The Cinema Show" are born. Based on a guitar riff of Mike's in 7/8, "The Cinema Show" will become a huge stage favorite for years to come. Also completed at Chessington is a song we began at Una Billings during the *Foxtrot* sessions, "I Know What I Like (In Your Wardrobe)."

The resulting album, *Selling England by the Pound*, is released in October (again I sing lead vocal on one track, "More Fool Me"), and we're already back on tour. We won't stop until May 1974, by which time "I Know What I Like (In Your Wardrobe)" has given us our first Top 30 single in the U.K.

In the studio the song didn't strike us as particularly "pop," though it was of pop-single duration. We had got hold of a sitar-guitar, something used by The Beatles. Steve played the basic riff, which sounded good, I started to play a Beatle-ish groove, and it went from there. Peter's lyrics came in quite late, because they were influenced by the Betty Swanwick painting (*The Dream*) on the album cover. On the track, my voice is in there, in a kind of duet with Peter. And that's it. Genesis have their first hit. *Top of the Pops* here we come.

Except we don't. We decline an offer from the BBC's weekly in-stitution because we think our fans will object to us appearing on such a mainstream show. Fundamentally, we object, too. We're forg-ing our own path and, for the same reason we don't trust festivals (we can't control the staging, it's not our audience), we don't trust television. Plus, by now we pride ourselves on our presentation, and "I Know What I Like" doesn't readily lend itself to much in the way of presentation. Not yet, anyway. Touring the album, Peter will don a pointy hat, somewhat reminiscent of a Boer War military helmet, and, with some straw clamped between his teeth, mime the mowing of a lawn along with the drone that starts the song.

It's around this time that Adrian Selby's poor bookkeeping catches up with us and we discover that Genesis are in debt to the tune of £150,000. A fortune in those days, around £2 million in to-day's money. But we still say no to the biggest bit of TV promotion in the land.

This is where Tony Smith enters the picture. Just to clarify: he's not to be confused with Tony Stratton-Smith. Strat was our man-ager, and also boss of our label, Charisma. He'd kick-started things and kept Genesis rolling for a good while, but inevitably that created a conflict of interest when it came to negotiations between manager and record company. So although we all love and trust him, we have to be businesslike and consider our future. Especially when there are eye-watering debts to consider.

Tony Smith, on the other hand, is a partner in an established concert promotion business with Mike Alfandary and Harvey Goldsmith. Tony's dad, John, was a promoter too—he promoted The Beatles and Frank Sinatra—and Tony had a top-of-the-range apprenticeship with him. In fact, they also promoted the Charisma Package Tour. So Tony knows all the people to befriend, or to avoid, including notorious managers like Don Arden and Peter Grant. But he decides to sacrifice all that sure-fire concert income and manage a band which is clearly going places—most notably at this point, the bankruptcy court.

The *Selling England* tour is the first of Genesis' epic treks around North America, and Tony Smith's first major undertaking with us. We'd done a month's worth of shows there on the *Foxtrot* tour, but here's a shock: it was going to take a lot more than that to "break" the U.S. and Canada. So off we go.

The French Canadians love us. We start the tour with two shows in one night in Quebec; I think of them as the beatnik crowd, enthralled by our artiness. The Tower Theater in Philadelphia is also a great gig for us. We play a lot of shows in and around upstate New York, and around the Northeast, many arranged by a young promoter named Harvey Weinstein, the same Harvey that now runs The Weinstein Company and is one of the most successful film producers of all time.

Over the following months we end up being quite popular on the East Coast. Almost deliriously popular. That said, we can take nothing for granted. We have an awful show with The Spencer Davis Group at the horribly carpeted and acoustically dead Felt Forum underneath Madison Square Garden. We'd hoped for something like the real Garden but instead got its ugly cousin. Boston still seems to hate us, though they'll come round eventually.

Generally speaking, over the U.S. as a whole, in the likes of Ypsilanti, Evanston, Fort Wayne and Toledo, we play to quizzical faces. We are, in short, swimming against the musical tide. They've never really heard something like us before. We're not as noodly as Yes. We're not as virtuoso-driven as Emerson, Lake & Palmer. We're far quirkier than anybody else out there, and we pay the price.

By the time we get to Los Angeles, we're ready to let our hair down. We stay at The Tropicana, a real motel (excitement for us English boys). We go from room to room, spliffing up—this is LA!—and eat downstairs at Duke's coffee shop, a famous eatery to which all the visiting bands gravitate. LA is all we expect it to be. All the landmarks are clearly visible: the Whisky a Go Go, the Hollywood sign, the Capitol Records Tower. Palm trees and warm weather and the odd tequila sunrise and we're all very happy.

We do six shows at The Roxy over three days. This club is situated on Sunset Boulevard, and boasts a very chic, members-only club above it called On The Rox. Here, Jack Nicholson, Warren Beatty, Joni Mitchell and a host of other eminent hipsters gather nightly. The Roxy itself sounds grander than it is. It's only a 500-seater venue, and it's probably the same 500 people at all six shows. But at least the label, Atlantic Records, entertain us: they lay on a boys-only party, and screen the hottest film of the previous year. I don't mean *The Godfather* or *Cabaret*. I mean *Deep Throat*, even then one of the most notorious porn films of all time. That said, none of us are *au fait* with cinematic porn, and all I can remember is: a lot of hair. It's pretty gruesome. There's some embarrassed shuffling in the English area of the room, but it's all strangely un-erotic and not far from being a biology lesson.

When all is said and done, I can't say that this is a grueling tour-bus schlep through the highways and byways of America, because it isn't. We're not on a tour bus. We have two stretch limousines.

Tony Banks hates flying—he'll get used to it in later years—and the rest of us aren't so keen either. The idea of living the rock'n'roll dream by gigging across the States by bus leaves us unimpressed. We're not rock'n'roll, for one thing. Boozing and shagging on the team bus doesn't really interest us. "Clean sheets and cocoa," Mike Rutherford used to say if the hotel was to his liking. On a bus I don't think any of us can sleep easy wondering if someone's still awake at the wheel of this coffin-shaped box full of bunks.

So two stretch limousines it is, each driven by a guy called Joe (that's a coincidence rather than a prerequisite).

Now I come to think of it: perhaps it's no wonder Genesis are £150,000 in debt.

Generally, a stretch limousine is a fine mode of transport by which to travel the length and breadth of North America (unless you're at the bottom of the pecking order and end up sitting in the middle at the back, above the axle. Gee, wonder who that might be). The only hitch is that two limos full of unwashed, hirsute Brit musos can attract attention, particularly at border crossings.

Canadian Customs are among the toughest. They're used to musicians crossing over from America with a little stash of dope. Bands tend to forget that Canada is another country, which is perhaps one reason for Keith Richards' infamous Toronto bust. Inevitably, as we enter Canada, en route to Toronto, Customs pull us over at the Peace Bridge, at the Niagara Falls border crossing. Our lighting guy, Les Adey, a highly diligent and enthusiastic toker, is white as a sheet. Soon our equally white-as-a-sheet English bodies are on display as we submit to a strip search. Our tour manager, Regis Boff, supposed to be a pillar of strength, is shaking like a leaf. Things don't look good.

Then they look worse. As they start going through my stuff I suddenly remember the little spliff-end I'm saving for a rainy day in my dad's wallet, a memento mori I'm now carrying.

Customs promptly find this brown dog-end. As I stand there with my Y-fronts round my knees in the interrogation room, I have one thought: "I'm not making it home for Christmas." Mercifully, the chief customs officer brushes my mini-spliff off the desk. Even for pen-pushing Canadian Customs, this paltry drugs haul is too tame a reason to bust us. We get let off, albeit with the fear of God in us.

The Two Joes Tour, as Genesis still laughingly describe it, is nevertheless a success. Some of the audiences are coming round to our way of doing things, and we are developing into a band with a decent cult following. Speaking logistically, it also underlines our conviction that we don't need to follow the herd and tour by bus. Later on, we'll even drive ourselves. I think Tony Banks is still paying off his American speeding tickets from the seventies.

We plow on. Genesis play Bill Graham's Winterland Ballroom in San Francisco—a legendary gig, but not for us. This is Jefferson Starship and Janis Joplin country. They don't go for limo-riding English beardies. There is a wild lack of interest from the audience. But we have to go to these places, because we're not getting much radio play. There are pockets of DJ support—New York, Chicago and Cleveland spring to mind—but little more. This lack of reaction is, understandably, mirrored at a lot of our shows. In cities where we're played on air, there is an enthusiastic crowd. Where we're struggling for airplay, we struggle to get an audience.

There is antipathy in the South, a continental hinterland that's lethal for Genesis. They just don't understand what we're about. We're the height, or the depths, of English foppery. What are they singing about? What are they playing? And is that make-up the singer's wearing? All that's missing in some places is the chicken wire in front of the stage.

In New York we play three nights at the Academy of Music. But after our first show, our guitars are nicked overnight. This feels like a major violation. Our precious gear, gone. We have to have a lie-down. We even cancel the second show, just to aid our recovery, and give Mike time to buy new gear. Borrow some? Are you mad? It'd be like playing with someone else's wife. We eventually recover, play the third show and go on our way.

Back in the U.K., and the work rolls on. We play five nights at London's Theatre Royal, Drury Lane, and Peter decides to really go for it. After all, this is a theater, where they're used to flying Peter Pan around on cables. He pulls together a silver outfit, and a white painted face. When he throws off his cape and his fluorescent box head at the climax of "Supper's Ready," he soars into the air.

What Peter's not counted on is the fact that while he's dangling there, he's going to slowly rotate. So he's frantically kicking his legs to try to face the audience—". . . *and it's hey babe* . . ."—and he completes the song in that manner, jiggling and wiggling. Although the effect is spoiled somewhat, we make the front page of *Melody Maker* again, so we still view it as a great success. The visuals aren't getting in the way. Not yet.

Within four or so weeks of the end of that eight-month tour we start work, in June 1974, on the album that will break us, in every sense. We're in Headley Grange in Hampshire, built in 1795 as a poorhouse, but more recently the place where Led Zeppelin and Bad Company have recorded. Whichever band was in last has left it in a horrific, stinking state. Taking advantage of this are the rats. They're everywhere, leaping up and down the creaky staircases, rustling up the creepers covering the trees, scurrying up the vines covering the house. Dozens, hundreds of them. And that's just the ones you can see. It's still a poor house.

The only redeeming factor about this place for me is the fact that John Bonham recorded his incredible groove to "When the Levee Breaks" in the stairwell. I can almost smell it. Instead I smell rats. Thousands of 'em. I arrive last, the best bedrooms already chosen, of course. So I have a shitty room, with hot and cold running rats. At night I can hear the scampering of tiny feet above and below me.

Because "Supper's Ready" went down so well on the *Selling England* tour, we decide to stretch the idea of a story song or suite of songs to a double album. It's the era of *Tommy*, *The Rise and Fall of Ziggy Stardust* and *The Dark Side of the Moon*, when concept albums roamed the earth. It's not daunting, or ridiculous, not to us anyway. For me, *Tommy* soars above the rest. I'm a die-hard Who fan, and they had more magic than they knew what to do with.

Out of left field, Mike has the idea of doing something based on the classic children's novella *The Little Prince*, but that goes nowhere. So more narrative ideas are kicked around. Peter and Tony must have come to blows at some point, because Tony in particular does not want Peter writing all the words. But Peter's argument is: if it is going to be a story album, it should be one person writing the story, and therefore the album.

Peter wins, and sets to writing what will become the surreal-cum-allegorical story of Rael, a Puerto Rican kid living in New York. He will title it *The Lamb Lies Down on Broadway*.

We set up the gear in the main living area, while Peter installs himself at a ropy old piano that's gathering dust in another room. The four of us jam, he jots down his lyrical ideas, and I record everything on my trusty Nakamichi cassette recorder.

We write some great music—"In the Cage," "Riding the Scree," tons of good stuff—and a lot of it comes while Peter is in another room, hammering on the piano, writing the lyrics. It's a weird process, but it seems to be working.

Unfortunately Peter is getting snowed under, and not just with the workload.

Things are bad at home—his wife Jill is having a difficult pregnancy, which is not something I'm aware of at the time. The result is that he's occasionally absent, which means we crack on without him. This doesn't facilitate us thinking as one for such an ambitious project.

Simultaneously, while we're still in the writing stage, an offer comes in from an unexpected direction: William Friedkin, director of *The Exorcist*, and an Oscar winner for *The French Connection*, wants to make a sci-fi film and is looking for (as Peter will later describe it) "a writer who'd never been involved with Hollywood before." He's read the sleeve notes on the back of *Genesis Live*—a typically fantastical short story by Peter—and been caught up in his surreal, dry humor. He thinks maybe Peter can collaborate. We all went to see *The Exorcist* on the *Selling England* tour and loved it, so we know Friedkin is someone to be reckoned with.

For Pete it's a dream come true: the chance to collaborate with a visionary artist at the top of his field in another medium, to work from home, and also be there for his wife. He asks, "Can we put the album on hold? Give me time to do this, then I'll be back." He doesn't say he's leaving.

We all say, "Sorry, Peter, 'fraid not. You're in or you're out."

From my point of view, if it comes to it, Peter leaving needn't be the end of the world. My stoutly practical solution is that we reconfigure Genesis into an instrumental four-piece. At least that way the music can finally be fully heard.

To this suggestion, the other three's reaction can be summed up thus: "Don't be so fucking stupid. Us, without singing, without lyrics? Get back in your box, Phil." And of course they're right.

Before anything concrete can happen, word reaches Friedkin that his offer might result in the demise of Genesis. He doesn't want that, especially as his sci-fi project is only a nebulous idea. A couple of weeks after the offer is made, the plug is pulled.

So Peter is back. But he's back because a better offer didn't work out. Not the best circumstances under which to reconvene. We carry on working, forgive and forget, or at least pretend to.

We then go in to record this stash of music at a Welsh farm, Glaspant Manor, with Island Mobile Studios, again with John Burns. We've realized that the recording studio environment was stifling us, and we were struggling to be as exciting on record as we were in concert. In using John and a mobile studio, we make a move that brings a freedom of sorts. He's almost beginning to feel like part of the band.

Peter is still writing lyrics while us four are recording, but it's a relaxed interlude, especially as it's a great opportunity for Peter, Mike and Tony to indulge their love of country walks. Often on tour we'd pull over, buy some onions, carrots, cheese and bread, and go to a field somewhere and have a picnic. It sounds a bit hippie, but there's nothing wrong with a good slab of Cheddar and an onion.

Back in London we mix *The Lamb Lies Down on Broadway* in Island Studios, Basing Street. After two months recording this epic in Wales, we're glad to be on home turf. While laying down the tracks, word gets to us that Brian Eno is recording in the studio upstairs, working on his second solo album, *Taking Tiger Mountain (By Strategy)*. I'm not much of a Roxy Music fan, but the rest of the guys love them. Peter goes up to say hello and asks if we can put some vocals through his computer. In return Eno asks if I can go up and play on a track of his called "Mother Whale Eyeless." I don't mind being pimped out.

Eno and I hit it off. He's a very interesting character, not in the normal mold of a "pop" person, which is perhaps one of the reasons he left Roxy Music, and I'm drawn to his way of working. I end up playing on his albums *Another Green World*, *Before and After Science* and *Music for Films*.

During the mixing sessions at Basing Street a schism develops, between daytime Genesis and night-time Genesis. Peter and I sometimes mix till two in the morning, then Tony comes in the next day, hates it and scrubs it. Sometimes we're still recording when we're supposed to be mixing. Time is short, the mood is tense and everyone is tired. There's too much music, there are too many lyrics, we're rushing to get finished, the narrative nuances of this double-vinyl concept album are a mystery to all of us (including, we suspect, Peter)—and any minute now we're due to go on tour. A tour on which we've decided to play this entire album. A tour with a big production attached.

Inevitably, unavoidably, *The Lamb Lies Down on Broadway* show promises the grand unveiling of a 23-track double album that no one has ever heard, played by a band who are themselves running to catch up, punting a concept on which the paint is still wet, tricked out with an ambitious production that's entirely untested, on a world tour booked to run for 104 dates.

Cut to Dallas . . . Genesis are rehearsing at the headquarters of Showco, who are renting their sound and light equipment to us. We're trying to get the lighting right, and trying to make sense of the slides that will supposedly illustrate the entire *Lamb* narrative. Even before we've started it's a disaster. Getting the three screens to work in sync, long before the advent of reliable technology, is proving impossible. And if it's not working in rehearsals, it's not going to work on the road. Plus, as has been previously established, a lot of the theatrical stuff is kept from the rest of us. Peter has been plotting his costumes, and some of them are simply wildly impractical, to comical effect. When he's wearing the "Slipperman" costume—a rather nasty outfit comprising a body piece with inflatable balls (as in testicles. It has an almost Elephant Man look)—he can't get the mic near his mouth. When the "Lamia" prop, a revolving colored gauze encasement, descends from above, the microphone cable is forever caught while it's going round and round, meaning many a gig is spent frantically trying to tug it free. Everything is rushed, and we never have time to troubleshoot.

Cut to Chicago . . . On the opening night of the *Lamb Lies Down on Broadway* tour, midway through the set, I notice something large filling with air just next to me. It's a huge inflatable penis. But of course it is. Next thing I see is Peter, dressed in his Slipperman costume, crawling through it.

Cut to Cleveland . . . Five days into the tour, we're staying in Swingos, a trendy though tacky hotel in Cleveland. Each room is decorated in a bizarre fashion—stripes, polka dots, whatever. In one of these bizarre settings, Peter tells Tony Smith he's leaving the band. Tony persuades him to see out the tour.

Cut to Scandinavia . . . The pyros get out of hand. Too much bang, too little smoke, and bits of wood from blown-up speakers everywhere. We're suddenly one crew member down. (Just to clarify, he wasn't incinerated, he was fired.)

Cut to Manchester . . . In the sedate Midland Hotel, Peter finally tells me he's leaving. I can't hide my sadness. He and I have a pretty solid relationship in and out of the band. Also, we're fellow drummers. Us drummers stick together.

Despite the impending departure of Peter, most of the snapshot memories I have of the *Lamb* tour are great. A lot of the time, truth be told, I'm in heaven. I'm wearing headphones so I can hear myself sing, and I have a wonderful sound mix. Some of the pieces of music are really great to play: "The Waiting Room" is fresh and different every night, and Tony's keyboard piece "Riding the Scree" and the mellow "Silent Sorrow in Empty Boats" are ambient pieces that are also a joy.

Yet the overall feeling is one of a band chasing their tails. The album had come out in the U.K. on November 18, 1974, and the tour started in Chicago two days later, so even the most ardent fans don't have much time to digest four sides of ambient-prog conceptualism. It's an enormous amount to chew in one piece at a gig. Behind closed doors, everything is getting a little fractious at this far-from-auspicious way to start any tour, far less a tour of this ambition, magnitude and expense.

But bless the fans, they do their best. By the time the ninety-minute spectacular finishes, with two versions of Peter onstage for the closing number "*it.*" (a song whose title is lower-case, italicized and accessorized with a full stop), everyone is seeing double. We triumph, but not in the way we would have, had the music been known and the plot more accessible.

The *Lamb Lies Down on Broadway* tour will become mythologized, not least in *This Is Spinal Tap*. This tour would be perfect fodder for the scriptwriters and actors. When that pod doesn't open? I've been there, stuck on a stage with malfunctioning props and an irate guitarist. Is it perhaps no coincidence that Derek Smalls, Spinal Tap's bass player, is a ringer for Steve Hackett at this time?

Out front, we occasionally play to half-full houses. In the back, Peter has his own dressing room, with make-up and a mirror, and the four of us are welcome visitors. He's no prima donna, but there are a lot of record company guys coming into the dressing room afterward, huffing and puffing, "Great show, Pete!"

Their blowing dry ice up his arse also gets up Tony's nose, and mine too. Peter is being viewed as the glorious architect. Genesis are in danger of being overshadowed by him. That said, I don't remember Peter ever taking the bait of stardom. Backstage, despite his separate dressing room, he remained one of us.

Finally, France and, to everyone's relief, the end of the tour. Just before we go onstage in Besançon, a small, inauspicious town close to the Swiss border, Tony Smith tells us that the last gig, in Toulouse, is canceled due to lack of interest. This seems to sum it up. So the penultimate show, in Besançon, becomes the last show. It suddenly dawns on us: this is more than likely our last time performing the likes of "The Colony of Slippermen" and "Here Comes the Supernatural Anaesthetist." It's our last gig with Peter. It's the last time we'll see him crawling through a big cock. It is May 22, 1975.

Peter plays "The Last Post" on his oboe. It's all rather anticlimactic. *The Lamb Lies Down on Broadway* and, finally, it doesn't get up again. And then there were four.

Do I resent Peter for leaving? Absolutely not. Personally, he and I are as close as we were when I joined Genesis five years previously, and for all the difficulties and unwitting comedy of the *Lamb* tour, I've enjoyed myself. Professionally, if anything, the challenges have bonded the rest of us even more closely. There's never any question of Tony, Mike, Steve and me calling it a day. The four of us are committed to carrying on. We don't know how. But we will. So we need a new singer and frontman. We'll cross that Rubicon when we come to it.

We all amicably agree to keep schtum about Peter's departure for as long as possible. We want to be ready, with new material, before word gets out.

And *The Lamb Lies Down on Broadway*, now? It's one of the few Genesis albums I can put on and be surprised by, not that I can ever remember having listened to it in its entirety. But it's a high-water mark for the band in some respects, and even the *Spinal Tap* reference is a compliment, backhanded or otherwise. To quote Peter's final lines onstage with Genesis: "It's only rock'n'roll, but I like it."

As for me, I'm excited about what tomorrow might bring. After all, I now have other, personal obligations. On the Canadian leg of the *Selling England by the Pound* tour, I had reconnected with an old flame, and was delighted to discover she came with a plus-one: an infant daughter.

We're halfway through the seventies. The decade began with me finding a band, continued with me losing my dad, and now, at its midpoint, has me recast, out of nowhere, as a family man.

8

FAMILY MAN, FRONTMAN

Or: trying to keep everyone happy. Results: mixed

PAUSE, REWIND, REFLECT.

It is March 1974, fourteen months before Peter leaves Genesis. The *Selling England by the Pound* tour rolls into Vancouver for a show at the Garden Auditorium. I'm twenty-three and I'm excited: this city on Canada's distant Pacific coast is where Andrea Bertorelli, my on/off/on teenage girlfriend, now lives.

Andy, you'll recall, was in my year at Barbara Speake's Stage School. Being childhood sweethearts, we spent a lot of time at each other's family homes. I *loved* Andy's mum, and would happily hang out at the Bertorellis' whenever the opportunity arose. The Bertorellis were part of the famous London restaurant family of the same name, and both Mr. and Mrs. B. were fantastic cooks. The after-dinner refreshment was equally welcome: they didn't mind their daughter's boyfriend sleeping over. I was already part of the family.

In the late sixties, as Andy and I went our separate ways—courtesy, as usual, of my going back out with Lavinia Lang—so did our wider familial ties. After Andy's father died, her mother rekindled a friendship with a Canadian air force officer, once stationed in wartime Godalming, Surrey, married him, then emigrated to Vancouver. Andy, her sister Francesca, a Playboy bunny, and her brother John went with her.

By spring '74 I haven't seen Andy for three or four years. I know some of her news, though. Mrs. Bertorelli writes to my mum, and Mum relays that Andy had gone off into the wilderness, met someone, lived in a cabin for a short while, fell pregnant and was then abandoned by the father. Andy returned to the family home in Vancouver, and on August 8, 1972—two years to the day after I'd joined Genesis—had a baby daughter named Joely Meri Bertorelli.

Ahead of the band's arrival in Vancouver, I call to invite the Bertorelli family to the show. Andy's mum, hospitable to the last, insists that I stay with them during my brief stopover in the city. It's a wonderful reunion. I gladly accept Mrs. B.'s invitation to eat with the family. I meet the Canadian stepdad, Joe, a keen tenpin bowler (I will sponsor his team many years later), and I meet sixteen-month-old Joely, a little peach. We haven't even finished dessert before old feelings between Andy and I start to flicker and flare.

She's a beautiful young lady, with a beautiful body too. She's ragingly sexy, which is why she was good at breaking hearts. I have to confess that large chunks of the lyrics to Genesis' 1986 song "Invisible Touch" were written about her.

Andy's pleased, I'm pleased, and Mrs. B. is pleased—she always wanted me for a son-in-law. By the time Genesis leave Vancouver, Andy and I are once again a couple. And I am, I suppose, a father. Life has changed, quickly, but I don't look back or sideways. Andy has a piece of my heart from school. She has a daughter? I don't think twice about it.

The next show is in New York, six days later, back at the Philharmonic Hall, so I'm on the move again quicksmart. But over the following month we stay in touch by phone, falling in love all over again. My life has reset, both to my teenage days, but also to the future.

The tour loops back toward New York, where it ends with the three scheduled nights at the Academy of Music. Andy joins me. Joely sleeps in the bed between us, and I remember her looking at me, as if to say, "What are you doing here?"

It's been less than six weeks since our reunion in Vancouver, and we have decided: we are getting back together, and Andy is returning to the U.K. with me. I've gone off on tour a single man and I've come back hitched, and a dad. We are a family and I couldn't be happier.

Back in England, Genesis have a month off before we start writing and recording the album/concept/vision/milestone/millstone that will become *The Lamb Lies Down on Broadway*. Before long, Andy and Joely join me in my rented one-bedroom flat in Epsom. We'll discover that it's not a great place for a young family. Mercifully, we soon relocate to Headley Grange . . . where we're confronted by the horrific sight of all those rats in that stinky old house. I don't have time to dwell on the conditions, as I'm immediately plunged into work. Which is fine by me, of course—I'm working *and* my new family is going to be with me. But what is it like for Andy and Joely? They've been uprooted from a family home on the other side of the world, dropped down into the chaos of a band, then left to their own devices, with nothing to do except sit on the grass and count the rats. Daunting, overwhelming, frightening—take your pick.

This is not the best of environments for partners, to say the least. As Peter will find out with his (literally) embryonic family, within Genesis there is no such thing as compassionate leave or family time. We work evenings, weekends, any or all of the Sabbaths. Then, habitually, we up sticks and work some more. That's the way it is.

As ill fortune has it, recording *The Lamb* pretty much overlaps with touring *The Lamb*, so things in Genesis world are even more frenetic than normal. Bearing in mind the chaos, and the cost of the show, Andy and Joely are unable to join me on tour anywhere near as much as we'd like. From the outset of our relationship she's being forced to be alone. From day one she's a rock'n'roll widow. However, I don't recall this seeming to affect Mike or Tony, or their partners; they seem omnipresent. Maybe I just wasn't assertive enough.

We manage to move out of the Epsom pit, to a house in Queen Anne's Grove in Ealing. But we have to wait until the following year, till the end of the *Lamb* tour, to be married, which we are at East Acton Registry Office. The beautiful bride wears white, the groom a carnation, neatly trimmed beard and brand-new Converse All Star sneakers, bought specially. True to form, there's no time for a honeymoon.

Meanwhile, with Peter having left, Genesis still have to solve the tricky problem of finding a singer. We place an advertisement in *Melody Maker*: "Singer wanted for Genesis-type group," the wording, we hope, artfully maintaining secrecy, while also throwing the press off the scent.

The lore is that we receive 400 replies to the ad. I don't believe that figure, but maybe Tony Smith's office sifted out more chaff from the wheat than I know.

I do know we get all sorts. Tapes by the bucketloads. Guys singing along to our records. Playing guitar to our songs. Some guys doing a bit of piano, bit of this, bit of that. Some people send tapes of them singing over Frank Sinatra or Pink Floyd. We whittle them down to a presentable bunch before we start auditioning.

Simultaneously, we're squirreled away in Maurice Plaquet's basement in Churchfield Road, East Acton, familiar to me from my brief drum-lesson days. We dive into the songwriting for the band's seventh album, our first as a four-piece, though Steve is missing initially while he adds the finishing touches to his first solo album, *Voyage of the Acolyte*. My sense is that he wanted more of a shout as a songwriter—Tony, Mike and Peter monopolized the writing of the material for the band, and frankly they wrote better stuff than Steve. Better stuff than me, for sure. But up until *The Lamb*, I've barely been writing at all, so I have no issues. Steve, though, wants an outlet, so, without any grumbles or dissension from us, he plows a solo furrow. Mike and I even play on *Voyage of the Acolyte,* and I obligingly sing lead vocal on "Star of Sirius." It's all quite amicable.

Even working without Steve at first, to our huge relief it's clear quite quickly that we're going to be OK without Peter. The songs are coming like the old days, and it's good stuff. We have "Dance on a Volcano" even before Steve rejoins us. "Squonk" and "Los Endos" follow, a strong opening salvo for the album we will title *A Trick of the Tail.*

Then, disaster: another Peter front page in *Melody Maker*—"Gabriel Quits Genesis." News has leaked before we've had time to regroup.

The whisper in muso circles is that this means the end of Genesis. Of course it does: how can any band survive the loss of a frontman, especially one as charismatic and creative as Peter Gabriel? We have to move fast, in case the idea of us as a dead duck gains a traction from which we can never free ourselves.

All the accompanying press and available facts help bolster the opinion that Genesis are finished as a going concern. Just prior to this, in October 1975, before we've had a chance to even start recording *A Trick of the Tail*, Steve's album comes out. Also not helping matters is the fact that I choose this period to start seeing another band.

My on/off affair with Brand X begins in late 1974 when I get a call from Richard Williams. The former *Melody Maker* writer is now head of A&R at Island Records. He tells me he has an interesting group, a jam band he's not long signed, and they're looking for a new drummer.

I join them for rehearsals, and we have some fun. At the time Brand X are more funk than jazz. They have a singer, but for much of the time there's nothing for him to do, so he jumps on the congas (with a shudder and the sudden specter of Phil Spector, I empathize). There's lots of improvising around a groove and one chord. *Hours of it.*

Nonetheless, I like these guys, and I like the freedom they offer, so I agree to join Brand X on a part-time basis, even though I don't really know what I'm joining. There are no gigs and only distant rumors of a record. But eventually the guitarist and the singer say their farewells to do something else, leaving bass player Percy Jones, keyboardist Robin Lumley, guitarist John Goodsall and me.

When the four of us instrumentalists start playing, Brand X become a whole different thing. These are the days of fusion and jazz-rock, some of which is definitely too noodly and self-indulgent for me. But we will make a few interesting records, notably the first two, *Unorthodox Behaviour* (1976) and *Moroccan Roll* (1977).

But right now, in the autumn of 1975, the members of the Peter-less Genesis are all-for-one-and-one-for-all united. Our defiant feeling is: *we'll show them.* All Peter, was it? He wrote everything, did he? Well, just because the fox's head is gone, doesn't mean we are. We might have to find a singer, but the new material he'll have to work with is great. Rumors of Genesis' death have been very much exaggerated.

We step up a gear, and every Monday at Churchfield Road we audition four or five potential singers. I teach them the vocal parts, singing along while Steve, Tony and Mike quietly play the music. We choose a few pieces that might indicate their talents. *Selling England by the Pound* track "Firth of Fifth" is one, and "The Knife" from *Trespass*, another—a couple of touchstones to show range and quality. Just snippets, but even so these ask a lot of any would-be front-man. We have to do it this way: we're a demanding band, and Peter's are big boots to fill.

We're not just looking for someone with the vocal chops. We're asking ourselves, will he be a good writing partner? What will he bring to the band? We're trying to suss out whether we want this person in our family. Because right now Genesis, with our backs against the wall, are very tight. A band of brothers.

I begin to enjoy these Monday routines, having the opportunity to sing. It's always been a given that on this album I might front a couple of the acoustic songs—"Entangled," say, or "Ripples." But I know I'm not ever going to be able to pull off "Squonk," "Dance on a Volcano" or any of the heavier material.

Yet this isn't an issue: we need a new singer, and are doing our damnedest to find one. It doesn't occur to me—or to any of the guys—that I'm even remotely frontman material.

Not least, of course, because we've just come off *The Lamb Lies Down on Broadway*: a big, bold double album with a lot of singing—a lot of elaborate singing—and with a theatrical production to match. How on earth would I scale that cliff? I couldn't. And frankly, I have no interest in scaling that cliff. I'm happy at the back.

Equally, I'm still ready to pull out my joker: I'd rather be in an instrumental band than take over the microphone. Unfortunately that idea is, again, quickly shot down. Tony and Mike have long had aspirations to be songwriters—that is, songs with lyrics, lyrics that need to be sung. More than that: they want to write *hit* songs, singles that will reach the pop charts. They've always wanted that; always wanted to write like The Kinks and The Beatles. You can't do that if your band doesn't have a singer, or lyrics, or choruses.

It's a development of some irony that it takes almost ten years for their songwriting skills to "mature" and come up with hit singles—exactly coinciding with another emerging reality: I'm becoming the singer-by-default, in the basement of Churchfield Road at least.

Every night I'm going home to Andy.

"Find a singer yet?"

"No. No one that meets the requirements."

We audition for five or six weeks. We've seen about thirty guys. It's starting to become tedious. With the clock ticking—unsurprisingly, there's already talk of another tour—we have no option but to commit to studio time. At least we've written some strong material.

We go into Trident with a new co-producer, Dave Hentschel, and record at a cracking pace. I'm most involved with "Los Endos," which I model on the groove of Santana's "Promise of a Fisherman," from his just-released jazz-fusion album *Borboletta*. "Squonk" is really Zeppelin-esque. And there's "Robbery, Assault and Battery," proving there's still a place for the "story" songs for which Genesis are known.

We're really pleased with these songs. They're sounding strong, fresh and a bit different. We feel like a new band, and we're sounding like it.

Then we're briskly back to business, dividing up the backing tracks and deciding who's writing lyrics for which song. There's added time pressure now, because the tracks are recorded and there's still no singer. That said, we finally agree to let one vocalist past the front door. Mick Strickland is a bit better than the rest, and we ask him into Trident to have a crack. We give him "Squonk" to sing. The very first line of that vocal is a bitch: *"Like father, like son . . ."* We don't ask his key or his range. We just give it to him. Take it away . . .

Poor guy. It's not remotely his key. We have to say, "Thank you and goodbye . . ." Looking back, I feel bad for Mick. I've been that soldier that has to sing the song in the key I'm given. In those days, though, we didn't even consider that an issue.

But "Squonk" is new and it's a groove I like. More pertinently, right now we've no other option, nothing left to lose, and there are studio hours racking up. So I say, "How about I have a go?" And the rest of the guys shrug: "Might as well."

Deep inside, I know I can do this, but *actually* singing it—that's another thing entirely. Sometimes your brain says yes, but your voice screams no.

But I have a go, even if Mike's lyrics do have me guessing. Mike and Tony later tell me it's like one of those cartoon lightbulb moments. They look at each other in the control room and their eyebrows say it all: *By George I think he's got it!* Looking back it was a defining moment for me. The studio environment was great, allowing us to hammer away at it until the vocals worked and the music clicked. I still didn't want to go out front and sing, mind.

And yet, and yet . . . We're still dazed and confused. The guy we thought might, finally, manage the vocals has proved a bust . . . and now the drummer's had a pop and it doesn't sound bad . . . but over the whole album? Is that wise?

We try a few takes, finesse it, come back in the next morning, have another listen and all agree: it still sounds good.

I'm *very* unsure, but could it be that we might just have found a singer? Albeit in a manner reminiscent of finding a fiver down the back of the couch.

Casting doubts aside for the time being, we have to plow on. We knock the songs off one after the other. "Robbery, Assault and Battery" is a stand-out and works really well from the off—I add a bit of my Artful Dodger into the vocal delivery. Slowly, I'm showing that I can not only sing these songs but bring in something else. A bit of character, in every sense of the word. I can inhabit them, without resorting to Peter's visual accessories.

Some songs are especially demanding. "Mad Man Moon" is one of Tony's, and his melodies are out of my usual comfort zone, especially if you have to learn them on the fly in the studio. I would get used to this over the next few years. "A Trick of the Tail" is also his, but feels more natural for me. All in all, though, singing the album comes easier than I would have thought.

Suddenly, we've finished. Yet all I'm thinking is that it's a one-time-only deal. As a stopgap I've managed to sing the album, but doing it onstage will be another matter entirely. So, really, we still haven't got a singer.

I go home to Andy and Joely in Ealing.

ANDY: "How's the album going?"

ME: "I've been singing them all and it sounds great."

ANDY: "Well, why don't you become the singer?"

ME: "You must be mad! I'm the drummer. I refuse to go out the front and wiggle my bum. I have a safety blanket between me and the audience—my kit—and that's the way I like it."

Once we've finished recording we have another rifle through the audition tapes. "Are you *sure* there was no one in here?"

No, there wasn't, and there isn't.

Eventually I say, "Fuck, well, I suppose I could be the singer, but . . ."

We're caught between a rock and a soft place. Having explored every other angle, it seems like the drummer is the last-ditch, last-resort-only option. None of us can take this entirely seriously. The "backman" is going to make a good frontman? Surely some mistake?

I'm just as conflicted, especially because I really enjoy playing the drums. That's where I live. Yet there's no denying the truth: I *can* sing the songs.

Finally, a compromise: I might consider this if I can get a drummer that I like, because I don't want to be looking over my shoulder the whole time, checking and quietly critiquing. And I'm not up for double duty—that looks crap. Don Henley did OK for a song or two, Levon Helm did great for a song or two. But neither would have been able to sustain contact with an audience throughout a two-hour set. The lead singer singing from behind the drums is alienating for an audience. There's a whacking great kit getting in the way of any connection between vocalist and crowd.

Tentatively, reluctantly, with some caveats and teeth slightly gritted, I'm coming round to this idea. And in the end, I am the agent of my own doom.

Bill Bruford, late of Yes, is a good friend who's turned me on to a lot of jazz drummers. He comes down to one of Brand X's rehearsal sessions—we're writing *Unorthodox Behaviour*—and he asks, "How's things in Genesis? Found a singer yet?"

"Not really. I've done the album, and they want me to try out as the singer. But to do that we need to find a drummer."

"Well, why don't you ask me?"

"You wouldn't want to do that. A bit too Yes-y for you, surely?"

"Yes I would."

And suddenly Genesis have a new drummer.

Now I've no excuse.

We all shuffle about a bit and get used to this new line-up and configuration. There's no great ceremony about it. It just happens. I don't even remember the rehearsals, or any announcement.

Bill fits in well, although he's the kind of drummer who likes to play something different every night. Although I sympathize with him wanting to keep it fresh, some drum fills are *cues*, something Tony, Mike and Steve rely on.

Then, boom, we have lift-off. Another tour, another chapter.

A TRICK OF THE TAIL comes out in February 1976. This new Genesis are definitely feeling like underdogs. Perhaps that's one of the reasons it's reviewed favorably: expectations about the future viability of the band have been very, very low. Then people hear the record, they think it's great, and these underdogs might have the last bark: the album reaches number 3 in the U.K. charts, which, reassuringly, matches the achievement of *Selling England by the Pound*.

The following month we decamp to Dallas for live rehearsals. The first date on the *Trick of the Tail* tour is looming in London,

Ontario, Canada, on March 26. I'm not especially nervous about the singing, nor about the sheer fact of doing it in front of an audience. I'd got used to that on *Oliver!*, way back when. But performing with just a microphone stand instead of a row of cymbals between me and the audience—that's the thing to overcome. If you're not predisposed toward bat-wing headgear and flying in the air, what do you do when there's no singing?

There are other practical concerns. I've already made it very clear that I'm not going to be able to do what Peter did. I will not be sporting Andy's camisole or a badger pelt. But what *will* I wear? The workman's overalls that did the job when I was just the drummer? Or is that too, well, workmanlike? I can wear a flat cap and Edwardian coat for "Robbery, Assault and Battery," but that's as theatrical as I'm prepared to go.

It's suggested that I have some clothes made. These are ready in time for the opening show, but I'm not going to go onstage for the first time as singer wearing something not *me*. I have to feel totally at ease. Workman's overalls it is.

Then another concern. Peter became very good at regaling audiences with little stories while Mike, Tony and Steve tuned up. He was the "Mysterious Traveller." But I'm more "Uncle Phil." So on the car journey from Toronto to London, I'm frantically scribbling ideas for things to say between songs. "This song's about, ah, er . . . Fuck, nothing to say about this one . . ."

The house lights go down at the London Arena. I curse quietly and gulp loudly. What's this going to be like? Everybody is terrified. I've taken the responsibility seriously, so there's no quick, confidence-building drink, and certainly no quick spliff. Suddenly the enormity of this moment hits me. Genesis are going onstage with a new singer. Most bands wouldn't even risk that, far less survive it. A lot of people have assumed we won't, writing our epitaph already: "Genesis: in the beginning was the word . . . and in the end was a disaster when they tried to replace a brilliant singer with an accomplished drummer. May they rest in pieces."

I spend almost the entire show hiding behind the microphone stand—I'm a twenty-four-year-old, drumstick-thin slip of a thing.

And I don't even touch the microphone. To take it out of its stand would be too . . . *singer-y*. But I get through the show with only minor cuts and bruises to my fragile sense of myself as a frontman.

For the second show, in Ontario's Kitchener Memorial Auditorium Complex, I pull out one of the outfits that's been made: a mustard-orange one-piece jumpsuit. Flared, buttons up the front, slightly too small so my tom-toms are showing—which, trust me, is very intimidating for a whole show. Further, it's made of a synthetic material that stinks as soon as I sweat.

It's awful from the minute I step onstage. I'll never wear that again. Ever. Promise.

That wardrobe malfunction aside, those first two shows go fantastically well. We do *The Lamb* medley—let's give the audience something they know—but none of the material is daunting. I know it all very, very well. I've heard it to death. And it's incumbent on us to play the fan favorites, no matter how tricky, epic or heavy. We have to telegraph as best we can the key message: *For Genesis it's business as usual.*

Still, my hands stay jammed in my pockets for long periods when I'm singing. It will be some time before I touch the microphone, remove it from its holder and actually walk around with it. Only when that happens do I feel it's official: I, Phil Collins, am a singer.

It's a six-week tour of the U.S., and again it's the first leg of a world tour. America is still very much our priority. We're getting blank stares in Germany—it's not until *Duke* in 1980 that they like us—but we know that we can, just about, make money in the States.

Ahead of us are Led Zeppelin; they've already climbed the mountain. Our British peers are Yes, Emerson, Lake & Palmer, Supertramp et al. But we still haven't had an international hit single. We're still only being played on FM radio. We're a cult band. A large cult band.

I take heart from the reviews and interviews, and also from the encouragement of Andy on the occasions when she and Joely come to visit me on tour. Everyone is surprised at how good it is. "Wow," people tell me. "You sound great. It sounds like Peter." I'm not sure whether to take that as a compliment. But at this point, I'll take *anything*.

The great reactions keep coming. From London, Ontario, onward, Genesis and our fans collectively breathe out. We're hugely reassured to discover that our de facto solution to the problem of Peter leaving has worked better than we might have hoped. Replacing Peter from outside would have been very difficult. Arguably, replacing him from the inside is just as tricky.

In May we return home and, after a month off, on June 9, 1976, I make my British debut as the singer with Genesis, at the first of six nights at Hammersmith Odeon.

On the one hand I'm somewhat bedded in as vocalist. On the other, after a long run of U.S. concerts, you get used to their boisterous audience response. The ambient noise the Americans make during the show is surprisingly loud. Returning home to Europe the band is hit by a reverent silence: *Fuck, they're listening.* Everyone tightens their belts.

But Hammersmith is great. By now I've decided on my uniform: white dungarees and white jacket. That's what I feel comfortable in. I'm sliding into the spotlit role quite easily. I become more and more at ease onstage, even if I'm still not removing that microphone from the stand yet. The communication with the audiences is getting better as well. Which is a useful skill to develop as I'm now the person that people want to interview. This is flattering of course. Finally I can tell the world how things really are. It's only later that I realize doing six interviews on a show day might hinder my singing that night.

Hitting my stride (a bit), I devise a different way of hitting a tambourine. Somewhere in these heady days of gigging and more gigging, I start bashing my head with it. Not once, not twice, but many times. In rhythm, at the end of "I Know What I Like." This craziness will develop into a routine known as The Tambourine Dance. It's a cross between morris dancing and John Cleese's Ministry of Silly Walks. A bit of music-hall fun that both the audience and I love.

All told, Genesis have survived from within. More than that: we're rejuvenated.

The tour finishes in the summer of 1976, and by September we're in Relight Studios in Hilvarenbeek, the Netherlands, recording Genesis' eighth album, *Wind & Wuthering*, again with the essential Dave Hentschel producing. It's our first time recording outside the U.K., and we complete all the backing tracks in twelve days. Our momentum feels doubled.

It's even apparent to the American record-label publicist charged with writing a press kit. "Despite all this activity, the unstoppable Phil Collins still managed to fit in gigging and recording with his 'second' band, Brand X," bugles the *Wind & Wuthering* publicity material, "as well as doing other sessions . . ."

From being a slightly dubious frontman, I'm now confident without (I hope) being cocky. We are charged with new material and we run with it. Once again the writing credits are shared. Steve and I co-write "Blood on the Rooftops," and we all chip in with ". . . In That Quiet Earth." I push for the Weather Report groove on "Wot Gorilla," with Tony and me sharing writing credits. But it's during these sessions that Steve starts to feel the pinch as a writer.

However, by far the most important thing in my world at this time is the fact that any day now, Andy is due to give birth to our first child together. This would obviously be momentous at the best of times, but for me, having been so far away for such a long time, it has added emotional resonance. With Andy being pregnant since the beginning of 1976, she couldn't join me on much of the *Trick of the Tail* tour. While she's been stuck at home in Ealing, I've been out in the world, trying to become a frontman.

Simon Philip Nando Collins is born on September 14, 1976. Philip after me, Nando after Andy's dad. In theory Genesis could have delayed the start of the album so I could be home for the birth without any panic or emergency dashes back over the North Sea. But this is Genesis, and the show must go on. In hindsight I could have said, "Fuck Genesis, I'm off to look after my wife." But we're all expected to give everything to the band, even if there are, later, recurring attempts to reverse-engineer such situations: "Well, if only you'd told us, we could have moved the start-date." But while I've been emboldened as a performer by becoming the frontman, behind closed doors I'm too timid to speak up. Old pecking orders, domestic or professional, die hard.

To put it another way: all musicians are created equal, but some are more equal than others. I'm out front, giving it all I've got—frankly, I've been instrumental in saving the band from disintegrating—yet I still feel like I shouldn't rock the boat. The Collins insecurity biting back again.

Luckily, I get the call early enough to make it home in time for Simon's birth at Queen Charlotte's Hospital in Hammersmith, west London. He's quarantined for a short while due to a skin condition. I visit him and Andy regularly. I'm there for a few days, but I'm soon needed back in Holland to rejoin the troops. My all-too-brief visit only increases Andy's growing feeling that she's playing second fiddle to the band. But from my point of view, just at this moment obligation takes precedence over emotion: there is another album to finish, and another personnel issue to face.

Bill Bruford opted out after the *Trick of the Tail* tour to form his own band, U.K., so we're a band in flux again. I call the great American drummer Chester Thompson. I've seen him with Weather Report and heard him with Frank Zappa on his live album *Roxy and Elsewhere*, where he was joined by a second drummer, Ralph Humphrey. They play a fantastic double drum riff in Zappa's song "More Trouble Every Day"—I want some of that in our band.

I call Chester, he says yes, never having met us, we do some rehearsals, and that's it, he's in. Chester will stay with us until the end of our reunion tour in 2007.

Wind & Wuthering is released in December 1976, and we start 1977 as we mean to go on: the tour begins on New Year's Day, and we've stepped up our live production. We now have lasers, and 747 landing lights. Genesis are becoming a jumbo-sized touring operation.

For me as the frontman, all these bells, whistles and lasers are used in the best possible taste. It's not distracting. In fact, these visuals replace the Peter gear. Enough light and magic—not forgetting a brace of new material—and audiences seem to have already forgotten that the frontman in Genesis used to be known for dressing like a centurion or Bill (or Ben) the Flower Pot Man.

We're booking big shows now. In London we play the Rainbow—reputedly 80,000 people apply for 8,000 tickets. Three nights at Earls Court. New York's Madison Square Garden. We go to Brazil for the first time, where we play to 150,000 people and are each assigned an armed bodyguard to prevent us from being kidnapped. This is a whole new experience. We tangle with military police, are nearly flattened by a lorry on a freeway, jam with local musicians in bars, enjoy record company extravagance next to poverty-ridden favelas, and flirt with voodoo. The whole trip is interesting and terrifying. I buy some traditional Brazilian percussion (including the surdo, a large hand-held bass drum that I'll one day play on Peter's "Biko"). And, of course, a stuffed piranha.

The months blur by. We finish the *Wind & Wuthering* tour at Munich's Olympiahalle on July 3, 1977, have August off, and in September we start work on our ninth album. Simon is one that month.

The Genesis fan base is increasing big time, and all the time. We're playing arenas now, and professionally things couldn't be much better. However, home life is diminishing due to my continued absence. With two young children to mother, Andy is housebound and her frustration is showing.

During this time Steve's frustration has also become apparent. He's released his solo album, but rather than reduce the pressure, it's increased it. He wants to have more songs on the Genesis albums. One man's meat is another man's poison: the new configuration of Genesis has unexpectedly thrown up new songwriting avenues, and while I'm feeling increasingly confident as a writer, Steve still isn't getting the creative space he believes he deserves.

That summer, we're in London, mixing *Seconds Out*, a live album recorded during our four-night stand at Paris's Palais des Sports in June. I'm driving from Queen Anne's Grove to Trident, and I see Steve in the street in Notting Hill.

"Want a lift to the studio, Steve?"

"Ah, no, I'll call you later."

I arrive at the studio and relay this odd encounter.

"Oh, didn't he tell you? He's left," says Mike.

I think Steve was too embarrassed to tell me. But also, I later learn, he feared that I might have been the one person who could have persuaded him to reconsider.

So, Steve goes, another one biting the dust. But if we could survive the loss of a singer, we can survive the loss of a guitarist. We roll on, undaunted, with Mike working hard on bass *and* lead.

That autumn we're back recording in Hilvarenbeek, and by the end of the year we've finished recording another album, ...*And Then There Were Three*.... Genesis have never been more successful. The threesome is working, and me being singer is working. The sense is that we could be about to break through to another level. If only we're prepared to put in the legwork. Yes, even more legwork than we've put in already.

Those home fires? They're dying down, and also flaring up. With two young children to mother, Andy has endured a lot—*a lot*—of being alone. On the rare occasions when I'm home for anything like an extended period, the atmosphere is tense. We can't speak more than a couple of sentences before we're arguing. We love each other, to be sure, but sometimes it's plain we don't *like* each other.

In a relationship it's vital for each partner to complete the other. This isn't happening in our marriage. I'm not one for suspicions or, dare I say it, paranoia. Andy, though, picks up on a strange look, or something someone said, and it goes under the magnifying glass for careful, endless, tiring scrutiny. I don't cope with this very well, and the drawbridge comes up.

Indeed, neither of us is coping very well. I'm pulled this way, I'm pulled that way. I've gone from drummer to rock star, but I'm still a family man at heart, and a dad to my core. I look into Simon's cot and think, "You have no idea what's happening." When I think about it, neither do I. I want my son and daughter to have a father and a normal family life. But the way it's looking, we're all going to be disappointed. Genesis' success is conspiring against us.

Less than four years have passed since my teenage girlfriend and I reconnected in Vancouver. In that time we have absorbed seismic changes: a transatlantic relocation, the creation of a family, the departure of a frontman, the elevation of a drummer, the transformation of a cult band beloved by students into something of an international rock phenomenon. My becoming the singer in Genesis has supercharged my working life in ways I could never have imagined. But it looks like it's also accelerating the demise of my personal life.

But do I regret or resent what the band has become, or what it's done to me? I can't say I do. There was no alternative. I had to take over.

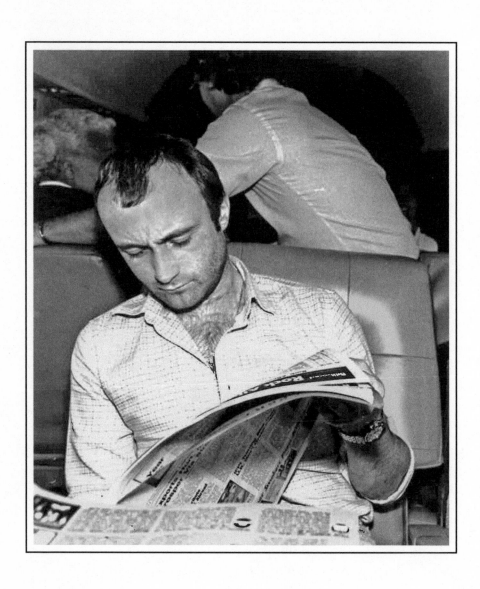

9

THE DIVORCE THAT ROARED

*Or: how multiple American tours end my first marriage, kick-
start my solo career and wrench out "In the Air Tonight"*

EARLY 1978 and, as our new album title tells it, ...*And Then
There Were Three....*

Tony Banks, Mike Rutherford and I have just finished recording,
and Tony Smith calls a band meeting. These are usually convened
to discuss our future, and usually involve us gathering at the band's
HQ in London, grumbling a bit and drinking tea.

Genesis meetings are always a good forum for an argument.
Smith will suggest something and I'll reply, "How many times do I
have to tell you, I don't want to fucking do . . . *insert name of tour/
promotional obligation/*Top of the Pops *gig*. And, by the way, contrary to your schedule, a month is four weeks, not five, so we can't
fit in all that work." And then I cave in.

For once, however, we are all in firm agreement about something
(maybe because there are now fewer of us to disagree with): Genesis are not being played enough on American radio. Not enough to
break out of the big metropolitan centers—New York, Philadelphia,
Chicago, Los Angeles. And we are not breaking out of those cities
because we are not, frankly, rock'n'roll. We are studious, sometimes
overly so, occasionally indulgent English long-hairs who tend to in-

spire our audiences to vote with their bums and sit down while they watch us play.

So if we want to spread into the South, and heartland America, Genesis will have to try by other means. We will have to put our plimsolls firmly on the ground, get on the road and voyage deep into the USA, hitting the so-called secondary and tertiary markets.

In short: in order to break America, we have to play everywhere in America.

Of course, no thought is given to the possibility that America might break us. Or, specifically, break one of us, and his marriage.

Smith and our long-term agent Mike Farrell duly book an intense American tour. Then another. Then another. And then there were three American tours, in quick succession. And two European tours. And a short Japanese tour at the end.

I say, "OK," caving in again.

I go home and report back to Andy. "Darling, great news— Genesis have a fantastic chance to make some serious inroads in America . . ." To me, the professional logic of touring our arses off for the best part of a year is impeccable. The emotional, personal, matrimonial logic? Let's say I am perhaps less clear on that front.

Andy's response can be paraphrased thus: "Well, if you do that, we're not going to be together this time next year."

Granted, of course, people have feelings. But here's my feeling: *This is what I do for a living.* And now that I'm the frontman in Genesis, this is what I do for other people's livings, too.

I put it to Andy (somewhat gingerly) that when we got married, she knew that this was my job. That I have to go away, regularly, repeatedly, to earn a crust. I gently suggest that she has signed up for this. But the great thing is (I press on), once Genesis have completed this rather epic bout of touring, we won't have to do it again. Honestly, being away for the best part of a year isn't establishing the pattern for our life. It's about getting Genesis over that hump, breaking into those smaller U.S. markets, so that life gets easier.

Andy and I have just bought a house, Old Croft in Shalford, near Guildford in Surrey, which is a bit farther out of London than we'd originally intended. Located up winding country roads, it's almost on a par with Peter's parents' house. I've gone from end-of-the-line to end-of-the-lane. Still, at this time I am far from wealthy. *A Trick of the Tail*, two years previously, was the album when Genesis started to credit the writers individually, so there are individual royalties coming in. But even now, with ...*And Then There Were Three...*, I'm still not a big earner on the songwriting side. Now here we are with a big mortgage, and a young and expanding family—Simon is one and a half and Joely is five.

Another reason for me doing all this touring is less tangible, and something my upbringing has ingrained in me. Despite dodging the loathsome prospect of working in the City, I'm still my father's son. I'm the breadwinner, the provider, and I need to go out and work for my family. Not to buy a guitar-shaped swimming pool or a champagne-colored Rolls-Royce. Just because, quite simply, it's my responsibility.

So I go away on tour, and Andy gets on with the job of building a home. Her first order of business: Old Croft needs fixing up. A lick of paint, and the rest.

Handily, one of Andy's relatives, Robin Martin—nice guy, I get on great with him—is a decorator. But he can't do the whole job, so he gets in some cheap labor. One of them is this pipe-smoking, slipper-wearing, ex-public-school chap. Your typical painter and decorator, right? He's out on a limb, out of work, so Robin employs him to work on our newly purchased marital home.

And that's how the affair starts.

And I find out.

And unfortunately I remember finding out—in the course of a particularly heated phone conversation—during one of the tours. But unless I want to abandon the tour and shoulder all the financial aftershocks, I have to carry on and hang on for dear life.

I come home knowing I have to face this disastrous turn of events, but with the knowledge that I have to go back out on another tour pretty much immediately. And touring in the seventies isn't like touring now. There's no email, Skype, FaceTime or mobile phones. We're not that far from the days of the telegram.

Consequently, when I arrive home, we have, to put it mildly, a lot to discuss. But when we try to communicate, we get nowhere. I know this isn't how Andy sees it, but this is honestly how I remember it.

One afternoon Andy calls me at the house while I'm there with the kids, and says, "I'm not coming home tonight. I'm staying out." And I know who with.

I go ballistic. I punch a wall, making a fist-sized hole. If it wasn't the wall it would have been something else. I've reached that point. The next morning she turns up and I'm livid. I'm also very, very sad. Because I now know that it's over. She's quite matter-of-fact about this, in the "Andy" way I've got used to. I can't stop thinking of what probably happened the night before. She seems to be unaffected by what she's done, and all the obvious ramifications. The fact that I'm unhinged by her actions doesn't seem to bother her. She seems to be saying, "I told you this would happen. It's your fault."

There's all this loose change in a little tray by the phone, and lest I lash out at another wall, I launch it across the hallway. I don't intend to get physically violent, and this is as close as I come.

This can't help but affect the kids. Later, I hear Joely and Simon playing mums and dads in the dining room. Simon arrives in his pedal car. Joely says, "What are you doing back? You're not supposed to be here!" Out of the mouths of babes.

Nonetheless, believe it or not, I'm still desperately keen to make all this—our marriage, our family, our new home, the band—work. Spinning one plate in the air while watching another wobble toward the floor.

I'm pleading with Andy: "Just wait until I finally get back. There's only two more weeks to go on the tour. Just wait, and we can discuss this when I come back."

Andy says, "OK, I'll wait."

By the time we're in Japan on that final leg, it's not just the plates that are spinning. As Mike Rutherford will later write in his book, *The Living Years*, I'm legless in Japan, having discovered sake, though I'm never unable to perform. I also discover the head-melting nature of being so far ahead of GMT. For the average European, Japan forty years ago is like being in a completely alien world, not knowing or understanding anything; blind to language, customs, rules; grappling with a time difference that makes it nigh impossible to get hold of anyone at home. It's utterly disorientating. So I cling to sake in a nightmare haze.

Finally back in the U.K. at the end of 1978, my abiding memory is of a restaurant in the village of Bramley in Surrey, not far from Old Croft. It's strange what you remember in a time of crisis. I remember I ordered risotto. I remember not being able to eat it. I also remember being told by Andy that it's all over between us. Not only that, she's taking our kids and moving back to Canada.

I'm dreaming of a gray Christmas: that not-so-festive season, Andy leaves for Vancouver. But I'm not giving up on my marriage without one last fight. I ask some of the Genesis road crew to pack up the Old Croft furniture because, in early 1979, I decide I'm going to follow her there. I will live in Vancouver, buy a house and woo back my wife.

Before leaving for Canada I have a meeting with Tony, Mike and Smith in The Crown pub in Chiddingfold, Surrey. I say, "If we can carry on the band while I'm in Vancouver, we've still got a band. But as that's almost 5,000 miles, eight time zones and a ten-hour flight away, I doubt we can do that. So I guess that means I have to leave Genesis."

But Tony, Mike and Smith ask me to hold my horses. If I need some compassionate leave, I can take it.

So I set off for the Canadian west coast. And none of it—the expat-living, the house-buying, the wife-wooing—makes any difference. After four months, nothing changes. My marriage is over.

BY APRIL 1979 I'm back in Shalford, tail between my legs, boxes still packed in this house in which I've barely lived. The paint is still practically wet on the walls. The paint applied by the guy who's been sleeping with my wife. We've gone for wooden floorboards and brick interior—*très* late-seventies chic—so it looks even more desolate. Everything, myself included, is stripped back to the core.

I'm rattling about in this house, just me and the cardboard boxes.

I would have jumped straight back into Genesis, but Mike and Tony have taken advantage of my emotional sabbatical to begin making the solo albums after which they've long hankered. In the course of 1979 both spend time in Stockholm, recording at ABBA's Polar Studios. They hadn't considered that my love-dash to Vancouver would be so abortively short. Nor had I.

Lest I go completely off the rails, I start channeling my energies into whatever musical distraction I can find. Someone recommends me to English singer-songwriter John Martyn, he of the seminal 1973 folk jazz album *Solid Air*. John asks me to drum on the album that will become *Grace & Danger*. As we become close, he discovers I can sing a bit, and I add background vocals on the beautiful "Sweet Little Mystery."

I fall in love with John and his music during these sessions. He and I seem to musically hit it off—so much so that two years later I produce his next album, *Glorious Fool*. But before that, *Grace & Danger* ends up being arguably one of his best works. Unfortunately, Chris Blackwell, boss of Island Records, isn't so sure about it. Like me, John is working his way through a divorce, which is probably one of the reasons we form such a strong bond. But Blackwell feels the songs are a bit too close to the bone. John and his wife Beverley made records together for Island, and Blackwell is very tight with them both. As a result he's loath to release such an emotionally raw bunch of songs.

But *Grace & Danger* is finally released, albeit a year later. With plenty of time on my hands, I go on the road with John and the same guys that made the record. For me, at this time, it's a wonderful release. It's rejuvenating, not least because it's a million miles from the juggernaut that is Genesis. We have great fun, perhaps sometimes too much fun. John likes to drink, as is now well-trodden musical history. He's also partial to other substances, which can make him extremely, but lovably, unpredictable. If you are simply *around* him in those circumstances, you can just walk away. But for those of us working close to him, it seems like he's hell-bent on self-destruction. And you can't help but be somewhat dragged in.

In this period John comes to stay and play at my house many

times, and we take it in turns to call our soon-to-be-ex-partners. It always ends in shouting and the phone going down.

So we open another bottle.

So it goes on.

I also reconnect with Peter Gabriel. He has a very expensive American band on retainer. I say, "If you ever need a drummer . . ." I end up going down to Ashcombe House, Peter's home in Somerset, and me and some other musicians live with him for a month or so. We help him spitball the ideas that are going to become his third album, and we do some gigs: Aylesbury, Shepton Mallet, Reading Festival. During these shows I leave the drums and join him down front for "Biko," "Mother of Violence" and "The Lamb Lies Down on Broadway."

Considering all the historic interest in supposed tension between Gabriel-era Genesis and Collins-era Genesis, it's not often noticed that I play with Peter a lot at this time. If I may be so bold, I'm the best drummer he knows. He can rely on me. With Peter being a drummer himself, he's pretty picky.

But our connection is deeper than the merely musical. Contrary to what people might like to think, there was never any bad blood between us. We were great friends. But as they say in the muckier newspapers, never let the truth get in the way of a good story. After leaving Genesis he may occasionally have voiced his feelings— "Finally, I'm free of the bastards!" (I'm paraphrasing)—but he didn't have anything against any of us personally. Within Genesis he and I bonded closely. I was someone he could always rely on to be his stooge for comedy routines during his stories. Unlike he and Tony Banks, we had no baggage. Perhaps Peter was pleased that it was me that took over vocal duties in the school band, rather than some new-boy incomer. Not that he ever voiced an opinion before, or after, his leaving. He always just seemed to accept my assuming the frontman role. Sure, compared to the Charterhouse chaps, I was a grammar-school oik. But I was *his* grammar-school oik.

Later in 1979 we continue the reunion at London's Townhouse Studios, where I play drums on four tracks on his third solo album, which is being produced by Steve Lilywhite and engineered by Hugh

Padgham. Notably I play on "Intruder," the song on which we develop the so-called "gated" drum sound. More of which anon.

Meanwhile, back home, for moral support two of the Brand X guys, Peter Robinson and Robin Lumley, move into Old Croft. Not, in retrospect, a particularly wise decision. They're far more party animals than I am.

Robin brings his American girlfriend Vanessa, and she and I start to have a thing together. (Robin is quite happy about it. He's a bit bored with her. And we are *très* late-seventies chic, remember.) Peter lives down one end of the house, and Robin down the other in what would have been one of the kids' rooms. I move into what would have been the master bedroom. Alone. The marital suite never felt less sweet.

Before our first short American tour, Brand X record an album, *Product*, at Tittenhurst Park in Berkshire. This is the John Lennon pad of "Imagine" video fame, which he then "gave" to Ringo Starr. Although still Ringo's, it now runs as a studio, and when Brand X are in residence, it runs as a studio twenty-four hours a day. There is daytime Brand X, and there is night-time Brand X. I'm on the day shift.

I also start living at the Queen Victoria pub in Shalford, every lunchtime and many an evening. The landlord and landlady, Nick and Leslie Maskrey, become great friends and confidants who nurse me through the difficult times. I will end up spending many a session there, some of those in the company of Eric Clapton. He's a country neighbor in Surrey, but I first met him earlier that year, when I was in the studio in London with John Martyn.

Our introduction went like this: John has played with Eric and knows him well. One tiring day during the *Grace & Danger* sessions, he's looking for something to, ah, brighten up his day and thinks Eric can help. So John calls and asks if the pair of us can come over to Eric's house in Ewhurst, not far from Old Croft. Eric must have said no—John is the kind of chap who has a tendency to overstay his welcome, and here he's suggesting popping down to score with me, a complete stranger.

So we meet in a pub in Guildford. Eric doesn't know me from a bar of soap, but I do remember sitting with a pint of Guinness oppo-site one of my heroes. Me, quaffing pints in the pub, with the guy I'd idolized at the Marquee . . . Unfortunately, for a while thereafter I fear that Eric assumes I'm just someone who hangs about with John when he's shopping for drugs.

But by the end of '79, Eric and I are very close. The friendship is partly fostered after I'm introduced to Hurtwood Edge, Eric and his wife Pattie Boyd's house in Ewhurst, by one of their friends, song-writer Stephen Bishop, whom I'd met in LA on a Genesis tour.

In these post-Andy dog days of '79, robbed of any Genesis dis-tractions, I visit Hurtwood Edge most days, often staying into the night. I befriend all of Eric's Ripley pals, friends from his teenage years. We often travel en masse up to London to see football matches at Tottenham and West Ham, though Eric is a diehard West Brom fan.

One memorable Sunday after a long session in his local pub in Ripley, Eric is too loose to drive. I've gone with him in one of his prized Ferraris, and we have to get it home. He takes the passenger seat, I take the driver's. I've never driven a Ferrari. Eric says he'll change gears, and all I have to do is use the clutch, brake and accel-erator, and steer. This would be a challenge, even if I wasn't the chap forbidden from driving the Hillman Imp or Mini Traveller in Gen-esis. It's chaos, and I start to feel sorry for the Ferrari's precision-engineered gearbox. But somehow we get to his house, and both the car and I breathe out.

Other times we play pool until the early hours, drinking and laughing, then laughing and drinking some more. We have blues nights at The Queen Victoria, which follow my blue days. It's the start of a beautiful friendship, not to mention a short-term lifesaver for me, and Eric and I will come to play significant roles in each other's lives, personally and professionally, for years to come.

In a way I enjoy this unforeseen, unwanted freedom. I've never much before just "hung out" with fellow musos. My career hitherto has been about me joining a line-up—I've never formed a band with a bunch of mates. This larking about with pals is new to me, and I take to it like a duck to champagne.

At Old Croft there is partying, of sorts, in that we do stay up all night, but mainly to endlessly watch *Fawlty Towers*. It's just me and the Brand X guys, sitting around, awake till morning, in this house down a gravel lane in Surrey, where the nearest other resident—a retired army chap, General Ling—has a lovely cottage. You should have seen his flowerbeds. Picture postcard. There are fun and games, and toy gunfights, which must have been somewhat discomfiting to our war veteran neighbor.

Brand X even do that on record—on *Product*, Robin is credited with "gunfire and chainsaw"—and onstage, where the boys play jazz cowboys and Indians. We do slightly crazed gigs that are very *Python*-esque, with bleating sheep and barking dog sound effects. Brand X do a good job of saving me from myself a bit, for a bit.

But these high jinks, funny and indeed useful though they are, must eventually come to an end. I like working, making music, too much. So I knock their partying on the head, and the guys move out. And I set to writing . . . well, I don't know what I'm writing. Not yet.

MEANWHILE, BACK AT the ranch: when Genesis were in Japan we were offered, gratis, the newest drum machines by Roland, straight off the conveyer belt. The CR-78 is at the forefront of the emerging music technology. I'm told this is the sound of tomorrow. To me it's a step on from the cabaret/lounge-bar drum machine, but still very limited. Mike and Tony took one each. But I'm a drummer. Why would I want a drum machine, a future that would consign me to the past? I said, "Thanks but no thanks."

But back in England, all three of us have started thinking it would be beneficial to Genesis if we could each record our song ideas at home. It's becoming a bit of a late-seventies "thing" to have your own studio environment.

One of our long-serving crew, tech/studio boffin Geoff Callingham, investigates the best home-recording kit, and we all buy a set-up. And lo, suddenly I *do* want one of those CR-78s. I decide that the master bedroom—what would have been my marital bedroom—is going to be my studio. That feels like an appropriate change of use.

I move my great-auntie Daisy's 1820 vintage, straight-strung Collard & Collard piano up there. I also have a Fender Rhodes piano and a Prophet-5 synthesizer. Handily, the previous owner of Old Croft was an old navy chap, a captain of not inconsiderable girth. I bump into him in The Queen Victoria one night (he's only moved down the lane), and he mentions that he'd had the joists strengthened upstairs. For him it was about accommodating his sizeable bath; for me it's about supporting the weight of Daisy's piano, and of my future, in whatever form that may take.

I also have a drum kit, jostling for space alongside that drum machine I said I didn't want. But soon that old faithful kit is cast aside as I grow to like the CR-78. Maybe this coming technology won't put me on the employment scrapheap after all.

In my ad hoc studio in my empty, echoey, house-is-not-a-home gaff in leafy Surrey, I'm just playing, in every sense of the term. Tinkering. My ambitions are low. My technical knowledge stops just before I open the instruction manual. If I see the desk meters moving, and I can hear something play back, I'm happy. It means I've actually managed to record something. At this stage it doesn't really matter what.

I program some pretty simple drum-machine parts, and I mess about on the eight-track. Come back from the pub at lunchtime—after two pints of bitter, max—and mess about some more. Over a year these doodles of mine slowly take shape. But they are doodles. Nothing is really prepared, or finished.

Yet nonetheless, gradually, without me even noticing really, doodles become sketches become outlines become mini-portraits. Become songs.

The words? They just come out of me unbidden. This is true stuff. This is like *jazz*. I improvise, the lyrics coming off the cuff when I record the guide vocal. Sounds roll around in my mouth, become syllables, become words, become clauses, become sentences.

One day, from out of the ether, I get together a nice chord sequence. It's the opposite end of the scale to "The Battle of Epping Forest." As I feel my way around my new studio, fiddle about with the sounds emerging in my head, the memories of early Genesis songs like that, and like those on *The Lamb*, are bleating in my head—music that was written with no idea of what would go on top, so it was all a bit busy.

There was never too much "space" in Genesis music. Whereas I covet space. For sure the songs I might eventually record will have room to breathe. This embryonic number, built round this nice chord sequence, is the perfect example of the space I'm looking for. Without even thinking about it, I soon have a working title based on the lyrics I've sung: "In the Air Tonight."

This still-tentative song is the classic example of where I'm "at" as a fairly wet-behind-the-chords songwriter. What's it about? I have no idea, because with the exception of maybe one or two lines or words, it's totally improvised. I still have the sheet of paper with the original scribblings, with the letterhead of the decorator—not *that* one; the original one, Robin Martin, who hired the undercoating cuckolder—at the top. I'd write down what I'd just sung.

"In the Air Tonight" is 99.9 percent sung spontaneously, the words dreamt up from out of nowhere.

"If you told me you were drowning, I would not lend a hand": that comes from a place of resentment and frustration, I know that much. That is what was going on. *"Wipe off that grin, I know where you've been, it's all been a pack of lies"*: I'm firing back, refusing to take it lying down, giving it as good as I've got.

This is a message to Andy. Whenever I call to speak to her in Vancouver, I have difficulty getting through, literally and figuratively. I don't seem to be reaching her.

So I communicate in song. When Andy hears these words, she will realize how fucking hurt I am, and how much I love her, and how much I miss my kids, then she'll understand. Then it'll be OK.

And there's more where that came from: "Please Don't Ask" and "Against All Odds" are also among the songs written at this time.

Then again: I have also just told her that if she was drowning, I wouldn't lend a hand. These are up and down times. What I write is dependent on the phone conversations we've just been having, or trying to have.

There isn't any distinct pattern to the song sketches that I slowly accumulate throughout 1979, just as the idea that I'm Making My First Solo Album remains abstract and remote. The emotions, and the intention, change from day to day. One day Andy might really piss me off by repeatedly slamming the phone down. Then, that night in the home studio, I'd be in full "fuck you" mood. But the next day I might write something like "You Know What I Mean." Something more plaintive, heartfelt, broken, bereft.

Out of raw emotion emerges instinctive truth. The lyrics and the message of "In the Air Tonight," I later appreciate, are considerably greater than the sum of their parts. *"I've been waiting for this moment all my life, oh Lord . . ."* This is all subliminal, subconscious. Those words fit the music. The verses have a bit of a storyline, but there's no link necessarily between them and the anger. And those words have been dissected by many, many people over and over again. Some guy gave me a thesis he'd done for his college degree; he'd analyzed how many times I'd used the word "the." Other people suggest conspiracy theories about an actual drowning I seemingly once witnessed.

What does "In the Air Tonight" mean? It means I'm getting on with my life, or trying to.

10

ACE VALUE

Or: how some tunes knocked up in my bedroom shift a few copies

W HAT DO TONY and Mike make of my DIY scribblings?
Do I give them the option of using "In the Air Tonight"
for the Genesis album that will become 1980's *Duke*? Do I, in short,
show my solo hand?

The jury's still out. My 1979 batch of writing is finished. These
songs are by no means properly recorded, but the demos are done.
And after this year of each of us recording on our own, Mike and
Tony have finished their first solo projects, *Smallcreep's Day* and *A
Curious Feeling* respectively, and they're raring to go with the next
group project. Which is fine by me—at this time I'm still not thinking of this collection of newborn compositions as an "album." But
one thing I am clear on: these are the most personal songs I've ever
written, created amid the emotional rubble of my wrecked marital
home. The upshot is, by the time we begin work on *Duke* as the seventies bow out, I'm a little protective of these compositions.

I have the idea of moving the writing sessions for this new Genesis album into the second master bedroom at Old Croft, a suggestion to which Tony and Mike agree without complaint. In terms of
group songs, the cupboards are bare. Apart from a couple of bits,
Mike and Tony have used up all their good material on their solo al-

bums. That said, their solo-album period has been great for Genesis. A great relief, a great releasing of pressure. Previously when Tony came in with a piece that was already finished, he'd kind of steam-roller it through: "This is a song I've written so this is what I want Genesis to do." It wasn't said as such, but it was implied.

The three of us have a chat and come to an agreement that any-thing we've finished writing as an individual, we'll keep to ourselves for future solo projects. Any incomplete but promising ideas, we'll bring in and put to the band committee.

Mike offers up a couple of songs that are really strong, "Man of Our Times" and "Alone Tonight," as does Tony: "Cul-de-Sac" and "Heathaze." I play them half a dozen demos, and they say, "These two are great—'Misunderstanding' and 'Please Don't Ask.'" In the former, they hear a kind of Beach Boys thing, which they like. The latter is a very personal song, my version of the conversational device David Ackles used in "Down River." I thought that was an unlikely choice for the band—it's so intimate, and very unlike anything Gen-esis have done before.

But hand on heart, I do not remember not sharing "In the Air Tonight." One reason I'm sure of this is that at this time I don't view it as particularly special, as any kind of rare peach—my '79 compositions are all peaches as far as I'm concerned. To be honest, I don't really want to give any of them away, as I have quite strong ideas as to how they should sound. But at the same time, I'm still far from certain that I'm going to make a solo record, so this next Genesis album might well be my only shot at getting these songs out there.

But what I also know is that I might never have this kind of in-song space again. Because once you put any song ideas to the band committee, Tony and Mike come in and add their ideas. And al-though we're a million miles away from the fiddly, fussy days of "The Battle of Epping Forest," we are not far enough away for me to say, "Do whatever you want to 'In the Air Tonight.'"

Still, just to reiterate, I have no memory at all of keeping it in my back pocket. I think I play them pretty much everything I have, apart maybe from "Against All Odds," because for me that's only a B-side. And based on that recollection, they choose not to choose "In the Air Tonight." Mike has no memory either way, but Tony maintains he never heard it—otherwise he would have grabbed it for *Duke*.

So we'll never know definitively.

But one thing I do remember Tony saying quite often is that my songs only have three chords in them, and as such they are unworthy of being "Genesis-ized." In that telling, without the drums and the ornaments, "In the Air Tonight" is just a drum-machine part and three chords. Accordingly, it's quite probable that it just doesn't register with him.

From Old Croft we move, in late 1979, to Stockholm, to Polar Studios. The material we've come up with for *Duke* is really strong, and I'm on a massive learning curve as a songwriter. I only started writing "properly" a year previously. Yet apart from bringing in "Misunderstanding" and "Please Don't Ask," my role in Genesis is as it was before. Tony and Mike like these songs, but I feel I'm still regarded as primarily the band's arranger. I am gaining in confidence, though, gently pushing forward.

Mike has this slow guitar riff in a funny time signature, 13/8, and I suggest speeding it up. That becomes "Turn It On Again." I use the CR-78 on "Duchess," which is the first time we use that drum machine in the studio. I've used it on my demos, and after a year in my bedroom with it, I know what it can and can't do. It's incredibly limited, but it works really well on "Duchess."

At one point "Behind the Lines," "Duchess," "Guide Vocal," "Turn It On Again," "Duke's Travels" and "Duke's End" are tenuously joined as one thirty-minute track about this character named Albert. He's the figure in the album cover art by French illustrator Lionel Koechlin. But we know a single piece of that length is only going to be compared to "Supper's Ready," so we opt not to go there again. It's a new decade and maybe "suites" that take up a whole side of an album won't be indulged quite so readily anymore. A clean sweep is called for.

Duke is the band's commercial breakthrough, particularly in Germany. It starts Genesis mania there, which leads into Phil Collins mania. It will sell hugely in Britain, too, but gets a terrible review in *Melody Maker*, and on a couple of occasions I'm anointed "Wally of the Week" in the music press.

Why? There's the old saw that the "inkies" (as *Melody Maker*, *NME* and *Sounds* are collectively known) are automatically suspicious of anything that becomes hugely popular—the perception is that something has been dumbed down so as to appeal to the masses. Equally, "prog" is fast becoming *genre non grata* at the indie-, post-punk- and New Wave–loving music papers. As frontman with Genesis, I am a target for such ire. Equally, I will hold my hands up and admit that, with all the success, it's quite possible that I have been giving off an unintentional smugness.

By the time the album is released, on March 28, 1980, we've already started the *Duke* tour. That particular day is the middle of three nights at London's Hammersmith Odeon, which is when Eric Clapton—who attends at Pattie's suggestion—finally realizes I'm more than a pool-playing drinking pal and mangler of Ferrari gearboxes. He actually sees that I'm a fellow musician, a revelation about which I later hear he's a little surprised. The tour runs the length and breadth of the U.K. until early May, pauses for a week, then resumes in Canada for a North American leg that runs until the end of June.

The third Canadian show is in Vancouver, and when I'm there I take the opportunity to call on Andy. Though the divorce is trundling on I'm still holding a candle for her, and desperately missing my kids. I'm thinking, "This could be the time we fix things." The band have around three days in the city, and I stay with her mother. We've always been close, and I love Mrs. B. with or without her daughter.

In a final, optimistic attempt to woo back my wife, I book into Vancouver's Delta Inn for a night, invite Andy over, put on my compilation tape of irresistible songs—Chris Rea's "Fool (If You Think It's Over)" and all of the other deathless torch songs that I know—and crack open the champagne and roses. The romantic in me thinks, "This is bound to work." If nothing else, who can deny the power of these all-time great songs of love and loss?

It doesn't budge her at all.

HOME IN THE U.K. that summer of 1980, I turn my attention back to the songs I wrote the year before. Time to put my recordings where my heart is.

The way I make the album that will become my first solo set establishes the tone of what I will do in the future. Record all my vocals at home. Sing in that improvised way. Play it back and write down what I sing—or what it seemed I was trying to sing. You're jotting down a sketch of what you've just sung. Sometimes it's almost fully formed, other times it's useless. A song develops, slowly or quickly. You can feel it coming in the air tonight. But only sometimes.

From here on I do that for every record I ever make.

And yet this isn't going to become an album until I have twelve or thirteen songs, put them on cassette and play these demos to someone else. Eventually I let Tony Smith hear them one day on my Mini's car stereo, and I play them for Ahmet Ertegun, our American label boss at Atlantic Records. Truth be told, I revealed my homework to Ahmet before we went out on the *Duke* tour—but only because I drew the short straw and was given the Genesis job of driving up to London to the apartment he keeps while he's in the U.K. and playing him *Duke* for the first time.

We have a drink or ten, Ahmet asks how I am—he knows about the impending divorce—and I tell him I'm OK, and that actually I've been doing some writing . . .

I hadn't really anticipated playing anything of mine to Ahmet. But I always had a tape in my car, so I could listen to the demos and come up with new ideas to add. Anyway, Ahmet listens to these demos and declares with emphatic enthusiasm, "THIS IS A REC-ORD!" Suddenly he forgets the new Genesis album. "Phil, you've GOT to make this into a record. Anything I can help you with, I will. But this has to be a record."

Wow. It's incredibly important to have this man, whom I respect so much, saying this. Ahmet discovered Aretha Franklin, Ray Charles, Otis Redding, and now he's telling me I'm a winner, too. He's produced numerous records I've held close to my heart, and he likes what I've done. It doesn't get much better than this.

And I need it. I've been through the mincer with the marriage split, feeling like a fool . . . I'd told the guys I was off to Vancouver to patch things up, and I'd come back having done no such thing. Then Tony and Mike were off on new solo musical adventures, and there I was, just the singing drummer again.

So, yeah, I've been feeling pretty bad about myself. Yet here's one of the greatest record executives in history telling me that what I've been doing on my own is fucking great. Ahmet's thumbs-up finally convinces me that, as soon as I'm done with *Duke* obligations, I will record my first solo album.

Still, I'm not blind to one final irony: had I not been battered by the breakdown in my marriage, my debut collection of solo compositions would have taken on a very different hue. It probably would have been a Brand X–type, instrumental jazz thing along the lines of Weather Report. If it wasn't so sad it would be funny.

Nonetheless, not all the songs I've written are doom and gloom. "This Must Be Love" ("*Happiness is something I never thought I'd feel again / but now I know / it's you that I've been looking for*") and "Thunder and Lightning" ("*They say thunder / and they say lightning / it will never strike twice / but if that's true / then why can't you tell me / how come this feels so nice?*") are the songs that move the personal narrative onward. These are the Jill songs.

I meet Jill Tavelman in mid-1980, in Los Angeles, after Genesis play the Greek Theatre on the *Duke* tour. Tony Smith is going through a divorce, too, so we're both brand-new bachelors. Generally the management and I never hang out after the shows, but uncharacteristically, he and I go out on the town together.

This particular night we decide to do something different for both of us: we have the limo drop us at The Rainbow Room on the Sunset Strip. It's an LA rock'n'roll institution: not so much a hangout for bands but for their crew. It's also a place to pick up girls. These facts could be related.

We slide into a booth and sit there, quenching our post-gig thirsts. I stretch my arms above and behind my head. Suddenly there's a pair of hands grabbing my hands. I look back and there's this girl, short hair, very cute in a Tinkerbell sort of way. She's very happy. And she's with another girl. Before long we're all sitting at the same table.

Eventually, the four of us hop into the waiting limo and repair to L'Hermitage, the LA hotel of the moment. I still don't quite know how this happens, but later that night I'm in bed with Jill and her girlfriend. That hasn't happened before, or since. I should stress that there is no hanky-panky. My abiding feeling is: "What am I supposed to do with two?" For other people, *this is the life*. Not for me. I'm too embarrassed, I guess. For young(ish) Phil Collins, it's stage-fright time.

Jill is a well-educated Beverly Hills girl, twenty-four years old, with her own distinct musical tastes (Iggy Pop is one of her favorites). I recognize that she's special, and deserving of more than casual sex. It seems like the feeling is mutual. We have a couple of dates and, before I leave LA, Jill comes by the hotel to say goodbye. She gives me a Steve Martin book, *Cruel Shoes*. She knows I'm a big fan. I find out that her godfather is Groucho Marx. I have a funny feeling about this girl.

I invite Jill to join me on tour and, five days later, she flies into Atlanta. Unfortunately, there is another Collins staying at the Hyatt Regency, and Jill is given the key to his room. He's a proper musician—a Scottish bagpipe player, in town with his clan to play in full Highland regalia—and when she arrives in his room, he's in the shower. On hearing a female voice, he perks up, thinking it's in the small print of his contract. By a whisker reasonable modesty is preserved, although Jill is cruelly robbed of solving the mystery that vexes most Americans: namely, what a Scotsman wears under his kilt.

All of a sudden it looks like we're an item. I respond in the way that is fast becoming second nature to me: I write about her, with "This Must Be Love" and "Thunder and Lightning" emerging with loved-up ease. We talk on the phone regularly and then, a few months later, when I'm back in LA to record horn parts for my work-in-progress solo album, Jill comes to the studio. She brings along her mum and introduces us. Afterward, her dear mum Jane will say, "Well, darling, love is blind." That stings a bit, but I turn my pain to gain: the line will reappear in the lyric of a song, "Only You Know and I Know," on 1985's *No Jacket Required*.

I make a list of who I want to help out on this still-abstract, non-jazz solo album: Eric Clapton, David Crosby, the horn section from Earth, Wind & Fire, Stephen Bishop (who will later return the favor by giving me "Separate Lives"), string arranger Arif Mardin, jazz bassist Alphonso Johnson. All my heroes, basically.

Working with Eric is easy. He and Pattie's Ewhurst home is only fifteen minutes away from Shalford, so I often sleep over. Pattie takes a real shine to me, and I've always had a soft spot for her, ever since first clapping eyes on her as a schoolgirl in *A Hard Day's Night*. So much so that one time Eric jokingly tells Mick Fleetwood at a New Year's Eve party that I'm fucking Pattie while he's away on the road—and I'm fucking Mick's ex-wife Jenny (Pattie's sister) in the bargain. Mick gets the joke, but of course I'm embarrassed by the crack, especially as Joely and Simon are standing beside me.

So I'm round there all the time. We drink, and Eric sometimes has to be put to bed, but it never gets out of hand. That's the kind of person—the kind of drinker—he is. He goes to the edge. I'm too sensible. I leave the edge to others.

Eric plays on two tracks I've earmarked for this still-as-yet-untitled solo album, "If Leaving Me Is Easy" and "The Roof Is Leaking," but only I know he's on the former. He comes over to my place one night and I play him the demo. The lights are down and we've had a few too many drinks—he's a committed brandy-and-ginger guy, and we've already been out to the pub. That's the way we are most of the time.

I play him "If Leaving Me Is Easy," and the thing with Eric is, he only plays when he's got something to offer. He plays a guitar part, but ol' Slowhand takes it slow. I was hoping he'd play more, but he says, "I didn't want to play, I didn't want to mess it up."

Even though I intend to make a virtue of my inexperience and produce these songs myself, I know I'll need an assistant producer and an engineer. So I meet with Hugh Padgham. Hugh is a bass player but he loves drums, and we'd developed that groundbreaking sound on Peter's track "Intruder." With hindsight, I now know that that day or two we'd spent working on Peter's third album in Townhouse in 1979 was life-changing.

I tell Hugh, "I can't face recording all this stuff again. A lot of emotion has gone into it, and I like the way it sounds. So I want to use my demos." So we copy my eight-tracks onto sixteen-track, state of the art for the time, and throughout winter 1980/1981 we carry on overdubbing at Townhouse.

We fool around with "In the Air Tonight," but at the moment there's no big drum fill, so none of that gated drum sound, just me coming in on the drums for the last choruses. That's the way I assume it will stay.

But then I'm sitting in the Townhouse live room. You can control how much "liveness" you want in the recording by closing heavy curtains to deaden the sound. And if you put the microphones in the top corners of the room, you can make the drums sound much more live. But for "In the Air Tonight" we say, "Let's try that sound we had with Pete . . ." What we actually end up with is nowhere as extreme as "Intruder." Even if you place the mics in the same place, and try for the same sound, you'll always end up with a different animal. Different day, different result.

As for that drum fill: people ask about it all the time. A landmark in percussion, in production, in *ba-doom, ba-doom, ba-doom, ba-doom, doom-doom.* Imagine seals barking it next time you're at a zoo. It's pretty cool, as that gorilla in the 2007 Cadbury's advert would agree.

But back in Townhouse, at the dawn of the eighties, I know for sure that I never say, "I know what's going to work . . ." I just play it. Hear it. Love it. That's it. What do I know? Remember, I think "Against All Odds" is a B-side.

But I soon realize that nobody has heard drums like this, as loud as this, and with that kind of sound. Beyond that, lyrically too, the song has that something about it that nobody really understands. Not even me. Maybe because I'm not a songwriter—not yet, not really—it's outside the box of traditional songwriting.

It's simple, it's ghostly, it's full of space, it's a *cri de cœur*. It should definitely not be a single.

I have to come up with a title for the album. It's obvious that most of the songs are autobiographical. So I have an idea to call it *Exposure*. Or *Interiors*. They sound appropriate. But I then remember that not only is *Exposure* a Robert Fripp album, but it's a Fripp album that I played on. And *Interiors* is a Woody Allen film. I still liked that for the title, though. But then, might calling it *Interiors* make the painter and decorator think it's all about him?

For the cover, I have the idea of seeing inside my head, right through the eye sockets. What is going on inside this person's mind? That, and not any egotistical reason, is why it's a close-up. And, of course, it's black and white. That cover image in turn underlines an idea I've now had for the title: *Face Value*.

Because this is such a personal record, I'm committed to every aspect of it, fully responsible for all the nuts and bolts. For one thing, there's the choice of label that's going to release it—and that's not going to be a label that has anything to do with Genesis. Even if that means letting down our Charisma label boss and my old pal Tony Stratton-Smith, the man who, a hectic decade earlier, pointed me in the direction of the Genesis gig in the first place.

I have a sad liquid meeting with him in his room at L'Hermitage to break the bad news. He's in LA because the *Monty Python* crew are performing at the Hollywood Bowl, and John Cleese stops by to say hello to Strat. It's a very *Fawlty* scene, with him dressed in a Pittsburgh Penguins hockey shirt. "Sorry . . . sorry . . . didn't know you were busy . . . not to worry, come back later," splutters Cleese. The whiskey of our meeting does not mix well with the tequila of our Mexican lunch. A Strat cigar finishes me off. I'm as sick as a Norwegian parrot on the pavement. Maybe it's appropriate penance for ditching my old benefactor.

Anyway, onward. Tony Smith shops *Face Value* around in the U.K. and Virgin are desperately keen. I sign on the dotted line with

Richard Branson's label, the home of *Tubular Bells* and *Never Mind the Bollocks*. I can fit somewhere in between those. To the casual observer, this is a new Phil Collins.

I go to the cutting and the mastering. I write by hand everything that has to be written—the track listing, the sleeve credits, even all the legal stuff that goes on the disc label. I get the record company to give me some blank labels that go on the middle of the vinyl and I write around the edges. If I run out of space, I start again. If I have too much space, I start again. Attention to detail. It's my first solo album. It might be my last solo album. I'm going to give it everything, and it's going to be all me.

Still, I have low-to-no expectations. People close to me have heard *Face Value* and they all say what Ahmet said: "*Wow.*" But they're biased. And really, I know none of them expects anything, critically or commercially. In America the label doesn't even want to release "In the Air Tonight" as the first single. They plump for "I Missed Again."

I go to New York and meet with Ahmet to discuss how to promote this hard-to-pin-down album. I've stayed with Atlantic for the U.S. release, largely because of Ahmet. He loves me and my music, and maintains that enthusiasm for as long as he lives. He gives me a lot of courage and reassurance over the years when I'm getting stick left, right and center. Whenever he has new artists in his office, Ahmet will play "In the Air Tonight" and say, "Now *this* is what I would like from you."

My question for Ahmet and his team: how can I open doors that are closed to Genesis? After all, the initial radio reaction sheets from American disc jockeys to "I Missed Again" are promising, along the lines of: "Hey, this is a mover!"

I think, "There's no reason this album couldn't appeal to R&B fans. It's got the Earth, Wind & Fire horns on it!"

So I organize a meeting with Henry Allen, the label's head of black music. "Listen, I would like this record to go to R&B stations."

"Yeah . . . but they're not gonna play you. 'Cause you're white."

"Yeah, but they won't know that if you don't put me on the cover. Bill it as 'Phil Collins and the EWF horns.' Or even 'The

EWF Horns with Phil Collins.' I don't care how, but I feel this can cross over."

"No. *They'll know.*"

This racial delineation is a shock to me. This is not the fifties or the sixties, it's the eighties. But I soon learn that old prejudices linger. When Earth, Wind & Fire's Philip Bailey is preparing to come over and make his album *Chinese Wall* with me in the producer's seat in 1984, he has meetings with Frankie Crocker, the famous black disc jockey, and with Larkin Arnold, the head of CBS's R&B division. They both tell Philip, "You're going to London to work with this Phil Collins? Well, don't come back with a white album."

At the end of October 1980 I invite Jill to move over to England, and as 1981 comes round we're ensconced in Old Croft. She's sacrificed her last year of college, where she was studying to be a high school teacher, to come and live with me.

Face Value comes out on February 9, 1981, shortly after my thirtieth birthday. I don't go out on a solo tour. Too soon for any of that, and I want to have more music in my repertoire. Besides, it's a little daunting to think of a *solo* tour.

Meanwhile, Genesis have decided to bite the bullet and get our own studio-cum-headquarters. We buy a lovely Tudor house in Chiddingfold, our minds made up in no small part by the large, multi-car garage in the garden. This we can convert into the recording space of the complex we will call The Farm. While the building conversion takes place we settle into the house's low-ceilinged living room and begin writing what will become Genesis' eleventh studio album, *Abacab*.

During the writing of *Abacab* news slowly filters through of *Face Value*'s unexpected success. This makes things a little awkward. I'll come in all bubbly, and genuinely gobsmacked: "My God, 'In the Air Tonight' has reached number 1 in Holland!" Not only that, it's becoming a smash all over the world. *Face Value* keeps selling and selling. As Tony Banks pithily says in the 2014 BBC documentary *Genesis: Together and Apart*: "We wanted Phil to do well. Just not that well."

Here at the start of the eighties I can glimpse, already, how things might change in the band. I guess maybe the guys are thinking, "Well, that's it—Phil's going to leave." Not that anyone says as much, although Tony Smith pointedly tells me, "I think Genesis is really good for you." Another singer leaves Genesis? To lose one frontman is careless; to lose two . . . Certainly Genesis wouldn't survive another schism like that.

Smith, being a great manager, is right. And he'll stay right for a long time after. Each career—solo and band—reinforces the other.

Plus, of course, I'm *enjoying* this unforeseen solo success. Before now I labored under that ongoing sense of being the junior partner in Genesis. I realize years later that I underestimated the guys' opinion of me, which I find out when reading Mike's book: "If Phil had an idea, we listened." This is a revelation to Mr. Insecure. We'd never had that kind of discussion. Emotional candor was not something we displayed in front of each other.

For a long time, though, I will still feel sheepish with Genesis when it comes to writing—"I've got this tune, is it good enough?" But with my songs, coming thick and fast as the eighties kick into gear, I'm starting to prove myself. "Misunderstanding," the first full song I wrote for the band, is released as the third single from *Duke*. It becomes our biggest international hit.

Face Value continues to sell. It's a number 1 in the U.K., something which impresses us all. We've always wanted a number 1 for Genesis.

Are Tony and Mike jealous? Not that I'm aware. And that sense of humor—"We wanted Phil to do well. Just not that well"—is how we are with each other. Nobody is allowed to get above themselves.

Me (gasps): "Fuck! 'In the Air' is going to number 1 all over Europe!"

Tony (sniffs): "Yeah. Still only got three chords in it."

Me (shouts): "FOUR, ACTUALLY."

And what does Andy think about me airing our dirty laundry for the edification of countless millions around the world? Well, she's not the kind of person who buys *Sounds* or *Rolling Stone*, so she won't necessarily have read anyone's dissection of my lyrics. But I have no reservations telling interviewers/anyone who asks what this album is about.

And then I'm on *Top of the Pops* with a tin of paint.

About that tin of paint: "In the Air Tonight" comes out as a single in the U.K. on January 5, 1981. Within a week it's number 36, and I'm at the BBC, appearing on their nation-uniting weekly chart show (times have changed). How am I going to perform the song? I'm still not comfortable standing there with a microphone, especially on TV. So I'll play keyboards. And my engineer, roadie and factotum Steve "Pud" Jones says, "I'll get a keyboard stand."

"Nah, looks a bit Duran Duran to me. Get a Black & Decker Workmate. That'll do."

"OK. What'll we put the drum machine on?"

"Um . . . a tea-chest?"

The tin of paint? That's because we're going for rehearsal after rehearsal, and the *Top of the Pops* producers are desperately trying to make this tea-chest look interesting. So Pud just keeps adding little bits.

"A paint pot . . . ?"

So there is, indeed, a DIY theme to that (in)famous *Top of the Pops* appearance. But it has nothing to do with Andy going off with the decorator. That performance, and that paint pot, have come back to haunt me time and time again.

While I'm kicking about the BBC studios, I chat to that week's host, Radio 1 DJ Dave Lee Travis. He watches one of the rehearsals of "In the Air Tonight" and goes, "Cor, this is going to be massive."

"Are you sure?"

"Oh, yeah, this is going to be Top 3 next week."

And it is. Then it goes to number 2. It looks like it's headed all the way to number 1. Then John Lennon gets shot and puts everything into perspective. Life will never be the same again. One of my heroes, gone.

11

HELLO, I MUST BE BUSY

Or: the imperial years, and more hits, more tours and more collaborations than are probably advisable. Sorry about that

WHERE WERE YOU when MTV began broadcasting, on August 1, 1981? What were you doing three days previously, when Prince Charles married Lady Diana Spencer at St. Paul's Cathedral?

Throughout the eighties, me and my videos, both solo and with Genesis, will become a fixture on this revolutionary new TV channel. I will somehow end up as Charles and Di's go-to entertainer. No weddings or bar mitzvahs, but I'll play a few royal birthday parties, at one point performing an unwittingly inappropriate divorce-heavy set around the time there were, infamously, three people in the heir to the throne's marriage. Yet despite the prominent role in my life of both institutions—Establishment and anti-Establishment, if you like—I struggle to remember the precise details of my whereabouts and activities that summer of '81 . . . and at various points over the ensuing half-decade.

I can't blame encroaching senility—right now, six months after the release of *Face Value*, I'm a sprightly thirty years old—and nor can I blame rock'n'roll naughtiness. It's simply, I think, that I'm too busy to remember it all years later. And I'm about to get busier still. So busy that I'm not even aware that I'm busy. I just know that pulling double duty as a solo performer and as singer with Genesis is, from out of nowhere, asking more of me than I'd ever anticipated. More than anyone anticipated, maybe. Few people before or since have enjoyed a hugely successful solo career concurrent with a hugely successful band career.

As if that isn't enough, I enthusiastically embrace a third career: record producer. Band success begets solo success begets lots of people wanting a bit of whatever perceived "magic" I've got. These aren't any old people; these are offers I'd be stupid to turn down from artists I class as friends and/or heroes. Eric Clapton, John Martyn, Anni-Frid from ABBA, Philip Bailey—they all want me to produce their new albums or, in the case of Robert Plant, seek my recording studio counsel.

In between, shoehorned into the bursting schedule, I'm becoming more and more involved with The Prince's Trust. This commitment to the cause means nights out, playing for or socializing with various members of the House of Windsor. No hardship whatsoever, but it does paint me as a conservative, monarchy-loving, brown-nosing lackey. My good pal Charles tells me to ignore the naysayers—or to just say the word and he'll happily instruct Mummy to decree: "Off with their heads!"

Treasonous joking aside, I'm wholeheartedly committed to the work undertaken by The Prince's Trust. The charity was formed by Charles in late 1976, his concerned response to inner-city riots that reflected the growing frustration among British youth. In its early days it was customary to use concerts and film premieres as fundraisers for the Trust. Aware of the power of a pop or rock show to connect with youth both young and old, Charles invited me to join as a trustee.

One such concert is the Michael Jackson show at Wembley Stadium in 1988. Charles and various Trust bigwigs are in the royal box, and I'm sitting behind HRH with some other anointed commoners. Halfway through the show he turns to me: "I'd like something like this at my party. Could you arrange it?" Slightly stunned, I reply automatically, "Yes, sir, I'll see what I can do." Suddenly I'm organizing Prince Charles's Jacko-inspired fortieth birthday party and in charge of booking the entertainment. Will he be expecting moonwalking and crotch-grabbing?

I call one of the Genesis booking agents, Steve Hedges, and he sends me some cassettes of turns that might be appropriate. If they're a covers band who do a decent version of "Beat It," they're instantly on the shortlist. I eventually choose an outfit called The Royal Blues. They sound good, can play all the hits of the day, and their name will give pleasure at the palace. I find out from them later that they're the same band that played at Charles's twenty-first birthday party. So far, so good.

The party is to be held at Buckingham Palace and about a month beforehand I'm summoned to a pre-party walk-through of the schedule. I meet with Charles's equerry and Nigel, the briefcase-toting leader of The Royal Blues.

We discuss tactics. It seems I am to be the "surprise" entertainment come party night. I therefore won't be in the receiving line, which is a bummer—no chance to doff my cap to the Queen Mother or the Queen, nor ask whether they preferred Genesis with Peter singing or me.

Cometh the regal hour, cometh the surprise guest: emerging onto the party floor from my bolthole in a Buckingham Palace anteroom, I'm instantly struck by the presence of so many of pan-European royalty's greatest hits. Every continental monarch worth their crown seems to be there. Diana is standing front and center, Elton and Fergie are sharing tiara tips at the side of the small stage, and Prince Charles is somewhere not entirely close to his wife.

I've invited guitarist Daryl Stuermer to join me to make it sound a bit more professional, and we've rehearsed a set that includes all the songs I'm able to play with this reduced line-up. Unfortunately this means most of my saddest, most break-up-y songs. This doesn't particularly get them dancing in the aisles. Even at this late stage in their married life, and despite being reasonably close to their inner circle, I'm probably the only person present at Buckingham Palace that night who doesn't know Charles and Di are on the verge of splitting up.

Before I leave for home, I commit two more cardinal sins. The first is to approach the Queen and introduce myself. One has to wait for the Queen to approach one. I also address her as "Your Highness" instead of "Your Majesty." Neither faux pas seems to bother her, and she's quite friendly, referring to me as her son's "friend," which tickles me no end. I'm just starting to glean her views on the use of the 9/8 time signature in "Supper's Ready" when a beefeater intervenes.

As I finally exit, propelled forcefully in the direction of something called "the Tower," I watch as the Queen and Prince Philip jive to "Rock Around the Clock." Not an image I'll ever forget.

My crew, meanwhile, stay till breakfast is served with the traditional "carriages" at around 1:30 a.m. The guys are holding their plates full of sausages and beans, looking for a place to sit. They see three empty seats and go to sit down, only to find Her Majesty Queen Elizabeth II sitting in the fourth seat. "Sit down, sit down," she commands. And a good old full English fry-up was had by all.

I have another encounter with Princess Di at her thirtieth birthday luncheon at the Savoy in July 1991. Again I'm booked as the entertainment, and again I play a set of completely inappropriate songs, notably "Doesn't Anybody Stay Together Anymore." I sit at her table and ask for her autograph, another no-no as far as royal protocol is concerned. But in this period we seem to meet quite regularly, at Prince's Trust shows and related events.

Just to be clear, I certainly wasn't the fourth person in their marriage, but we're familiar enough for Diana to reveal some intimacies. Around this time I'm at the dentist in Harley Street. I'm emerging with my longtime assistant Danny Gillen after some major tooth work when a BMW pulls up and the window slides down. It's Diana and, sitting in the driver's seat, an officer-class chap I recognize as James Hewitt.

"What are you doing here, Phil?" she says, smiling. Then, light as you like, "I've just had a colonoscopy. It was great. You should try it."

Danny and I look at each other. "Did that really just happen?"

BACK TO 1981. A year that began with my unexpectedly successful first solo album now ends with *Abacab*, a chart-topping Genesis album that has mixed things up a bit—it features songs that are, generally, shorter, punchier and less synthesizer-heavy than what we've done before. I've entered my thirties, but my Tiggerish enthusiasm for change, and adventure, is undimmed. I won't become Eeyore for some time yet.

The beginning of 1982 brings more change, and more challenges. ABBA's Anni-Frid Lyngstad, stunning in a huge fur coat, visits me at The Farm. She's been going through a divorce, too, from Benny Andersson. With her personal life splintering, and with ABBA's future looking equally rocky, she wants to make a solo album. I get the impression she's lived under the oppressive weight of the ABBA phenomenon, and of songwriters/producers Benny and Björn Ulvaeus, for so long that she wants to stretch and be her own woman.

She doesn't reveal much of this during our meeting at The Farm, only that she has chosen me to help her realize her goal. She's seemingly listened to *Face Value* incessantly, so she believes I understand and can relate to what she's going through.

I tell her I can, and also how much I love her fur coat.

Easily flattered by her enthusiasm for my work, I agree to return once more to Stockholm's Polar Studios to produce her first ABBA-era solo album. I've put together a crack team of musicians: Daryl on guitar, Mo Foster on bass, Peter Robinson on keyboards and The Phenix Horns from Earth, Wind & Fire. Jill will also come for several visits over the eight-week recording/mixing period, although declines the opportunity to stay. Sweden is lovely, but Stockholm isn't the most exciting place to be for an extended length of time. Jill likes traveling with me, but not that much.

Sitting together at the studio, Frida and I choose the songs, but she has certain pre-booked numbers that preclude any argument. ABBA's management put out a worldwide call for compositions and, from the hundreds of responses, an eclectic selection has been assembled. I've thrown in one by my pal Stephen Bishop, and she's chosen a Bryan Ferry number; a Giorgio Moroder co-write that appeared on a Donna Summer album the previous year; a Dorothy Parker poem set to music by the guy who would go on to found Roxette; a song that was the British entry for the 1980 Eurovision Song

Contest; and a rework of my *Face Value* track "You Know What I Mean." Talk about a *smörgåsbord*.

One day while recording at Polar, Benny and Björn come to visit. It's a little awkward, to say the least. They're naturally rather possessive. Frida is somewhat fragile, the divorce is still reverberating, they've produced her all her adult career, and now, professionally speaking, she has a new man in her life. A man who's producing, playing drums, singing with her and giving her a far rockier sound than ABBA ever had. And why is the album called *Something's Going On*? No one knows at the time that ABBA won't outlast the year, but the writing is on the wall.

Maybe that's why Stig Anderson, the band's manager and owner of Polar Music, is such an arsehole. Once the album is finished, he invites us all to his house for dinner. When we arrive he's completely drunk. We listen to *Something's Going On*, and at the end he snorts, "Is that it?"

Frida bursts into tears, and we all want to thump him. And I'm mob-handed—all the Genesis road crew are there, including beefy Geoff Banks, one of our boys with the telling nickname "Bison." We've all come to love this fine lady, and we all feel protective. But cooler, more sober, less Scandinavian heads prevail and we leave, although Stig's response has soured the whole evening for us.

Something's Going On will sell well, with the single "I Know There's Something Going On" becoming a hit in multiple territories around the world (and a favorite source of samples for hip-hop artists). But I'm fast learning that the producing game comes with its own peculiarities. Maybe being a self-produced solo artist is the easier option after all.

Back home at Old Croft in spring 1982, the phone rings. "Hi, Phil. It's Robert Plant." Despite my being a fan of Plant and Led Zeppelin from way back when, from their very first London gig at the Marquee, Robert and I have never met.

Led Zeppelin split at the end of 1980, after the death of John Bonham. That tragedy came only two years after the death of another of my teenage drumming heroes, Keith Moon. Shortly after Moonie's demise, I was working with Pete Townshend at Oceanic in

Twickenham, helping on tracks for an artist from New York he was producing, Raphael Rudd, a brilliant pianist and harpist.

At that time Pete was running around London clubs with New Romantic gadabout Steve Strange. He wasn't in great shape, partying all night and recovering all day. Pete was still sleeping when I arrived at the studio for the session. But once he was up I grabbed him: "Who's gonna play drums for The Who now? 'Cause I'd love to do it."

"Oh damn, we just asked Kenney Jones to do it."

It was a serious offer, and I was a little disappointed. I'd have left Genesis to join Pete, Roger Daltrey and John Entwistle. It's The Who, man! I grew up with that band. I just loved the energy and I know I could have done it and made it work.

Denied the chance to play with one set of childhood heroes, here's Robert Plant offering me another. He wants me to guest on his first solo album. He sends me a bunch of demos with Jason Bonham playing, and he's fantastic. It's just like listening to his dad.

Jason and I had bumped into each other at various Genesis gigs around the English Midlands. He was in his mid-teens, and he was a fan. Jason would later tell me that his dad made him listen to "Turn It On Again," released just before he died, and made his son try to play it. I never would have thought that John was even aware of me as a drummer.

I jump at the chance of following in the footsteps of one, if not two, Bonhams. I spend a couple of weeks at Rockfield Studios in Wales playing on six of eight tracks on the album Robert will call *Pictures at Eleven*. We have lots of laughs between recording. Here are a great bunch of guys, and I'm in a band again, albeit for a short while. Robert's players are a group of Brummies, all good solid guys, and not in awe of the Zep thing at all. Robert is trying to reinvent himself, something I can understand.

Home in Surrey again, I start on my second album. I don't have much to work with—the previous year I'd gone from *Face Value* to recording *Abacab* to producing John Martyn's *Glorious Fool* to the *Abacab* tour, and then into the Frida album and the Robert album. There's been no time for reflection or songwriting.

Then I hit the proceedings for Andy's divorce from me. Or they hit me. Legal letters seem to arrive with ponderous regularity. There are demands for a slice of this or that fortune—a fortune that doesn't exist. Although *Face Value* has made big impressions and big sales, it will be a long time before the record and publishing companies, as is their business model, finally hand over the royalties.

For a while Andy returns to London with Joely and Simon, and rents a house in Ealing. Her new Canadian boyfriend follows her. He and I get on OK (you have to live my life to believe it), certainly much better than Andy and I get on. Poor Simon and Joely, more often than not, seem to be almost pushed out the front door to greet me when I come to collect them.

I'm trying to maintain an even keel, but I admit I'm on a short fuse, and there is lots of shouting. Shouting that will resound in the kids' ears for many a year.

It's a frustrating, enraging situation—one that, alas, won't be ending any time soon—but also an inspiring one. Soon I have songs like "I Don't Care Anymore," "I Cannot Believe It's True," "Why Can't It Wait 'Til Morning" and "Do You Know, Do You Care?" The last thing I want to do is make a second "divorce album," but being someone who writes from the heart and not the head, right now I have no option.

The next emotion I have to deal with is my own fear: I have to follow a solo album that wasn't meant to be an album, far less a hit. Writing another may not be a task I'm up to. I wasn't expecting to make a second record.

Neither, it seems, was the listening public. "Thru These Walls," released in October 1982 as the first single from my second solo album, *Hello, I Must Be Going!*, limps into the U.K. charts at number 56. In America it fares even worse—my stalwart supporter Ahmet's label doesn't even deem it worthy of release. On my part there's no panic but a little disappointment, and some resignation.

Luckily, Motown saves me, as it had done so often in my youth—as a teenager the label and its artists were the soundtrack of my life, as filtered through The Action's set-list. Paying tribute, I include on *Hello, I Must Be Going!* a cover of "You Can't Hurry

Love." I think of it as one of the forgotten Supremes songs, a bit of a dark horse; the likes of "You Keep Me Hangin' On" and "Stop in the Name of Love" seemed to get the most plays and the most affection.

Aided by a video featuring multiple chirpy versions of myself (yes, even in a single video I'm all over the place), "You Can't Hurry Love" finger-snaps to number 1 in the U.K. It's the only hit from the album (it also reaches number 10 in the U.S.), but it helps push *Hello, I Must Be Going!* to number 1 in Britain. Disaster averted. Or is it? I'm very happy but underlying it is the thought: "A song I wrote went nowhere as the album's first single, but this very poppy Motown cover has gone to number 1. Is the number up for my songwriting?"

In August, prior to the release of *Hello . . .* , Genesis go on the road for two months in America and Europe. It's a tour in support of a live album, *Three Sides Live*, of which *Rolling Stone* comments, "Where once Genesis represented art-rock at its most fatuously spectacular, they now show how lean and compelling such music can be." On the tour we do our best to minimize fatuous art-rock, and I try my utmost to be lean and compelling.

We're still trying to give it lean and compelling on a soggy Saturday in autumn 1982, despite Genesis' line-up doubling in size and the British elements doing their best to dampen our spirits.

On October 2, at Milton Keynes' National Bowl, the three of us are joined for a fourteen-song set by Peter and, arriving late from South America, Steve. For the first time since 1975, the "classic" line-up of Genesis are back together, for one night only, our ranks rounded out by Daryl Stuermer and drummer Chester Thompson.

As reunions go it's an odd one, but it's for a good cause—a benefit concert that's an emergency response to a unique set of circumstances. In the summer, Peter had put on the first festival by his two-year-old organization WOMAD (World of Music, Art and Dance). Featuring an appropriately eclectic line-up of artists including Peter, Echo & The Bunnymen, Nigerian high-life star Prince Nico Mbarga and the self-explanatory Drummers of Burundi, it was a critical success but a financial disaster. Peter had creditors threatening his life. As he later said, "When the shit hit the fan, people identified me as the only fat cat worth jumping on so I got the aggro, a lot of flak, nasty calls."

Still a band of brothers seven years after his departure, we all gladly pitch in to help, and the Bowl is packed with 47,000 fans for this once-in-a-lifetime gig. Talk Talk and John Martyn drew the short straws and have to open for us, and the incessant rain does its best to ruin the day. We've only had time for a couple of afternoon rehearsals during Genesis' recent gigs at Hammersmith Odeon, the song selection necessarily draws mainly from the Peter era, and the whole idea feels better on paper than it does in practice. But we have to laugh when Peter insists he comes out in a coffin over the intro to "Back in New York City." Typically Pete, and typically dark and humorous, but I'm not sure the audience get it.

Overall, though, the fans are pleased, and so are the critics: "It probably fell some way short of Genesis and Gabriel's standards of perfection. But this was an unrepeatable bargain"—*Sounds*; "A reunion that is unlikely to ever happen again. The rock event of the year"—*Melody Maker*. More importantly, we've helped stop our mate being jailed, or worse, and helped WOMAD live to fight another festival. It becomes the biggest annual event on the world music calendar.

After Milton Keynes I'm just home long enough to see "Thru These Walls" stiff as a single, and then my second solo album comes out in November. Hello, I really must be going: I immediately embark on my first solo tour, which runs until February 1983.

This, I'm realizing, is what happens when you're a solo artist and simultaneously in a band. There's no time to stop and smell the roses, or to rue the failures and process them.

There is, however, time for nerves and apprehension. I've been touring with Genesis since 1970 so, after twelve years, I need to assemble another great band to help stave off the anxiety of being "on my own." I pull together The Phenix Horns, Daryl on guitar, Mo on bass, Chester on drums, Peter from Brand X on keyboards. The setlist is just as strong. I have two albums of material to choose from. The hits are still hits, and the ones that weren't hits become something else live. "I Don't Care Anymore," for example, grows into a huge stage song.

Guildford Registry Office, Surrey, August 4, 1984, with Jill on our wedding day. I had stayed the night before at Eric's and Patti's house, and Patti wouldn't let me leave without ironing my wedding shirt.

With Bob Geldof backstage at Live Aid, 1985, in a photo taken by the legendary David Bailey. I don't think I'd performed yet, so this was before the madness started. Even Bob looks relatively calm at this point.

The Heavy Mob: Lionel Richie, Michael Jackson, Quincy Jones and I at the Grammys, 1985. I had just performed "Sussudio" on the show, and Michael leaned over and asked me who had arranged the horn parts.

Presenting a small tour jacket for the baby Prince William (future King of England) to Diana, Princess of Wales, at a Genesis show on the *Mama* tour at Birmingham NEC in 1984. This is a pretty heavy photo, as William is now knocking at the door of the throne. Maybe his son George now wears that satin *Mama* jacket.

Trying to teach HRH Prince Charles how to play the drums during a Prince's Trust week at Caister in Norfolk. Thankfully, he was useless and I kept my job.

Mum, Carole and Clive in happy times at the *Buster* premiere at The Odeon in London's Leicester Square. They were very proud that I had made a good film, especially with someone like Julie.

Tommy: From left to right, my Uncle Ernie, Billy Idol's Cousin Kevin, Pete Townshend, Elton's Pinball Wizard, Roger Daltrey, John Entwistle, Steve Winwood's The Seeker and Patti LaBelle's Acid Queen. Difficult job to live up to Keith Moon, but I tried the best I could.

With Steven Spielberg on the set of *Hook*. He's trying to talk me down from the ledge after informing me that he wants to do my scene in one shot: no cutaways, no chance to regroup and to get it right. Tremendous pressure.

Mark Knopfler, Eric, Sir George, Macca and I at AIR Studios in London rehearsing for the 1997 Music for Montserrat concert. As always with these kinds of events, the atmosphere was friendly and without ego.

With my good pal Planty, who presented me with an International Achievement Award at the Ivor Novello Awards in London in 2008. I love Robert. We share a great sense of humor, and he is, like George Harrison was, a little suspicious of fame and the blind faith that comes with it.

With Orianne on our wedding day in 1999. I was so in love with her. It's a lovely story that we're back together now. We have two wonderful sons, and I don't want to be with anyone else.

Baby Nic on my lap, playing my drums. Nic had a small kit when he was about two. He would stand at it and play.

Oscar night, 2000. I'd seen Elton at a MusiCares event the week before. He'd told me where his Oscar party was going to be, and that if I got lucky, as he believed I would, I was to come and show off. I did get lucky and I went to his party, Oscar firmly in hand.

The dynamic trio: Steve "Pud" Jones, Matt and Danny Gillen. As I'm writing this, Pud has been with me for forty-one years, and Danny since *Buster* in 1987. I can't imagine doing things without them.

At the Alamo with Nic and Matt, looking for traces of enemy bombardment on the church columns. You can see where the Mexican cannons hit the church, and that was a great education for the boys to see how the battle actually happened.

The lovely Lily finally getting her dad to dance at the Crillon Debs' Ball, 2007. By this time, Lily had made quite a mark for herself with modeling and was about to become an actress with similarly impressive results.

Joely, Dana and Lily at Twickenham rugby ground on the Genesis reunion tour, 2007. Genesis is a long-serving band with plenty of history. Children have been born and have grown into adulthood in the band's lifetime.

The only photo in recent times of the original Genesis. I'm the young, good-looking one at the top of the stairs. It's quite extraordinary to think that these five people were together in some shape or form for forty-six years, and we're still great friends.

My idea of heaven: playing drums with The Action, my favorite band of all time, Beatles excluded. We posed for this photo outside the back of the legendary 100 Club in London in June 2000. My biggest drum hero was Roger Powell (on far left). Sadly, since this photo was taken, bassist Mick Evans (second left) and singer Reg King (far right) have died. These guys formed my musical taste with their versions of Motown and soul classics.

PG with PC, his stooge till the end. I think this photo says a lot: Peter the serious thinker, me with the funny hat and goofy smile. I consider him a great friend, and I would like to think he feels the same.

Left: My sixtieth birthday in London, 2011, with all my children at the Tower of London. Dana and Lindsey had arranged a weekend of fun with the entire Collins family involved: Clive and Carole and partners, Mum, all the nieces and nephews—everyone. *Right:* The adorable Zoe and Grandpa in Vancouver on her fourth birthday. I love reading to children and helping to build their confidence.

Sister Carole's husband Bob, Nic, Carole, me, Clive's wife Lynne, Matt and Clive in London for a family weekend. All my kids have a great sense of family, and we all get together whenever we can.

Taken in Geneva after landing from Miami, en route to Lausanne for the Little Dreams Foundation show in June 2016. I am so happy to be back with my sons and their mum. I think it shows.

This was taken on June 2, 2016, at a concert for the Little Dreams Foundation in Lausanne, Switzerland. It could be viewed as me putting my foot back in the water to see if I liked it. Well, I loved it, and I'm sure more will follow. What I'm most proud of, though, is the guy in the background behind me. Nic has played three shows with me now, and if I do more, he'll be there. He was magnificent, stepping up to the plate and filling big shoes.

I feel like I hit the ground running as a solo artist. I've never been short of confidence, but I become more of a performer, leading from the front and filling the stage. Somehow I'm able to reach out to the Genesis fans who bought *The Lamb Lies Down on Broadway*, and to the pop fans who bought "You Can't Hurry Love" by that smiley, cheeky Phil Collins chap. I'm able, too, to dig deep for the encores— every night we finish with a version of Curtis Mayfield's "People Get Ready" and Brand X's ". . . And So To F . . .," which is pretty fantastic with horns, and which gets a long-overdue shout on the 2016 *Hello, I Must Be Going!* reissue. Everyone goes home happy.

But if I'm honest, this is the blurriest time for me, and my recollections are fuzzy. Is it possibly because this is when things go stratospheric, and because it's now that I really start putting in the solo miles in America? The *Hello* tour only has six European shows, four of them in London, and the rest—through December, January and February—are all in North America.

Or are my memories dim because that's how I feel about the album? Fundamentally, *Hello, I Must Be Going!* doesn't tick many boxes for me, even though I know there are some songs that are huge for fans. But there are no real stand-out memories of writing it or even recording it.

I know what my second album did for my career, though: it brought my first nomination at the Brit Awards (British Male Artist), and my first Grammy nomination (Best Rock Vocal Performance, Male), for "I Don't Care Anymore."

But what did it do for my art and heart? Not much. I got the second solo album blues.

Back in the U.K. in early spring 1983, I reconnect with Robert Plant. Again I go to Rockfield, again I play on six of the eight tracks on what will become *The Principle of Moments*, his second solo album. This time, Robert decides to go on tour, a six-week run around North America. Would I like to join him? You bet I would. After the craziness of my day job—day jobs—back to being just a drummer, sitting behind everyone else, will feel like going home. And doing so for Led Zeppelin's former singer is an honor I'd be mad to turn down. It's a muso gig, as distant as it's possible to get from this new pop gig I now have, and I jump at it with both sticks. It's the deepening of a great relationship. Some people, rock stars especially, drift in and out of your life, but Robert has stayed a good friend.

In this period, not only am I away from home all the time, I'm away in multiple directions. Jill is accompanying me on a lot of these adventures—she loves the Plant tour, it's her kind of music—but not all of them, and probably not enough of them. But we're getting on like a house on fire. Love is still in the air.

Home, briefly, in May 1983, I meet up with Mike and Tony at The Farm. After all my running around it's good to be back with the guys again. As we embark on what will be Genesis' self-titled twelfth album, now that our studio is fully operational we have the luxury of both time and improvisation. Mike plays around with a new toy. As he later describes the harsh rhythmic sound he comes up with: "I programmed that with the very first big Linn drum machine. And I did something the Americans would never do: I put it through my guitar amplifier, a small one, and I turned it up so loud that it was jumping up and down on the chair. What the English do well is take a sound and fuck it up. That's a prime example. It's just a horrible but great sound."

He's not wrong. Straight away it works. We all fall in love with it and, inspired, I do my best John Lennon impersonation, and I also take a vocal cue from Grandmaster Flash and the Furious Five's "The Message," adding in the maniacal laugh.

And that's "Mama," the lead single from the *Genesis* album. Our biggest ever U.K. hit, both of its time and timeless, and an enduring stage classic. It's followed by "That's All," the writing of which begins with a piano riff of Tony's and becomes our first U.S. Top 10 single. Released in October 1983, the album is another U.K. number 1, and sells 4 million copies in the U.S., by some margin our biggest at that point. At this time we're just very lucky. Whether it's my thing or the Genesis thing, it just keeps getting bigger. One profile is reinforcing the other, and our songs seem to be exciting more and more people.

By the time February 1984 rolls around, I'm looking a bit greedy. Before Genesis have even finished our five-night stand at Birmingham's NEC, the last dates of a four-month tour spent mostly in North America, I've released a new solo single in the U.S. At least at home I do the decent thing—"Against All Odds (Take a Look at Me Now)" isn't released in the U.K. until after the completion of the tour, at the end of March.

Well, I say "I've released." The idea that the artist has any control over release dates for singles and the like is one of the great fallacies surrounding the music industry. If I had my way, I wouldn't even be involved in choosing which songs are released as singles. On the one hand I'm not sure I'm very good at these kinds of decisions—if you'll recall, I'd ignored "Against All Odds" when I was recording *Face Value*, viewing it as a B-side at best. It didn't even get a look-in on *Hello, I Must Be Going!* a year later. Then it becomes my first American number 1, wins my first Grammy and secures my first Oscar nomination.

On the other hand, in 1983–4 I have so many other things going on that it barely occurs to me to think how this release date reflects on that touring schedule, how this solo obligation impacts on that band responsibility. I've just got my head down, getting on with it.

The serendipitous tale of "Against All Odds" goes like this: in December 1982, during my first solo tour, Taylor Hackford—the future Mr. Helen Mirren—comes to meet me in Chicago. He's the director of *An Officer and a Gentleman*, which is a big film that year. Hackford wants a song for a new film he's shooting, a would-be noir-ish romantic thriller. I tell him that I can't write on the road, but I have an unfinished song with the working title "How Can You Sit There?" Might this demo cut the mustard?

Hackford loves it. I haven't seen a script, but he feels the lyrics are already perfect for the main musical theme for his still-in-production film. So I wrestle together a proper recording. The piano and orchestra are recorded in New York under the supervision of the legendary Arif Mardin (he's worked with everyone from Aretha Franklin to Queen); then, at Music Grinder in LA, I record the drums and vocals. Arif is a lovely man and a fantastic producer, able to get great performances in the most effortless way. I'm thrilled to work with him, I want to impress, and he coaxes out of me a powerful vocal.

I already have most of the key lyrics, notably the *"take a look at me now"* line. But Hackford reminds me his film is called *Against All Odds*, so I incorporate an approximation of that, using the phrase "against the odds." Hackford, though, is precise: he insists I have to title it, and sing, "Against All Odds."

The director is thrilled with the end result, and I'm pretty pleased, too. In a short space of time I seem to have become known as a writer who can crystallize emotional turmoil. I'm the Phil Collins of Genesis lore, but to more and more people, I'm the Phil Collins who's written "In the Air Tonight" and "Don't Let Him Steal Your Heart Away," who can write with space, and also with dramatic, cinematic sweep.

The song is big, way bigger than the film. It's now viewed as a paradigm of the eighties power ballad, that phenomenon from the decade when the hair was big, the emotions were bigger, but the shoulder pads were biggest of all. Barry Manilow covered it on his album *The Greatest Songs of the Eighties*, and Bazza knows what he's talking about.

"How can I just let you walk away / just let you leave without a trace / when I stand here taking every breath with you / you're the only one who really knew me at all . . ." Why do these words and this song mean so much? Well, it was written at the height of my troubles with Andy, and forced at gunpoint to analyze it, I'd have to say it's a good break-up song, with universal resonance and empathy. People hate a break-up, but they love a break-up song. "Against All Odds" pins down how it feels to be broken-hearted, and it's one of the songs most often mentioned when people write to me, describing how it helped them through the trauma of heartbreak. And it's a big vocal: impactful, raw, real. Courtesy of Arif, that was a good day in the studio in LA. I don't remember having the pain and misery coursing through me as I stood in the vocal booth, but I must have drawn it from somewhere. That's what the song needed, so I went for it.

Singing it onstage for years thereafter, I can't say that I'm dragged back into painful memories every time. If I was feeling that much pain night after night, I'd be a crackpot. Onstage you're just trying to sing it—keep in tune, get the lyrics right. I don't always manage. *"How can I just let me walk away / when all I can do is watch me leave"*—I've sung that more than once or twice, which is pretty impressive as clangers go.

A year after its release, "Against All Odds" is in the running for an Oscar for Best Original Song. Normally, the nominated artist sings their nominated song. But 1985 is the year the Academy decides to change things: they're going to have the songs performed by other people.

The dispute starts small—a note from my label or management to the Academy, professing our willingness to stop over in LA en route to an Australian tour and perform on the telecast. Soon it escalates, and the letters are flying back and forth. One is addressed to a "Mr. Paul Collins." Eventually Ahmet Ertegun writes to Gregory Peck, who's president of the Academy at the time. This has gone right the way to the top. For as long as I can remember, I've watched the Oscars, and I'm an avid movie buff. I'm privileged to be in this exclusive group of nominees. I have no intention of upsetting anyone by inviting myself to sing my song. But suddenly, I'm unwittingly in the middle of an Oscar meltdown.

The Academy gives "Against All Odds" to a dancer to lip-sync. To be fair, she's not any old dancer—she's the hugely experienced Ann Reinking, ex-partner of master choreographer Bob Fosse. None of that prevents the whole thing being a pig's ear.

It's all very unseemly by the time I finally get to LA, because it looks like I'm the one who's been writing the letters. I go to the award show and everyone in the business knows about the kerfuffle. As soon as Ms. Reinking comes on to perform the song, everyone turns around to look at me, to gauge my reaction. I'm just embarrassed, at what she's done to the song and at what they think is my argument. Stevie Wonder wins, for "I Just Called to Say I Love You." But at least "Against All Odds" wins the 1985 Grammy for Best Pop Vocal Performance, Male.

That said: I didn't even know it was nominated for a Grammy. I only found out when the award arrived in the post. "What's this? Something else for Paul Collins?"

12

HELLO, I MUST BE BUSY II

Or: still hard at it

L ET'S GO BACK twelve months, to the period after the end of the *Mama* tour in February 1984, and after I've finished promoting "Against All Odds."

Simon and Joely are growing up into great kids. That said, I'm all for hard graft, so I'm a bit of a taskmaster with Simon and his maths homework throughout the school holidays. Just to encourage him I've bought an old-fashioned, Victorian-era school desk and chair for his bedroom. He sits there, his back to the window, laboriously working through his algebra while the sun shines outside. Sorry, mate, I thought I was being a responsible dad. And for sure that algebra will come in useful later in life.

As for Jill and me, we're settling into a lovely home life together, and she's wholly supportive of my overlapping working commitments. Even though these are becoming, I have to concede, a bit much.

Between May and the end of '84 I produce Philip Bailey's *Chinese Wall* album at Townhouse in London; produce Eric Clapton's *Behind the Sun* in Montserrat; write and record most of my third album, *No Jacket Required*; and take part in the recording of *Do They Know It's Christmas?* by Band Aid.

Why does Philip Bailey want me to produce his album? It seems I'm deemed to be the hot guy. Plus, the Earth, Wind & Fire horn players have told him about working with me. Philip and I have met a few times, although thankfully we've got over the inauspicious occasion when EWF's management mistook me for the band's drug dealer.

I was in New York, and EWF were playing Madison Square Garden. *Face Value* wasn't out, so I wasn't "Phil Collins" yet. I've worked with The Phenix Horns on the album though, and they invite me to the show. I arrange to meet them beforehand in the lobby of Le Parker Meridien Hotel on 56th Street.

First to appear is tour manager Monte White, brother of band leader Maurice White. Soon all the band members arrive, then take off in their limos. Finally the Phenix guys appear, looking for their allotted car. Monte, meanwhile, has assumed that this shifty, loitering Englishman is the Horns' drug dealer. He informs Don Myrick, the sax player and leader of the section, that under no circumstances is anyone other than the horn players to be in the car. But after he leaves, Don insists I jump in with them, which I do, albeit a little uneasily—the White brothers run a notoriously tight ship.

We arrive at MSG, drive up the inner ramp, and Monte is waiting with a checklist. He gives me the death stare: I don't have a pass, and I certainly shouldn't be getting out of the Horns' limo. Abandoned at the backstage entrance, I suddenly feel very alone. Mercifully the union crew and the local security recognize me from Genesis, and they welcome me into the cafeteria. To this day the respect and affection goes both ways.

Back to business: in early summer 1984 Philip Bailey flies over from Los Angeles. He checks into Bramley Grange, a small country hotel in the sleepy Surrey village of Bramley, very close to my home. English country living is a new experience for Philip, quite a paradise, although we don't seem able to accomplish what we set out to do, which is to co-write songs—there are too many other cooks involved.

In the end we only manage to write one song together, and that comes right at the end of the sessions. We set about this mission, and start improvising. Philip starts directing us, I sing something about a "choosy lover," which becomes the working title. We record a rough and energetic take last thing at night, just so we remember it the next day. The following morning we like what we hear and that, pretty much, is the finished version. I'll write the lyrics and it's eventually retitled "Easy Lover," and released as a duet between two Philips. The single reaches number 2 in America, kept off the top by Foreigner's "I Want to Know What Love Is." It hits number 1 in the U.K. just about the same time I'm grimacing my way through Ms. Reinking's interpretation of "Against All Odds" at the 1985 Oscars ceremony.

Before *Chinese Wall* is released, I'm already otherwise engaged: Eric asks me to produce his new album. It seems that legendary producer Tom Dowd had mentioned to him that he should get a bit of "that Phil Collins thing" on his next album, not realizing that we were buddies. So Eric decided to cut out the middle man and come straight to me. Frankly I had no idea that he respected me that much and would trust me with his new album. Even before learning that we'd be recording in Montserrat, I'm firmly on board. To quote the old sixties graffiti, Clapton is God, even if he is your country neighbor and drinking buddy. If I'd had a crystal ball and foreseen the troubles ahead, I'd still have said yes.

Eric's previous album, *Money and Cigarettes* (1983), hadn't done much for me. His music was just starting to sit there. It didn't have much fire in it, to my ears. So I start extolling to Eric the virtues of having a little home studio, a place to write. Inspired, he installs a set-up like mine at Hurtwood Edge. I don't think he ever uses it. I think the idea is a little alien for Eric at this point, a little too complicated to run on his own. He just wants to play, whereas I want him to express himself, and not just cover other people's songs.

AIR Studios in Montserrat is, as one would imagine, idyllic. Opened by George Martin in 1979, it's a beautiful place, perched on a hilltop with views of the ocean and the sleeping volcano—which stops sleeping in 1997, when it erupts and destroys much of the island, including the studio. It's a great feeling being here in this paradise as producer for my mate and his band of legends.

We have the lovely Jamie Oldaker on drums and, on piano, Chris

Stainton, longtime server with Joe Cocker's Grease Band. Stax bass player Donald "Duck" Dunn is part of the group, and his playing and character add to the sense of both fun and occasion. This guy is a true legend, part of the original Booker T. & the MG's that backed Otis Redding at Monterey, Sam & Dave, Eddie Floyd and so many more. I had got used to bass players traveling with multiple basses, and assumed it was the bass player's version of penis envy. I ask him why he only has the one. "I used to have two," he replies in his Southern drawl, "but one went down with Otis," he says, referring to the 1967 plane crash in which Redding died. He also tells me that he's never changed the strings. Ah, the good old days.

Before we jet off to the island, Eric tells us the rules. Firstly: no women, so Jill's left at home. However, during the course of the recording, he has a relationship with the studio manager, Yvonne, with whom he will have a baby girl, Ruth.

Secondly: no drugs. Which is fine by me, but then, a few days in, Eric thinks (wrongly) that I'm holding out on him, and artist gets a bit grumpy with producer. There's a bit of an angry confrontation, Eric and I discuss the matter, and I am cleared of all narco charges against me.

I follow Eric's lead, producing in a manner sympathetic to the songs he's written—songs that are not full of endless guitar solos. We had long chats at Hurtwood Edge about writing, and I was urging him to write more. But it transpires that endless guitar solos is exactly what his new label—burned by the low sales of *Money and Cigarettes*—have been holding out for. Neither artist nor producer got that memo. Well, perhaps artist did, but he didn't pass it on to producer.

The "finished" album is delivered to the label . . . and then rejected by the label. They put a rope around Eric's neck and drag him to LA, where he records some new songs written by Texan singer-songwriter Jerry Lynn Williams. Lenny Waronker (president of Eric's American label) keeps close guard and does additional production.

It's my first taste of record company interference, and I still have the bruises. Only later that year, when I'm still smarting from the accusation that Eric and I have dropped the ball, do I understand why he might have been distracted enough to let the label dictate the creative terms so forcefully. As close a friend as I am to them both, I don't know that he and Pattie are splitting up. To me, they're the perfect couple.

Before the album is finally delivered, Eric rings me one day: "I've written a song that has to be on the record. It's called 'Behind the Sun.'"

He comes round to Old Croft with his guitar and sings it to me. I'm floored. It's fantastic, and clearly deeply personal and pained. I say, "How are we going to record this? The sessions are over; the album's done, everyone's gone home."

Eric says, "We'll do it now."

Suddenly I'm not his producer, not the singer with Genesis, not a solo star. I'm not even his mate. I'm a kid again, the straggly fifteen-year-old who, in 1966, stood waiting for a bus outside The Attic in Hounslow and heard Cream shake the walls. Now, here's Eric Clapton wanting to record in my pretty basic home studio. It's a great song, and he wants it to be the album's title track, so I'd better not fuck this up.

He plays it once or twice, no more, and I record it. The meters are moving: that's good. Then I have to record his vocal. Again I see the meters moving: that's a relief. At least it's recording. You have to understand that usually I do this on my own, for me, and a little bit of messing up doesn't matter. But here I am with Eric, clearly in an emotional maelstrom, and I, as his friend/producer, want to help him make the best album possible.

Now we have to mix it. It's only him and the guitar, but for mood I put a little synth on it, nothing more than sustained strings. Old Croft is definitely not a good mixing studio, but Eric likes what he hears. It's put at the end of the album, and it's a coda, a meditation on the end of his and Pattie's marriage: "*My love has gone behind the sun . . .*"

It's a sweet way to end the record, a nice turnaround. All this happens after the LA intrusion, so I feel a little vindicated. Then, years later, Eric tells *Mojo* that "Just Like a Prisoner," one of our

Montserrat tracks, was his best guitar-playing in as long as he can remember. I'm proud I was there.

After finally finishing *Behind the Sun* I start thinking about my third solo album. Over the course of 1984, I'll work through ideas and record my little demos. I have a notion of what I want to do: break out of this "love song" box that I've found myself in. I'll make a dance album. Or, at least, an album with a couple of up-tempo tracks.

I program a drum-machine track and improvise some syllables over the top. The rhythmic word "sussudio" comes out of nowhere. If I could have a pound for every time I've been asked what the word means, I'd have a lot of pounds. I can't think of a better word that scans as well as "sussudio," so I keep it and work around it. I ask David Frank of The System, a New York electro/synthpop duo that I like, to take my demo of "Sussudio" and make it into a dance track.

But old habits die hard: I've also written a bunch of emotional songs—"Inside Out," "One More Night," "Doesn't Anybody Stay Together Any More," the latter a response to the demise of Eric and Pattie's relationship, and the splits being endured by, it seems, quite a few of my friends. At least Jill and I are happily entwined; I never want to go through that trauma again.

The new album's title, *No Jacket Required*, is inspired by a couple of incidents. Jill and I are on holiday at Caneel Bay on St. John in the American Virgin Islands. We go to eat at the hotel's open-air restaurant. When I get to the front of the queue, the *maître d'* gravely informs sir that sir needs a jacket.

"I haven't got a jacket, mate. I'm on holiday. In the Caribbean."

There are a couple of fellow vacationers in front of us, and the husband turns round and gives me the raised eyebrow. "Jacket required," jokes Reuben Addams, a doctor from Dallas. I don't forget the phrase, and I don't forget Reuben or his equally lovely wife Lindalyn.

In the same period, on Robert's *Principle of Moments* tour, we stay at the Ambassador East in Chicago. He's wearing this very loud, check Williwear suit, and I'm wearing a brand-new leather jacket and jeans. We go to have a drink at the hotel bar, and the barman gravely informs sir that sir needs a jacket.

"I am wearing a jacket."

"A proper jacket, sir . . . Not leather."

Percy Plant's dressed like Coco the Clown, but he's all right. I'm in designer leather jacket (very modish, I'll have you know) and I'm lowering the tone.

So this idea of "jackets required" seemed to be turning up everywhere. I've always hated stuffiness and snobbery, so *No Jacket Required* becomes my album title and, yes, why not, ethos.

Doing the rounds of American chat shows to promote the album, the story about the Chicago hotel is the one I trot out for David Letterman and Johnny Carson. Eventually the manager of the Ambassador East writes me a letter, requesting that I stop talking about their daft dress codes. I can come in anytime, wearing anything I like, just please stop talking about them. They send me a jacket, too, garishly patterned to look like it's splashed with multicolored paints, just so I know they're not being 100 percent serious. I wonder if Robert might like it.

I'M IN THE middle of recording *No Jacket Required* at Townhouse when Bob Geldof calls. I've never met him, but he's straight to the point: "Did you see the news?"

"No, I've been here working." When you're in the studio, you're cocooned away from the outside world; you're "in the woods," as Quincy Jones would say. Geldof tells me about Michael Buerk's BBC news report on the famine in Ethiopia. Then he explains his idea for an all-star charity single. "We have to do something, and I need a famous drummer, and you're the only one I can think of."

He mentions Midge Ure and George Michael and that's about it. A few quick days later, on Sunday November 25, 1984, I go down to SARM Studios—formerly Island Studios in Basing Street, Notting Hill, where Genesis recorded *Foxtrot* and *Selling England*, and mixed *The Lamb*—to join the good and the great of the mid-eighties British pop scene.

It's nerve-racking. Everyone and their Top 40 dog is there, from Spandau Ballet to Bananarama to Status Quo to U2 to Sting to Culture Club. Most of the track has already been recorded, so it's just my drums that are being laid down today, followed by all the vocals. I have to come up with a drum part on the spot, while the cream of *Smash Hits* features pages hover, watching and/or applying make-up (and that's just the men). But sometimes fright can make you lift your game. I'm looking around and there's a warm feeling of admiration from the musos in the room. This is gratifying, but also scary, as I've not been told what's required of me. Geldof just says, "Start here and play what you want." I do my drum track, and there's applause. I go into the control room and Midge says, "That was great." I say, "Let me do it one more time." "No, we don't need to do it again." "Oh, OK . . ."

That was it, one take.

I meet Bono for the first time, and get talking to Sting. The former Police man and I click. Remembering that I have an album to finish, I ask Sting if he'll help me out with a bit of singing. He ends up doing backing vocals on "Long Long Way to Go" and on "Take Me Home," where he's joined by Helen Terry and Peter Gabriel.

No Jacket Required comes out on January 25, 1985, a week before my thirty-fourth birthday. Why the red face on the sleeve? Because it's a hot album, club-friendly and pumped up. The beads of sweat on my forehead are part actual sweat, part glycerine. The songs and the sentiments are true, but the cover, I confess, needed just the slightest bit of fakery to make me look hot and bothered. Not sure why—I've barely stood still for three years.

The album is an instant hit. When "Sussudio" is released, I top the singles and albums charts at the same time in the U.S., and I do the same in the U.K.—but in the U.K. it's "Easy Lover" that's the number 1 single; a song that's not even on this album. *No Jacket Required* is at number 1 for seven weeks in the U.S., and sells over 12 million copies there. Worldwide to date it's sold 25 million copies.

I only know this because I looked on Wikipedia. In the eye of the tornado, and for years afterward, I couldn't really care less about chart achievements or sales figures. I'm just running to stand still.

These are the years when I'm everywhere, all the time, monopolizing the airwaves, MTV and the charts, even the bloody Oscars.

Try as you might, when you turn on a TV or radio, you can't escape me. If you take a charitable view, I simply write a lot of hits. If you take a pragmatic view, me and my music just won't give it a rest.

The *No Jacket Required* tour starts at the Theatre Royal, Nottingham, on February 11, 1985. Backed by a band I dub The Hot Tub Club, I play all over the world for five months and eighty-three shows. Multiple nights at London's Royal Albert Hall and other venues in the U.K., then the rest of Europe, Australia, Japan, then a big run in America—including three nights at Universal Amphitheatre in LA, two nights at Madison Square Garden—all the way through to the summer.

Not enough? Don't worry, coming down the pipe is another project, another single, another inescapable Phil Collins hit.

Stephen Bishop is a good friend and a great songwriter, and I recorded an acoustic version of his song "Separate Lives" for *No Jacket Required*, but it didn't really fit on the album. But the song hangs around, and eventually Atlantic's Doug Morris calls and says, "Would you be interested in recording 'Separate Lives' as a duet with Marilyn Martin?" I don't know her, but Doug is president of Atlantic Records, and I trust his judgment. The plan is that the song will be featured in another Taylor Hackford movie, *White Nights*. Here at the height of the Cold War, the world badly needs a ballet/spy mash-up.

"Separate Lives" is another American number 1, which means that in 1985 I have more American number 1 hits than anyone else, and Stephen receives an Academy Award nomination. That same so-called award season, *No Jacket Required* wins three Grammys and I win my first Brit Awards: Best British Album and Best British Male Artist. But even before those award shows take place in early 1986, by the end of '85 I'm already back in Genesis world, making the album that will become *Invisible Touch*. And off we go again.

BUT FIRST THOUGH, during my summer break in 1985, I get a call from the office. It seems that the popular American detective series

Miami Vice wants me to appear in a cameo in one of their episodes. The show used "In the Air Tonight" in their pilot episode, and it worked brilliantly—so much so that many people started referring to it as the theme song. In fact Fred Lyle, the series' music producer, has used my music quite a few times.

A handful of music people have played cameos already—Glenn Frey and Frank Zappa to name two—and I think it might be a hoot. But when they send me the script, I come out in a cold sweat. Instead of being a cameo, I'm on every page, and in almost every scene. My character is called Phil the Shill. I don't know what a shill is, but it's clear that it's been written with me in mind. I then find out that a "shill" is a spiv, someone who'll do anything for a buck. I don't know why they thought that was me.

I call them and say that I haven't acted in years; I don't know if I can handle this. Director John Nicolella brushes away my concerns. "Just come over, it'll be fine. We'll have some fun."

So I do, and we do have fun. Don Johnson is particularly nice to me, and my female counterpart is Kyra Sedgwick, wife of Kevin Bacon. Even Jill gets a role in the party scene. It's all over in ten days, and I'm back home for the summer.

Thinking back: I can't believe I managed to do all these things, that they were all successful, that I was busy across such a range of projects. If it's tallied now, in simple numerical terms, I was one of the biggest pop stars in the world. But at the time, on the inside, it didn't feel like that. *No Jacket Required* was number 1 for *how long*? Could have fooled me.

The word that is constantly used to describe me is *workaholic*. I'll deny it till I'm red in the face and have glycerine sweat running down my forehead. Simply, I'm asked to do things I can't possibly turn down.

I'm not producing Duran Duran, or duetting with Boy George, or touring with Cyndi Lauper. I'm not chasing another *Top of the Pops* slot or craving another zero on my bank balance. Robert, Eric, John, Philip, Frida—these are people I've grown up with, people I'm fans of, and/or people who look great in a fur coat. People I class as icons and true artists. Working with them is an honor. That's the reason.

Still, I understand that in some quarters I am an exemplar of the high eighties. But I'm not a yacht-going conspicuous consumer of Ferraris and penthouses. There are some dubious suits, but everyone has them in the eighties. So what if Brett Easton Ellis's Patrick Bateman views me as all that is glorious about the music of that giddy, gaudy decade? He's a psycho.

One of the best things about this time is that Jill is able to travel with me, and enjoy the fun, so our relationship becomes stronger and stronger. She never once complains about the amount of work I undertake. Joely and Simon are ensconced in Vancouver with their mum for much of this time, and I check in on them as often as I can. They always seem happy, which makes me happy. But I miss so many important times with them. Looking back, I can't quite believe it. If there's a dark side to the success, that's very much it.

WHERE WERE YOU on August 4, 1984, in the middle of the Los Angeles Summer Olympics, the games that were marred by the Eastern Bloc boycott, itself a tit-for-tat retaliation for the American-led boycott of the 1980 Moscow games?

I certainly know where I was: I was getting married to Jill Tavelman. The lovely bride wore a beautiful white wedding dress, the groom a smart black suit. My best men were Eric and Tony Smith, and the bride's maids-of-honor were her friend Megan Taylor and Pattie. The wedding was at Guildford Registry Office, and then there was a blessing at our local church. Simon and Joely were there as usher and bridesmaid.

We had the reception in our garden at Old Croft, where an all-star band played into the night. Eric, Gary Brooker, Robert Plant, Stephen Bishop, Ronnie, Daryl, Chester—so many good mates chipped in. Even the unanticipated arrival of the man from Dyno-Rod—someone's blocked the downstairs toilet—couldn't spoil the atmosphere.

We honeymooned on a yacht in the Aegean, cruising the Greek and Turkish coasts. My professional life was flying, and so was my personal life.

And where were you when Live Aid happened on July 13, 1985? Well, I know that one, too . . .

13

LIVE AID: MY PART IN
ITS DOWNFALL

Or: the show-off must go on

ROBERT PLANT AND I meet in the Mandalay Four Seasons in Dallas. I'm rehearsing for the *No Jacket Required* tour. We're happily reminiscing about recording and touring his solo albums together, and about that time in Chicago when my expensive leather jacket fell foul of the hotel dress code but his multicolored monstrosity passed muster.

Word has started to circulate about a "global jukebox" event being put together by Bob Geldof, a follow-up to Band Aid that will apparently comprise huge, star-studded concerts on the same day in the U.K. and the U.S. I've been reading about it and thinking, "This is never gonna happen. Too fantastical." It's 1985, the early days of simulcast concert technology, and to produce a live concert on both sides of the Atlantic just seems too ambitious.

I've heard nothing directly from the unstoppable Mr. Geldof—not a man to sit on his hands—so I've assumed it's pie-in-the-sky stuff, or that I wouldn't be involved. To be honest, though, I'm busy enough elsewhere. Frankly, *No Jacket Required* has been flying since its release at the start of the year.

Then suddenly Geldof's giving press conferences, declaring that so-and-so will be performing—without actually having spoken to so-and-so. Then he's jumping on the phone: "Bono's doing it, so will you do it?" Or, actually, because it's Geldof: "Bono's fucking doing it, so will you fucking do it?" Which, in the end, is pretty much how the offer to perform in some capacity at this global jukebox comes my way.

In Dallas, Robert asks me, "Are you doing this show that Geldof's putting together?"

"Yeah, I think I am. Dunno what though."

"Oh," says Robert. "Can you get me on it?"

"You don't need me to get you on it—you're Robert Plant! Just call Bill Graham," I say of the legendary American concert promoter. He's booking Geldof's U.S. show, which will take place in Philadelphia, while the equally legendary Harvey Goldsmith is booking the London show.

"Oh no, I can't call Bill. We don't get on with Bill. Bill hates us."

Then I remember the "Oakland Incident": the notorious backstage fight at a Led Zeppelin show in 1977 in which one of Graham's team was assaulted by members of the Zeppelin crew. But that was the "dark cloud" world of Led Zeppelin, not the infinitely lighter world of Robert Plant.

So I say, breezy as you like, "I'm sure it'll be OK. Bill will be fine!"

Then Robert says, "You, me and Jimmy could do something."

To me, this suggestion seems (a) casual and (b) reasonable. I'm busy all over the place; I've been performing with everybody, plugged into projects with Robert and Eric and even Adam Ant (I produced and drummed on his single "Puss 'n Boots," from his 1983 album *Strip*). So, even if I am already playing under my own steam, I can do something else too. Why not?

The syllables "Led" and "Zep" are never uttered. There is no talk at all of reviving Led Zeppelin, who haven't fired a riff in anger since the death of John Bonham five years previously. No reunion. Nothing. So, no talk of making a big deal of this, and no talk of rehearsing. There's no need. It's just me and Planty, who have a history, and Jimmy Page coming in on guitar, to have a bit of a blow. What could possibly go wrong?

And from such innocuous acorns are mighty oaks of global juke-box argy-bargy grown.

Not long after Dallas I'm on tour somewhere in America, and I get a phone call in my hotel room. It's Sting. "Are you doing this Geldof concert, Phil?"

"Yeah, I am . . ."

"Well," says Sting, "do you want to do it together?"

After connecting at the Band Aid recording, and me then asking him to sing backing vocals on *No Jacket Required*, I'd returned the favor by working on some demos for Sting's first post-Police album, *The Dream of the Blue Turtles*, which will also come out this summer of '85. Now that he's broken with his past and is in the process of launching a solo career, Sting's in no mind to immediately rejoin his old band mates, no matter how big or global this jukebox is. Equally, he doesn't want to be up there all alone. I get that.

"Sure, Sting, why not? We'll do a couple of yours, couple of mine." Again, this request seems reasonable and, just as importantly, doable.

That spring and early summer we all go off on our individual journeys. My U.S. tour finishes a week before the date of Geldof's event—now called Live Aid—and I go home to Jill. Sting and I talk on the phone and decide to rehearse at my house. Sting, wife Trudie Styler by his side, arrives ready to rock.

Jill and I have a pool. It's an outdoor English swimming pool, it's July, so possibly the sun is out. But we're not on the Riviera, and the water is barely heated. But to be hospitable, and remembering how nice Mrs. Gabriel was to me the day I auditioned for Genesis, I say, "If you want to have a swim . . ."

Without batting an eyelid—or fetching a pair of trunks—Sting does just that. Off with the trousers, a slight rearranging of the underpants, and in he slides, smooth as an otter, making barely a splash. Jill tries to avert her eyes, but not entirely successfully.

After a few easy lengths he pulls himself out, dries off, and instantly looks immaculate once more. Flash sod. I briefly consider taking up yoga but, mercifully, common sense prevails.

We sit down at the piano in the front room. I refresh his memory

about what we're going to do together—"Long Long Way to Go,"
which he sang on *No Jacket Required*—and I manage to throw together a passable solo piano version of "Against All Odds." Then we
do "Every Breath You Take." I can't remember the words, so Sting
tells me what to sing, and I write it down.

Meanwhile, over in Plant and Page world, one thing has led to
another. Harvey Goldsmith and Bill Graham have got involved.
"You, me and Jimmy maybe doing something together" has become
The Second Coming of History's Greatest Rock Band. This is a development of which I am blissfully ignorant. Robert hasn't called, so
I don't know that John Paul Jones is coming too. And all of a sudden, it's LED ZEPPELIN!

Just to add to the drama, there has also been another parallel
conversation. Someone asks, "It would be great if you could do
something else at Live Aid, Phil—any thoughts?"

"Well, really, I'd prefer to just play drums with someone" is my
honest reply. I'm used to that. I can slip on to that stool, into that
role, no problem. I don't have to worry about my voice. "Where are
Eric and Robert playing?" I ask Harvey Goldsmith.

"Eric's in America. So's Robert."

So, I'm thinking, that's that. I'm here and they're there. That's
not going to work. "Well, I'm back in England after a long tour in
America," I say, "so I don't fancy going back so soon. Plus, I'm committed to playing with Sting at Wembley."

Then the plotting begins. Goldsmith goes away, looks at the logistics and announces to Tony Smith, "It *is* possible, if Phil takes
Concorde, that he can get to Philadelphia before the show ends. He
can do his thing with Sting at Wembley, fly over to America, and finish the day onstage with Eric and with Robert."

Hearing this, I think, "Great, getting to play with all my mates—if
it's possible, I'll do it."

With Eric, I have no worries. We've done *Behind the Sun*, I've
played with him many times, and I know his drummer, Jamie Oldaker. Plain sailing.

Then, another word comes down the pipe. I finally hear that
Robert and Jimmy want to rehearse.

Rehearsing is the last thing I want to do, especially as that would need to happen in America. I've just come off that two-month tour, and I want to spend some time this summer with my kids. Anyway, I know these songs. I saw Zep's first gig. I'm a fan!

I later find out that they've also asked former Chic drummer Tony Thompson to play, but Robert still wants me on board. I wonder if it's because he doesn't want to let me down as a mate. Or has Goldsmith sold him on the gimmick of me doing both shows? I don't know; I never ask. But I do know I still don't want to rehearse, even though I can totally understand why, with so much at stake, Robert might want to have a bit of a run-through. Perhaps I might have thought differently if I hadn't underestimated the "Led Zeppelin reunion" juggernaut.

Anyway, I tell Robert, "You rehearse it, tell me the songs, and on the plane over, I'll woodshed it. I'll listen to the songs on my Walkman."

IT'S JULY 13, 1985, the day of Live Aid. I wake up at Loxwood, our new house in West Sussex.

It's a beautiful day. The whole country, indeed the whole world, is anticipating this once-in-a-lifetime event. For months the preparations have been front-page news across the globe, but the start of that day is the same for us as it is for millions of others: we have childcare issues.

Jill and I have decided to leave Joely and Simon at my mum's. Over thirty years later, Joely still won't have forgiven me. Simon is eight, but Joely is twelve-going-on-thirteen, and Live Aid and the line-up are right up her street. But I just anticipate a logistical nightmare—it's going to be a long day, involving huge amounts of traveling and obligations, plus commitments by the Concorde-load, and it won't end until I collapse in a hotel in New York at 5 a.m. U.K. time, almost twenty-four hours since setting off from Sussex. I'm not sure I can be a parent *and* the global jukebox's ocean-hopping drummer.

So, ducking Joely's stadium-sized adolescent strop, we drop off her and Simon at Mum and Barbara Speake's place in Ealing, and Jill and I head toward Wembley Stadium. Right across London everyone is out on the road, having street parties and building a fabulous carnival atmosphere.

Backstage at Wembley, there is a dressing room–compound comprising lots of caravans parked in clusters. For some reason—is it the hair?—I'm lumped with representatives of the New Romantic mob—Howard Jones, Nik Kershaw—and with Sting. Before show time, the BBC's world music champion Andy Kershaw comes back to interview us, clearly through gritted teeth. He tells the BBC Live Aid documentary years later that he would sooner have been talking to the cool guys like Paul McCartney or Queen or The Who. The ones who'd be a bit more fun, a bit more cred. Instead he has these wallies.

After a few last-minute discussions, Sting and I go onstage around 2 p.m. As we walk on there's a huge roar. Compere Noel Edmonds mentions that as soon as I finish here, I'm taking Concorde to Philadelphia to play there as well. More cheering.

I'm biting down on my nerves. There's the logistics—are we actually going to make this flight? And there's the immediate challenge of not ballsing it up in front of this global telly audience of 1 billion.

Just before we go on, casual as you like, Sting says, "By the way, sometimes I mess around with the words . . ." Next thing I know, I'm standing at the piano, singing, and he's off on a tangent on the other side of the Wembley stage, singing, "*Every breath . . . every move . . . every bond . . .*" I'm singing the correct words, but the flash sod is, metaphorically speaking, once again improvising in his underpants. Meanwhile, the viewing millions are howling, "Shut up, Collins! You're singing the fucking wrong words! You should have rehearsed!"

If only that was the last of my problems that day.

The stage is white, and it's a very sunny day, so it's blisteringly hot up there. I'm so sweaty that my finger slips off the piano key on "Against All Odds." It's a real clanger, and I can almost hear 80,000 people in Wembley wincing. It's the bum note that's heard around the world. With that, and the "Every Breath" lyrical "confusion," I'm already looking a bit of an amateur.

But I'm offstage before I know it. Then some hurry-up-and-wait—we might have to get across the Atlantic sharpish, but I still have to wait an hour or so for Noel Edmonds and his chopper to pick me up and get me to Heathrow. Even Geldof can't tell air traffic controllers to pull their fucking fingers out.

I had been reassured I wasn't the only one making the trip to Philadelphia—I definitely didn't want to give the impression that I was the solo show-off playing both concerts. I'd been told not to worry—Duran Duran would be going as well.

But for some reason Duran Duran are now only playing in America. So all of a sudden, I'm the only one, and the vibe changes. In the Live Aid rock and pop aristocracy, everyone is equal, but some are more equal than others. So, off Jill and I go in a car to Edmonds' chopper, which is lurking in a field nearby. Of course there's television coverage of every step of this journey. "And here's grinning Phil Collins, still in his stage clothes, still sweating, and already he's on his way to Philadelphia. What a guy!"

Into the chopper, up in the air, a quick hop to Heathrow, where we land right next to Concorde—all of this still on camera.

It's a scheduled Concorde flight, so there's a planeload of passengers waiting to take off, when suddenly this sweaty rabble pile on. Most are aware of what's going on because it's been in all the papers, and a few are nudging each other, whispering, "He's a lot shorter than I thought he'd be."

But not all of them, it turns out, know what's going on. Halfway along the aisle, on the way to my seat, I see Cher. She clearly hasn't the slightest idea what the fuss is about. She's in her civvies. She doesn't look like "Cher." She clocks me, trailed by this posse of journalists and photographers.

I'm a bit star-struck. Wow, *Cher*. I don't care if she isn't wearing her battle make-up. But plainly she cares. So, as I'm getting out my chunky eighties Walkman, and my cassettes of the Zeppelin albums, she's making her way to the bathroom. And before we've taken off, she's coming back again, having made herself look like "Cher," bless her heart.

During the flight she comes back to see me.

"Hi, Phil, what's happening?"

"Um, you don't know about this big Live Aid concert? Global jukebox thing, Wembley, Philadelphia, one billion viewers around the world . . . ? We're just on our way to play the American show."

"Oh," says Cher. "Can you get me on it?"

I'm thinking, "Again? What am I, a fucking talent agent?"

So, like I said to Robert, I tell her she doesn't need me. She's Cher! I'm sure it's not a problem.

Now, there are rumors about this Concorde flight. Notably that I was out of my brain on cocaine, my own version of the mile-high club. I would never have been able to do everything I had to do at Live Aid if I was off my head. But I can see where the myth might have come from. It's high-flying rock stars! It's the eighties! It's the decade for that. But I'm working all the time, and the reason I'm working all the time is not because I'm speeding out of my box.

I keep my hands very clean when it comes to my responsibilities. Especially on July 13, 1985, this day of all days. I don't even have my free glass of Concorde champagne. Maybe Cher nabbed it.

Halfway through the flight, it's been arranged that I'll do a broadcast from Concorde using the pilots' communication systems. So I head to the cockpit. These pilots are at the top of their tree, and they're saying to me, "We're not supposed to do this, so don't tell anyone . . ." I'm thinking, "We're about to do a live broadcast around the world!" Clearly the captain hadn't thought through the practical mechanics of this global jukebox either.

Back in the TV studio in London, the BBC presenters are stoking the excitement. "And now we're going over live to Phil Collins in the cockpit of Concorde! How's it going, Phil? What's it like?"

"It's all right, we're halfway there . . ."

There's puzzlement from the studio guests, Billy Connolly, Andrew Ridgeley from Wham! and Pamela Stephenson. All they can hear is this muffled squawk and static. Connolly is skeptical. "It could be fucking anybody! He could be anywhere!"

Before I know it, we're landing. Straight off Concorde at JFK Airport in New York, no Customs, straight on to another chopper, and off we go to JFK Stadium in Philadelphia. It takes almost as long to get from New York to Philly as it took to get across the Atlantic.

We drive in, and backstage I meet my old mate and right-hand man Steve "Pud" Jones. He tells me everything's OK with the drum kit. I pop round to Eric's dressing room and sense that even his band are all muttering, "Fucking show-off . . ." But I find out what we're playing, and it's a breeze. I'm buzzing on adrenaline and it's all forward momentum. It's too late to stop now.

Then I'm buttonholed by Kenny Kragen, Lionel Richie's manager. He's in charge of the finale performance of the USA for Africa song "We Are the World," which Lionel wrote.

"Phil, would you sing a line in the song?"

"Ah, well, what time is it gonna be?"

"It's just one line, no big deal."

"OK, yeah, I'll do it."

Then I start making my way to the Led Zeppelin caravan. There's no goat's head over the door, but I can see the black clouds gathering before I get there.

Here's how it is. Robert on his own: a lovely bloke. Robert and anything to do with Zeppelin: a strange chemistry happens. It's like a nasty strain of alchemy. Everything becomes very dark—sulfurous even. It's immediately obvious that Jimmy is, shall we say, edgy. Jumpy. It's only later when I watch the clip that I see him dribbling onstage—actual saliva. And he can barely stand up as he's playing, which I believe is possibly his "thing." Keith Richards does that, and it's beautiful to behold. But Jimmy just looks like a baby giraffe.

But that fun is all in front of us. Right now I'm introduced to John Paul Jones, who's quieter than a church mouse. Then I'm introduced to Tony Thompson. He's very cool with me. But not in a cool way. I believe the term is *froideur*. I mention to him the pitfalls of playing with two drummers. I've done it for years with Genesis and my own band, and know full well how badly it can go awry. The secret, I've learnt through hard experience, is to keep it simple.

But the look from Tony suggests he's not interested in "tips" from any ocean-hopping carpetbagger who's just swanned in off Concorde.

It slowly dawns on me: these guys have been working pretty hard in preparation for Live Aid, and Tony's been rehearsing with them for at least a week. It's a big deal for all parties, except this party who, perhaps naively, has not quite grasped how much is riding on this performance.

Then Jimmy looks at me. "So," he says, part drawl, part growl, "you know what we're playing?"

"Ah. Yeah. The only bit I'm still a bit green with is the flamenco guitar part before the solo on 'Stairway to Heaven.'"

"Well, what is it then?"

"I think it's this . . ."

"No, it's not!" smirks Mr. Page.

I'm thinking, "OK! Be helpful. Don't tell me what it isn't. Tell me what it is!"

I feel like I've failed a test. What I think Jimmy's actually saying is: "Do we really need this guy? Do we really need him to be playing with us?" I'm made to feel like the guy who's gate-crashed the party.

I'm looking at Robert and wondering, "Have you told him? Have you told anyone why I'm here? I'm here because you asked me to get you on this fucking gig, and then you said, 'Maybe you, me and Jimmy can do something?' That's why I'm here! I didn't come here to play with Led Zeppelin. I came here to play with a friend of mine who's morphed back into the lead singer of Led Zeppelin, a very different animal from the one who invited me."

With regards to Robert's vocals, you have to be match-fit, especially if you're doing what he's doing, all this high-range stuff. But it's clear to me that he is *not* match-fit. Then there's this other undercurrent from Page. Yes, I was Robert's drummer, and I've played with him on the road. But this isn't the same. *This is Zeppelin.* You don't fuck with Zeppelin.

Now I'm caught up in the ceaselessly toxic, dysfunctional web of Led Zeppelin interpersonal relationships, ongoing to this day. But I have no option but to shrug off the doubts and get on with it.

The set with Eric is great fun and problem-free. His drummer Jamie and I keep out of each other's way, and the result is a beautiful thing. Then, before the Led-Zep-not-Led-Zep show, I have to reprise my two-song set from Wembley. This I manage, and with only a hint of a sweaty finger/clunky note.

And then: the fateful reunion.

I know the wheels are falling off from early on in the set. I can't hear Robert clearly from where I'm sat, but I can hear enough to know that he's not on top of his game. Ditto Jimmy. I don't remember playing "Rock and Roll," but obviously I did. But I do remember an awful lot of time where I can hear what Robert decries as "knitting": fancy drumming. And if you can find the footage (the Zeppelin camp have done their best to scrub it from the history books), you can see me miming, playing the air, getting out of the way lest there be a trainwreck. If I'd known it was to be a two-drummer band, I would have removed myself from proceedings long before I got anywhere near Philadelphia.

Onstage I don't take my eyes off Tony Thompson. I'm glued to him. I'm having to follow—he's taking the heavy-handed lead and has opted to ignore all my advice. Putting myself in his shoes, he's probably thinking, "This is the beginning of a new career. John Bonham isn't around anymore. They're gonna want someone. This could be the start of a Led Zeppelin reunion. And I don't need this English fuck in my way."

I'm not judging him, God rest his soul. Thompson was a fantastic drummer. But it was very uncomfortable, and if I could have left that stage, I would have left, halfway through "Stairway . . .," if not earlier. But imagine the coverage of *that*? Walking off during The Second Coming? Who the fuck does Collins think he is? Geldof really would have had something to swear about.

After what seems like an eternity, we finish. I'm thinking, "My God, that was awful. The sooner this is over, the better."

There's one more moment of horror. Backstage, MTV VJ Alan Hunter is waiting to interview Led Zeppelin. The sweat still damp on our brows, the bad taste still ripe in my mouth, we gather outside the caravan of doom. Back in the studio, he's teed up the interview with the words: "On a day for reunions, probably the most anticipated is the Led Zeppelin reunion. Now right here, an interview with the reunited members . . .”

Hunter starts asking questions, and it's quickly obvious that nobody is taking him seriously. Robert and Jimmy are being difficult, giving vague, cocky answers to straight questions; John Paul Jones is still quieter than a church mouse.

I feel sorry for Hunter. He's live on air, a worldwide audience is waiting with bated breath, and these guys are making him look like an idiot. So I try to come to the rescue by steaming in with answers. Answers to some questions I'm not really qualified to answer.

Hunter's probably getting urgent instructions off-camera: “We don't want to talk to Collins!” But I'm thinking, “What the fuck? Why are Robert and Jimmy being like this? The guy is just asking questions. If that onstage debacle wasn't bad enough, this interview footage is going to be even worse.”

In a shutting stable door after the horse has bolted style, Led Zeppelin won't let the performance be included on the official Live Aid DVD. Because, of course, they were ashamed of it. And I find that I am usually the one blamed for it. It couldn't possibly be the holy Led Zep who were at fault. It was that geezer who came over on Concorde who wasn't rehearsed. He was the culprit. That show-off.

Backstage again, I start planning to scarper. Eric is now holed up in Bob Dylan's caravan with Ronnie Wood and Keith Richards—that other lot who didn't do very well that day. Lucky I didn't see that shambles (although it might have made me feel a bit better). I'm tired and thinking, “What the fuck was all that about?” I've played with an awful lot of musicians, and a lot of awful musicians, but I've never experienced anything like that.

Then, shattered, and utterly deflated, like the plug has been pulled, I suddenly remember: “Oh, man, I've got to sing ‘We Are the Fucking World’ with Lionel Richie and Harry Belafonte.”

I tell Kenny Kragen I can't do it. Certainly from where I'm sitting, amid the wreckage of a crashed Led Zeppelin, we are very much not the world. I need to get out of here, and get the last helicopter back to New York.

Tony Smith, Jill and I clamber wearily aboard. We land at the he-

liport on Manhattan's West Side and tip out onto this riverside wasteland. After everything that's happened today—Wembley, Heathrow,
Concorde, JFK Airport, JFK Stadium, four performances, one of
them the gig from hell, helicopter back to the city—we get out, and
it's tumbleweed: *no car*. Someone has forgotten to book a driver to
meet us. No cabs either. Not round this part of town at this time of
night. Just when I thought things couldn't get any worse . . .

Eventually we manage to flag down a cab and we make it to the
hotel. I turn on the TV. It's the death throes of the Philadelphia
show. Who do I see onstage?

Cher.

It's the mad end to the whole mad day. Not only did she get in,
she got a microphone. And she's singing "We Are the World." Maybe
she's singing my line.

The next day, we get Concorde back and collect the kids—
they've just about finished sticking pins in my effigy. Back home in
West Sussex on Sunday, July 14, 1985, it's just Jill, Joely, Simon and
I, and the beginning of the school summer holidays. "What do you
want to do? Shall we get the Lego out?"

Now the really challenging stuff begins.

14

THE GREAT BRAIN ROBBERY

*Or: trying to maintain domestic bliss while filling stadiums
(collectively), becoming a leading-man film star (briefly)
and embarrassing the heir to the throne (inadvertently)*

DADDY'S HOME! THE post–Live Aid summer of 1985, I try
as best I can to go back to being a family man. I usually have
Simon and Joely for the long school holidays, and given that they live
the rest of the year in Vancouver, and that I'm always busy somewhere, these summer months when we can reunite are sacrosanct.
Even though Joely, Simon and I speak regularly, every visit is a surprise. They both have bigger personalities, become more fashion-
conscious, more aware of their hairstyles and, of course, taller.

I have many home videos from that era, and it's fascinating to
listen to their evolving accents. Joely in particular gradually goes
from prim and English to more mid-Atlantic. They are both turning into lovely young people with fine manners, although, of course,
with these changes come problems—problems I wish I'd been there
to share. For me and my geographically distant children, there are
growing pains on both sides.

"Home" now is Lakers Lodge in Loxwood, West Sussex. We
decided to move from Old Croft while I was recording *No Jacket
Required* in London. Jill took on the major task of finding us a new
base while I was otherwise detained in the studio. It wasn't quite the

same as my mum buying a new house and moving the family into it in the course of one of my dad's nine-to-five days, but, well, it is a bit.

Lakers Lodge dates from the early eighteenth century, when it was called Beggars Bush. Grade II listed, it's a big old Georgian house, sturdily built, with twelve acres of land and a formal walled garden. We later dig a lake, enabling me to do with my children what my dad did with me—mess about in a boat. This house was the local nerve center during the Second World War—I have pictures of the Home Guard detachment doing rifle drill on the lawn.

The property comes with a small staff, a middle-aged couple called Len and Joyce Buck, who've lived in the grounds for twenty-five years. Len is a quiet and justifiably proud gardener of the old school who knows exactly when to reap and when to sow. Joyce is the housekeeper and the boss.

The previous owner had told them they would not be wanted after the sale, but I didn't want this house unless they came with it. They're as loyal as could be, and help Jill and I settle in. Over the ensuing years we become happy members of the community. We host big Christmas parties to which we invite the whole village; we become regulars at the lovely pub, the Cricketers; and I join the "celebrity" team who play cricket on the green on occasional Sundays. All the locals become good friends, and years later they come en masse to my fiftieth birthday party in Zermatt, Switzerland.

August also brings my and Jill's first wedding anniversary, so there's added reason to bunker down near heart and hearth. As I've been bouncing from project to project, country to country and collaboration to collaboration these past four years, she's generally been traveling with me. Coming on the road was pretty exciting for her, though not as overwhelming as it might have been, given that she has a slightly showbiz background: her dad was a Hollywood outfitter, making suits for the rich and famous, and her mother was an actress and dancer. When I was recording a snippet of "Over the Rainbow" as a little coda to *Face Value* and had a sudden blank on the lyrics, Jill was able to phone her mother, who knew the lyricist, Yip Harburg. He dictated them to her over the phone. Straight from the mouth of Dorothy, as it were.

The thrill goes both ways. I love having Jill with me on my travels, a wingwoman by my side. The first half of the eighties has been a very busy time, but it could have been a very lonely time, too. Jill gives me strength and support and encouragement.

This has meant that for much of the first year of our marriage we've been together. Yet it has also meant that, courtesy of all the professional distractions, we've been apart while we've been together. All things considered, then, summer '85 is a time for the four of us to be as blissfully domestic as we can.

Us having children is, by mutual agreement, not on the table right now, and won't be for a few years. Firstly, we have Joely and Simon to consider. They're still young—with her being born on August 8, in the school holidays, I generally get to celebrate Joely's birthday with her; conversely, I usually just miss Simon's birthday, which falls on September 14—and we don't want to complicate things further before they're ready to deal with yet more change.

I have huge admiration for Jill: it's been very difficult for her inheriting a family. It's difficult for the kids, too, taking Jill as a stepmother. In fact, technically Joely now has a stepmother and a stepfather, but not since day one have I ever thought of myself that way, and neither has she. I'm her dad, she's my daughter, that's it.

But this fragmented, internationally scattered family—something we'll joke about years later, when it's even more fragmented and scattered—is more than just a traditional "mum and dad got separated" set-up. It's tricky, and I try to keep things peaceful, functional and above all loving.

Anyway, the summers are time off and a break for me—but they're not particularly a break for Jill. Suddenly she becomes a mum. She's very good with it, but it's not without its trials all round as the kids try to reconnect with an unavoidably absent father and connect with a new mother figure. When they're older, Simon and Joely tell me that they found it harder than they made it look at the time, even during the brief spell when they were living back in the U.K. with Andy. In fact, Simon reveals to me that he regularly ran away from primary school in Ealing because he hated school so much. Or maybe he hated his life so much. Either way, I can't help but carry the guilt.

No one tells me this at the time. But I do, I belatedly realize, have photographic evidence. In a school photo, Simon is positioned at the end of the line; in fact he's sitting a good meter away from the rest of his schoolmates. It couldn't be more symbolic if he was clutching a vinyl copy of *Face Value* under his arm. I still wince at that photograph of my little boy.

So, working hard to make up the dad hours that I have so painfully lost through trial and circumstance, I spend a lot of time with the kids. I sometimes think this might cause a problem for Jill. We're together but apart once more. But I can't stop thinking about the inevitable: Joely and Simon leaving to go home to Vancouver. So I cherish every minute they're with me in England.

Jill and I have our time, after Joely and Simon have gone to bed. We'll watch a movie or talk, but as they grow older the bedtimes get later, and the time we have alone together shrinks—like most couples with kids.

When the school holidays are over, I reluctantly drive Joely and Simon to Heathrow and wave them off on the long-haul trip back to their mother, unaccompanied minors on a ten-hour flight to Vancouver. I wouldn't dream of doing that with Nicholas and Mathew now—I'd get on the plane with them. I don't know what I was thinking of. I apologize to Jo and Simon here and now for my selfishness. It didn't feel like that at the time, I promise, especially as I was doing battle on another front.

I've become used to bargaining with Andy, bartering about when I can have the kids. Divorce can be cruel to children, pawns in an adult game. They hear one side of a conversation, the shouting, the phone slamming down, then have to listen to Mum or Dad berate the other. It's bad enough their parents not living together anymore; they certainly don't want to hear them arguing now that they're apart. But wisdom comes with age, and I now feel I have a master's degree in divorce and people management. I will come to view my adult life as forty years of negotiation.

. . .

THE SUMMER HOLIDAYS done, I'm ready to go back to work. Not that I resent this in any way. Unlike my dad, who was frustrated and I think ultimately damaged by the job he was forced to do, what I do for a living is what keeps me living. I love my job.

With the kids safely back in Canada, Genesis come together at The Farm that October to start work on the record that will become *Invisible Touch*. Now that I'm ensconced at Lakers Lodge, Mike, Tony and I all reside near each other, and we can all drive to the studio within ten minutes.

If ever I was going to quit Genesis in favor of my solo career, in theory this would be the time, with the tailwind of *No Jacket Required* still blowing hard. But at the same time, I've missed the guys. Tony and Mike have become more lovable as time goes on, which is the reverse of the traditional rock-band narrative. Tony, formerly rather diffident and difficult to talk to, has become a great friend, funny and witty. He's a different person, especially with a glass of wine in him. Mike, too, has loosened up.

So I've missed them, and I've missed our magical way of working in the studio. We have nothing planned, so we go in and improvise. We *play*. It's not like John brings in a song and Paul brings in a song. I don't know any other band that works like we do, sitting round, improvising together, until something forms. Every other band seems to be more organized—more boring—than that.

I think, "I can't do this anywhere else." We have something special here.

Genesis is also a safe haven. I'm back in the group, surrounded by friends (it's the same road crew I have on my solo tours). We work together, we relax together, we eat together. You come into the studio in the morning and the roadies have some breakfast waiting. When you're making an album, there's a lot of time where you're not doing anything, especially once you start recording, so a couple of hours later you might wander over and see if there are any cold beans and sausages left. Then there's curry in the evening. You put on weight making an album. Love handles aside, the only problem is having to clock off each day.

We start with a blank sheet of paper, and the lovely big control room that's been built in The Farm since we last recorded here. We also have a live room for my drums, but we start to use drum machines more than on any previous album. This frees me up, both in the writing of the songs and the singing of them.

The track "Invisible Touch" is one example. Mike has this insistent guitar riff, I start singing, and instantly I have this phrase: "*She seems to have an invisible touch* . . ." This touch "*takes control and slowly tears you apart* . . ." This is someone dangerous and destabilizing. This is Andy, and it's Lavinia. Someone who will come in and fuck up your life, man, which is the line I will end up singing onstage, much to the audience's general whooped appreciation and my kids' embarrassment.

But "Invisible Touch" isn't bitter or angry—it's an acceptance. Sometimes when Simon's had relationships that haven't gone well, I'll say to him, "She seems to have an invisible touch . . ." and he'll laugh. He appears to have relationships similar to the ones I have. Even with my son Nic and girls he's meeting at school, I tell him there are certain people you shouldn't go out with. But you find yourself attracted to them.

Yet while there's a haunted, fever-dream quality to the lyric, there's a bounce to "Invisible Touch," its sound influenced by "The Glamorous Life," a big American dance hit from 1984 by Prince's sometime percussionist and co-singer Sheila E. It's one of my favorite Genesis songs, and when it's released as the first single from the album in May 1986 it becomes our first—and only—U.S. number 1 single. In fact it's the first of five American Top 5 singles from *Invisible Touch*, which to this day is Genesis' bestselling album, released one year after *No Jacket Required*, my bestselling album.

Oddly, the worlds of Genesis collide in other ways in this period. Having dominated the American sales and airplay charts that summer, we're knocked off pole position in the singles chart by Peter's "Sledgehammer," which is taken from his brilliant fifth album, *So*. He's a long way from a fox's head, but he does now have a stop-motion animated head in the classic video for the song.

Hands up: I do envy Pete. There are some songs he's written that

I wish I'd written—for one thing "Don't Give Up," his gorgeous duet with Kate Bush. But even here at the height of my success it seems that, for every achievement or great opportunity that comes my way, I'm starting to accrue bad press as a matter of course. Pete seems to get good press seemingly equally automatically. It seems a bit unfair, which I appreciate is a pathetic word to use in this context. A few years later, in 1996, when I release *Dance into the Light*, *Entertainment Weekly* will write: "Even Phil Collins must know that we all grew weary of Phil Collins."

Between the completion of the recording of *Invisible Touch* and the start of the ensuing tour, I hook up again with Eric. It seems like we've both been forgiven for *Behind the Sun*, because I'm allowed to drum on, and co-produce with Tom Dowd, his new album. It's to be called *August*, as that's when his son Conor was born. We record in Los Angeles under the watchful eye of Lenny Waronker, to make sure there's lots of guitar. *August* becomes Eric's bestselling album to date, a happy outcome we might attribute to better song choices, Waronker being right, my being a much better producer, or a magical combination of all three. We carry that momentum into a run of live shows in Europe and America on which I become part of Eric's touring line-up. It's fantastic fun playing with Eric, Greg Phillinganes and Nathan East—we're in such raptures we call it The Heaven Band—and a lovely, relaxing prelude to what is about to happen.

The *Invisible Touch* tour starts in September 1986, with three nights in Detroit at the 21,000-capacity Joe Louis Arena. It won't be over for ten months and 112 shows.

This is the tour on which we start to have underwear thrown at us onstage. Prior to this we'd get the odd shoe—were people limping home?—but now it's underwear. Why? Five American Top 5 singles have brought us a younger, more liberated audience? The passion in the lyrics of "Invisible Touch" is getting to people? Tom Jones isn't touring this year?

Round the world we go, three nights here, four nights there, five nights at Madison Square Garden. Days off on tour? Not really interested. I'll hang around the hotel, maybe go to the cinema, and not much else. It's not because I might get bothered by fans in the street;

it's because I'm just counting down the hours till that night's gig. That's what I'm here for. Alternatively, I sit in my room and listen to the tapes of the previous night's show, checking out the sound mix, alert to any sloppiness or mistakes from any of us onstage. Eventually I will realize that each show is its own time and place.

Sometimes, at the suggestion of the best throat doctors rock'n'roll money can buy, I'll take myself off to the nearest steam room. Now that I'm playing so many shows, solo and with Genesis, and increasingly in large venues, I live in fear of losing my voice, and the steam helps.

Probably, then, I'm not much fun to be around on tour, so I always encourage Jill to go out—do some shopping, see the town, get a feel for this latest pit stop on our ongoing global wanderings. This also helps me to have some time alone and recharge my batteries. I'm obliged to give so much of myself onstage, I need all the "me" time I can get.

I know how it looks. There I am, sitting alone in my room, in silence, listening to last night's show, or trying to find something to watch on American TV. I sound like Greta Garbo.

In Australia our routing overlaps with that of Elton John, and I spend an instructive evening in his dressing room in Melbourne. He's playing with the Melbourne Symphony, and it'll be broadcast all over Australia. Elton throws a moody because he thinks he's lost his voice. It looks like he's about to pull the gig, no matter how this might impact on the dozens of orchestral players and the tens of thousands of fans. He calls for his limo, is driven round the car park in a low-speed huff, but in the end comes back and takes the stage.

Post-show, back in his dressing room, I tell him I only noticed a slight vocal wobble in one place, during "Don't Let the Sun Go Down on Me." He's pleased to hear that, but I sense a tantrum remains but a tickly tonsil away.

For me, it's an illuminating interlude. Most times the audience just don't notice these subtleties—I'd barely noticed and I *knew* he was hoarse. You need to think twice before letting a sore throat mushroom into a diva-shaped cancellation. There are few excuses that will cut it with 20,000 fans, short of actually dying in the steam room pre-gig.

The *Invisible Touch* tour finally ends back home in July 1987. But only six of the 112 shows are in the U.K., so we'd better knock it out of the park. Dauntingly, those parks are the national football stadiums of Scotland and England: Hampden in Glasgow and Wembley in London.

For a football fan, these are special moments. At Hampden they let us use the trophy room as our dressing room, and I'm thinking, "This is where England and Scotland played . . . I wonder if Jimmy Greaves sat here . . ."

Wembley is tremendously atmospheric, and the four nights we play there are easily the triumph of the tour. When you're on-stage in front of 86,000 people—at the legendary home of English football—and you lead them in lovely, daft crowd antics ("woo-ooo" when the lights come down during my introduction to "Domino," for example), it's a thrilling, intoxicating sight. I feel very powerful that night. Top of the world, Ma. And my ma was there, as she was at every Genesis show in London, even when, her sight failing and her legs going, she had to be pushed there in a wheelchair.

After most shows I'm down to earth with a thump. But there is something strange at Wembley that I never feel anywhere else. This place was so important in my early years that to actually walk around the stadium, to walk the turf, is just a wondrous feeling.

So how do I alchemize my four-nights-at-Wembley golden-god status? Not with champagne, cocaine, supermodels and speedboats. During the *Invisible Touch* tour I've been visiting local model-railway shops the world over, shipping fun-sized rolling stock back to the U.K. There I intend to fill the basement of Lakers Lodge with a Lilliputian layout that will have Rod "the Mod" Stewart sobbing with HO-gauge envy.

I also take the opportunity to revisit something I swore I'd never touch again: acting. I've just done ten months on some of the world's biggest stages—*of course* I can be a leading man. And surely this time no one's going to edit me out of the action?

I WAS TWELVE years old in 1963 when the Great Train Robbery happened. I remember skimming the headlines in Mum and Dad's newspaper the day after the heist. I knew it was important. Most of Britain seemed to quite like the audacity of the fifteen-strong gang of thieves stopping the overnight Glasgow to London mail train in such a simple manner—by tampering with the signal lights—then relieving it of its cargo of banknotes, the princely sum of £2.6 million. That's about £50 million in modern terms. Very, very princely.

After their capture, the members of the gang landed outrageously long prison sentences. The swinging sixties were just starting and the country's mood was changing, so the popular feeling was that they were made an example of by the British Establishment. One of the incarcerated thieves, Ronnie Biggs, disparagingly known inside the gang as "the tea boy," escaped from London's Wandsworth prison and fled to Paris, then Australia, before settling in Rio de Janeiro, where he made quite a name for himself as the celebrity train robber. In 2001, almost forty years after the robbery, he finally returned to the U.K. and to justice.

Two of the main members of the gang managed to skip the country even before Biggs, fleeing to Mexico, where they too became folk heroes to some people back home. One of them was the gang's leader, Bruce Reynolds. The other was first mate Buster Edwards.

So it was that one day in 1987 I received an offer from a film company. They were making a movie based on the life of Buster, who, after returning from Mexico skint and homesick with his family, had spent nine years in jail before going straight and running a flower stall outside Waterloo railway station in London.

As the film-makers saw it, Buster's story was a romance. Throughout his life of petty crime and the accompanying jail time, he and his wife June were inseparable. They wanted to tell the couple's story, with the Great Train Robbery simply as background.

Would I consider taking the role?

Of course I'd consider it. I might have been well rid of acting at the twilight of my teens and the tail end of the sixties—I'd had more than a few bad experiences on-screen (and on the cutting-room floor), plus I was more interested in making it as a musician—but that's a long time ago now. A new creative challenge is appealing.

Why me? It seems that the director, David Green, was watching TV one night when my episode of *Miami Vice* came on. Within a few minutes his wife said to him, "There's your Buster."

Green already has his June: Julie Walters, the talented and much-loved British actress and comedian. She won a BAFTA and a Golden Globe, and was Oscar-nominated, for the title role in 1983's *Educating Rita*. Her involvement is a mark of approval on this project, and overcomes any lingering doubts I have.

One of my first tasks is to take a false nose for a test-drive. The real Buster had terrible cosmetic surgery when he was on the run in Europe. The idea is that I'll start the film with a fake nose, then it'll come off and my real nose will act as the post-surgery nose for the bulk of the action. Still with me? This makes sense for the filming, but does suggest that my real nose is deemed to be rather comedic. I try not to take offense. We actors have to have thick skins, darling.

Immediately after I emerge from make-up, a lunch is organized at Wembley Studios for producer Norma Heyman, David Green, Julie and me. Still wearing the prosthetic nose, this is the first time I meet Julie, and the idea is to see if we can connect. She's pleased to meet me and my fake nose, and I instantly fall for her. She's so attractively funny, all her genius *Acorn Antiques* and *Wood and Walters* sketches flooding fondly back. But a little bit of "falling" is OK, because leading men and women need to have chemistry, right? Enthralled by such an experienced actress, and a lovely one at that, I'm secretly anxious as to whether my old acting skills will be up to scratch. I don't want to let Julie down.

As if the mortification of having to meet her wearing a dodgy false nose isn't enough, Green and Heyman suggest that we dive into a rehearsal. Specifically, the rehearsal of a kissing scene. Under normal circumstances this would probably please me no end. But as there wasn't much kissing required in *Oliver!* or *Calamity the Cow*, I don't know how you stage-kiss. What are the parameters? Are there tongues? And what happens if my nose falls off?

As I'm trying to get my head, and my lips, and my nostrils, round this, the director is leaning in, barking instructions: "Harder . . . closer . . . you're married, remember . . . watch the nose!" Green and Heyman are shouting at me from about a foot away. This is all very intimidating.

Finally, we're done, and without Julie being too traumatized. Luckily, the nose is blown and we do the film without it.

This is when Danny Gillen enters my life. Belfast-born and a big man with a big heart, he's hired to pick me up every morning at 5:30 in West Sussex, drive me to the locations in various parts of London and look after me throughout the day—not least to make sure none of Buster's old "pals" decide to come say hello—then drive me back home. We become inseparable friends throughout all this, and remain watertight to this day. From *Buster* onward there will be many experiences, and not a few scrapes—involving everything from paparazzi to over-eager fans to junkie Australian burglars—that I will only manage with the tireless help of Danny.

I must confess that I find the part of Buster Edwards easy to play. I suppose he's an extension of The Artful Dodger, a cockney wideboy. But there are tempests off-screen.

Overnight between October 15 and 16, 1987, a huge storm batters England. That night at Lakers Lodge I feel the sturdy Georgian house shaking and the apocalyptic crashes of trees being blown down. I lose about twenty in all, but other people are far, far worse off—across the country an estimated 15 million trees are felled and, in modern money, £5 billion-worth of damage is done.

The next morning Danny and I can't drive to the film set in London as most of the roads in rural Sussex are blocked by fallen trees. Finally, late in the afternoon, we manage to find a way through, and the scenes that meet our eyes are horrific: trees broken like matches, even in central London, destroyed houses, flattened cars, lives uprooted everywhere. We try to do our best with the scenes that day, but everyone's head is somewhere else: most of the cast and crew have suffered damage to their houses and they're trying to reach relatives, emergency services, utilities companies and insurers.

In the end we reshoot the scene a few months later, by which time Julie is almost seven months pregnant. But we manage to act around the elephant in the room.

The producers didn't want me to meet Buster himself before filming, lest I become confused in my portrayal; the script is, after all, a bit of a fairy-tale-cum-sitcom telling of his life. I do, however, briefly encounter him before we start, at the pre-shoot soirée where the cast and crew get to know each other. That lack of familiarity does mean there are a couple of key missteps in the film. I play him as a keen smoker, as it seemed everybody smoked in the sixties; plus it gives me something to do with my hands when we're filming. But I discover that Buster was the only one *not* smoking in the sixties. Much worse, there's a scene in Mexico where I smack June/Julie. When he sees this, Buster is appalled. "I'd never do that to my June," he says to me, rightly offended.

More broadly, ultimately Buster and June consider the film to be nothing like their real life—Buster confided in me that it was not as *Lavender Hill Mob* as it was written.

Buster's partner-in-crime Bruce Reynolds attends the same cast and crew party, and later occasionally drops by as we film on location. We become quite friendly and one day, when we're shooting at a place similar to Leatherslade Farm, where the real robbers holed up after the crime, Bruce sidles over and whispers, "This is a choice place, Phil. I'll have to remember this address." It seems he's still open for business.

Meanwhile, the soundtrack to *Buster* has been encountering its own turbulence. The film-makers' first thought is to ask me to sing the theme song. They want the Phil Collins package: actor, singer, writer. I'm firm. "No, I don't want people to think of me as a singer when they see me acting." I'm taking this job seriously. It's going to be a tough enough gig without my band/pop persona elbowing its way onto the screen.

I offer some alternatives. I know some people who can provide authentic period music. I've just met one of my heroes, Lamont Dozier of Holland-Dozier-Holland Motown fame, on the *No Jacket Required* tour. He came backstage in LA and we exchanged love and phone numbers, and vows to work together. Beatles producer George Martin is a good friend of mine, too.

For some unknown reason the producers seem underwhelmed by the idea of George, but Lamont they like. So I ask the Motown legend and he agrees to write some songs. He flies to Acapulco, where we're filming scenes from Buster's exile, bringing with him a couple of musical sketches: an instrumental with a title, "Loco in Acapulco," but no lyrics, and another piece which has neither title nor lyrics. Overnight I write the lyrics to both, give the second a title, "Two Hearts," then go up to Lamont's hotel room and sing them to him.

"Well," Lamont says, smiling, "you're going to have to sing them now, they're your songs . . ."

As it's to be placed in the middle of the film, I refuse to sing "Loco in Acapulco." I eventually ask The Four Tops, and produce them with Lamont. I have the unnerving job of singing the melody to Levi Stubbs, one of the most incredible voices of the sixties. I come under heavy pressure, however, to sing "Two Hearts." Eventually I say, "OK, but it's not going to be before the end credits, is it? I want people to decide whether I can act before they hear me singing."

Then, I shoot myself in the foot. I say, "We also need a love song from that period somewhere, something Buster and June might hear on the radio—a crooner like Andy Williams singing a ballad like, say, 'A Groovy Kind of Love.' "

"Great idea, Phil!"

"Yeah, but not me," I clarify, panicked.

"OK, but can you give us a demo of it, so we know what you mean?"

I call Tony Banks and ask him for the chords of the song, record a quick half-hour demo version, then send it to the producers.

"This is fantastic, Phil!"

"But you'll get someone else to sing it, right?"

"Sure we will."

I go to see a rough cut of the film and there it is, my demo, playing over a romantic goodbye kiss between Julie and me. I protest. But because it works so well in the film, I'm stuck with it. So we re-record "A Groovy Kind of Love," with orchestral maestro Anne Dudley producing, and that version is released as a single.

To paraphrase a far greater sixties-set British film: I was only supposed to blow the bloody doors off . . . Instead I end up with another number 1 single in the U.K. and the U.S., and a lot more stick for doing another middle-of-the-road sixties cover, even if it was just a project for a movie.

But, in the scheme of things, so what? After the film comes out in November 1988, I'm pleased to see Buster Edwards become a different kind of folk hero. He and June are a lovely couple, and they become firm friends of Jill and I, visiting Lakers Lodge a couple of times a year. When Buster commits suicide in 1994, I'm devastated. The tabloids run terrible stories about him, but my feeling is he was just depressed and bored. He'd say to me, "Fuck, Phil, I'm selling flowers outside Waterloo Station. None of the excitement of the old days . . ."

Buster is a classic minor Brit-flick: a nostalgic, romantic romp in a swinging-sixties period setting that does well at the U.K. box office. Julie and I paired together was great casting, and I'm thrilled at the experience. Finally, my first lead role.

Before its release, my performance receives decent advance notices, so I'm pleased to be able to do something with this new-found (and no doubt fleeting) cinematic clout. In another part of my life, I'm still a trustee of The Prince's Trust. Having become quite close to Prince Charles and the Princess of Wales, I do the obvious and invite them to attend the opening of the film in aid of the Trust.

But then the tabloid press kick in. During the Great Train Robbery one of the gang coshed the train driver, Jack Mills. He died seven years later, but people said he was never the same after the robbery. The newspapers run stories along the lines of "Royal Film Glorifies Violence," and suddenly there's an embarrassed back-pedaling.

One night I arrive home from performing "A Groovy Kind of Love" on *Top of the Pops* and Jill says, "There was a phone call for you. You have to call Buckingham Palace." Blimey. Clearing my throat and putting on a shirt and tie, I dial the number given, ask for this or that equerry—"We've been expecting you, Mr. Collins"—and am put through to Prince Charles.

"I'm ever so sorry," says Prince Charles in that Prince Charles way. "It's stupid, a stupid fuss about nothing, but Diana and I can't come."

Postscript: *Buster* tanks at the U.S. box office. They don't know Buster Edwards from Buster Keaton, or the Great Train Robbery from Casey Jones. But the soundtrack gets some love at the Grammys—"Two Hearts" wins the award for Best Song Written Specifically for a Motion Picture or Television and is also nominated for an Oscar. And at the Golden Globes in 1989, the year of *A Fish Called Wanda*, this means John Cleese is in the audience, nominated for Best Actor in a Motion Picture Musical or Comedy.

Bounding onstage at the Globes in LA to collect the award for "Two Hearts" (Best Original Song), I say, "This is fantastic for me. This is actually from a British movie called *Buster* that sank without a trace, mainly because of the company that was distributing it. But as I always say, forgive and forget. Or at least pretend to."

Hearing this, one voice pipes up, laughing. It's Cleese, recognizing one of his Basil Fawlty lines. That makes my night: I've made John Cleese laugh.

15

BUT SERIOUSLY, FOLKS

Or: current affairs, and an actual affair

MY 1989 ALBUM ...*But Seriously* has that title for a couple of reasons. For one thing, on March 18 that year, Jill gives birth to our daughter Lily. I'm suddenly enveloped all over again in feelings of parental responsibility and doting fatherhood. I'm looking inward at my family, but I'm also looking outward at the world in which Lily will grow up.

These thoughts are mirrored in the songs I've been writing. "Another Day in Paradise," "That's Just the Way It Is" (both of which will feature the wonderful David Crosby singing with me), "Colours" and "Heat on the Street": four socially and politically engaged songs about, respectively, the homeless, apartheid, the Troubles in Northern Ireland and inner-city unrest. You can divine my state of mind by my expression on the cover art, which, as ever, features nothing more than my face. I'm wearing my heart, and my seriousness, on my album sleeve.

Still, when I look at that cover now, I think, "Why the long face, Phil? Did you perhaps have a sense of a gathering emotional storm?"

In making these rare forays into "issue"-based writing, I wanted to sound like me. I didn't want to sound like Paul McCartney sounded when we recorded his song "Angry," a little self-conscious and barely committed.

Post–Live Aid, I was invited down to Paul's East Sussex farm to play on his new album. I didn't know what he was looking for, only that Hugh Padgham, who was producing this new McCartney record, had suggested me to Paul to give the music a bit of a kick.

Pete Townshend also got the call, so he and I arrive to guest on what would become Macca's 1986 album *Press to Play*. I'm loath to use the dreaded eighties phrase "conscience rock," but the three of us are switched on, engaged, mature men of the world. We've all been around the block, and around some of the planet's biggest stadiums. Us millionaire musos, we know all about despair, poverty and injustice. We must do. We've all done Live Aid.

In the studio Macca declares, "When I was doing Live Aid, I felt *angry*. And I wanted to write a song about it. I felt I should be angry about something. So I wrote this song. It's called 'Angry.' "

At best, you might say it's a very sixties attitude. I'm thinking, "Either you're committed about something, or you're not." I like McCartney—he was a hero of mine growing up—but he's got a few quirky issues. He's very aware when you're talking to him that he's a Beatle, and that it must be hard for whoever's doing the talking.

Here at the fag-end of the eighties, this is still very much the era of rock'n'politics. Sting, Bono, Peter: they're known for flying the flag, beating the drum, fighting the good fight, for the right cause. Or causes, plural. Fair play to those guys, and huge respect to those causes.

I'm happy to stand up and be counted when asked. My enthusiasm for, and commitment to, the work of The Prince's Trust is a passion of forty-odd years' standing. But generally I do not feel confident enough, or smart enough, to lead the charge on this or that campaign. To my mind, if you're going to do that, you have to be prepared to offer ideas and solutions, and answer hard questions. To be an activist, you have to be fully engaged with the issue. That's not what I'm good at.

Case in point: during my 2004–5 *First Final Farewell* tour, I have consecutive gigs in Beirut and Tel Aviv. But due to the situation on the ground in the Middle East, we can't fly direct from Lebanon to Israel; we have to fly via Cyprus. There are important issues at play here about a conflict that is both ongoing and millennia old. But I'm just a rock person, in town to play some tunes to the faithful. What am I going to add to the debate? Yet when we arrive in Tel Aviv, I'm reluctantly led into a press conference. Standing in front of popping flash bulbs, I feel out of my depth.

"What did they say about Israel in Beirut?"

"Um," I pause, "they didn't say anything."

The questions, and my responses, are all along those lines. It's a ludicrous situation. So I scrupulously try to avoid any sense of offering my half-cocked tuppence-worth.

I'd rather do it in my smaller, more personal way, in song. And I'm the first to hold my hands up and say that my lyrical jabs at this on ...*But Seriously* are pretty basic, possibly naive. But then again, sometimes a clear-cut, straight-ahead viewing of things isn't a bad way to go. It's how a lot of people think. Occasionally, the obvious way is the right way, the last thing anybody thinks of.

I can't remember what the ...*But Seriously* reviews were like. Probably not very good, as was coming to be the pattern. But I had a good time making the album: I said what was on my mind; I wrote "Father to Son" for Simon; Eric helped out on "I Wish It Would Rain Down" (you could hear him this time, *and* he appeared in the video). Then "Another Day in Paradise" goes on to strike a global chord. It's a hit all over the place.

The origins of that song lay in Washington, DC, when Genesis played the Robert F. Kennedy Memorial Stadium during the *Invisible Touch* tour. We land from Pittsburgh in snow, and as we're coming in from the airport I ask Myron—a preacher as well as our driver, a good man who becomes a good friend—about the cardboard boxes lined along the pavements in the shadow of the Capitol Building.

"Homeless," he replies.

I'm gobsmacked. Homeless, so many of them, so close to all this wealth and power? An image is planted and fixed in my mind. I start to become aware of boxes—the homes of the homeless—wherever we play. Homeless charities all over the world ask to use "Another Day in Paradise" in their campaigns. Much later, we film the 1994–5 *Both Sides of the World* tour rehearsals—held at Chiddingfold's Working Men's Club—and sell the video on the tour itself. All the proceeds go to the local homeless shelters at each stop on the 169-date, thirteen-month tour. These organizations also collect at the shows and I match their takings. It's the beginning of an important relationship.

If I'm "political," this is how I prefer to do it—very much with a small "p." To this day all record royalties I earn in South Africa stay there. They go to the Topsy Foundation, which works with the HIV-affected poor in rural parts of the country.

Back in the pop/rock world in 1989–90, there's a feeding frenzy. "Another Day in Paradise" breaks through from "Phil Collins fans" to become one of those records that's always on the radio and that everybody seems to have.

I've been busy elsewhere, too. In 1989 I finally get the chance to try following the great Keith Moon. Pete Townshend having had no need of my services after Keith died in 1978, this year I finally do join The Who temporarily, for two special re-stagings of *Tommy*. At Los Angeles's Universal Amphitheatre and at London's Royal Albert Hall I take on the role of dodgy Uncle Ernie, first played by Moonie himself.

At these performances I really go for it. Pud and I work hard to nail the "look": dressing gown, worn half-open over boxers; blacked-out teeth; an empty bottle of cooking sherry; all topped off with a look of leery lust. Townshend sees me staggering onstage in character, rolls his eyes and smiles. Another loony. Roger Daltrey looks slightly terrified when I approach him and get on my knees.

In February 1990 I attend the Brits ceremony at London's Dominion Theatre and perform "Another Day in Paradise." I win Best British Solo Male Artist, and "Another Day in Paradise" wins Best British Single. I'm wearing a nice Versace suit (they did make them, once) and the hair is greased back (I did have some, once). In my acceptance speech I feel it's only right that I make a nod to the lyrical content of the song. I point out how we all grumble about First World problems: coffee's a bit cold; steak's a bit underdone; bus is a bit late. But that's nothing.

It's hardly a nuanced, Bono-worthy rallying cry. But to me it's pretty reasonable as a broad-stroke comment about the sentiments that inspired "Another Day in Paradise." I'm counting myself as a normal bloke, and how this is just another day for you and me, compared to the plight of those poor souls on the streets with cardboard boxes for beds.

With hindsight, I can see it differently: a rock star who has it all, tritely lecturing his fellow jewelery-rattlers on a glittering showbiz night about the travails of the homeless.

But don't take my word for it. Here's Billy Bragg: "Phil Collins might write a song about the homeless, but if he doesn't have the action to go with it he's just exploiting that for a subject."

At the 1991 Grammys, "Another Day in Paradise" takes home Record of the Year, which is nice—especially as I'd won none of the other eight Grammys for which I was nominated. It's the last award of what feels like a day-and-night-long ceremony. By the time Hugh Padgham and I troop up, the audience has thinned out fairly dramatically. Everyone has gone to the post-show party. The awards have been a Quincy Jones fest—he's released his first album in years, and it's swept the board. There's a lovely picture of Quincy and me at the party. He's won it all, and he's commiserating with me. Friends till the end.

It's the close of the eighties and the beginning of the nineties. And on both sides of the Atlantic, I bestride the changing of the decades like a Versace-clad, five-foot-eight colossus. "Another Day in Paradise" is the last number 1 of the eighties on the Billboard Hot 100, and ...But Seriously is Billboard's first number 1 album of the nineties. It's the second bestselling album in America in 1990, beaten only by Janet Jackson's Rhythm Nation 1814. In the U.K. it's number 1 for fifteen weeks in total, winding up the bestselling album of 1990.

As the new decade begins, I hit the ground running. The 121-date

Seriously, Live! tour begins in Nagoya, Japan, in February 1990 and ends that October with seven sell-out nights at New York's Madison Square Garden.

All, I think, looks good . . . especially as it now seems that I'm on Hollywood's radar. Not because they mistake me for Bob Hoskins—that comes later—but because *Buster*, despite bombing in the U.S., has brought me to the attention of casting directors and producers around town.

As is the Hollywood way of things, I do lunches, I take meetings and I audition. A theater manager in *Sister Act 2*; a buddy movie with Mickey Rourke; a part in the Mel Gibson/Jodie Foster/James Garner Wild West gambling drama *Maverick*; a Russian serial killer—I don't get any of them. But I do make one film, Roger Spottiswoode's AIDS drama *And the Band Played On*. I play a gay Greek bathhouse owner opposite Steve Martin, Lily Tomlin, Richard Gere, Ian McKellen and dozens more. It's an all-star cast, although I fear more people were in it than watched it.

I also land a couple of animation gigs. In *The Jungle Book 2*, the famous "John, Paul, George and Ringo" vultures from the original 1967 *Jungle Book* are joined by a "fifth Beatle," a wisecracking cockney corvid who is, yes, just a little Artful Dodger–esque. In *Balto*, an animation about a hero dog, I play not one but two polar bear cubs, Muk and Luk. Talk about challenging dual roles (although one of them doesn't speak). Yes, I have a great face for cartoon voice-work.

Around this time I'm "developing my own projects" too (this is also the Hollywood way). One is a live-action telling of the tale of "Goldilocks and the Three Bears." This idea began during the *No Jacket Required* tour, when more than one review remarked on my similarity to stocky, balding English actor Bob Hoskins. Then other reviews compared me to Danny DeVito.

Rather than take umbrage at these libelous comparisons with *no basis whatsoever* in physical facts, I have a sudden brainwave: the three of us could play the Three Bears in a movie.

This idea burbles along for an age until I find myself sitting next to Hoskins at the London premiere of *Scandal*, the 1989 film about the Profumo affair. I mention the idea, he loves it, and he suggests we approach Robert Zemeckis, who's just directed Hoskins in *Who Framed Roger Rabbit*.

Somehow, word goes round about this "project." Kim Basinger gets in touch—she wants to be Goldilocks. All this and we don't even have a solid script.

The next time I'm in LA, DeVito summons me to his office. He asks me to write a song for a film he's directing about a battling divorcing couple (why did he think I'd be good for that?), *The War of the Roses*. I'll go away and write "Something Happened on the Way to Heaven," but DeVito passes so I keep it for ...*But Seriously*.

Then he says, "So you think I'm a bear? It's a good idea. Zemeckis, eh? That's also a good idea. We should all get together."

I start having meetings with DeVito, Zemeckis and his writers. It takes a long time for nothing to happen. I see "my" film gradually getting more and more expensive, and cruder in its humor, and more remote. It's like trying to grab smoke. To paraphrase what would have been one of Papa Bear's best lines: "Who's been fiddling with *my* project?"

Finally, though, a film comes good. Not long after the end of *Seriously, Live!* Steven Spielberg's office contacts Tony Smith's office. The director offers me a part in *Hook*, his reboot of the Peter Pan story that's to star Dustin Hoffman as Hook, Robin Williams as the grown-up Peter Pan and Julia Roberts as Tinkerbell. Spielberg wants me to play a John Cleese-esque London policeman. Steeped as I am in the British comedy of Tony Hancock, Monty Python and *Fawlty Towers*, I grab this opportunity with both hands.

Spielberg sends me the pages of script and I enthusiastically commit them to memory. In February 1991, on the plane over to LA (the film is shooting on nine sound stages at Sony Pictures Studios), I act out the dialogue over and over again, trying it this way and that. Apologies to whoever was sitting next to the lunatic on that flight.

At this point I have forgotten the two things Michael Caine once said to me: "You're a good actor, Phil. And remember—never learn the whole script. 'Cause they're gonna rewrite it." But I'm terrified, so I do learn the whole thing. Also, I'm a musician: this is a song, so I'm going to learn how it's played.

I arrive on-set and I am handed a fifteen-page script. "Ah, no, it's OK, I've learnt it."

"Steven rewrote it last night."

"You're joking?"

"Yeah, he just had some new ideas . . ."

In the dressing room I'm panicking. I'm about to work with the great Robin Williams, one of my comedy heroes; I don't want to mess this up, not for him and certainly not for Spielberg. I frantically scan the pages and it's basically the same thing, but in a different order. Which is even worse.

After an hour shitting myself, I'm taken to the set. Spielberg doesn't recognize me, which is one good thing—I've decided to disguise myself as much as possible. I don't want people to see "Phil Collins" in this film.

Spielberg, a very nice man, tells me not to worry about the new script—however, we are going to film this scene in one long shot.

I'm now double-dreading it. But we do a rehearsal and all the right people are laughing at all the right moments. Everyone except Hoffman.

He's not even in the scene, but he's sitting there, his feet up, with his own scriptwriter/assistant at his elbow, a guy who comes in and makes the script more "Dustin." First thing Hoffman says to me: "Where d'you get those pants, man?"

"Ah," I begin, flattered, "they're Versace . . ."

"Hey, make a note of where he gets these pants . . ."

But I'm soon less flattered. Hoffman pipes up to Spielberg: "Are you sure he should be saying all that?" Spielberg ponders this, and then says, "Hmm, yeah, maybe we should do a short version too . . ." One version of my scene is longer, and very funny, and people are laughing, and I'm able to do what I've been working on endlessly in the run-up to filming. The other one's had all the meat, and the jokes, cut out of it.

Spielberg says, "OK, we've only got Phil for the afternoon, maybe we should shoot both versions."

We shoot the two versions, and I say to Spielberg, "I'd love to come and see how this looks."

"Sure, come see the rushes tomorrow."

When I turn up the next day, Hoffman is there, attached to Spiel-berg's elbow like a Versace pants-wearing limpet. We watch both versions of my scene and, gulping slightly, trying to be casual, I offer: "The longer one's the funniest . . ."

With a bit of Method tutting, Hoffman makes it clear he doesn't agree. I know there and then that my long version is history. I was ready for my close-up, but Rain Man rained on my parade.

At *Hook*'s LA premiere in November 1991, Spielberg is very nice. At the after-party he tells me he had to use the short version. So, yes, not quite another cutting-room-floor rejection for Collins, but nearly.

IN MARCH 1991, the month after I film my *Hook* cameo, Tony, Mike and I begin recording *We Can't Dance*. It takes an uncharac-teristically long time to write—four or five months—but we're in our own studio, The Farm, so we can take our time. And, frankly, after a non-stop few years, I'm in no rush.

Plus, while I have no problem being bandleader in my own group, it's a nice change of tone coming back to the boys. Always good mates, there is the usual cheery, relaxed atmosphere between the three of us, something which is creatively inspiring. Upon its release that November, *We Can't Dance* becomes the band's fifth consecu-tive British number 1 album.

The commercial success is obviously nice, but the most impor-tant song on the album to me is not one of the hit singles. I wrote the lyrics for "Since I Lost You" for Eric. It's about the death of his four-year-old son, Conor, a lovely little boy whom I'd last seen when I was visiting Hurtwood Edge with Lily.

We were in the early stages of making *We Can't Dance* when I got the call telling me that Conor had died after falling from the window of his mother's fifty-third-floor Manhattan apartment.

Eric was dry at the time and I told him one of my concerns: that the easiest thing for him to do after this terrible loss would be to start drinking again. He said that, no, "that would be the hardest thing."

In the studio the next day, Mike, Tony and I, all of us good friends of Eric's, are talking about this unimaginable tragedy. We're working on a new piece of music. I start singing a lyric: "*My heart is broken in pieces* . . ." Lily turned two earlier that same week, and I'm thinking of all the times I'm separated from her. I write from the perspective of a dad who is often a long way away from his kids, and who has to entrust their care to others. It's a gnawing feeling that's always preyed on me—I've long said to all my kids, "Remember when you're crossing the road: stop, look both ways. I know it sounds dopey. But chances are, I won't be there."

I tell Mike and Tony what the lyric is about. They confirm something I'd already thought: I need to run this by Eric. If he has any problem with the song, it won't go on the album.

At the mixing stage, I go round to Hurtwood Edge, sit with Eric on his sofa, explain what I've done and play him "Since I Lost You." We both start crying. "Thank you, man," he says, "that's lovely."

Then he says that he's written a song, and that his label want to release it as a single. He's not sure, so he wants my opinion. Eric plays me "Tears in Heaven." It's a beautiful song. In his grief, Eric has pulled together something extraordinary. Another reason to love him.

In May 1992 the *We Can't Dance* tour begins. Genesis are now firmly in the big league, notably in the U.S., where we're generally playing stadiums.

In June the tour passes through Vancouver. While we're in town I phone Andy. We're almost on speaking terms, and really I have no choice, because I want Simon and Joely to come to the show. Andy asks where we're playing next.

"Tacoma, then Los Angeles."

"Oh. You know Lavinia lives in LA, don't you? Do you ever see her?"

A quarter of a century on from those heady mid-sixties days at Barbara Speake's, Andy knows my lingering thing for Lavinia lingers on. But at this point I haven't seen her for over twenty years. She had joined British dance troupe Hot Gossip—once a sexy fixture on anarchic TV sketch program *The Kenny Everett Video Show*—

and eventually married one of American sibling group The Hudson Brothers. We'd all moved on. At least that's what I thought.

Now, all these years later, Andy is telling me that Lavinia is still living in LA with her husband. My ex-wife gives me her number. She is also giving me a hand-grenade. I will later come to wonder whether she knows this.

I get to LA and I call. A voice comes on the line. My brain freezes, my heart stops.

"Is that you, Vinny?"

"Is that you, Phil?"

"How did you know it was me?"

"*I just knew it.*"

In that short exchange, a cosmos of longing. It's *Brief Encounter* by way of Shakespeare. Two star-cross'd lovers, snagged on the horns of circumstance, torn apart moons ago on a steam-shrouded, black-and-gray railway platform. Something like that. I mentioned that I was at stage school, right?

In all the times I went to LA—playing, recording, buying a house with Jill, producing other people's records—we never reconnected. And now, years later, here we are again.

Trying not to sound like I'm bragging, I tell Lavinia that Genesis are playing Dodger Stadium the following night. Would she like to come? She'd love to.

"Can I bring my husband?"

"Ah, of course, sure . . ." Anyway, this isn't going to go anywhere. She's married and has kids, just like me. Course it isn't going anywhere.

The next day I pass my LA guest list to our press officer, Sheryl Martinelli. I mention Lavinia: "An old friend of mine, make sure you give her great seats."

I call back later. Did Lavinia pick up her tickets? Sheryl replies, "*Wow.*"

"Oh, still nice, is she?" I say, hoping to concrete my schoolboyish excitement under a slab of casual insouciance.

"Oh, yes. Beautiful girl."

During the show, I know Lavinia is out there, though I don't know where. I think I see her at one point, amid the crowd of 40,000, but I'm not sure. It's been twenty years. But just in case, I keep an eye on this particular person in the audience . . . only to establish, come show's end, that it's not her.

Still, it's a very good gig. Afterward, for the first time ever, Tony Smith says, "That was a good show. Pulled everything out of the box."

"Really?" I say, that casual insouciance vibrating hard.

Did I mention that Jill is also in Los Angeles? With Lily, who's now three? They've been traveling with me, on and off, on the tour. Just to add to the fun, my mother-in-law Jane is also there.

Backstage, after the gig, a scrum—a menagerie—of LA celebrities. Kevin Costner stands out. He's a fan, fresh off a big year winning seven Oscars for *Dances with Wolves*. I don't know who else is there, because, frankly, I'm not interested.

My eyes swiveling around the inner sanctum of the after-show, I say to Sheryl, "No sign of Lavinia?" Sheryl says she'll go and have a look. I'm standing there, absent-mindedly glad-handing the well-wishers, craning my neck. I'm talking to Stephen Bishop, I'm talking to Costner, I'm listening to neither.

Then, as if by magic, Sheryl arrives with Lavinia.

"Kevin, mate, *Dances with Wolves*, loved it, but I've got to go . . ."

Sheryl leads Lavinia into the inner sanctum. She doesn't have her husband with her. She's brought Winnie, her best friend. Lavinia says, "I gave Winnie my bag 'cause I wanted to have both hands free and ready for this . . ."

She gives me a hug and a kiss. Time stops, then rattles backward, fast, dizzyingly, to teenage dreams in Acton, west London, nineteen-sixty-something. I'm thinking, "Oh my God . . ."

I am not thinking about my nearby wife, three-year-old daughter and mother-in-law.

I know that recounting this makes me sound like a right shallow bastard. But I'm not that way. I'm very loyal. Very committed. I've fought in the prog wars, survived the giddy, groggy seventies and kept my nose clean. I'd married young, and I'd wanted to stay married, only to be betrayed. Now here I am, happily married, but betrayed again, although this time by the feelings I still have for someone pivotal in my formative years.

Seeing—hugging—kissing—Lavinia again, the cliché is true: it's electric. In a flash I've gone from *We Can't Dance* to I can't breathe. Another cliché: suddenly, in this crowded scrum of an LA aftershow, there's no one but me and my schoolgirl sweetheart.

I lead Lavinia out of the throng, over toward my caravan—Genesis have four or five of these dressing rooms on tour, but I usually have my own for my clothes and hair gel—and we talk excitedly, harking back to the old days. Stephen Bishop sidles up. He's clocked our hug. He whispers to me, "Wow, that was electric. What's going on there?"

"Oh, she's just an old girlfriend . . ."

Meanwhile, I'm looking around to see if Jill has noticed all this. Of course she has. There may be trouble ahead.

Lavinia and I talk a bit more, and I am very aware I am being watched. But she always was a physical girl, touchy and tactile, and I can't help but reciprocate. Or, as Jill might interpret it, I can't keep my hands off her. Left to my own devices, I might be glad of that personal caravan . . . But there are forty other people around, all of them, no doubt, thinking, "What's going on here?" That magnetism, the aura, is powerful enough for everyone to sense.

Eventually Lavinia goes, and it's like two hands parting at the last possible second, Romeo and Juliet style. Funnily enough, when Franco Zeffirelli was directing his 1968 adaptation of Shakespeare's great tragic romance, Lavinia was up for the female lead (she was a great friend of Olivia Hussey, who eventually landed the part). I was in the running for Romeo. Yes, really. It was a long time ago, OK?

So we get in the limo to leave—Jill, her mum, Jane, and Lily. Jill states matter-of-factly, "That was that Lavinia." She's never met her, but she's heard of her. She knows.

"You never told me she was that beautiful."

I never knew she was that beautiful! I haven't seen her for twenty years.

The next day I call Vinny, ostensibly to say goodbye. Instead I say, "How can we see each other again?" I am already desperate to reconnect. Something has been rekindled. What happens now? I'm married, she's married.

She gives me her mum and dad's number back in London. Shortly afterward Lavinia arrives in the U.K. to visit her parents. Jill and Lily are still in LA; Jill's working on the restoration of the house that we've recently bought on Sunset Boulevard, the former residence of Cole Porter. I crowbar open that window of opportunity and get together with Lavinia a few times. An affair is born.

Please don't let me be misunderstood: it's hard to explain just how much a school love affair can stay with you throughout your life. As much as I loved Jill and Lily, I adored Lavinia. She was attractive, sure, but there was something else that drew us together. So why did I sacrifice my personal life at this time? Unfinished business-of-the-heart, I suppose. To have one last try at something I felt should have gone all the way, all those years ago. I wasn't able to resist the chance.

My life suddenly revolves around trying to see Lavinia. I'll call her at three or four in the morning. I'm perennially distracted, from the tour and my family. It's awful. I'm awful.

Things move very quickly: I'm going to leave Jill, Lavinia's going to leave her Hudson brother, and we'll run off into the hills together. Unknown to Jill, I have reached the point of no return. Before this I have never been unfaithful. But I class Lavinia as a genuine exception—I have good reason to do this in my misty eyes. She's the love of a younger life, the one that got away.

I'm back with my childhood sweetheart, the way it always should have been.

Only three or four intense weeks after our first meeting, the *We Can't Dance* tour reaches Scandinavia. I phone home to LA with the "Dear Jill . . ." call.

Alas, from dizzying highs to nausea-inducing lows. The speed of this whirlwind romance—albeit one that was twenty-five years in the making—causes the wheels to clatter off. Lavinia comes back to me, having spoken to her husband, and says, "He's not gonna kill me, but he's gonna ruin my life: he'll take the kids."

As quickly as it was all on, it's all off. Of course the children have to take precedence. Jill and I stay together—kind of. I'm not sure things will ever be the same again between us. Sure, we'll give it a try, but it won't be easy. From going up the long ladder, I've gone down the long snake. And it hurts.

16

FAXGATE

Or: divorce my wife by fax? Of course I didn't

I T'S THE MORNING after the affair before.

The emotional turbulence has left me hollow. It's not the rejection that's killing me. It's the loss. Little wonder that my head isn't wholly in the game by the time the *We Can't Dance* tour finishes in Wolverhampton on November 17, 1992. The mammoth run of globetrotting shows may have finally ended, but I'm still all over the place—a feeling not helped by a surreal detour to Neverland.

That December I'm in LA to present the Billboard Awards, which is not something I've ever done before. The big winner on the night will be Michael Jackson. He's swept the board with *Dangerous*. On top of that, it's the tenth anniversary of *Thriller* and Billboard wants to honor its ever-more-astronomical sales figures.

Unfortunately Jackson is off on tour the day after the awards, so the plan is to pre-record my presenting him with the trophies at his Neverland ranch in Santa Barbara.

The opportunity to meet the man properly, and see what Neverland is *really* like (are there monkey butlers?), is hugely exciting. Even getting there is exciting, if by "exciting" you understand that I mean "alarming": the helicopter ferrying Jill, Lily and me gets lost in fog en route, we have to make an unforeseen landing several miles shy of the ranch, and are then limousined the rest of the way.

When we eventually de-limo, we're met by a pair of greeters dressed in Disney-esque uniforms. There's Muzak tinkling in the gardens, and children running around in the on-site amusement park.

We're led into the house and parked in his living room to wait for the maestro to come downstairs. There are photos on the wall of him in his *Thriller*-era pomp, and various family portraits. There's also a huge oil painting of Jackson surrounded by animals and birds, the King of Pop giving it some St. Francis of Assisi.

Eventually Michael descends and introduces himself. He's very sweet and friendly. All thoughts of the weird things I've heard disappear in an instant, and I don't bat an eyelid when he invites Lily and Jill to play upstairs in his toy room. He and I go to his studio complex, where the camera crews are setting up—in addition to the Billboard Awards team, there's his own team who film for his archives everything he does.

While we wait we make small talk, and he apologizes for his pale make-up. It's for a skin condition, he tells me. I get the impression he feels safe with me—and not just because, as the *LA Times* later notes in its report on the telecast, I'm an "English paleface."

After we finish filming the somewhat stilted awards presentation—he has to pretend he didn't know about the second award—we walk back to the house and Michael says his goodbyes.

It's only a brief encounter, but I'm left with the feeling that Michael Jackson, though clearly not the same as us mortals, is not the weirdo we've been led to expect. A brilliant musician and a nice guy who's had to live an extraordinary life from the age of five. But, even though I have no direct knowledge of the murkier side of Michael's life, I have to say that there's probably no smoke without some kind of fire.

In January 1993 I'm at home in Lakers Lodge, considering my next moves. Genesis have never been bigger, yet I've never felt smaller. The confusion is rattling around in my brain just like the trains rattling around the rapidly expanding model railway set-up that I built for Simon (and for myself) downstairs in the cellar.

I've apologized profusely to Jill, explained that Lavinia was a bolt-from-the-past aberration, and promised to be a better, truer husband.

In my studio at the top of the house, as I contemplate the beginnings of the songs that might make up my next solo album, I'm having different, darker thoughts. If it was anybody other than Lavinia, I'd be able to put it out of the way, to banish the thoughts and bury the ache. But this is Lavinia. She's something special. The painful truth? I'm deeply confused. Might the first love of my life still be the last?

I write a lot in my little room, with calming views of our newly renovated barn. Just me and my twelve-track Akai recorder. I sit on my stool, and I sing spontaneously. I sing out, and I sing loud, without using headphones, just using the speakers. The words, the music and the emotions pour out of me at once. I write "Can't Turn Back the Years" ("*the perfect love was all you wanted from me / but I cannot turn back the years . . .*") and "I've Forgotten Everything" ("*I've forgotten everything about you till someone says your name . . .*"). That's my version of Hoagy Carmichael's "I Get Along Without You Very Well," and it's a song that I create and record so fast I don't even write it down.

I write "Both Sides of the Story," and its bold appeal for understanding all the circumstances surrounding a scenario gives me the title for the album: *Both Sides*.

The emotions that are firing these new songs are similar to the ones that gave *Face Value* its power, impact and, ultimately I hope, resonance. They're me, laid open and laid bare. On my first solo album, and on this, my fifth, I put it all out there. In the long run this is why *Face Value* and *Both Sides* are my two favorite albums, and why *No Jacket Required* doesn't come close for me.

Specifically, on *Both Sides* the rage and hurt of *Face Value* is replaced by the pang of regret, heartache and nostalgia. Lyrically, to my mind, I hit some of those emotions pretty perfectly on the head. I love the simplicity and the purity of the songs.

As I'm writing I come to a decision. With songs this personal, so close to home, no one else will be playing on or recording them. This is private, and I'm going to keep it that way for as long as possible. The irony, of course, being that, if I've done my job properly and written movingly from the heart, I'm fearful that as soon as Jill hears *Both Sides*, our marriage will implode.

I suppose that, in keeping the creation and recording of these songs purely to myself, I'm trying to delay that moment for as long as I can.

I play all the instruments myself, record the vocals and work up my home demos into an almost releasable state before taking them to The Farm to add the drums. There I will continue to keep them close to my chest by producing the album on my own, and doing so with some briskness. The musicianship is, you might say, amateur- ish. Or, better, intimate. But that works for these songs; that's part of the charm.

While I have an idea that writing these songs will have ramifica- tions that are earth-shattering for my personal life, I have no clue that recording them in this manner will have an equally tumultuous impact on my professional life. That will come a little later. But for now, the album is finished.

Then, some breathing room before I go public with *Both Sides*. In early 1993 the phone rings with an enticing invitation: a young Australian director, Stephan Elliott, has seen *Miami Vice* and wants me to play the lead in a film called *Frauds*, a black comedy about a perverse insurance inspector who terrorizes the lives of a couple he suspects of fraud.

In the window between finishing recording *Both Sides* and its release, I travel to Sydney for the shoot. It's great fun and a welcome change of headspace after the *We Can't Dance* tour, and from what's been happening at home. Hugo Weaving is my co-star, and soon he'll rocket to fame in *The Matrix* series, while Elliott goes on to di- rect genius, ABBA-channeling musical *The Adventures of Priscilla, Queen of the Desert*.

In October 1993, "Both Sides of the Story" is released as the first single from *Both Sides*. It's long, almost seven minutes on the album. Even edited for radio purposes it's still five and a half minutes. The Americans want "Everyday" as the first single because "it's more like what Phil Collins does." I dig in my heels. I don't care if this album isn't as commercial as my four previous albums. It's not meant to be. It's a defiantly, proudly personal record, made entirely to my script and my specifications. It's my heart on my sleeve, as ugly and messy as that must necessarily be.

I don't view *Both Sides* as a public statement that I have closed the doors on my second marriage. That's certainly not the message intended for Jill. Rather it's an honest account of the turmoil I've been experiencing. I'm just acknowledging what happened, and doing so the only way I know how.

"Both Sides of the Story" is a hit—just. It's the only hit single from the album. *Both Sides* still reaches number 1 in the U.K. but, broadly, the innermost thoughts and feelings of this haunted, guilty man are not clicking with the record-buying public, certainly not compared with the surreally huge sales of what has gone before. I don't care. I've done what I set out to do.

In any case, I have more pressing concerns. To be painfully honest, I've realized that my marriage to Jill is over. I've undermined everything, and I can't see a way back. I'm so sad for Lily, who is trying to make sense of all this mess her dad has made. I will always be sorry for that. I know that confessing to these feelings will unmoor Jill and Lily's lives, so I make the difficult decision to take the coward's way out: I say nothing.

THE *BOTH SIDES OF THE WORLD* tour starts in spring 1994, on April Fool's Day. Given what soon unfolds, it's an auspicious date on which to kick off a 169-show tour that will run for thirteen torrid months.

The first three weeks of the tour are uneventful, other than the fact that the concept for the show is going down brilliantly with the fans. The gig is in two halves. The first half I title "Black & White," featuring as it does songs from *Both Sides* and other, similarly reflective and/or downcast numbers: "One More Night," "Another Day in Paradise," "Separate Lives." The second half, "Colours," despite beginning with "In the Air Tonight," is more upbeat and fun: "Easy Lover," "Two Hearts," "Sussudio." The home straight.

They're long and demanding sets, taxing from the opening moments. I enter the stage through a fake door, hang up my coat and sit down at what looks like a pile of rubbish but which has drums hidden inside. Drummer Ricky Lawson, in the band for the first time, enters playing a kit of pads hidden inside his waistcoat. There's a call-and-response drum piece, and seamlessly we segue into "I Don't Care Anymore." And we're off. I'm enjoying throwing myself into the performances. The distraction, certainly, and the expelling of energy and emotion, are welcome. Receiving rapturous responses night after night can't fail to cheer me up.

On April 26 I fly into Geneva. I have a show tonight in Lausanne, Switzerland's fourth biggest city, located on the shores of Lac Léman. I'm in Lyon the day after tomorrow, and three days from now the tour reaches Paris. There I'm booked for three shows at the Palais Omnisports arena, playing to 20,000 people each night.

Tony Smith, booking agent John Giddings, tour manager Andy Mackrill, Danny Gillen (still by my side seven years after joining me during the making of *Buster*) and I land at Geneva, at the Global Jet Aviation hangar, the private part of the airport.

As at every other airport at which we land, we're met by cars driven straight onto the tarmac, usually containing a local record company employee or some such.

So we deplane, and split into two groups. There waiting, as scheduled, are two Renault Espace vans with drivers . . . and this very attractive woman. Girl, really.

She's very smart, formally dressed in a gray skirt suit, and very beautiful. She introduces herself as Orianne—an unusual name, I think to myself—and says she's been hired by the local Swiss concert promoter, Michael Driberg, to translate during our stay in Lausanne. She has an Asian look (her mother is Thai, I later learn) and speaks great English with a French accent.

We climb into the back of the van and settle in for the forty-minute drive from Geneva airport to Lausanne. I'm reading the book that accompanied the documentary *Listen Up: The Lives of Quincy Jones*. I love Quincy's big-band stuff, and am mulling over the idea of having my own big band, so I'm hoovering up anything I can find on the man and his music.

Well, I say I'm reading Quincy's book. I'm *holding* Quincy's book. Really, I'm drinking in this incredible young woman in the front seat. I nudge Danny and raise my eyebrows. He gives me the look: "Yeah, I know." I ask her name again—Oriel? Orion? I'm not messing, I really can't remember her name.

She's not a translator by profession, even though everyone will come to describe her that way. Orianne is twenty-one and works in the Geneva offices of Capital Ventures, an investment company. But because Driberg knows her, and knows she speaks excellent English, he asked if she would get me from the airport, take me to the hotel, escort me to the show, then deliver me back home again, all the while meeting my linguistic needs.

And I'm not lying or exaggerating: on the way from Geneva airport to Lausanne's Beau-Rivage Hotel, I become besotted with Orianne Cevey. There is no flirting, in part because I've never been any good at flirting. She's giving me no signals. I'm not even talking to her. Stupid, really.

Obviously in real, practical terms I'm thinking, "This isn't going to go anywhere." Yet at the same time: *I would love this to.* This feeling reminds my forty-three-year-old self of being a teenager. With light-speed certainty and blood-rush irrationality, I know I want to take this further. And this is not just about sex. It isn't even the conversation, or any intimacy, because no one's speaking, and she's in the front, and I'm in the back, with big lump Danny and big hero Quincy. This stranger's presence, in this crowded car, for forty quick minutes, is enough. As I later learn in French, it's a *coup de foudre.*

We arrive at the extremely elegant Beau-Rivage. Get out, check in, and I now take the opportunity to appreciate the full splendor of this young woman. Half my age, half Asian, half a whole world away. But numbers don't mean a thing.

I have an hour or so before soundcheck, so Orianne arranges to come back with the driver and collect me for the gig. Danny and I go upstairs and, for the first and only time in our entire history of touring, we have connecting rooms. We open the doors between the suites and excitedly chat.

"Did you see her, Danny?"

"Yeah. Lovely girl, lovely girl."

"*Wow.*"

Frankly, I can't think about much else. An armchair therapist might suggest that right now I'm predisposed to a reaction like this, given the emotional turmoil I've been experiencing (and yes, of course, I brought all that on myself). But I'd tell the armchair therapist to take a running jump. This woman seems special, and so are my feelings.

I manage to unpack, get my head together, remember that I've got a gig that night. At the appointed hour, we go down to the lobby and find Orianne waiting, still looking businesslike but smiling sweetly.

Back in the car, on to the gig at the Patinoire de Malley arena, into the dressing room. Orianne hangs around because her job is to take care of me. It's soon apparent that as well as being beautiful, she's intelligent. It's only in the far reaches of my silly, hopeful imagination that anything has happened, but already I'm riddled with the old Collins chestnut: *guilt.*

Backstage it's like a pebble has been dropped into a pond. The ripples are radiating outward. Our wardrobe lady, Carol, says to me, "Who on earth is that?" She's floored by this vision of loveliness, too. Carol disappears for a few minutes and primps up her hair and make-up. There's another woman backstage and she will not be outshone.

John Giddings comes to the dressing room. "Who's that?" he says, mouth agape.

"She's the lady that's helping me out with my French. Hands off." Andy Mackrill echoes Giddings' stupefaction: "*Who's that?*" Then all the guys in the band start taking an interest. Our trombone player, a true gentleman, wants her name and number. I can hear the others mumbling, "Man, she's beautiful . . ."

After soundcheck is when I brush up on my locally sourced stage patter. French, German, Italian, Japanese—everywhere we play, I prepare a little spiel in the native language, a little respect to, a little nod to the locals. I've always done it, just as Peter did it in Genesis.

Carol says to me, "Do you want to do your French now?"

I'm trying to be casual. "Ah, yeah, could you get Orianne?"

"Yeah, she's lovely, isn't she?"

Orianne comes in, sits opposite me and asks, "What would you like to say?"

We go through some lines for the concert—"*Bon soir . . .*" And *mais oui*, perhaps that *soir* I put a bit more effort into learning some passages. Frankly, I want to drag it out. But finally I can't detain her any longer. And at the end of it I say, "Have you got a boyfriend?"

"What do you mean?"

"Have you got a boyfriend?"

"Yes."

"OK . . . But I'd love to take you out for dinner."

She's a little bit flustered, but seems to agree. Then, quickly, she's on her feet and heading for the door. "But at least I said something," I think, "made some sort of personal, non-work contact." Just before she disappears, just to be sure, I say, "I'm going to see you afterward, right?"

"Yes, I'll take you back to the hotel."

We do the show, and I'll hold my hands up: there is a little bit of pouting on my part. More so than normal. I'm trying to make it the best show possible. I may even have thrown a few more athletic shapes than is customary.

Because this is a cavernous ice-hockey venue, there are several doors leading from the arena floor to the hot dog stands, bars and merchandise stalls. During the gig I see Orianne and a friend standing by one of the doors nearest the stage. She's dancing a little bit, moving in time to the music, enjoying herself. I'm schoolboy-pleased.

Show's over and I'm backstage, getting changed. I ask Carol if she's seen the translator girl. Carol, possibly with lips a little pursed, says she has no idea where she is. Danny comes in with the bags. Am I ready to go? Not really. Where's that translator girl? Danny says he can't find her but that we have to vacate the premises. Reluctantly, I head back to the hotel. It's fair to say that my mood is somewhat crestfallen.

Up in our adjoining rooms, at my relaxed-but-also-insistent request, Danny phones the back office at the venue. "Is that translator girl around? The promoter's girl? Oh, she's there?" It seems that Orianne had been waiting for us, but had missed us in the crush of 10,000-odd fans tipping out of the venue and a ten-strong band and thirty road crew scurrying about their post-show business.

Danny hands me the phone so I can speak to Orianne directly. I ask for her number. After some hesitation she gives me her work number. "And can I have your home number?" Also: "What are you doing tomorrow? You're working? What about after that? I've got a day off!"

"Well, I'm supposed to . . . I don't know. Call me tomorrow and we'll talk about it."

I'm ecstatic. That's enough for me.

I call her the next day, and she's not there. I'll end up getting to know Les, her boss at Capital Ventures, very well. He tells me she's out on assignment. I don't have a nuanced understanding of the Swiss finance industry (or even of Swiss cheese or chocolate), but I gather her job is to go and charm money out of businessmen.

That evening I call her at home. Her dad, Jean-François, answers, a lovely Swiss man who barely speaks English. So he puts on her Thai mum, Orawan. "Who is it? Phil? *Phil Collins!*" She's flustered. "Orianne told me you may call. She's not here."

Orawan goes off to get a number for her. Only later do I find out that in her hurry to find me the number, she's left the dinner cooking on the stove. The dinner burns, and the kitchen catches fire. Dad, not unreasonably, loses his rag. One minute the phone's ringing, the next minute the fire alarm's ringing. "It's OK," toots Orawan through the din, smoke and flames, "I have Phil Collins on the phone!"

She gives me the number for Christophe, Orianne's best mate, whom she's currently out with. I call, and Christophe passes the phone to her.

"Can I meet you for dinner tonight?"

"I can't. I have to see my boyfriend."

"OK. How about afterward?"

"Maybe. I'll call you at your hotel later."

I appreciate that in the cold light of the printed page, this might all come over a little, well, *stalker-ish*. What can I say? She already had me by the heart.

Danny and I book a great table in our hotel's well-regarded restaurant, and immediately order a lovely bottle of wine. We sit and sip and wait. And we wait. The waiter hovers. "Another bottle of wine, sirs?" I'm feeling chipper, and not just because of the Chateau Orianne.

Another waiter comes up. "Monsieur Collins, there's a phone call for you."

It's Orianne. She says she can't come. Why not?

"Because my boyfriend heard about you and he hit me."

I later find out that she'd been in the process of breaking up with him. But right now's he's punched her in the face and she has a fat lip. I express my outrage and my sympathy, and I've a good mind to dispatch Danny to sort out this fucker. I tell her I don't mind how she looks—she should just come to the restaurant.

"Maybe later."

Danny and I have something to eat, then go up to our adjoining rooms. Eventually the phone rings. Orianne is in the lobby, with Christophe. He's a lovely big guy who I will grow very close to. He wants to make sure that his best friend is OK, that she's not messing around with some jerk, especially after the evening she's had. Maybe he's already heard about the Ceveys' kitchen going up in flames, too.

The four of us rendezvous for a drink in my room, and eventually Christophe looks at me and says, "Phil. You're a nice guy. I'll leave you alone. But I'll be waiting in the car."

For the next couple of days, I'm like a dog with two tails. But at the same time: I'm about to go to Paris. And in Paris I'm due to meet my wife and our five-year-old daughter, who are flying in from London.

What have I done? Well, I know what I've done. I've betrayed my wife and child. Again. And I've set sail for perilously uncharted waters. "Meet Phil Collins' new mystery girlfriend. She's young enough to be his daughter." Ticks all the midlife-crisis boxes.

My dalliance with Lavinia has already pulled the carpet from underneath my marriage, and I was really kidding myself if I thought I could make things right again with Jill after that. This doesn't make the guilt any easier to deal with, and it won't make it any easier to deal with for years and years after. My love life is a cauldron of conflictions of which I am far from proud.

In Paris, from the window of my hotel room, I watch Jill and Lily get out of the limo. I feel like a complete shit.

If my marriage to Jill wasn't over with the Lavinia episode, it is now. With my actions in Los Angeles and Lausanne, I've made sure of that.

Considering I've been on the road pretty much my whole life, up until Lavinia I'd never been unfaithful. Why now? I don't buy the "midlife crisis" thing. Maybe Jill and me being a couple had run its course?

Separations are chaotic and difficult at the best of times, but they're much more complicated here. I'm barely a month into a mammoth tour that will last for another year. It's not an option to cancel a leg, or even rearrange a run of shows, so that I can return to the U.K. and sort through the legal and logistical mess of my matrimonial breakdown. This is of no comfort to my wife—in fact it worsens things—but I have professional obligations coming out of my ears and I have to look at the bigger picture. These are huge shows, employing dozens and dozens of people, performing to hundreds of thousands of fans around the world. The juggernaut must go on.

Two weeks after Paris, in mid-May 1994, I'm on the other side of the Atlantic. I'm starting the North American leg with four nights at Mexico's Palacio de los Deportes, a fantastic, 26,000-capacity circular dome built for the 1968 Olympics. It's a phenomenal venue in which to start an intense, three-month run of shows. I've never played Mexico before, neither solo nor with Genesis, so there's huge anticipation. The concerts become something of a national event. For 100,000 Mexican fans—some of the most enthusiastic music-lovers in the world—I have to keep one set of emotions in check, while giving full vent to another. I've let down my family. I don't want to let down the fans, too.

The *Both Sides of the World* tour rolls on, as it must. My schedule is, often literally, up in the air, and we're now also contending with tricky and ever-changing time differences between the U.S. and the U.K. So there are few times when I can sit down in peace and quiet and make the difficult phone calls home. I want to speak to Jill, I want to speak to Lily. I also want to speak to Simon and Joely and explain the situation to them, but that means going through Andy, which is a whole other world of pain.

But on the rare occasions when I can call Jill, it's difficult to get through. That said, Jill still occasionally joins me on tour in the U.S.—Lily wants to see me. Bless her, she's trying to snow-plow through it all and, in her young heart, thinking that whatever's wrong will soon be all right. On more than one occasion I'll be standing center stage, singing "Separate Lives," which is obviously a hugely emotional moment in the show. And whenever Jill is in the audience, she makes a point of walking down the side aisle and standing by the stage, staring at me.

Three weeks into the North American leg, six weeks after Paris, I handwrite a four- or five-page letter in which I try to outline the way I feel about us, about the future. The most reliable and quickest way to get this letter to her is to fax rather than post it. So that's what I do. But it doesn't help. Things are still messy and complicated, communication lines still fractured.

The situation doesn't improve when the tour comes back to Europe at the start of September. In fact, by the end of that month, when we reach Frankfurt, they're worse. Jill is rattling around a big house in the English countryside, single-handedly parenting our daughter. Meanwhile, her faithless husband is out and about in the world, playing giant shows to adoring fans, living the high life— and, I suppose she presumes, taking his pretty young girlfriend along for the ride. The truth is that only occasionally does Orianne join me; most of the time she's working in Geneva. Still, that's bad enough.

Now, in Frankfurt, we're playing three nights at the 100-year-old Festhalle. I'm in one place for seventy-two hours, and there's only an hour's time difference between Germany and Britain. So I figure this is an opportune moment to catch up with Jill and sort out a few things. But I can't get through. I never seem to be able to get through. Thinking I have no other option, I fax her again at Lakers Lodge.

By this point on the European leg of the *Both Sides* tour, whenever I have the odd day off I'm jetting to Switzerland, where I stay in a little hotel down the road from Orianne's parents' house. Early one morning I'm woken up in this hotel by the phone. It's Annie Callingham, my secretary. "What's going on, Phil? You're all over the front page of *The Sun*."

"What is?"

"The fax."

"What fax?"

"The fax you sent Jill."

"How did that happen?"

All hell has broken loose. *Somehow* Britain's biggest-selling tabloid has got hold of the fax I sent from my dressing room in Frankfurt. What *The Sun* has edited and used from what I actually wrote has given them the headline "I'M FAXING FURIOUS," and the story that I was faxing for a divorce.

More all hell breaks loose. The press queue up outside Orianne's parents' house. Her father is dying of cancer, and this is the last thing they need.

Reporters doorstep my mum, my brother, my sister. Anyone who knows me is contacted for comment, and the story becomes a national talking point. Actually, scratch that—an international talking point. I become used to never entering a hotel via the front door, lest I'm ambushed by the paparazzi.

The recently installed twenty-nine-year-old editor of another tabloid, *News of the World*, gets in touch. Piers Morgan oozes oily blandishments: it's my chance to tell my side of the story, I'll have copy approval, I can be reassured that this will set the record straight, in a grown-up manner, blah blah. Of course, it still comes out *News of the World*-ish. Oily Piers pours some of that oil on the flames.

This scrutiny is hard enough for me to take, especially as the crux of the story is untrue; for Orianne, however, a twenty-one-year-old suddenly enmeshed in a world of which she has no experience or comprehension, it's hellish. She has to look behind her wherever she goes.

In timing that's so perfect it's painful, just as "Faxgate" hits I'm booked to perform an *MTV Unplugged* show at Wembley TV studios in London, to promote the U.K. leg of the tour. I'm contractually obligated; otherwise it would be the last thing I'd do right now. Walking onstage in Birmingham, a few days later, I'm still thinking this is the worst possible moment to be starting a tour at home. I've gone from being Mr. Really, Really Nice Guy (Albeit a Bit Ubiquitous and Annoying) to Mr. Bastard.

As I mentioned before, the show opens with rubbish on the floor: corrugated iron, bins, scrunched-up newspapers. Having played the drum duet with Ricky, the first number is "I Don't Care Anymore," from the *Hello, I Must Be Going!* album. That song was written about my first failed marriage, when Andy and I were going through the legals. The lyrics, accordingly, are caustic, and I perform it appropriately moodily, scuffing my way through the rubbish scattered on the stage.

But now everything takes on added resonance. The lyrics are nothing to do with Jill or our marriage. But when I kick those newspapers, I'm apparently kicking the tabloids.

After that opening song, I sit on the edge of the stage at Birmingham's NEC and say to the audience, "Listen, this is all very embarrassing, but you mustn't believe everything you read in the papers . . ." I don't know if that sets anybody at ease, maybe not even me. I was always told in the theater: "Never make apologies to the audience. Just get on with it." But I like to think there was a little bit of a sigh of relief. "Thank God we got that out of the way."

But then, introducing "I Wish It Would Rain Down," from *...But Seriously*, I do my take on a skit by politically incorrect, intense (and intensely funny) comedian Sam Kinison (a friend, who'd died two years previously). It's about a couple in a car, arguing about an old girlfriend of the husband's they've just seen. My thinking: it's me, doing a bit of acting, talking up my love of comedians, segueing into a song in a characterful manner. In my ignorance, I don't see that this is a bit too close to the bone for some. That it might look like I'm dancing on the grave of my marriage. I'm just desperate to make the audience laugh, or defuse the tension that I feel is there. To my shame, I don't understand that, in the circumstances, it's in poor taste.

The European leg, and 1994, ends with eight nights at Wembley Arena. Sounds impressive, and on lots of levels it is. But a London crowd are a crowd apart; at the best of times there will be a bit of that "so impress me" vibe. But now, every night there's a portion of the crowd for whom I'm a villain.

In spring 1995 I resume the tour, in South Africa. This final leg is called *The Far Side of the World*, and it will also take in Asia and South America. Professionally things are going great. I play football stadiums, and I play places I've never been to: Indonesia, the Philippines, Puerto Rico. Here on the far side of the world there's relief, too, from the endless barracking I've been getting in the U.K. press. Back home it feels like Faxgate is the scandal that will not die.

Orianne joins me whenever she can arrange a few days off from Capital Ventures. She flies in, seemingly impervious to jet lag, and we stay up all night, just talking and catching up. These are moments, hours, of bliss in the maelstrom of a thirteen-month world tour and the hurricane of a collapsing marriage.

There are no winners in this situation. I'm fortunate enough to be able to bury myself in my work. Unfortunately my work necessitates being out front and center, in front of thousands of people who are reading all this terrible stuff about my terrible private life.

Night after night, peering into the gloom beyond the stage lights, I don't see the tens of thousands enjoying themselves. I see the odd huddle who are having the intense conversations: "I used to like him. But now he's left his wife for this young girlfriend, and she's a bimbo, who he's trying to mold into what he wants. But he's not getting our money for nothing—we're still going to the concert! Let's see how far he's fallen! Oh, I like this song. But what a bastard. Oh, this is a good one too . . . but it's about his first marriage! Another ex-! Can't faxing Phil Collins sort himself out?"

Paranoid? At the very least my guilt is making me highly sensitive to the psychic energy, real or otherwise.

This is the damage Faxgate does. It messes up my head, and in my confused mind it blows out the foundations of my career. I certainly didn't like being Mr. Nice Guy, the Housewives' Pal. But as soon as I wasn't that guy anymore, I missed it. Now I'm pop public-enemy number one. Rod Stewart shags around, serially, and it's just Rod being Rod. Mick Jagger does it and, well, of course he does—he's Mick. Phil Collins does it and *what an arsehole.*

Now I don't know where I am. I feel like I've lost control. My standing as a human being—my dignity, or lack of it—is being buffeted by stuff that's reduced to headlines in newspapers. The cumulative effect is I just want to write myself out of the script. I want to scrub the blackboard clean and say, "I don't want any part of this. Because this is now too much. I carry too much baggage."

That wound festers, and deepens.

After ...*But Seriously* and *Both Sides*, people begin saying, "Phil, we don't want this. Lighten up, mate. You are 'You Can't Hurry Love.' You are 'Sussudio.' You are the cheeky chappy who makes us laugh onstage and romps for two hours. That's what we love. No more dark nights of the soul, please. We have other people to go to for that."

And Lavinia? I never gave her a heads-up as to what *Both Sides* was about. So I don't know what she thought of it. After that phone call, I never hear from her again. But I still love *Both Sides*. It's not clouded or tarnished by the events that inspired and surrounded it. It had its little day in the sun.

Despite the personal cataclysms, I don't think of the album as being an unhappy experience. It was very pleasurable to make. Writing and playing and recording entirely on my own was utterly liberating. Which is why I decided to liberate myself in other ways. During the promotion of *Both Sides*—before the tour, before Orianne even—I tell Tony Smith that I'm leaving Genesis.

17

TAXGATE

Or: I've fallen in love with a Swiss woman.
And I follow my heart, not the money

SHOULD I STAY or should I go? Do I leave Jill . . . do I leave Genesis . . . do I leave the U.K.?

The three years between reconnecting with Lavinia in summer 1992 during Genesis' *We Can't Dance* tour and finishing my *Both Sides of the World* tour in spring 1995 have been more than a little tempestuous. The imperial eighties have become the emotional nineties. Which decade thrilled me more, and which messed me up more? Even now it's hard to say.

Casting my mind back to the *We Can't Dance* tour, I realize now that the weight of leading the band finally got to me. From the start of that global run of Genesis' biggest-ever shows, there was a sense of nostalgia, a sense of "look how far we've come." This was most apparent in the footage we showed on the screens during "I Know What I Like": lots of archive film, stretching back through the Peter era. It was moving stuff.

But also from the off, there were problems and niggles.

After the opening night in the Texas Stadium in Irving, Texas, we move on via Houston to Florida. I develop a sore throat, so I try acupuncture backstage at Miami's Joe Robbie Stadium. The next night, in Tampa, I only manage one song, "Land of Confusion," before apologizing and exiting stage left, my singing voice in tatters. So much for acupuncture. Half the stadium is shouting "awwww," in sympathy. The other 20,000 are bellowing something along the lines of "Bastard! I've paid my money, sing the songs!" I scuttle back to the dressing room and cry. It's just too intense. I've let everybody down, from fans to crew to caterers to the entire team working in and around the stadium. It's a very heavy responsibility, a very heavy moment. It's all on me. One week in, and in my mind I've already scuppered Genesis' biggest-ever tour.

But as I routinely feel compelled to do, I battle on and the tour steams forward. As we tick off the world's enormodomes and super-stadiums, a thought sets in: do I really want this, this pressure, this obligation? Can I keep this up—the singing, the banter, the larger-than-life performances required—right through a grueling summer schedule, all the way to an eye-wateringly gargantuan, outdoor homecoming show at Knebworth?

The truth is, I hate stadium shows. You're not in control. These venues are built for sports, not for rock tours. You're at the mercy of the elements; a bit of rain can ruin everyone's evening, and if the wind picks up, God help the sound. There's so much activity every-where in the place, all of which catches your eye from the stage. The queues for the hot dogs, the overpowering smell of frying onions, the endless lines for the toilets, the ranks of cops and security. If there are 40,000 people in the place, 10,000 of them are moving at any one time when we're playing.

I remember going to see Bad Company in Texas in the seventies, walking around the arena floor and being amazed by all the stuff going on: people scoring, people fighting, people puking up. Some were even watching the band. By the time Genesis are touring stadi-ums in the eighties, fans are following the performance on huge telly screens at the side of the stage because really, for most of the punt-ers, it's either watch some matchstick men in the distance or watch them on the big screens—only the image on the screen doesn't quite sync with the sound blasting from the house-size speakers. In these conditions, it's no surprise no one's wholly invested in the actual music. "I'm off for a bucket of fizzy beer and a tray of nuclear-orange nachos."

A whole tour of this size demonstrates the staggering popularity of Genesis in the early nineties. But actually having to do it is a giant pain in the arse.

And then, what next? What happens on the tour after the stadium and arena tour? When you've done four nights at Wembley and six nights at Earls Court, what's the next goal, the next height? Anything less, we've peaked. Anything more, we're knackered.

Plus, for most of the tour, I'm having to wow those stadiums while putting on a Jumbotron-friendly brave face. If there's such a thing as vertigo of the heart, I have it bad.

That is the mindset I take into the writing and recording of *Both Sides*.

All this time Tony Smith has been walking on glass. He's one of the few people who knows what happened with Lavinia. He is also aware that, as a result, Jill and I are on very dodgy ground. He knows the emotional state I'm in has resulted in this rather downbeat solo album, and that chipper eighties pop star Phil Collins is dying on the inside.

Ever the attuned manager and confidant, Tony is right to worry, but not about my personal life.

In late 1993, Tony and I are on a private jet, flying to fulfill some album promotion obligations. We are the only two on board, sitting together at a table at the rear of the plane. Though I've already made up my mind on my future, I haven't told anyone. I'm promoting *Both Sides* with media interviews, and I'm enjoying it. This, to my mind, is my finest hour, a very personal album full of songs with lots to talk about.

Above all, I'm relieved I've made the decision.

"Tony, I'm leaving Genesis."

He isn't surprised; he's been anticipating this moment for a few years now, so his response is measured.

"OK. We don't have to say anything yet. Let's see how you feel after the *Both Sides* tour. Then we'll take a view."

I suspect his interior monologue went like this: "I know Phil. He'll come round. He'll get the album out, get out on the road, get all that off his chest. Then, having realized the error of his ways, he'll get back in the saddle, just like he always does."

But I know how I feel, and I know how I'll feel after the tour. I've made the leap, and revealed my true feelings. I won't be changing my mind. But I agree to keep it quiet, until such time as we *have* to tell the world.

Jetting about to promote *Both Sides* in late 1993, my life is all over the place. I've made what I consider to be my best album, but at what price? The inspiration came from the perspiration of trying to work out where my head and heart lay. These are songs of separation, of a love lost. Moreover, the freedom I had making them is also giving me feelings of anticipation. What if I do more records like *Both Sides*, personal and self-sufficient? Why do I need to make more band albums?

In sum, for reasons positive and negative, after devoting half of my life to the band, it's time to leave Genesis. I just can't tell anyone about it.

So I keep schtum for over two years, during which time I come back down to earth with a bump. *Terra infirma*. In Switzerland. Now it's time to address the women in my life.

I'VE ALWAYS HATED the "divorced wife/divorced band" view of me at this time, as if the two could be yoked together. It's a pithy headline, but far from the truth. At the time I convinced myself that I was in control of both sides of my life, but that each was a separate issue. "At the time" being the operative phrase.

Those around me, I sense, think I'm mad. Tony Smith especially can see that quitting Genesis and quitting my second marriage will cost me dearly, two times over and in every sense. I don't care. I need out.

I don't blame Genesis for the serial traumas in my personal life. I may have felt a perennial obligation to agree to tours and schedules and projects, to keep everybody happy and everybody employed. But fundamentally, the buck stops with me. I could have said no to that follow-up album, to that final leg round America, to that latest invitation to produce. And I could have said no to Orianne—or, rather, not pursued her with quite so much vigor.

During the *Both Sides* tour I decide that, once I'm finished, I will go and live with her in Switzerland. To a man who's been pilloried in the U.K. press, bolt-holes don't come much safer or welcoming than the small, mountain-and-lake-ringed, democracy-loving country where discretion is one of the core natural assets. In search of a clean break from all my adult relationships, domestic and professional, there aren't many places cleaner than Switzerland.

That's how observers might think I think.

The next thing people automatically assume is that it's a money move. Cue another round of headlines: "Millionaire rock star Phil Collins skips the country to avoid paying his taxes, thereby denying the U.K. government money to keep the lights on and the hospitals open." I still get it now—"Tax Exile Phil Collins (Who Divorced His Wife by Fax) (What a Bastard)."

But in all honesty, none of the above has occurred to me. I haven't mused, "Where am I going to get noticed less? Where can I hide easier?"

It's simply that Orianne lives in Switzerland. So I go where she lives. The "only" thing I'm guilty of is being a forty-four-year-old married man who's fallen in love.

I try to say as much in a couple of interviews. I tell a U.K. newspaper that if Orianne lived in Grimsby or Hull, I'd have gone there. The paper promptly seeks out inhabitants of Grimsby and Hull for their views on my quotes—their implication being that The Faxing Tax Exile is now laying into honest-to-goodness English burghers. Hey presto, another round of hostile press, followed by a barrage of abusive letters from Grimsby and Hull: "What's the matter with our towns?"

Still, the coincidental advantage of moving to Switzerland is that, generally, people do keep themselves to themselves, and leave you alone. If they don't, you can quite legally shoot someone if they come into your garden. Right now, something about that rather appeals.

I'm immediately very, very happy in Switzerland. While, obviously, I have a huge self-made mess to clean up, here on the ground life simplifies in a flash.

Waiting for Orianne to finish work each day in Geneva, I frequent a nearby bar. The barman says to me, "What do you want to live here for? We're all trying to get out." The reasons they want out are the reasons I want in. The natural beauty, the slow pace, the deafening peace—all bliss to me. After twenty-five years being public property, now I get to be private property. It's taken some drastic measures, but I've written myself out of the script.

Our first home is on the southern side of Lake Geneva, in a rented townhouse in a medieval village, Hermance, right on the French border. There are four floors, one room on each floor, and no straight walls. It's lovely, a little skew-whiff paradise.

In Switzerland, life is more family-oriented, in a warmingly old-fashioned way. Orianne's dad had been suffering from cancer when I met her, and tragically he died the night I played in Stuttgart on the *Both Sides* tour. I'd flown to Orianne immediately after the show.

Now her family are closer than ever. We go to her mum's every weekend for a family lunch. Aperitif, glass of white wine, nice meal, nice conversation. Obviously I don't talk as much (my French is *un peu* basic, but I am learning) but the feeling is wonderful. I'm transported to my childhood, to the suburban west London of the late fifties and early sixties—to those happy Sunday lunches with Reg and Len, Mum killing the vegetables and Dad fighting with the dishes. It's a little step back in time, and I love it.

With Mum and Dad separating, then Dad dying in 1972, then me spending the next twenty-odd years on the road, this sense of being part of a bigger family is something I've missed for almost a quarter of a century, almost my entire adult life. Andy's family were in Vancouver, Jill's in LA. Here in Switzerland, everyone's together. This is something comfortable, familiar, that's nothing to do with who I am or what I do.

The rest of my family? Complicated, to say the least.

It's terribly hard for Jill to deal with this mess. One of the first things she says when I tell her I'm moving to Switzerland: "You don't speak French!" She's right, but it doesn't matter to me. I can learn, and I do.

I try to see Lily, who's now six, as often as I can. I fly back to the U.K. and stay in bloody awful Holiday Inns or airport hotels. I pick her up from school and we sit in the car and talk, or listen on repeat to the soundtrack to the latest Disney film, *Aladdin*, waiting for the Italian restaurant in Cranleigh, Surrey, to open. A difficult, sad thing for all concerned.

The first time Orianne meets Lily is in Ascot—I can't stay in London because the press are still stalking me, so I book a little country hotel, not far from Tittenhurst Park, the former Lennon house I'd rented with Brand X.

I introduce Lily to the difficult subject of the new lady in Daddy's life by telling her: "I've met a lady who looks just like Princess Jasmine from *Aladdin*." She's wide-eyed at this. "Wow!" That helps Lily and Orianne have an instant connection.

Orianne doesn't meet Simon or Joely for a while. Baby steps. Inheriting a family can be traumatic for all concerned. But Orianne, a bright, intelligent woman, takes it all in her stride.

Mindful of the fact that I need to solidify things—I want my kids to be able to come visit as soon as possible—we begin looking for a proper, family-friendly place to live. But the Swiss are careful about this sort of thing. A foreigner can't simply arrive in their country and buy an enormous family house—you must have what's known as a C permit. To acquire a C permit you have to demonstrate a commitment to staying in Switzerland by having a B permit for five years, thereby showing that you are not just swooping in and buying a property as some sort of tax-friendly holiday hideaway.

It takes awhile, but eventually we find just the home. It's surrounded by vineyards, in the small village of Begnins, halfway between Geneva and Lausanne. Clayton House is a 7,000-square-foot mansion with seven bedrooms, six bathrooms, a tennis court, swimming pool, pool house and great views of Lake Geneva and the Alps. Unfortunately someone already owns it: motor-racing legend Sir Jackie Stewart.

Luckily, Sir Jackie is a mate, and he and his wife Helen are keen to move back to the U.K. For a while, we rent the house from Jackie, but after I've convinced the Swiss authorities of my bona fides and my commitment to their lovely country, I buy Clayton House.

I feel settled, stable and solid. First time in . . . *ever.*

I don't know if word of my new-found liberation has leaked, but I later learn that, in January 1996, my name is circulating in an odd new context. A TV movie of *Doctor Who* is in the works and, alongside Scott Glenn and Randy Quaid, I'm under consideration to portray the Time Lord's arch-rival, the Master. In the end, scheduling prevents me from being formally approached about playing the intergalactic baddie, which is probably a good thing. I can't very well swap touring with a band for traveling through space and time.

By now it's clear that we can't sit on the Genesis news any longer. I want to "out" myself as being a now former frontman, and Mike and Tony need to be able to move on with whatever they're planning next.

I fly to London, for a meeting at Tony Smith's house. I imagine that Tony and Mike have long ago been briefed by our manager about my intentions. But still, I'm nervous. These are my oldest musical friends. Two of my oldest friends, full stop. And I'm about to formally say goodbye to them.

We sit around Smith's kitchen table with cups of tea. There's a little bit of small talk, but we all know what we're here to discuss.

"I'm leaving."

Tony Banks replies, with true British understatement, "Well, it's a sad day."

Mike adds, "We understand. We're just surprised you stayed this long."

In my mind, it's an undeniable law of rock'n'roll physics: Genesis can't get any smaller. And then there were two? That won't really work. And while Peter leaving was a huge deal, Genesis now isn't like Genesis then. The well-regarded progressive rock group of the mid-seventies is now the stadium-filling phenomenon of the mid-nineties. I hadn't ever wanted to cause this outcome, but this is surely the end.

But no. Tony and Mike want to go on—they'll find another singer. Genesis are not over, not now, not yet.

Secretly, I'm thrilled that they're hatching plans to continue. I don't want the band to end, and I certainly don't want to be the cause of that end. I just want out.

We give each other a hug, wish each other well and say goodbye. We know that we'll see each other again, but not in the same light.

On March 28, 1996, the official announcement is made via a press release issued by our management: "Genesis end twenty-year experiment, decide to replace Peter Gabriel as vocalist . . . For the past twenty years, drummer Phil Collins has been temping as singer, to great acclaim . . ."

Funny, pithy, affectionate. It's the perfect goodbye. Cheers. And now that the news is finally out there, I enjoy a feeling I haven't felt in years.

Freedom.

18

BIG BAND, BIG APES, BIG LOVE

Or: I'm the king of the swingers . . .

HAVING UNSHACKLED MYSELF from a big band and all the heaviness that went with it, I decide to do the obvious: form a Big Band.

Genesis played the Montreux Jazz Festival in 1987, during the *Invisible Touch* tour, and I also played there the year before, with Clapton, as part of the four-piece line-up he put together to tour his *August* album that I'd produced. So I already know the lovely Claude Nobs, founder of this fantastic annual event. He's also Warners' man in Switzerland, which makes him my label guy in my freshly adopted homeland.

On top of all this, as a new resident, it seems only right that I should perform at Switzerland's—the world's—premier jazz festival. In fact, knowing the punctilious, jazz-loving Swiss, a gig at Montreux might have been part of the contractual small print that finally allowed me the right to buy the home at Begnins. No matter; when jazz calls, you don't say no.

Jazz, and particularly big-band jazz, has always spoken to me. In my youth, alongside The Beatles stood Buddy Rich and Count Basie, specifically Basie because I loved his drummer Sonny Payne—he was a huge influence. I listened to *Sinatra at the Sands*, with Quincy

Jones conducting, as much as I listened to *With The Beatles*. Growing older, my ears roamed far and wide, and I fell hard for John Coltrane, Weather Report and Miles Davis.

In that light, Genesis, diverse as we were in our writing, never satisfied the entire musical "me." Even though we were working a great deal in the seventies and early eighties, musically there was something missing. This explains the long stint I had in that period with Brand X.

Now, a decade and a half after Brand X stopped marking the spot where I could get my jazz kicks, here in Switzerland in the mid-nineties an old muscle is twitching. Happily, the Montreux Jazz Festival makes me an offer I can't refuse. Monsieur Nobs invites me to pick a day and do anything that I want.

"Well, Claude, I've always wanted to play in a big band."

He's instantly enthused, and just as instantly decides to involve Ahmet Ertegun in the planning. I'm only too happy to reconnect creatively with the man who was so pivotally enthusiastic at the start of my solo career. Ahmet's passion wasn't just professional or musical. If he loved you, he loved the whole you. You felt you were his long-lost, never-had son. This was a lovely feeling he engendered in a whole host of artists—something of which I became fully aware when I joined Eric, Wynton Marsalis, Dr. John, Solomon Burke, Ben E. King and a host of others to perform at a New York memorial concert after Ahmet's death in 2006. All I know is that he said it to me once: "Phil, you're the son I never had."

Ahmet flies in, and he, Claude, Tony Smith and I meet at the Beau-Rivage Hotel in Geneva. We discuss the nuts and bolts of what I'm already calling The Phil Collins Big Band: who are the wish-list participants, what will be the repertoire, where and how we'll perform, whether we'll do an album.

I say that I'd like to get Quincy Jones involved as conductor. I loved the records he made with his own big band in the sixties, and while on tour in Barcelona I'd sent him what he always refers to as a "love fax" after I'd checked out his *Listen Up* album. When I contact him and explain my plans, he understands that I'm serious and immediately offers his services. Handily, Quincy comes with some great players: in Europe he works regularly with a big band attached to a German radio station, WDR in Cologne, so we decide to use them as the core musicians.

But who's going to sing? While it will carry my name, this is definitely a big band, no one-man show. Partly through a deep-seated musical hankering, partly because of my recent personal bruising, I want to return to the back, to the safety of the drummer's stool. Equally, I also want it to be as authentic as possible, as true a tribute to the jazz heritage as we can muster. I don't want to be up front.

On the *Both Sides* tour, Tony Bennett and I started to come into each other's orbit. This was the beginning of the legendary crooner's new career as a hip, MTV-generation artist, a transformation savvily steered by his son Danny after he took over management of his father's career. At one point I saw him on TV, saying, "There are some great songwriters today, Phil Collins being one of them."

I remember thinking, "Blimey, Tony Bennett's heard of me."

As this idea gains momentum, I imagine a dream billing on the front of a concert hall: "The Phil Collins Big Band, conducted by Quincy Jones, with guest vocalist Tony Bennett."

One of the times our paths crossed was in Australia, when we were staying at the same hotel, and I left Mr. Bennett a note. I said I was thinking about forming my own big band, and should that ever come to pass, I'd be honored if he would consider singing with us. Word came back that Tony would be very interested in such a project.

Now that the idea has some flesh on its bones, we contact Bennett Sr. and Jr. And again, word comes back that Tony is keen. So, much to my amazement and honor, it seems that we have our headline artists, although Tony's son won't 100 percent confirm his dad's participation until the eleventh hour.

Now, what are we going to perform? Harry Kim, my trumpet player, has the foresight to hit the nail on the head: if we attempt the songs that Count Basie et al. had done, there is, frankly, a significant chance we'll fall well short. Those were some of the best players and vocalists in history. I know every note on Buddy Rich's *Swingin' New Big Band* album, having listened to it constantly since first hearing it in 1966. It was my gateway drug to a wonderful new world, and it set me on a path of discovery that would lead to Count Basie, Sonny Payne, Harold Jones, Jo Jones, Duke Ellington and so many more. I'm not about to trample on that sacred ground.

So, Harry suggests, let's do something that no one else can do: rearrange instrumental versions of my stuff, both solo material and Genesis songs.

Harry meets me in Hermance. He has lots of serious musical contacts who can help with the arrangements, and he and I discuss the choice of material. We decide that he will farm out the chosen songs to his contacts and see what comes back.

I round out the skilled line-up that will enable The Phil Collins Big Band to play Phil Collins material in a big-band style: joining Quincy and Tony as a special guest is David Sanborn on lead saxophone. The others in the band are Harry on trumpet, Dan Fornero (also trumpet), Luis Conte (percussion), Daryl Stuermer (guitar), Nathan East (bass), Brad Cole (piano), Arturo Velasco (trombone), Andrew Woolfolk (saxophone), and the rest will be made up by the WDR Big Band. That's around twenty players altogether.

With that number of musicians sharing a stage, I should have anticipated there might be some inter-personnel issues. I probably wouldn't have anticipated they'd come from the top of the tree.

We book eight shows, the first of them at London's Royal Albert Hall on July 11, 1996, as part of a concert being held to honor South African President Nelson Mandela's first official visit to the U.K. He had declared that he didn't want a state dinner—he wanted a party.

President Mandela will be in attendance, as will the Queen, Prince Philip, Prince Charles and the President's daughter Zenani Mandela-Dlamini. The evening will also raise funds for the Nations Trust, a charity set up to raise money to help disadvantaged South African youth. I might have picked a more low-key, less pressurized moment to unveil my new direction.

In early July the band gather in Montreux for rehearsals. We rehearse till we drop. We take this very seriously. It's a very serious business, this musical freedom. Tony Bennett joins us on the last day to run through his songs.

The plan is he'll come onstage in the middle of the show and sing a handful of his standards. I have no intention of asking Mr. Bennett to have a crack at "In the Air Tonight" or "Sussudio," no matter how jazzily artful the new arrangements.

During rehearsals, Tony is singing like a bird and dressed as sharp as a tack. To play drums behind him, singing his songs, is a dream come true for me. Quincy is as I'd expected he would be: unflappable and totally into the idea. He's a talismanic figure.

Claude is there, too, so it feels like a star chamber of jazz greats. Between run-throughs there are conversations around the grand piano, a swapping of personal anecdotes featuring walk-ons from some of my all-time musical heroes. "I remember the time Sinatra . . . Basie said to me . . ." I'm thrilled beyond belief. I feel like I've really grown up, a musician accepted at the top table, and also that I'm as far away from faxes, taxes and tabloid headlines as it's possible to get right now. It's a blessed relief.

After a few songs with Tony on solo vocals—including "Over the Rainbow," "Old Devil Moon" and "The Lady's in Love with You"—he suggests we do a song together.

"No, no, sorry, Tony, I'm not singing on this tour."

Tony persists, suggesting we do Duke Ellington's "Don't Get Around Much Anymore" as a duet.

"Ah, all right," I say reluctantly. "How does it go?" I'm not sure it really works, but maybe it gives Tony an idea of how it might work—fifteen years later he records it as a duet with Canadian crooner Michael Bublé, then again the following year with Panamanian actor/ singer Miguel Bosé.

We fly to London and the soundcheck for the Mandela gig at the Royal Albert Hall. I'm confident we're on top of our game and, despite the pressure, the show is great. Legendary South African trumpeter Hugh Masekela joins us for a version of "Two Hearts," and Quincy has a ball at what is, in fact, his first-ever appearance on a British stage.

Afterward there's a meet and greet with President Mandela and the royal family. It's been a groundbreaking evening, a great gig, an auspicious debut and a privileged encounter with a true political giant.

Our second and third shows are at the suitably swish Sporting Club in Monte Carlo. Unfortunately the front of the venue only announces the appearance of "The Phil Collins Big Band." No Quincy, no Tony. I panic. Neither will be impressed at their sudden lack of a billing. Some quick thinking is in order, and so is a rummage in the tool cupboard. Before the jazzers and nabobs of Monte Carlo begin to arrive for that evening's show, the correct billing has been mounted above the entrance: "The Phil Collins Big Band, with Quincy Jones and Tony Bennett." Their name isn't quite up there in lights, it's in black gaffer tape, but you'd never know it from the pavement.

Then another problem: post-show, one of Tony's team sidles up with a concerned look on his face. It seems that onstage I haven't been giving Mr. Bennett enough of an introduction. I need to ramp it up a bit, make more of a song and dance. OK, got it.

Then another problem. After the second show in Monte Carlo, Ralph Sharon, Tony's piano player for forty years, visits me in the dressing room.

"Phil, I got good news and bad news. It sounds fantastic . . . but it's a bit loud for Tony."

In rehearsals we were even louder, and Tony was happily singing his socks off. The first two shows were also conducted at a decent volume and, again, Tony seemed perfectly at ease. So I can't understand why and how this problem has arisen.

Then I'm tipped the wink: someone's told Tony that I'm a huge fan of Buddy Rich. In the great Frank vs. Tony rivalry, Buddy was always firmly in the Sinatra camp, as you'd expect from Ol' Blue Eyes' regular drummer. But apparently one time Buddy played with Tony, and at the end of Tony's four or five songs Buddy, being the (shall we say) *provocateur* that he was, shouted to Tony as he went offstage: "Nice try, Tony!"

So from then on, Tony hated Buddy, and here I am, seemingly trying to *be* Buddy. Which means that, by extension, Tony's now a bit unsure about my bona fides. I'd suggest it's a bit of a stretch to tar me with Buddy's brush, but I'm coming to understand that this new musical world I've entered has its own special rules. Among the big beasts of the genre, old memories and enmities die hard. All is fair in love and jazz. Rock'n'roll politics have nothing on this.

So we turn it down, night after night, on each of his remaining six shows. "Yeah, Phil, it's still a bit loud . . . ," says Ralph. We get so quiet we're barely playing. You could hear a tiepin drop.

In Perugia, Italy, there's just time for one more kerfuffle. Because Danny Bennett didn't confirm Tony's involvement until very late in the day, the Italian promoters had to go ahead and commission the concert posters without knowing fully who would be appearing. So, hedging their bets, they've printed them up using just my name.

Tony arrives at the venue, sees the poster bearing only the legend "The Phil Collins Big Band" and states to me in no uncertain terms, "I could walk right now."

"What's the matter, Tony?"

"My contract says 50 percent billing, but I'm not on any of these posters—and I haven't been the whole tour!"

"It's because your son didn't commit till the last minute!"

I'm out of my comfort zone here, not to mention thoroughly tired of all this pussyfooting. So I call in a professional. Tony Smith, skilled negotiator extraordinaire, sits Tony Bennett down, they discuss it, and they resolve it.

Mr. Bennett, though, old hand that he is, has the last laugh. As we're getting to the end of Tony's shows with us, I ask him for a picture and an autograph. He obliges, signing it: "To Phil, my 'buddy,'" the "buddy" pointedly in inverted quotes.

MEANWHILE, HOME LIFE with Orianne is blissful. For sure, the distant guns of my impending divorce from Jill can be heard booming on the horizon. In certain sections of the U.K. press, I'm still public enemy number one. But I'm head over heels in love, and I feel spiritually energized, nimbly creative and, in all the right ways, *loose*. Twenty-five non-stop years have, well, stopped. This new beginning in Switzerland is delivering everything I hoped it would.

Not least on the musical front. One morning I receive a call from Sir George Martin. As part of him winding down his career he wants to make an album, *In My Life*, featuring new versions of some of his favorite Beatles songs. We've known each other for years but never worked together, so I'm thrilled to be asked. He and his son Giles fly over to France to a house I've rented to use as a studio to record my next album.

It's decided that I'll take on "Carry That Weight/Golden Slumbers" from *Abbey Road*. First I play the drum parts, including the famous Ringo solo. We double the length of it, which George loves. Then we go about the vocal parts, full of close, three-part harmonies, with George saying, "This is what Paul sang . . . this is what John sang . . ." Working with this genuine musical legend and thoroughly lovely man is a treasured memory of mine.

My sixth solo album, *Dance into the Light,* is released later that year, in October 1996. The title and the sound are symbolic: this is an optimistic album, full of brightness and colors. I'm listening to a lot of Youssou N'Dour, and I'm also aware that guitar bands are back. This is the era of Britpop and, while I'm as far as it's possible to get from Cool Britannia and the new swinging London set— although I do feel close to Oasis's Noel Gallagher, insofar as he loves slagging me off—I'm inspired to experiment with guitar sounds on my keyboards. So I write a few "guitar songs"; that is, songs that are not of the type that Phil Collins would usually write. Now that I'm a full-time solo artist, I'm determined to fly that freedom flag as high as possible and mix it up a bit.

Shortly after the album's release I happen to meet Noel on Mustique. He's there on holiday with his first wife; I'm there with Orianne. Orianne and I frequent a small bar called The Firefly and befriend the owners, Stan and Liz. In conversation one night I suggest to Stan that the place could do with a bit of live music. He replies, "I'll get the musicians if you'll play the drums." Sounds fun, so I say OK.

I arrive on the proposed night to find a saxophonist and her piano-playing husband; they've boated over from a neighboring island. And sitting in the corner of this tiny bar are Noel, his wife, Johnny Depp, Kate Moss and a Labour MP (I don't know which one).

I introduce myself and ask Noel if he'd be interested in having a knockabout with us.

Noel's wife pipes up that she's seen the video for "It's in Your Eyes," the second single from *Dance into the Light*, in which I'd "played" guitar (one borrowed from Paul McCartney, a fellow left-hander). She airily informs me that she knows I'm not a guitarist and that I'm not fooling anyone. "That wasn't my intention," I reply, "it just felt good."

Now Noel speaks, dismissively declining the invitation. I retire to the bar, feeling not a little embarrassed. Credit to Kate Moss, though—she comes over and apologizes for the odd encounter. Our small trio starts playing regardless, and the Gallagher party up and leave soon after.

While *Dance into the Light* is a bit of a damp squid, the tour is a bit of a rocket. *A Trip into the Light* starts at the Ice Palace in Tampa, Florida, on February 28, 1997, and runs through North America till the end of April. After a five-month gap it resumes for a three-month run in Europe that takes me up to the end of the year.

These first couple of years post-Genesis bring another project with its share of struggles. But what's opportunity without struggle? If it's easy, it's not worth it. And knowing as I did their work and working methods, I wouldn't have expected any different from getting into bed with Walt Disney.

IN THE SUMMER of 1995, a team from Disney HQ in Burbank, Los Angeles, fly to Switzerland. They're a heavyweight bunch: Tom Schumacher, president of Walt Disney Animation Studios; Chris Montan, the company's executive music producer; Kevin Lima, part of the story team on *Aladdin* and *The Lion King*; and Chris Buck, an animator/character designer who worked on *Who Framed Roger Rabbit* and *The Little Mermaid* (and who would eventually co-direct 2013's *Frozen*, the highest-grossing animated film of all time). These guys will become close friends of mine by the time the project is finished in 1999.

We check into a conference room at the Metropole Hotel in Geneva. The men from Disney come with a proposal. They want me to write the music for the company's thirty-seventh animated feature, which will be an adaptation of Edgar Rice Burroughs' *Tarzan of the Apes* novels. As they used to say in Hollywood, this will be a major motion picture event. I later find out how major: with a budget of $130 million, when it's released *Tarzan* will be the most expensive animated feature ever made. But in a way, it needs to be: *The Lion King*, released in 1994, was a huge success, at the time the fifth most popular film in American box office history. Schumacher and his guys are gunning for similar levels of success.

On the blaringly obvious level, *what an offer.* At this point neither the Disney team nor the rest of the world are aware that I've left Genesis, so relatively speaking, my schedule is pretty clear. Equally importantly, I grew up with Disney; it's in my DNA. I've watched all the films with all my kids. I've even watched them without my kids: I remember being in LA with Tony Banks and going to see *Beauty and the Beast* as soon as it was released.

As a child, my brother Clive's future career as a cartoonist loomed large in my consciousness: the work of Disney's legendary animators, the Nine Old Men, was pinned to the walls on his side of our shared bedroom. Courtesy of my professional ice-skater sister Carole, the Collins family went to see the annual Christmas ice show at Wembley, which, more often than not, was based on the current Disney film. It became second nature to see the Fairy Queen (Carole) pal about with the rest of the Disney menagerie, including all of the Seven Dwarfs the year she was in *Snow White*. In fact, I got to know Dopey best of all—he came to live with us for the duration of the show's winter run at Wembley.

His name was Kenny Baker, and he also played in a musical comedy group called The Mini Tones. But he became best known via another gig: Kenny was R2-D2 in the *Star Wars* films. He had a six-foot girlfriend, Annette, who also stayed with us. Modesty prevents me from thinking what they got up to. I grew used to seeing them around our house, but our mongrel, Buddy, took a bit longer. Kenny would ring the doorbell, I'd open the door, and Buddy would find himself nose-to-nose with this human.

It wasn't just the cartoons and the characters that spoke to me. Like anyone who grew up after the war, Disney songs are part of my life. One example: as noted earlier, I remember my dad singing "Hi-Diddle-Dee-Dee" from *Pinocchio* the first time he let go of my saddle when I learnt to ride my bike. Much later, *Aladdin* was the soundtrack to those bittersweet marking-time interludes in the car with Lily after Jill and I split.

The memories are that specific, that totemic. These songs are in my blood. And that's before my mind zooms forward to the here and now, to 1995—this is the year Elton John, my near peer, has won an Oscar, a Grammy and a Golden Globe for his work on the soundtrack for *The Lion King*.

So when, as a songwriter, you get a phone call saying Disney want you to write for them, you think, "My God, I'm being asked to join a club I never thought I'd become a member of."

Then, immediately after that, you think, "My God, they're asking me to do something I don't think I can do."

The Disney quartet pitch me the story. It's *Tarzan*, and it makes sense to ask me: drums, jungle rhythms, percussion. On paper, it's a great fit. But still, I'm not sure. This would be a huge undertaking. And I'm not sure they're sure. Don't Disney know that my last release was *Both Sides*, not my first but my second rather bleak "divorce album"? And haven't they heard of Faxgate, not to mention Taxgate?

But these guys are American, so to a large extent they've been insulated from the charms of British tabloids. Also, *they're Disney*. They know what they're doing. It was the bright idea of Chris Montan, in charge of music production, to commission Elton for *The Lion King*, so he's clearly no fool. Plus, not many listeners caught on to the lyrical detail of *Both Sides*, and its perceived failure still amounted to around 7 million sales globally. I infer that Chris's key thoughts are: "This guy's hot, has been for a long while now, and we need someone reliably hot to do our film."

Nevertheless, ever the worrier, I find myself saying, "I don't know if I can write a song like 'Be My Guest' from *Beauty and the Beast*. I don't know if I can 'be' the candelabra singing to all the pots and pans. I can't do the show songs, and I'm not sure I can write the funny songs either."

Team Disney reply: "If we'd wanted that, we'd have asked Alan Menken [the pre-eminent American musical theater and film composer]. We want you to be you."

The mist clears. "Oh well, if you want me to be me, I can probably do that."

Then another realization: I don't have to leave home to do this. I can write *Tarzan* in my shed, in the garden, in my new Swiss home.

What's more, I'm being asked to do this as a writer. They want me for my ability to create songs with a distinctive voice. Best of all, they only want me to write the songs, not sing them. Which means I can continue with my plan to remain in the background of this or any other scenario.

The clincher comes when Disney tell me that there's no rush and that it's a long-term project. And they're not kidding: it will be four years before *Tarzan* hits the cinemas.

It's an offer I can't refuse.

Signed up to the Mouse House, I apply all of myself to *Tarzan*, approaching it with the seriousness and single-mindedness I applied to any of the band or solo albums. To me, this is not a children's thing. I'm being asked to do something that will last forever. That's the thing with Disney films: they move from generation to generation, usually (in the case of the great ones) becoming more popular as they go. You can't say that about many rock bands. I'm not suggesting that *Tarzan* will have the longevity of *Snow White*. But if we do it right—and, of course, the animators and storyboarders and scriptwriters are all equally on the hook—then this one could run and run. As is the multi-platform modern way of things, it could even become a stage musical.

But let's not get ahead of ourselves. In Switzerland in the autumn of 1995, once I'm over my initial crisis of confidence, I start to write. I keep writing. I write an awful lot of music. I write "You'll Be in My Heart" and "Son of Man" and "Strangers Like Me." The Disney team are over the moon at my enthusiasm, and at the depth and quality of the material. It's amazing what you can do when you're terrified.

This is a top-to-bottom, head-to-heart, deeply personal commitment for me. The lullaby "You'll Be in My Heart" began life as a melody I imagined singing to a baby Lily. And my engagement doesn't end with the initial songwriting. I've heard Elton's demos for *The Lion King*, and it was just him, a piano and a drum machine. But I really want to be part of the mechanism of how the entire soundtrack comes together. So I make the demos more than just simple home recordings, building them up into approximations of finished songs. Disney loves these. And when Disney loves you, you feel really loved.

Still, it's very much a creative back-and-forth. The making of a Disney film involves a cast of hundreds, which can mean a lot of "notes" on your particular patch of creativity. There is no such thing as a script, just pages. These can change, and they will, so a song needs to change. A character can be cut, so a song has to go. The narrative turns left, so your lyrics need to turn left. I don't have a problem with it. I was in a band for years; I'm used to writing-by-committee.

I've taken on this project on the assumption that the actor who plays Tarzan, and all the other voice cast, will be the ones singing the songs. This has always been the Disney way. The songs move the narrative along, so therefore you have to have the characters lead the songs. Even cartoons with talking animals have to possess an internal logic.

The next common-sense step is that I'll be present in the studio to help oversee the recording. Cut to a studio in New York as the process starts. I've sent the team demos throughout the writing. Unbeknown to me, they've grown very attached to these. So much so that it's becoming very difficult for them to see any other voice singing the songs. However, they're going to give it a try. Glenn Close, who's playing Tarzan's gorilla foster-mother Kala, is coming in to sing "You'll Be in My Heart," and Rosie O'Donnell (Tarzan's foster-sister Terk) is coming in to sing "Trashin' the Camp." Before we begin recording, I'm sent out to teach Glenn the song.

Before now I've never had occasion to consider this, but with "In the Air Tonight," for example, the drum machine does nothing on the down beat. So someone who's not a drummer would struggle to know where "one" is—that is, they'll struggle to know when to come in. Now I'm realizing that "You'll Be in My Heart" follows the same pattern. And Glenn just can't get it. She's singing on the down beat. She's a Broadway singer, and she can *sing*. But there's a basic rhythmic disconnect happening here.

Over the studio microphone I try to help, saying gently (I hope), "No, no, no, Glenn, it's like this . . ." But after a dispiriting number of failed takes, this group of Disney brass start looking at each other, telepathically screaming, "What the fuck are we gonna do?"

Glenn's frustration is also mounting. She's a lovely lady, no diva by any stretch of the imagination, but I can see through the studio glass that she's reaching the point of no return.

We record a duet version for the benefit of the cameras who are in here too (just to add to the pressure), filming for the press kit. It's very funny, and helps break the ice. But soon the ice refreezes.

A break is called and a quick discussion ensues. "Let's have Glenn sing-speak the first verse, then Phil will sing the rest." I nod, while thinking, "Yeah, but I'm not in the movie."

We record Glenn, almost a cappella; then I come in, with my drummer's timing. Finally, it sounds decent. But I'm still thinking, "What's really going to happen on the film soundtrack?"

Eventually, the Disney brass reach a decision: "Well, Phil, you're going to sing it." Moreover, once we've done "You'll Be in My Heart," it's decided that I'll sing four out of the five songs. The idea of characters singing goes out of the window, which is the first time this has happened on a Disney movie.

Most of the songs still work, and I breathe out. Now I'm singing more like the narrator of the story, albeit a narrator with no spoken lines of dialogue. We eventually manage to cajole Rosie into doing the scat, jazzy thing on "Trashin' the Camp," and she carries it off. But that's the only song in the movie that the character sings.

I won't lie: I'm thrilled at this outcome. Not only will my songs be in a Disney movie, my voice will too. On top of that, the songs will be performed as I wrote them. That has been my big fear—you write it and suddenly it's being sung by another singer in another style. Possibly a bugling Broadway musical style. This is, I learn, the art of writing for a musical, whether animated or on Broadway.

What I don't realize yet is that my singing the songs will mean singing them in a host of different languages. As the songs in the films are normally sung by the characters, usually the different voice talent in each territory sings the translated versions. But Tarzan isn't singing these songs in English, so he isn't singing them in Japanese either. As Disney is an entertainment force that knows no national boundaries, popular from Burbank to Bangkok to Beijing, that nameless narrator had better get his multilingual skates on. *Tarzan* is being dubbed into thirty-five languages, a record for a Disney film.

We compromise: I re-record the entire soundtrack in Italian, Spanish, Castilian Spanish, French and German.

The *Tarzan* commission has given me a feeling I've long hankered after, and long pursued: in being entrusted with the songs for an entire Disney film, I'm being taken seriously as a songwriter. For all my commercial success, the absence of this feeling is something I've always had a chip on my shoulder about.

On June 16, 1999, two days before the film's U.S. release, I'm awarded a star on the Hollywood Walk of Fame, outside Disney's own El Capitan Theatre. Not something an end-of-the-line boy from Hounslow could ever have imagined in a million years.

Tarzan is a hit, critically and commercially, grossing almost $500 million worldwide and becoming the fifth biggest film of the year. "You'll Be in My Heart" is nominated for an Oscar and wins the Golden Globe for Best Original Song–Motion Picture. At the Grammys, composer Mark Mancina and I win the award for Best Soundtrack Album.

Before the Academy Awards there is a small salute by MusiCares, the music industry charity, to Elton John in LA. Several previous honorees—including Stevie Wonder, Tony Bennett and Sting—perform a selection of his songs. I sing "Burn Down the Mission." Afterward, in the Elton receiving area, he and I discuss the upcoming Oscars, and what he felt when he won for "Can You Feel the Love Tonight," and what I will feel if I'm lucky enough to win. He tells me he felt "fucking great."

Come Oscar night 2000, I am, this time, deemed good enough to perform my song. Cher is presenting the music category. When she opens that envelope and says my name—I've won the Academy Award for Best Original Song—I stand there in disbelief.

All told, I count the four years I spent working on *Tarzan* as a brilliant adventure. I worked hard, stretched myself, met some great people, and I learnt a huge amount about working in a new medium.

As the nineties draw to a close, I feel like I can go anywhere. I've done a Disney film. I've made a colorful, optimistic solo album. I've done the big band—in fact, I've done it twice: in 1998 The Phil Collins Big Band goes out on tour again, this time for longer, and in America as well. In 1999 we release a live album, *A Hot Night in Paris*.

I also draw a line under my story so far. In 1998 I release ...*Hits*, and in 1999 Genesis release *Turn It On Again: The Hits*, both of which do what they say on the tin. That was then, this is now.

I'm moving onward, growing outward, growing up. I've been invigorated by my new love with Orianne. I'm learning French. I'm firmly, happily, settled in Switzerland. And, all these years after the halcyon days of the Converted Cruiser Club, I've finally got a boat. Shimmering blue Lac Léman isn't the muddy Thames, but it'll do. *Je suis vivant le rêve.*

Just before the new millennium dawns, on July 24, 1999, I make a commitment to the future. Orianne and I are married—twice, just to make sure, firstly in our home town of Begnins, and secondly in Lausanne, where we met. The bride wears white, the groom, a dark suit. We have a beautiful reception at the Beau-Rivage in Lausanne, with all our friends in attendance. I believe they're still talking about it.

That's it. I'm settled, I'm done, I'm happy.

19

GOODBYE TO ALL THAT

Or: earache, heartache and a final farewell

WHAT DO YOU call someone who hangs around with musicians? A drummer.

Did you hear about the drummer who finished high school? Me neither.

What's the last thing a drummer says in a band? "Hey, guys, how about we try one of my songs?"

It's not easy being a drummer. I've heard all the jokes. I know that it takes five of us to change a lightbulb—one to screw it in, four to talk about how much better Steve Gadd would have done it. I've yucked along to the one about the drummer who died, went to heaven, was surprised to hear some phenomenal drumming coming from behind the Pearly Gates, and rushed to St. Peter to ask if that was really Buddy Rich playing. "No, that's God. He just thinks he's Buddy Rich." I should have told that one to Tony Bennett.

I became used to the cracks early on. Us drummers have to develop a thick skin, especially on our fingers. We're the most physical guys on a stage, and we have to keep up. Post-show, the drummer is the one who's shattered, drenched in sweat in the dressing room, panting. I don't mind. That's our gig. Keeping the beat, feeling beat.

By the time I've completed the very physical *A Trip into the*

Light tour—a busy, in-the-round show—in 1997, and marshaled the troops on the second Big Band tour in 1998, I've kept the show on the road for almost thirty years. Although I have long since given over the drumming heavy lifting to either Chester Thompson or Ricky Lawson, both fantastic drummers, I still keep my hand in, making sure that at some point in every show on every tour, I play drums enough to keep my chops up. I always return to the warm embrace of the drum stool. She's my first love, the seat of all my power.

In three decades out there performing, I have barely ever faltered in brute physical terms. Blisters are generally as bad as it's got. After any length of time at home, you'd have softened up. A few weeks of bathing the kids, or washing up after dinner, and your hands that did dishes would feel as soft as your face. All of a sudden you'd have to go on tour again and your fingers would need to be gig-ready and hardened.

I remember the first time I went on tour with Eric, in 1986. We'd just started and I was complaining about blood blisters. He told me his ritual: a few weeks ahead of a tour he'd start filing the ends of his fingers. He'd literally scrape off the pads on his fingertips, they'd scab, then he'd scrape them off again. Eventually they'd be nicely calloused and EC would be ready for another run of blistering solos.

Being in pain and getting blisters is just an occupational hazard. The first few years of Genesis were physically arduous, especially when I was pulling double duty. Some singers physically switch off when there's an instrumental section in a song. Me? I would rush back to the drums and play. Things naturally eased up when the singing started to take over from the drumming. But when I reverted to pure drumming gigs with Eric and Robert Plant, that's when it was tough: non-stop playing, backing up frontmen who knew a thing or two about working with great drummers like Ginger Baker and John Bonham.

Some people—Stewart Copeland of The Police, for example— wear gloves. I could never do that. I need to feel the stick.

So fundamentally, there's no way round it. You just have to develop strength and resilience. On early tours, back in my hotel room, I'd play on pillows in front of the TV, endlessly, into the night, to strengthen my wrists. With the blisters, you have to push through. The blister breaks, then you get a blood blister, then that breaks and you're working with increasingly butchered flesh.

You have no option but to do it in the raw, in real time, onstage. Even if you've rehearsed—seven, eight, nine, ten hours a day—you won't get there. You won't find the angst, the nerves or the tension of playing a show. So the fingers won't get toughened either.

You could use New-Skin, a product like a thick nail varnish that's daubed on a piece of flayed epidermis desperate for some protection. You paint it on and it stings and it stinks. But once it dries, the nauseous medical pong fades, as does the pain, and you're armed with another layer of insulation. Then, when that comes off, it rips off another layer of real skin. You start all over again.

Although all of this may sound overdramatic, it's a reality that drummers live with. You play, and you play on, and on. You might, in desperation, stick on plasters, but the sweat makes them come off during the show, so you hope that you have bits of hard skin developing. If not, the salty sweat will make your cracked, bleeding digits feel like they're on fire.

Eventually—*eventually*—you've passed the worst. Now you have Tour Fingers.

So while as a drummer you might be mentally enfeebled, you're physically robust. Even when I became a singer first and foremost, I maintained that mindset, and that fitness. And after *A Trip into the Light*, with the nightly laps of honor around our huge, round stage, I feel in great shape. There's none of this personal-trainer malarkey. There's no gym addiction, as seems to be the way of the preening, peacocking modern pop star.

The voice, however, is a different beast. You can't put a sticking plaster on iffy vocal cords. So you have to try to transcend via other means.

Mercifully, while I never suffered from nodules on any of the giant Genesis or solo tours in the eighties or nineties, I did have a doctor in every port. I very rarely canceled shows, because I knew when it was time to pull the emergency cord and go for the injection of prednisone, a corticosteroid.

Your vocal cords are very small, like two tiny coins that rub together. If they become swollen, or abused, they won't meet to enable you to sing a note. Then you're in trouble. If you keep up the abuse, in their engorged state they eventually become nodules. But a quick steroid injection reduces the swelling and you're right as rain. In the short term, anyway.

I was forced to seek this recourse on a number of occasions throughout my singing life.

The conversation usually went something like this:

"Doctor, I can't sing."

"OK. When are you working next?"

"Tonight."

"Where?"

"A 40,000-seater stadium."

"Ah . . ."

So you're given a shot of prednisone, injected into your bum. The steroid will get you through the show, but once you're on it, you're on it for ten days. It will also get you a lovely cacophony of side effects: psychotic mood swings, water retention, moon face.

This happened in Fremantle in Australia, on the mammoth *Invisible Touch* tour of 1986 and 1987. Touring Australia is a huge undertaking—different time zones, major internal flights, upside down and back to front at the bottom of the world.

This is the tour where we bump into Elton John. My old percussionist friend Ray Cooper is a member of his band. We go to see him because we're playing the same venue soon after. Ray says, "Hey, man, you been working out?" Of course, I haven't. "You look great, you look great . . ." he adds hurriedly, protesting just a bit too much.

When I get back to the hotel, I check myself in the mirror. "I look OK," I think, at least to me.

However, I've picked up an injury on this tour. One night, at the end of "Domino," I jumped in the air and came down on the edge of my foot. The pain was excruciating, but it was just a sprain and I pushed through. Something—adrenaline, cortisone, insurance premiums, the threat of ruinous cancellation fees—helped me keep the tour ticking on.

Some months later, I see pictures of myself from the tour, and I realize what Ray was not saying. I look like David Crosby at the height/depth of his drug woes. No, I look like I've *eaten* David Crosby. Courtesy of the cortisone, I was taking on water like a blue whale sieving plankton. I've blimped out and no one had said a word.

Those pictures scared me stiff. I had not heeded the warning: "Do not operate heavy machinery while under the influence." And the machinery doesn't come much heavier than a Genesis stadium tour.

When I meet Ray a short while after that, at a show at the Royal Albert Hall, he admits that the only "working out" going through his mind in Australia was him trying to work out why his old mate Phil looked so "fucking terrible."

And it wasn't just that tour. As already recounted, the eye-wateringly long and climactic *We Can't Dance* tour was almost de-railed at the very start when my voice went in Tampa. The audiences on this tour were giant ones, and they knew the words better than me. I couldn't let them down. But on that occasion, even the needle couldn't save the show.

By this stage, I'd been dancing around the high notes for a while. This didn't happen so much on my solo tours since my music was written for me to sing. But portions of the Genesis set were written for Peter's voice. And for all the uncanny similarities between our voices, some songs were just difficult for my range. But even if Peter had been singing them, they would have been high even for him at this point in both our lives.

You could lower the key in certain songs, but that risked losing the magic. "Mama," for example: take that down too low and it really has no magic at all. It's all about the key it's written in, the place on the guitar where you play the chords, the resonance of certain keyboard sounds.

There were certain songs in the Genesis set-list that I'd be dread-ing coming down the pipe. "Home by the Sea" has a lot of lyrics. I had to make sure I remembered the starts of the lines as a crucial aide-mémoire. Tony Banks wrote that melody, and those words, but he'd never thought about how it would sound; he'd never sung it out loud. So to get through the show I had to gently weave my way round some of the accident black spots.

Tony always noticed. "Having a bit of trouble tonight?" he'd say after a gig, not unkindly. "Noticed you missed a few of my best notes . . ."

Even "I Can't Dance," a stupidly simple song, got tough. That opening high burst of the first chorus line—*ouch*. The reason I wrote that little bit was as a nod to Fine Young Cannibals' Roland Gift, who has a terrific soul voice. But singing that every night, I'd find myself skipping around the note. Otherwise the game would have been up. Shot myself in the vocal cord with that one.

Then there's "In the Air Tonight." If I sang that cold, it would sometimes be an effort to reach the emotive peaks that drive the song. Sometimes your body movements, and the shape of your mouth, could help you get there. But if I was drumming as well, the distraction would propel my voice to greater heights. In that regard, one helped the other: the drumming pushing the singing.

Mainly, though, I didn't allow myself too much time to think of these problems. For three decades I pushed on, and on, and on. What's worrying is that if I counted now all the times I've been pricked in the buttocks in the name of a good vocal performance, I'd have trouble sitting down. I'd have trouble getting back up again, too: as I would one day find out, too much cortisone can make your bones brittle.

IN 1998 THE *Tarzan* experience is drawing to a close, and we have to make a "pop" version of "You'll Be in My Heart" for the single release.

I book some studio time at Ocean Way in LA with Rob Cavallo, a producer who is also senior vice-president of A&R at Disney's label Hollywood Records (and son of the boss of the label). Cavallo's had huge, Grammy-winning success with Green Day's *Dookie*, and he'll go on to even greater successes as a producer (Green Day's *American Idiot*, Fleetwood Mac's *Say You Will*, My Chemical Romance's *The*

Black Parade, to name but three) and as an executive—in 2010 he becomes chairman of Warner Bros. Records.

One afternoon in Ocean Way we're listening back to a vocal take. I'm in the vocal booth, wearing headphones, when the engineer presses play.

Bang!

It's incredibly loud. Unbelievably so. Forget ear-splitting—this is head-splitting. The sound crashes from the headphones straight into me, overwhelming and explosive. I go deaf in one ear. As simple and as quick as that. In my left ear I can hear nothing. No ringing, no buzzing, just nothing.

Rather calmly, I say to the engineer, "Please don't do that again."

Somewhat dazed, I go back to the hotel, the Peninsula Beverly Hills. Lily, now aged nine, is waiting for me, which brightens things up no end. She and I start playing Spyro the Dragon—computer games are one of our new shared passions. I love them, and I love Spyro, although if push comes to shove, I'll declare myself a Crash Bandicoot man. As if by magic, the hearing in my left ear roars back. It's like I've been underwater, but the blockage is suddenly gone. Thank God for that.

That evening we go out for dinner at a little Italian place opposite the hotel. I'm about to enjoy my pasta when suddenly my hearing goes again. From that moment, I will never hear properly in my left ear. Game over, just like that.

I visit more than a few ear, nose and throat specialists. They all subject me to audiograms, and all, eventually, come up with the same thing: I have suffered what is known as an aural stroke, caused by an infection. It's nothing to do with the music. This is just bad luck. You work behind a sweet-shop counter, it could happen to you.

I learn that, in simple terms, the cells in the nerves that lead from my brain to my ear have been attacked by a virus. This has resulted in the loss of my ability to hear middle and bottom frequencies. If I'd dealt with it immediately—with a dose of my old friend cortisone, there's the possibility of kick-starting the cells' regeneration—it might have been different. But I left it too late, in true Collins tradition. It's what killed my dad in the end, him not dealing with his diabetes and heart condition.

Now, because this is a viral infection, the noise blast in the headphones was probably not the cause. However, as the months and years pass, it's the only hearing-related experience I have that's out of the ordinary, so I can't help but feel it's partly to blame.

On the advice of Disney's Chris Montan, whose son is chronically deaf, I visit the House Ear Institute in LA. The specialist asks, "Do you need to go on tour again?"

"Not really."

"Well then, why would you? Because anything could happen and you could go completely deaf. No one knows what causes this viral infection, and you would be putting yourself at risk again."

Am I panicked? Strangely, not really. For one thing, I'm thinking, "This will eventually be OK." For another, I'm having a deeper thought: "If it's *not* eventually OK, I can live with that."

I'm not entirely deaf, only 50 percent in one ear, so I can carry on working at home. If I was out gigging with a rock group, or leading my own band in a big pop extravaganza, it might be an issue. But I have no intention of doing either for the foreseeable future.

I'm happy here, bunkered in my garden on a Swiss hillside. I'm writing music for films. I've got my Big Band, who only play smaller venues and for whom I do barely any singing. I can take all the time in the world to make my next solo album. So, if I have to stop being the "Phil Collins" of headlines and headline-act (dis)repute, that's fine with me. Partly losing my hearing is my get-out clause.

I'm sanguine about this new, semi-deaf reality, which is baffling to my nearest and dearest. But the truth is, losing my hearing has given me something: *control*. It's disability-induced control, but I'll take that. After so many years of paying the piper but not entirely calling the tune, I can wrest back my destiny.

I've come to resent this "Phil Collins" doppelgänger, the one who was out there performing, showing off, hoovering up plaudits and (increasingly) brickbats. "Phil Collins" comes with aggravations, expectations, obligations and suppositions dragging round his ankles and hanging off his neck. He has splintered families and embittered partners and distant children. I don't like that guy. I don't want to be that guy. I've had enough of me.

Want me to go out and tour again, and be a pop/rock star again? Sorry, no can do. Doctor's orders.

Lost my hearing? Found myself. Or what was left of me.

Admittedly, I already have a pretty good fallback plan. The very day *Tarzan* was released in theaters in June 1999, Tom Schumacher asked me to come on board for another new Disney movie. *Brother Bear*—a yarn about Native Americans, the ancient harmony of man and nature, animal spirits and, yes, bears—would involve writing the songs and, even more interestingly, writing some of the underscore. That was a challenge I was itching to try. It more than compensated for Disney's other creative suggestion—that I might not be singing these songs in the film.

The making of *Brother Bear* is another drawn-out creative process, as I might have expected from a story that, in its earliest incarnation, had a *King Lear* subtext.

First off, Disney's music team insist that I get a computer in my life. Before this, I was working with tape. On *Tarzan*, every time they made edits to the film, it would affect the songs, which meant I had to go away and re-record the entire thing. Time-consuming, but I knew no other way. With computers you can shift around tempo and music at will.

I undergo a week's course with one of Mark Mancina's technical boffins, Chuck Choi. I take lots of notes and at first it seems a mountain to climb. But before too long, I've become a computer buff. I've developed my own new ways of working in a studio; plus I'm sitting elbow-to-elbow with guys who live and breathe this stuff. Mark is a seasoned score-writer, young and enthusiastic, and he's an old-school Genesis fan to boot. We click well, we divide up the music cues to be done, and I set to work—a very excited, soundtrack-composing, Disney-affiliated, partially deaf man.

Imagine now one of those old black-and-white films, where the pages of the calendar fly off, one after the other, month after month. A multitude of video conference calls with the directors and the scriptwriting and animation teams. Many late-night telephone conversations between Begnins, Burbank and Orlando (location of Disney's Florida studios), receiver pressed hotly against my (good) right ear. Lots of back-and-forth as I listen to the temporary score—used by film-makers when they're in production—and wonder whether it'd be best to copy it, mirror it or improve it.

Even more back-and-forth when Mark attempts to translate my pieces of underscoring into a real orchestral chart. We discover that parts I've written for a flute are out of the flute's range, or that my trombone part is really a French horn part. I'm learning, and learning fast, that for all my musical experience, when it comes to scoring a film, in some crucial areas I don't know my arse from my oboe.

Meanwhile, the writing of the songs is coming on just fine. I'm feeling quite breezy. But I do wonder: who's going to be the singing voice of the fish, the bear, all of the other animals? Ultimately those *Brother Bear* necessities are Disney's problems, not mine, although I'm included in all the discussions.

For "Great Spirits," the film's opening song, we call Richie Havens, a longtime hero of mine. He does a beautiful version, but it doesn't cut it for the team. After some more tryouts, we decide to ask Tina Turner. But she's just announced her retirement, so securing her services could be a struggle. Handily, I met her with Eric during the making of *August*—she duetted with him on "Tearing Us Apart." Also, she lives in Switzerland, which is another plus for stay-at-home Collins.

Tina says yes, and we hop to Zurich to record her. Being supremely professional and a true artist, she's learnt the song from the tape I'd sent. She gives it all she can and, after a couple of takes, we have it. Tina oozes musicality and class.

Another stirring piece, "Transformation," soundtracks the man-to-bear transition in the film. My lyrics are translated into Inuit and the song ends up being sung by the Bulgarian Women's Choir. On paper, an odd juxtaposition and a leftfield choice, you might say. In the finished film, extraordinary.

I do end up singing six of the songs as extras on the soundtrack album, so partially I'm satisfied. But for "Welcome," one of my best songs for the film, it's deemed a good idea to ask The Blind Boys of Alabama to sing it. It's for a hunting scene, where the bear clan welcome the hero bear to the wider ursine family with, basically, an orgy of salmon fishing. The salmon seem oddly unbothered.

This segment is the only one I feel doesn't work musically: the Boys were a little past their prime, and didn't have the groove for a song that I wrote as Motown-with-bears.

Still, when *Brother Bear* finally opens in October 2003, I do get to share a stage with Tina Turner at the premiere at Broadway's New Amsterdam Theatre. After the screening, I sing one of my songs, "No Way Out," and then introduce Tina, who sings "Great Spirits" with me on drums. It's quite amazing how Tina turns it on. She'll walk through the soundcheck, she'll "pretend" she's retired, and then she'll kill the song and give a solid-gold performance.

Meanwhile, back in the real (non-animated) world . . . In parallel with the *Brother Bear* work, I've been working at home—slowly—on the songs for my seventh solo album.

In late summer 2000, we discover that Orianne is pregnant. Nicholas Grev Austin Collins is born on April 21, 2001, "Grev" in tribute to my dad, and Austin for my brother Clive (it's his middle name) and our paternal grandfather. This glorious time inspires a new batch of writing. "Come with Me" is about Nic as a baby, but really it's about any baby. It's a rush of pure paternal love and care: don't worry about anything, come with me, close your eyes, it's going to be all right.

The lyrics are for any of my kids, or any kids anywhere. It's one of my favorite songs, the melody suggestive of a lullaby I used to sing to Lily in the back of limos in America. We make a music box for baby Nic, something to help him sleep, that plays that melody. I will then have to write one for his brother Matt and get him his own music box. Much to his frustration, at the time of writing, his melody has yet to transform into a song.

I decide to call this deeply personal new album *Testify*: a word that sums up how I feel about my life at the time. I want to tell the world about a woman I'm very much in love with and a new baby boy in the family. In this period I'm blissfully happy undercover in Switzerland.

It will therefore take something extraordinary to drag me, blinking, back to center stage. That extraordinary thing is a call from Her Maj.

In spring 2002 I'm asked to be the drummer for the house band for the Party at the Palace, a lavish concert being held at Buckingham Palace to celebrate Queen Elizabeth II's Golden Jubilee. Iffy ear or no iffy ear, I can't say no to that.

The brief outline is for a show celebrating the previous forty-plus years of British music. All the major artists from that period will be singing the songs that made them famous. Only Paul McCartney and Brian Wilson are bringing their own bands. For every other artist I'll be playing drums and acting as de facto bandleader for the in-house musicians.

We practice for a couple of weeks, a convoy of artists arriving in the rehearsal room adjacent to Tower Bridge: Ozzy Osbourne, Rod Stewart, Eric Clapton, Stevie Winwood, Ray Davies, Joe Cocker, Annie Lennox, Cliff Richard, Tom Jones, Shirley Bassey and many more.

Come show day, my hands hold up, my ear doesn't trouble me and everyone's in great form—even Brian May, who's playing up on the roof of Buckingham Palace and having to contend with wind that must be a nightmare for his sound, not to mention his hair.

Five months later, *Testify* is released. I testify before you now that it flops rather dramatically. The French, Swiss, Swedes, Germans, Dutch and Belgians, bless 'em all, show it some love, making it number 2, 3 or 4 in their national charts. But the rest of the free world, notably the U.K. and the USA, are less enthused.

I will also testify before you now that I am truly philosophical about this. I've had more than my fifteen minutes.

On the plus side, I've made an album that hymns my love for my wife and baby boy, I've made it mostly at home, and I've made it while grappling with sudden deafness that, for a minute there, looked like it might have ended everything. That has to count as a result.

And yet, and yet . . . In 2003, after *Testify* has rather quickly come and gone, I find myself doing some hard thinking.

On June 12, at New York's Marriott Marquis, I'm inducted into the Songwriters Hall of Fame. It was established in 1969 by the legendary songwriter Johnny Mercer, in collaboration with music publishers Abe Olman and Howie Richmond, as a body (to quote their website) "to shine the spotlight on the accomplishments of songwriters who have provided us with the words and music that form the soundtrack of our lives." To be deemed worthy of inclusion by my peers is a thrill. They're a discerning bunch—to date (2016) there are fewer than 400 members. My fellow inductees in 2003 are Little Richard, Van Morrison and Queen, while Jimmy Webb ("Galveston," "Wichita Lineman," "By the Time I Get to Phoenix" and countless other classics that don't feature place-names in their titles) takes home the annual Johnny Mercer Award. Good company.

It's a lovely validation, and it gets me thinking. If I am going to slowly retire this "Phil Collins" character, I should do so properly. Musically speaking, an underperforming solo album and a Big Band tour shouldn't be my last hurrah.

Another key factor in my decision-making process: by this time, three years after my sudden deafness, life is almost normal. My brain has adjusted, my right ear has compensated, my hearing disabilities have leveled out. I'm again able to listen to, and enjoy, music. And as I discover at Queen Liz's little gig, wearing in-ear monitors makes performing very much doable.

All things considered—and I do give this serious, serious consideration—I think maybe it's possible to go out on tour and, rather than disappear without a trace, say goodbye properly.

A final tour will also serve notice to my elders and betters and manager: when I say I want to stop, I mean it. I anticipate nobody will really believe me, because as we have seen, I have never stopped. But perhaps if I say it loud enough—over the course of a 77-date valedictory world tour, for example—I can alert those around me to the fact that I want to stop, properly, finally, forever, amen. After that, I will be free.

OK, calling it *The First Final Farewell* tour might confuse some people, and give them the idea that there's some wiggle room. But let's not allow the facts to get in the way of a good, *Python*-esque joke.

What I don't understand until later is that when I tell Orianne that I want to retire, that this tour is the end of the road for me, she has a sudden vision: *pipe and slippers*. She's only thirty-one, the mother of a toddler, and here's her old man saying he's hanging up his clogs. And he's half deaf! What's next, gout?

As I'm preparing for the tour in early 2004, I'm oblivious to all this. My head is very much elsewhere. But I snap back to domestic reality in spring, when Orianne tells me she's pregnant again. Fantastic news. For the first time in my life I embrace the concept of paternity leave: the tour scheduling is hastily rerouted to make sure we'll be at home for the birth, and around for a good while thereafter.

THE FIRST FINAL FAREWELL tour kicks off at Milan's Fila Forum on June 1, 2004. We tour Europe and America until the end of September, where I will say sayonara to the States at the Office Depot Center, Fort Lauderdale.

Before I leave America, though, I take advantage of a day off after the show in Houston. Aware that my retirement is nigh—meaning this might be my last visit to Texas—I make a special pilgrimage to San Antonio, site of the Alamo.

It's a half-century since I first saw the Disney film *Davy Crockett: King of the Wild Frontier* on TV as a five-year-old, piquing my interest in the battle between 185 Texans and a couple of thousand Mexican troops. But what started as childhood games featuring toy soldiers and a fort in the garden at 453 Hanworth Road has become, in adulthood, a serious hobby.

In 1973, during Genesis' *Foxtrot* tour, I took Peter Gabriel with me when I visited the historic site, to explore the reality behind the Hollywood myth. It was incredible, and incredibly moving, to witness firsthand the iconic church façade of the Alamo; to me, the scene of the bloody thirteen-day siege was hallowed ground. I couldn't wait to return and, on a subsequent trip to the city, I met a clairvoyant who was convinced that, in a previous life, I was one of those 185 defenders—a courier, John W. Smith. I'd have taken that with a pinch of gunpowder if it wasn't for the fact that I used to end my childhood games by setting fire to my toy soldiers—which, I learnt much later, was actually the Texans' fate.

On a day off in Washington, D.C., on another U.S. tour, sometime in the mid-eighties, I ended up in a shop called The Gallery of History. It sold historical documents and, among its cache of Nazi military orders and signed Beethoven scores, I found a letter written by Davy Crockett. It was priced at $60,000. Crockett was my hero, but I couldn't justify spending that amount on a piece of paper, no matter how thrilling it was to feel so close to the legendary frontiersman.

But I was intrigued and began casually looking around for other memorabilia related to the battle, although it wasn't until Christmas 1995 that I took possession of my first Alamo document, a gift from Orianne: a receipt for a saddle owned by the aforesaid courier Smith. He was out delivering final letters when the Alamo fell on March 6, 1836, and I couldn't stop thinking about how many miles that saddle had gone in the name of the state of Texas.

From then on I was a collector of all things Alamo, buying up weaponry and documents whenever opportunity and budget allowed—and occasionally when budget didn't allow.

Now, thinking that 2004 will be the last time I tour America, I charter a small plane to make another visit to the site. I drag Orianne, a three-year-old Nicholas and Danny Gillen with me. Leaving the Alamo after a ninety-minute private tour, I notice a store twenty yards from the northeast corner of the compound, scene of some of the worst carnage.

Inside The History Shop I get talking to the manager, Jim Guimarin. It's the start of a great friendship and a fruitful relationship—Jim will help me in my collecting endeavors over the coming years.

Sometime later, Jim—who's been renting the premises—mentions that he's sure that the ground underneath the store has never been excavated. So I do the obvious: I buy the store so I can dig it up.

Underneath The History Shop we find a treasure trove of artifacts: soldiers' personal effects, buttons, horseshoes and teeth, both human and animal. We clean and itemize them, then replace the floor and refit the store. It now houses an accurate model of the

Alamo as it was 200 years ago and, with a guided tour voiced by me, it attracts many a tourist.

AFTER THE AMERICAN run of *The First Final Farewell* tour I'm home for two months, and then Mathew Thomas Clemence Collins is born on December 1, 2004, in Geneva. I'm a supremely happy dad all over again. All my older kids seem to be as happy as me, and I am finally on the verge of giving up the touring life of a musician, eagerly ready to become a stay-at-home dad and help bring up the young ones.

I stay off work until October 2005, when we resume the last final leg of the tour at the Saku Suurhall in Tallinn, Estonia. The shows are fantastic. The closing run is especially great, not least because I'm playing places—Estonia, Lithuania, Finland—I've never played before. My hearing holds up fine, too, which is a huge relief. Everyone is having a ball. Me, retire, at my age (I'm a chipper fifty-four at tour's end)?

But my commitment to stopping is unwavering. I said this would be the end. I have to stick to my word. I have to go home. If nothing else, it's only fair—while I'm First Final Farewelling, Orianne is stuck at home, either pregnant while mothering a toddler or, in the second leg, nursing a newborn while mothering a toddler. With an absent husband, she has a lot on her plate.

I'm counting down the days to when I can come off the road, close the door on a lifetime of performing, go home and settle into a job I've craved, but never been able to enjoy, my whole life: that of a Proper Dad. A Full-Time Dad. On both previous occasions, with Simon and Joely, and then with Lily, I hadn't even managed to be a nine-to-five dad. We'd all paid the price for that. This time, with my two baby boys, I will do right by my children. I have a lot of loving to give and, for sure, a lot of making up to do. It's family time.

Simultaneously, Orianne is doing a lot of thinking, and a lot of worrying. She's convinced that my retirement will be total: no working for me, or for anyone.

But Orianne has no interest in giving up on a career, becoming a full-time mother and settling down as a full-time partner to an un-plugged and indolent retiree. She's creative, has a master's degree in International Management, and a bachelor's degree in Commerce, and has experience running her own business, an events organizing company called O-com.

Her dynamism was one of the driving forces behind a charity we launched in 2000. For years I'd been receiving letters from kids wanting advice on how to get into the music business and, other than giving them a couple of contacts, I really didn't know what else to tell them. Discussing this at home one night, Orianne and I hatched a plan to start a foundation that could help with tuition, coaching and guidance in the fields of music, the arts and sport. We contacted our friends in these areas and asked them to be godparents in their particular field of expertise. So began the Little Dreams Foundation.

All told, then, the idea of me stopping work and sliding into comfy dotage is not particularly appealing to Orianne. I can imagine her thinking, "This is not what I signed up for."

On top of these genuine fears and justified concerns, Orianne starts to have mood swings. She feels unattractive and useless. And, I'm appalled to admit, I don't have too much compassion. I keep flashing back to my dad's attitude to illness of any sort. "Pull your-self together," he'd say, "and get back to work."

Orianne's fears about what my retiring will mean for us as a fam-ily, combined with her "baby blues," mean that when I go home in the middle of the tour, she and I have very different mindsets. It's a tense household, we're both shattered, and the disconnection be-tween us increases.

If there's unhappiness at home, touring can be the hardest place to keep smiling. Still, by the time I resume the last two-month run in October 2005, there's part of me that's grateful for the distrac-tion. Perhaps a bit of distance will be good for both of us. I can take time to think more carefully about our future, and about Orianne's needs. She can take time to get better—albeit, yes, while looking after two small children.

But on the few occasions when she comes to meet me on tour, things are still tense. During the downtime at hotels, we're arguing. During the drives to the airport in the band van, the silences are icy and awkward, and magnified by the discomfort of the other members of the touring party. Joely, who's joined me for the tour, is especially aware of the discord. The celebratory shine of this *First Final Farewell* tour is dulling. The paradise of our marriage, and of our young family, is darkening.

There's a deep love for sure, but Orianne and I just can't find it at this time.

I can't help thinking, "I can't believe this. Here I go again. *Again* I'm on tour and *again* my marriage is rocky, if not worse. Third time unlucky. And what's the common denominator? Me. There can't be anyone else to blame."

If I have to sum up what's causing the breakdown between Orianne and me, I'd say that it's my fault for not hearing her crying out. I can't understand why we're arguing, I can't understand why I'm being pushed out of the marital bed. I just don't get it. I'm sorry.

Nic is four and a half, Matt not even one. If this goes the way I think it might go, my kids are going to be ripped from me. They have no idea. The feeling of déjà vu makes me sick to my stomach.

When *The First Final Farewell* tour ends on November 24, 2005, at Prague's Sazka Arena, Orianne and I are still together, in that we're still married, on paper at least. And we're still living in the same house, but we won't be for long.

What do you call a drummer who splits up with his girlfriend? Homeless.

What do you call a drummer who splits up with his third wife? A mess.

20

TURN IT ON AGAIN, TURN IT OFF AGAIN

Or: a Genesis reunion, a Broadway communion, a family disconnect

T HE FINAL SIX weeks of 2005 bring a traffic jam of conflicting pressures. Actually, more a car crash. In the resulting collision it's not only fenders that are bent out of shape.

In mid-November, the five core members of Genesis have a long-planned rendezvous in Glasgow, which is the latest pit stop on my *First Final Farewell* tour, to discuss a much-awaited, much-discussed reunion.

At the end of November, the tour finally says farewell, and I go home to a home that doesn't feel like my home anymore, and to a young family in urgent need of emergency TLC.

In December, Disney requires my presence post-haste on Broadway, to begin work on a theatrical musical adaptation of *Tarzan*—four months earlier than scheduled, and on the day after Christmas to boot.

In sum, my work-life balance is yet again well and truly out of whack. So much for retirement.

The Genesis meeting is to discuss the thirtieth anniversary of *The Lamb Lies Down on Broadway*, the band's now legendary moment. Actually, to be precise, 2004 was the thirtieth anniversary of *The Lamb Lies Down on Broadway*. Even three decades on, Genesis'

Finest Hour™ can't stick to a schedule. A suggestion has been float-
ing around for a while that the "original" line-up—myself, Tony,
Mike, Peter and Steve—get back together for a new staging of the
album that was Peter's swan song with the band. This time, though,
we'd be prepared. The best of modern technology will be utilized
to properly realize the theatrical vision contained within Peter's lyrics and the entire double-album concept narrative. On paper, that's
more appealing than a bog-standard, Greatest Hits, lap-of-honor,
cash-in comeback tour. Appealing enough, anyway, for five geographically scattered middle-aged men to submit to some furious
diary juggling, which is how the five of us come to meet at my hotel
in Glasgow on November 20, 2005. Even though this occasion comes
in the dying days of my so-called retirement tour, I'm notionally up
for this new project.

Live, *The Lamb* never had a fair shake of the tail. Personally, I
feel like I didn't say goodbye properly to Genesis, and nor did we say
goodbye properly to our fans. After ten years away, I miss Mike and
Tony. Equally, it would be nice to slide back behind the kit again
and just drum with the band. Crucially, too, an ambitious, expensive, multimedia theatrical presentation of *The Lamb* would not, by
definition, lend itself to a long tour of the world's biggest venues.
This would be both shorter and infinitely more artful than the original tour. It would be confined to multiple nights in a nice theater
somewhere, perhaps on Broadway even, with the rest of the global
interest assuaged by a live internet stream or cinema broadcast. The
possibilities are thrilling.

So, for the first time in thirty years the five of us sit down together. Also present: Tony Smith and Peter's manager, Mike Large.

The atmosphere is good. We're there to talk detail, and to pin
down solid dates to rehearse and perform—*if* Peter can decide
whether he wants to be involved or not. With him, it's a "go." Without him, it's a "no point."

As soon as talk turns to business, we quickly revert to long-
standing type: Peter still a little edgy, umming and ahhing; Tony
still digging a little at Peter; Steve still the dark one; Mike still the

cordial mediator; me still clowning and joking to defuse any tension. Same as it ever was.

It soon becomes clear that performing *The Lamb* set with today's technology—that's to say, with today's technology working properly—will require a huge amount of time, commitment and enthusiasm from everybody. Without as much being said, we all know that this means some kind of truce between Peter and Tony. The viability of this whole endeavor will revolve around who holds the reins and directs traffic. The potential is endless, but with rapidly evolving production technology opening up all manner of avenues, so are the pitfalls.

Equally, we all know that there can be no bickering about the ideas, but that—again reverting to long-standing type—Peter will want to explore all the creative options. Peter will therefore, unavoidably, take charge of some aspects of the operation. And with the best will in the world, there might be some resentment from some quarters at this. It won't just be the technology that will be pushed to the limits.

Then, courtesy of the management, we come up against hard economic and logistical realities: it will take months of preparation and a huge team to get this off the ground. And even if the shows are filmed and beamed around the world, the whole venture will not be financially viable if we only do four or five shows in one place.

Just as problematic is Peter's schedule, which seems to be very busy for a long time hence. He's spent thirty years trying to remind people to forget he was the singer in Genesis, and reinvent himself, a process with which he's still fully engaged.

After a couple of hours chasing lambs around the paddock, we decide to adjourn and have a think about it. Another one. Apart from it being nice to see old friends again, we've got nowhere.

As soon as Peter and his manager exit, followed by Steve's departure, Tony, Mike and I exhale and jovially wonder: "What the fuck was that all about?" We have a laugh about the five of us being incapable of doing the one thing we had all gathered in Glasgow to do: leave the room with a yes or no. So, with the benefit of the familiar, open, relaxed three-way environment we'd built over twenty years as a trio, we recognize the obvious and quietly put *The Lamb* to bed.

In fact we're so relaxed that, in short order, Tony, Mike and I decide that now we're here, why don't we three do something together?

There is a sense of unfinished business between us. After I left the band, Tony and Mike recruited a new vocalist, Scottish musician Ray Wilson (otherwise known as the frontman in grunge band Stiltskin), and made an album, *Calling All Stations* (1997). But after a tour in 1998 they decided, in 2000, to call it a day. And that seemed to be that, a rather anticlimactic end to the whole Genesis saga.

Within five minutes we have an agreement. The Banks, Collins and Rutherford-era Genesis will go back on tour one more time. And then there were three, again.

Personally, I have two key provisos. One, that this will be a sensible—that is, *short*—run of shows. Two, that I have time to fully meet my *Tarzan*-on-Broadway commitments before we restart the Genesis machine. This means not only booking the shows to commence eighteen months from now, in summer 2007, but also delaying for fully one year, to November 2006, the announcement that we're back together. That gives me a good, uninterrupted run of time to concentrate on *Tarzan*—and, most importantly, to try to bridge the widening gulf between Orianne and me.

But as *The First Final Farewell* tour ends its last lap and I face the prospect of returning to what's left of my home, I feel I'm losing, or have already lost, Orianne. I want desperately to reconnect with my wife, but whichever way I turn I find conflict, work battling real life.

Sadly, even once the tour is over, as so often in the past, work wins. When Disney tells me I have to be in New York on Boxing Day, I have no option but to agree. *Tarzan* is a huge Broadway production involving a cast of thousands, and I'm pivotal—it's a musical and it's my music. I'm barely home, and then I'm off again.

I establish myself in the Peninsula New York Hotel and, from the start of 2006, throw myself passionately into this new, third Disney project. I have to, as *Tarzan*'s opening at the Richard Rodgers Theatre has been brought forward by a couple of months. Being commissioned to write *Tarzan* on Broadway is the logical extension of writing the soundtrack to the *Tarzan* movie. But it comes with a huge amount of responsibility, way more even than with the film. It also comes with huge potential. I'm hoping that this kind of work will enable me to change my life, and help me be at home for my kids. If that's the case, the retirement of that "Phil Collins" character can continue apace. Maybe, just maybe, I can save my third marriage.

Creatively, working on a stage musical really lifts my game. I've gone from writing pop songs to writing material that's on a different plane altogether: material that's driving an entire stage production with an overwhelming number of moving parts.

I'm in the Richard Rodgers Theatre every single day. Rehearsing. Listening to the way the orchestra are playing my songs. Critiquing, giving notes, attending the recording sessions for the cast album. They all think I'm mad to be this deep, this committed.

In hindsight I should perhaps have done what Elton did on *The Lion King*: distance myself, go home and let Disney carry on with what it does best. But this is the obsessive me, who used to listen to gig tapes day after day on tour.

And what price my obsession? By early 2006 it's been made clear by Orianne that things between us are terminal.

Tony Smith brings a lawyer to New York and, one Friday, we have a short discussion about the procedures and responses should Orianne press the eject button. The following morning, just before the lawyer is due to return to Switzerland, I receive a registered letter from Orianne's legal representative, informing me that she has filed for divorce in Switzerland.

I'm dumbfounded. While I have been *contemplating* the future, she has been *deciding* it. This changes everything, so the lawyer and I have a last-minute meeting before his flight. All I'm thinking is: "Here we go again." And: "Why?"

But the fact is we've painted ourselves into corners, pride has got in the way, lawyers have become involved, the course has been set and the outcome is now . . . inevitable.

What I *should* do is get on a plane, fly to Switzerland and say to Orianne face-to-face what I tried to say to her over the phone: "*What are we doing?* I don't want to be without you. I love my children. I want this to work. What does it take? Me disappearing for six months while you try to feel good about yourself again? No problem."

But I never do. I just feel, well, that's that. There's no rationality, just resignation. Stupid bugger that I am.

And still the Disney juggernaut will not be stopped. After three months of rehearsals the *Tarzan* previews begin on March 24. They're attended by the great and the good of the New York cultural elite. As a desperate distraction to real life, I attend every single preview of "my" show. At one of these, Tom Schumacher introduces me to Dana Tyler. A news anchor on WCBS-TV's 6 p.m. newscast, she's a regular theatergoer. She also hosts a Broadway program on CBS, and the following day she interviews me for a segment.

Dana and I get on very well during the long, in-depth interview. Slowly, carefully, she and I start seeing each other. She's a lovely woman, bright-eyed and intelligent, and a grown-up from a very different world. We connect sympathetically and naturally. She helps restore my self-esteem.

I've started to dislike the person I've become, so when we start dating I ask her to call me Philip. Why don't I like "Phil Collins"? Because his life is a mess. He's a guy who's going through another divorce—a third one—and who's about to have a third broken family on his hands. After losing Joely and Simon in a separation, then Lily, he's about to lose Nicholas and Mathew.

I start to wonder what, or who, I am. If I give myself another name, another identity, I can most definitely write myself out of the script. I'm Philip, a new man.

Being with Dana hastens that feeling. As time goes on, after the boys have made a couple of trips to New York, I see that she's great with them. Joely, Lily and Simon all bond with her. My mum, my brother, my sister all come to love her. She's easy to be with. We even start playing golf together.

IN NOVEMBER 2006, six months after *Tarzan* opens, I fly to London to join Mike and Tony for the press conference announcing the European leg of summer 2007's *Turn It On Again* tour.

Things are slowly looking up. I have a show on Broadway and, professionally and personally, both Phil and Philip Collins are surfacing from the funk. Without doubt I'm still missing Orianne, and I ache for the boys, but I'm trying to move on. She's made it clear I have to.

Genesis gather in New York for rehearsals, and then later in Geneva. It's good fun, though not without its inherent problems. We're an odd bunch inasmuch as we never seem to be able to remember how the music goes. It's a lovely, honest "school band" attitude. Luckily, our long-serving guitarist Daryl Stuermer is usually on hand to help us with this sixth-form floundering as we look for the right notes and words. A rusty Genesis sounded oddly amateur when we started rehearsing for anything, but now, with a decade, a host of projects and two and a half divorces under the bridge, I find myself struggling to remember parts from songs written in the seventies. A lot of words, and another life, it seems. But being back with these old friends is a great reminder of why it was so much fun for all those years.

I attend these rehearsals to do what I need to do: get the words right, get my singing right. Tony and Mike, meanwhile, are grappling with the stage presentation—the great production artist and longtime collaborator Patrick Woodroffe is doing the lighting design, while acclaimed stage designer Mark Fisher is in charge of the sets. But I'm not engaged with, or distracted by, that side of things, much to the occasional visible annoyance of Tony Banks.

While this was always my stance with Genesis back in the day, now, I'll admit, there's an added underlying message to my semi-detachment. Yes, this is a reunion tour, but it's not a full-blooded comeback. I suspect that everyone else involved was hoping that, in the eighteen months between our Glasgow summit and the start of the tour, a new album might have been completed. But that's not been something I've been prepared to even contemplate. I adamantly do not want that. I've had enough on my hands, with the launch of a Broadway musical and the collapse of a marriage.

Fundamentally, too, we don't need to do an album to turn it on again. That would be a retrogressive step. I'm not rejoining Genesis. I'm saying goodbye. Hello, we really must be going.

In March 2007 the three of us pitch up in New York for another press conference. This one announces the North American leg of the tour, which will begin in Toronto in September. It's six weeks (a "month" in Tony Smith world) of venues with the words "Field," "Arena," "Stadium" or "Garden" in their names. Our plea to keep it simple and play theaters has long been booted into the long grass by agent Giddings and manager Smith.

Turn It On Again: The Tour starts in Finland on June 11, 2007. The first leg is twenty-three shows, including two in one day in the U.K., and climaxes a little over a month later with a massive free show in Rome's Circus Maximus.

From the off there's an amazing turnout and the audience reaction is fantastic. Europe's stadiums are full of young people who wouldn't have been born even when I took over the singing, and they're all very into it. The rain that seems to follow us all over the continent that month can't dampen their spirits.

It's my first time in a few places, most notably Katowice in Poland. There the weather is biblical, and dangerously so. The thunder and the lightning force the lighting guys down from their towers. Onstage at soundcheck we're soaked, but outside there are 40,000 Polish fans waiting to get in. We can't let them down. We play through the storm and finish with "The Carpet Crawlers," the entire drenched audience singing along with the drenched band. It's emotional, and Dana's in the audience to see Philip's old band, and their fans, at their best.

Less good: all-star charity show Live Earth. We're first on the bill at Wembley Stadium because we have to make it to Manchester for another gig that night. People are trickling through the gates when we troop on. It's a vast stage with a walkway, which is not normally the kind of thing I would use, but I gingerly feel my way out there during "Invisible Touch." I'm reminded why I retired—or tried to—from solo touring two years previously, and try to stave off a feeling of "I'm too old for this malarkey," but I'm only partly successful. The sooner it's over the better.

From the ridiculous to the sublime: that evening we're at Old

Trafford, Manchester United's theater of dreams. Manchester has always been a fantastic place to play and this is no exception.

The next day we're back in London for a show at another cathedral of sport, Twickenham, home of English rugby (also the place where a young Master Phil Collins competed as a sprinter at a long-ago athletics meeting for Nelson Infants School).

All these years later, we have a special addition to our band rider that night: wheelchair ramps. My mum, the only other person who calls me Philip, is in attendance. She's ninety-four, her eyesight is failing and she needs to be wheeled into the stadium. But she's there, as passionate a supporter of her youngest child's band as she ever was. This will be the last time Mum will see me perform. Two years later she has a stroke and will never be the same again. She tries to rally, but after more strokes she slowly starts to shut down. June Winifred Collins dies on her birthday, November 6, 2011. She's ninety-eight.

I thoroughly enjoy the whole European run. I have no collywobbles about being back as frontman, the voice holds up, I fall back in tune with the Genesis material, I enjoy being part of a band again and we all get on famously, as if we've never been apart. Exactly the way friends should be.

Orianne comes with the boys to two shows, in Paris and Hanover. Nic and Matt are both too young to have remembered *The First Final Farewell* tour, and they want to see firsthand what Dad does. After the show Orianne and I get on great, sharing a drink and enjoying the kids' excitement. Although we acknowledge that things have changed, it's nice to feel that we're still close.

And so to Rome, a fitting climax. It's something special to feel you're playing on ancient *territoire*. This is Circus Maximus, where entertainers lived in fear of the imperial thumbs-down millennia ago. Taking no chances, I've prepared all my Italian patter. But once I'm out there in front of half a million people, I realize that all the fans down the front are from Brazil, England, Germany—anywhere but Italy. But ultimately we get the thumbs-up, and these grizzled gladiators live to fight another day.

After a seven-week break, *Turn It On Again: The Tour* picks up in Canada. And then, after six weeks of outsized venues across North America, we finish in Los Angeles on October 12 and 13, 2007, with two nights at the Hollywood Bowl. It never rains in LA, but it rains for us.

The first night feels wholly average—I was never convinced a bowl designed for symphony shows was the right venue for Genesis—but the second night is much better. A good thing: we're all aware of the magnitude of this show. Everyone connected with Genesis is there— all the kids, the families, the crews. I'm thoroughly moved.

At the encore of "The Carpet Crawlers," with the audience as my witnesses, I tell Tony Banks and Mike Rutherford that I love them. These men know me better than anyone in the world and they understand what I'm really saying: this is it, no more. The end of the road. There's no more Genesis for me.

To be honest, rather than yet another big North American run, I would have preferred to have played Australia, South America and the Far East. But now my allotted time is up. At last I've come to the cast-iron conclusion that my personal life means more to me than any of that. A month and a half away from my young boys has been enough to shut that door and throw away the key.

My resolve is unshaken even after receiving some unwelcome news in the middle of the European leg: *Tarzan* will be closing after only fifteen months. Ticket sales have been healthy but not healthy enough to sustain an expensive show in the hyper-competitive Broadway market. Obviously I feel disappointed by this news, especially as I can't say goodbye properly to my baby. I'm stuck out on tour somewhere while all the cast gather in tears backstage in New York.

Ironically—bitterly, even—it closes on July 8, 2007, the night Genesis play Twickenham. A night of two halves.

Right up until the end, though, I feel pressure to change my mind about calling a halt. In managerial terms, Genesis haven't "maximized" the possibilities. My resentment at this is there in the reunion tour documentary, *When in Rome*. John Giddings and Tony Smith can't help but try to do their job. But if the agents and managers and promoters had anything to do with it, I'd still be out there now. So if I'm not firm, I know what this would lead to. It would become three, four, five months, then an album. It's why the documentary cameras catch me firmly standing my ground: "Don't fuck with me, John."

My name is Philip Collins and I will not be fucked with. Not by other people, anyway. Unfortunately, my body has other ideas.

SOMEWHERE DURING THE tour I develop a problem with my left arm. It gets to the point where I can barely hold the sticks for "Los Endos," the final song in the set on which I play drums. I try heavier sticks, and I try bigger cymbals. During the American leg I visit a few different medical professionals. I even go to see a faith healer. In Montreal, our long-serving promoter Donald K. Donald suggests seeing a massage therapist who's helped him through back surgery. I'll try anything to combat the numbness in my fingers and restore the strength in my hands.

But all to no avail: I can't produce the usual power.

After the tour, I stick to Collins family tradition: I do nothing about this health problem. It's bound to just go away.

It doesn't. It gets worse.

Back in Switzerland I go to my local clinic for an MRI. It takes the radiologist no time at all to see that the vertebrae at the top of my spine are in terrible condition. More than fifty years of drumming has worn away the calcium and crumbled the bone. If the diagnosis was alarming, the prognosis is horrifying: if I don't have an operation forthwith, paralysis and a wheelchair are on the cards.

In the Clinique de Genolier, I go under the knife. The surgeons slice open my neck below my left ear, root around for the crumbling vertebrae and screw them together with man-made calcium.

I recuperate, for a year. But after a year the fingers on my left hand are still numb. Forget holding a drumstick—I can't hold a bread knife. As a left-hander, I quickly come to appreciate how much I rely on my good hand. I go back to my local doctor, based at the Clinique, Dr. Sylviane L'Oizeau, a lovely lady who will go on to help me enormously, in various, life-affirming—not to mention lifesaving—ways. She sends me to Lausanne, to another specialist. Lo and behold, a new diagnosis. The problem is not in my neck, it's to do with the inside of my left elbow, where there's a misplaced nerve. It's been squeezed out of position, so in early 2008 I undergo two operations as the surgeon tries to re-lay the nerve. This time the inside of my arm is sliced open, followed by my left palm.

More recuperation. This is the longest I've ever not played drums since I was twelve. I know you have to get back on the horse, but I'm not sure the horse is happy at the prospect.

The years 2008 and 2009 are the best of times and the worst of times. I've bought a new home in Féchy, a village fifteen minutes from our old family home in Begnins. It's a comfortable, modest place and, as I'm on my own, all I need. With nightly work commitments, Dana is stuck in New York most of the time. She visits whenever she can, but unfortunately these trips are few and far between.

I see a lot of Nic and Matt, and relations with Orianne are cordial. Even if my days as a husband are over, my days as a hands-on dad have, really for the first time in my life, just begun.

On the downside, the recuperation from the neck, arm and hand surgeries is taking considerably longer than I, or any of the medical specialists, expected. If I had any lingering doubts about the wisdom of shutting up shop professionally, my body is making its feelings clear. It's waving the white flag.

I put my feet up.

Now another flag goes up, a red one. Tony Smith wants to know how I am. He's my manager, but he's also my friend. He wants to make sure I'm not slowing down to a complete and terminal halt in Switzerland. As soon as I said I was relocating there, I think it put him on high alert. Even though he knew I was really happy with Orianne, he feared Europe's most neutral country was going to kill my creativity stone-dead. He wasn't *completely* wrong and, to compound matters, now I'm on my own. But I'm not about to move. The boys are here, so I'm here.

"What are you doing?" Tony will say on the phone.

"I'm doing nothing. I'm flopped on the sofa, watching cricket."

I feel I deserve this, not least because my body is obviously demanding a rest. I *will* take this lying down.

So Tony plays his joker. "Why don't you do a covers album?"

As my very clever manager knows, this is something I've always wanted to do. The music of my youth, the stuff that set me on this path fifty years previously, still thrills and courses through me. So I suggest something along these lines: my interpretations of, and tribute to, the sixties standards that turned me on to soul and R&B, and that I loved when The Action peppered their set with their energetic, Mod-leaning versions. If this is to be my swan song as a recording artist—and I very much feel it will be—what better than to finish back where it all started? At the end of my music career, I'm digging back into my musical beginnings. I'll call this album *Going Back*, to underline the idea but also in tribute to the great Carole King and Gerry Goffin song "Goin' Back," which is one of the classics on my hit list.

Yes, it's nostalgia, a chance to do what I was trying to do with my school band, but—finally—do it properly. And it's nostalgia that makes me feel very much alive.

I'm quickly ears-deep in the project. I listen intently to hundreds of Motown tunes, and compile a longlist of songs to record: Stevie Wonder's "Uptight (Everything's Alright)," Martha Reeves & The Vandellas' "Jimmy Mack" and "Heatwave," The Temptations' "Papa Was a Rolling Stone." I'm determined to do justice to this cornerstone canon of American music by reproducing as best I can all the sounds—and doing so in my home studio.

It takes no time for me to realize that that's a skyscrapingly tall order. Even if my drumming and physical capabilities were fully up to speed—and they're patently not—I need some proper players to help me honor those brilliant original recordings. Amazingly, thrillingly, Bob Babbitt, Eddie Willis and Ray Monette—three of The Funk Brothers, players on so many of the Motown 45s I'd collected in my teens—agree to join me.

The recording sessions are a total joy. I work with an amazing engineer, Yvan Bing, and we have fun replicating those tracks. It's a reminder of a simpler, purer time. It's the authentic sound I'm seeking. I'm looking for the particular fill on "Dancing in the Street," that specific groove in "Standing in the Shadows of Love." There were three great Motown drummers, and I want to emulate all of them. Benny Benjamin, Uriel Jones and Richard "Pistol" Allen were jazz drummers, and if you're a drummer you can hear that each of them has a different *thing*. I want to be able to honor them all. I realize I just skimmed the surface with "You Can't Hurry Love." I want people to know that *this* is how Phil Collins does Motown. Because he knows it and loves it.

Of course the irony is that, when it comes to performing that drumming, I can't even hold a stick in my left hand. That's how weak I am. So I strap a stick to my hand with tape. Obviously that's not ideal. Fortunately, apart from each individual guy's trademark fills, the parts are pretty basic, which is an element of their ageless charm.

Working methodically through 2009, we eventually recorded twenty-nine songs. With the album more or less completed by early 2010, in March I'm back with Genesis. Just when I thought I was out, they pull me back in.

The band are being inducted into the Rock and Roll Hall of Fame in New York. Mike, Tony, Steve and I all fly in, but there's no Peter; he's busy with tour rehearsals in the U.K. We're not protesting too much when I say none of us are overly bothered by his absence. We've long become used to the fact that his schedule is what it is.

Also, he's done me a bit of a favor. With Peter unavoidably detained elsewhere, that stops dead any suggestion that the "re-formed" Genesis might perform at the ceremony. As my recuperation is limping slowly on, me drumming in public with a stick taped to my hand is surely not a good look.

Three months later I'm back in New York to collect another gong: the annual Johnny Mercer Award at the 2010 Songwriters Hall of Fame gala. I'm thrilled to bits, especially as songwriting is a craft I learnt relatively late in life. I'm also surprised: I'm not joking when I tell the BBC on the red carpet that when I got the call requesting my attendance, I thought they wanted me to present the award, not receive it. I'm still not sure I'm worthy, and there aren't many clubs I'd want to join that would have me as a member, but I'll gladly join this songwriters' guild.

Those two validations come just in the nick of time, because a couple of days after the Songwriters Hall of Fame event, I'm in Phila-delphia to begin a series of shows in support of the upcoming *Going Back*. It's a short run, only seven gigs (Philadelphia, New York, Lon-don, the Montreux Jazz Festival), but it's still too long. These shows should be wonderful, but my head isn't where it should be. To make matters worse, once I'm onstage, I inexplicably have trouble remem-bering all the words to these songs that I grew up with.

I try not to let that experience cloud my enjoyment of the album. *Going Back* is a personal, intimate and honest portrait of the fifty-nine-year-old artist as a young man. The cover art says as much: it's a photograph of me, aged twelve or thirteen, dressed in nice shirt and tie, sitting in our front room at 453 Hanworth Road behind my Stratford drum kit.

Two months after the shows, in September 2010, *Going Back* is released. My eighth solo album goes to number 1 in the U.K., mak-ing it my first chart-topping album of new material since *Both Sides* seventeen years previously. Collins is back! Not that he really wants to be "back."

Going Back, the tribute album I always wanted to make, is a full stop. My contract with Atlantic in America is up. I don't feel much kinship with the label anyway. With Ahmet gone, the place feels very different. Any personal connections between Atlantic and my solo career or Genesis have been whittled away by a succession of hired-then-fired executives. This, I realize, is the modern state of the record business. It's not a world that I relate to anymore.

Unfortunately, the other world that I thought I might be a part of isn't showing me huge love. The *Tarzan* musical hasn't led to a flurry of new commissions from the theatrical world.

All things considered, by the tail end of 2010, I'm starting to think that finally, this dog has had his day. My life onstage has pe-tered out with the underwhelming *Going Back* shows. But I can live with that. Just about.

I decide to give performing one last shot. My left arm and hand still aren't fully match-fit, but I tentatively step back into the ring. I'm asked to play with Eric at a Prince's Trust gala concert in Lon-don that's booked for November 17, 2010. I'm not sure I'm ready.

But my association with Eric goes back a long way, and with The Prince's Trust even farther. I can't say no.

But as soon as I sit down at the kit to play, I know it's a mistake. We're only doing one song together, "Crossroads," but it's one song too many. I have no feel. I think, "I'll never drum again."

So that's it. I've left my band. Drumming's left me. My glittering Broadway future isn't looking quite so glittering. Third time unlucky, my marriage is over. My girlfriend is stuck in New York. My life is empty.

What will I fill it with?

I know. I'll have a drink.

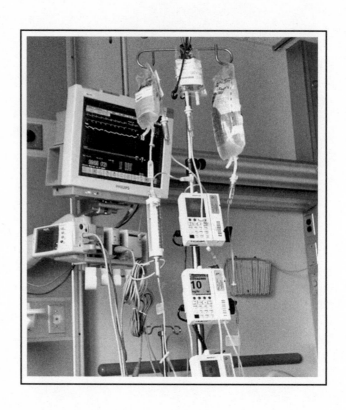

21

STRAITJACKET REQUIRED

Or: how I nearly drink myself to death

HAVE A HOLE, a void: where there used to be work there is now time. A lot of time. Stopping work so I can be with the boys will ultimately prove completely useless and destructive. It won't just upend my life. It will nearly end my life.

But let's not get ahead of ourselves.

The beginning of 2006 finds me alone at the Peninsula New York Hotel, working on *Tarzan* the musical. I'll be there, alone, for close to six months. Orianne and the boys are back in Switzerland. I go home, but I don't go home enough.

If I don't talk to the boys every day, I get edgy. I'm worrying, "Oh my God, what must they be thinking?" Of course it's difficult to get two words out of them when we do speak.

"How's school?"

"Fine."

The older ones also need me to talk to them. "I know I'm nearly an adult, Dad," Lily once said to me, "but I still need you to tell me you love me."

Why don't I go home? It's a good question. I think I'm so fucking obligated to the work in hand that I don't see the wood for the trees. Not for nothing are there endless phone arguments with Orianne.

When I do next go home to Switzerland, it's to walk out of the courtroom in Nyon a single man. I'm immediately thinking that thought again: "My God. Nicholas and Mathew are at school and nursery right now. And they have no idea that their lives have changed." I can't stop that thought. Nic's four; he knows his mum and dad have been arguing a bit. But that's it.

I feel terrible. What can I do? Confused, despairing divorcé that I am, orphaned for the third time from my kids, I channel myself. I dive into the Disney work, and I dive into the Bar Centrale, on 46th Street, a quick walk from the Richard Rodgers Theatre. It's a theatrical people's bar; you have to book. But our producer, and Disney Theatrical Group president, Tom Schumacher, always has a table. So I develop a daily routine. I walk from the Peninsula to the Richard Rodgers every morning; then I walk to Bar Centrale every night.

I also start to bury myself in the minibar, a little nightcap or three after an evening in Centrale. Occasionally I see the minibar man, filling 'er up. He says, "You *really* like vodka!" I don't particularly; right now I really like any alcohol, anything that'll numb the pain. I work my way through the miniatures, then the half-bottles, then the whole lot is gone. Well, I leave the Scotch. I don't drink everything. I'm thirsty, but I'm not that thirsty. Not yet.

But when you're drinking the miniatures straight from the neck, standing by the fridge, that's dangerous. Why dirty a glass? No mixer required. But at least I'm not buying carry-outs. That comes later, when I'm living in my apartment in New York.

The weekends when I'm not working I have what I call, in honor of Billy Wilder's great 1954 movie, the Ray Milland Lost Weekends. I drink, I sleep, I wait for the minibar to be restocked. Even when I am working I'll sometimes have a drink before I go to rehearsals. Poached eggs with a side order of vodka, straight from the bottle, at 10 a.m.

To be clear: I never indulge on the job. I'm professional, so drinking while working is off the menu. But that just means I have to drink with ever more vigor when I'm off the job.

The scary thing is my tolerance has gone through the roof. The vodka isn't touching the sides. How many do I have to drink before I feel something? No one knows, not even Danny Gillen, still by my side, still picking up the pieces and still looking out for me.

Danny tries: "Are you sure you want another one?" But he can only act when he sees me drinking. The difficulty for everyone is that I'm doing this in private. It's what Robin Williams said about his cocaine days. He didn't find it a social drug—he went home and did it, when it was just him. And that's what I do with drink.

Some people get morbid when they drink, miserable, aggressive, punchy. Not me. I just get happy. But the truth is: *I'm crying on the inside.* The cliché is true: I'm literally drowning my sorrows. Drink doesn't make me feel better. But it does make me sleep. And if I'm sleeping, I'm not thinking. That's what the lost weekends are all about. I'll drink, and that'll knock me out for the forty-eight hours until it's time to return to the sanctuary of work. I'm flooding the void in my brain and the hole in my life with booze.

After six months in the Peninsula New York—by which time I could have bought the place with my bar bill alone—and after *Tarzan* is up and running, I move back to Switzerland.

I don't have a home, so I stay in a hotel in Geneva, or in various hotels in Nyon. Day after day I try to remain part of the boys' lives, but often as not this boils down to simply ferrying them to and from school. And night after night I find myself lying on the bed, staring out of a skylight at gray Swiss skies, rueing my life. I'm all alone, save for my good friends Johnnie Walker and Grey Goose. "You've got everything," I think, "but you've really got fuck-all."

My mind is whirring, obsessed with an old, familiar scenario: *what do my kids think about when the lights go out at night?*

Eventually, in November 2008, I buy the small house in Féchy, fifteen minutes' drive from the boys. But for the first time in forty-five years, the days are long and empty. I bat away concerned calls from Tony Smith, who's keen to know what else I'm doing apart from lying on the couch, watching sport on TV and putting away bottles of wine. It's not quite the retirement I imagined, but it'll have to do.

That's not to say I'm endlessly sozzled. Life settles down, I have to pick up the boys after school and they stay with me for long weekends or holidays. So I still have that responsibility—I have to drive. And if I do step over the line, they're collected by Lindsey Evans. She's our tireless longtime nanny, although I don't think she expected to be nannying three boys.

And that, for the next few years, becomes my gig, a low-flying alcoholiday interspersed with only the occasional professional distraction and trips to New York to see Dana. In anticipation of more Broadway work, I've bought an apartment on Central Park West and we spend a lot of time there, or are out seeing new shows or having dinner. I never make it a secret that Orianne and I shouldn't have got divorced, a fact Dana seems to understand.

Then, out of the blue, in May 2012, Orianne announces that she's moving to America. She has a new husband and they want to start over. They're thinking Los Angeles. I'm thinking, "Hang on a fucking minute."

I say, "You're not going to Los Angeles. I'm not doing that all over again, a ten-hour plane flight to see my kids." Orianne knows as well as anyone I've already endured enforced separation of that distance (Joely and Simon were taken to Vancouver, Lily to Los Angeles) twice over.

I say, "I will fight you on this."

But Orianne goes through the divorce documents and says, "The lawyers say you can't."

So they decide to go and, "luckily," they choose Miami. It's at the bottom of North America, but on the "right" (European) side at least. Small mercies and all that.

It's summer 2012 and the kids are still in Switzerland, just. I'm suffering from severe stomach pains and am taken to the Clinique de Genolier. Dr. Loizeau's conclusion is swift and firm: due to my drinking I have acute pancreatitis and I need to go to the University Hospital of Lausanne immediately. I need to dry out, to detox, and this is a facility that is better equipped to cope with someone in my condition.

That "condition" is clearly of some concern to the medical professionals: they want me in the intensive care unit in Lausanne as quickly as possible, so they ferry me by ambulance helicopter. I stay there for what seems like an eternity. It's probably two or three weeks. Time drags when you haven't got a drink at hand.

This is not rehab, technically speaking (and when you're a serious drinker, you become expert in such nuances—"I've only had the one drink . . ."). But at the urging of Lindsey, Dana and Tony, I am looking at rehab facilities, albeit with not much enthusiasm. I don't need to go to rehab. I can just stop. And I do stop—a few times. I become very good at stopping. But I become even better at starting again.

In the University Hospital intensive care unit I'm wired up to an array of blinking, beeping machines. But even the best tech in town might not be enough: my pancreas is on the verge of shutting down and I am, it seems, close to dying.

Intensive care is truly awful. I'm having terrible dreams because of the very heavy medication. I can't move because I have wires and cables snaking from my nose, neck and penis—I'm on a catheter. I don't have a colostomy bag, thank God, but I have to, shall we say, work all that out. So going to the toilet is traumatic, the mortification of my public humiliation—I'm in intensive care, but not in my own room—mingling with the pain and fiddly horror of dragging behind me a spaghetti of tubing dangling from nearly every orifice.

But none of that is the worst. The worst is the fact that I'm trapped and strapped in this hospital when Nic and Matt depart Switzerland for a new life in Miami. I don't even get to say goodbye. For one thing, they have to leave home at 4 a.m. to make the flight connections. For another, Orianne, quite rightly, says, "You're not seeing the kids in this state."

My sons leave the country—emigrate—and their dad doesn't even get to say goodbye.

My heart and soul are racked with pain and guilt, but at least I'm not in actual pain: I'm up to my eyes on morphine. Please, Nurse, can I have some more?

"Are you in pain?"

"Ah, a little bit."

"OK, then."

One night, pumped full of opiates and completely wired (up), I try to rip the whole lot out. Alarms ring and in rush the nurses. I'm given a stern telling-off. Little wonder—it seems these cables and wires are keeping me going; they're literally plugging me into life's back-up generator.

I've gone from being stupefied with drink to stupefied with drugs and, unknown to me, I'm in so deep that various medical professionals are taking Lindsey gently but urgently by the elbow and asking her, "Is the will of Monsieur Collins in order?"

Two weeks pass. I say to the head doctor, Professor Berger, "Can I please go back to Genolier today?" She says no, maybe tomorrow. I'm desperate to get out. I'm on a ward where there are motorbike accident victims coming in on a Saturday night. There's only a curtain separating us and I can hear the moaning and the groaning, so I know the guy a few feet away is in a bloody mess. My dreams are already bad enough.

Throughout all this, mercifully, Dana has been a constant presence at the hospital. She's managed, via a sympathetic boss, to get some compassionate leave. She's there when I wake up, and there when I go to sleep. That helps, a bit.

Eventually I'm discharged and I start to have something like a relatively normal life. I'm on various medications—for hypertension, my pancreas, my heart. And against all medical advice, non-medical advice and sanity, I start to drink again—slowly. Slowly *at first*. What else am I going to do? My family have left me and I'm rattling around in Féchy, pretty much on my own. Dana will come and stay for a few days, Lindsey comes by, even though, with the boys gone, there's no reason for her to come. I know what she's doing. She's making sure I'm not dead.

With the boys now in Miami, I have to start visiting. That's when a particularly turbulent flight happens. Having hit rock-bottom, I'm about to go sky-high.

LINDSEY, DANNY AND I are scheduled to fly to the U.S.—Swiss International Air Lines to New York—then to travel by private plane from New York to Miami. Lindsey arrives in Féchy to take me to Geneva airport.

"Are you all right?" she asks.

"Sure I am!" I'm definitely all right, because I've got up and I've finished a drink from yesterday. I have no qualms about, first thing in the day, going to the freezer, getting a bottle of vodka, having a couple of sips—*oof!*—and carrying on.

We're booked on a midday flight, so we're in the Swiss lounge at around 10 a.m. Lindsey and Danny have both started to become the police. But I know the location of everything—by "everything" I mean the complimentary booze—and I know what I have to do, and how quickly I need to do it. While they're getting coffees, I make a break for it. Quick drink. Then another one. Standing by the fridge, I neck the vodka. They can't see me, there's no evidence.

This is where it gets a bit seedy, if it hasn't already reached that level. The new boss of Swiss comes in to meet me. *Apparently* I have my legs swung over the side of the lounge chair. Certainly I don't get up and say "pleased to meet you" and make small talk, which is what I would normally have done. I'm just uncharacteristically brusque, and everyone is very embarrassed.

The Swiss boss leaves. We get on the plane. "Glass of champagne, Monsieur Collins?"

"Yeah, all right."

Now, I am not drunk. *I promise you I am not drunk.* But according to the account Lindsey later gives me, I won't pull my seat forward for take-off. I point-blank refuse. Even before we leave the gate, the captain is looming over me. I'm oblivious, but he's been alerted by the obvious disturbance. Do we need medical assistance? Lindsey and Danny, true to form, cover for me by blaming a dodgy knee. It's the medication, honest, Captain.

They have to fasten the seat belt for me, and be content that in a few minutes we'll all be putting our seats back. This dynamic duo then have to spend the duration of the eight-hour transatlantic flight standing watch, making sure they don't lose me.

I have no recollection of any of that flight, not the take-off, not the landing, not the eight hours in between.

It gets better.

When we land in New York, I'm taken off in a wheelchair. Because for some reason, I don't understand why, I can barely be woken and I certainly can't walk. Nicoletta, the lovely Romanian lady who greets the first-class passengers, wheels me into the lounge where we make the connection for the private plane to Miami. Another journey of which I have no recollection.

By now I'm more than a little bolshy . . . *apparently* (in actual fact, I later learn, I'm awful). We arrive in Miami and check into the W Hotel. Clearly phone calls have been made, because word has reached Orianne. She appears at the hotel, scared out of her mind, with Nic and Matt. She's meant to be dropping the boys off for this lovely weekend we have planned. Dana has been alerted, too, and is whizzing her way south from New York to join the party.

Me? I'm very lively. I'm saying, "What's the problem?"

By now I'm in my room. A W hotel room has a kitchen, and in that kitchen there's whiskey. So I've opened the whiskey, had a few drinks. And this goes to show the tolerance I've developed. I've been on the go—on the booze—since before I left Switzerland. About eighteen hours.

Orianne's husband turns up to take the boys back. They're confused. "What are we doing? Where are we going? Daddy's here!"

In the time it takes for my boys to be taken away by their stepdad and for Francesca, a doctor friend of Orianne's, to turn up, I've gone into the bathroom, taken off my shoes, slid on my socks and the shower towel and hit the floor with an almighty thump.

I stagger out of the bathroom and Francesca orders me to sit down. I go to lie on my bed but I'm in too much pain. She says, "We're going to have to take you to the hospital." Turns out I've broken a rib. And the broken rib has punctured a lung.

I'm still protesting. "There's nothing wrong with me! I've come to see my kids!" But the doctor is persisting. And I'm spinning—even for a drinker of my heavy experience, this behavior is not my handwriting. I'm starting to wonder about the combination of my medication (which includes Klonopin, a powerful tranquilizer) and the alcohol.

Suddenly there are two burly guys in my room.

"I'm not going to hospital."

"Yes you are. These guys are gonna help you."

I'm thinking, "Nurse Ratched."

So they "help" me, almost kicking and screaming, to the wheel-chair. They take me downstairs. Lindsey is close behind. This is her worst nightmare.

Down in the lobby of the W, the manager who had been so nice and solicitous to me when I arrived is now looking rather anxious. "Are you all right, Mr. Collins?" But what she's really saying is: "Don't die here, please."

Dana has arrived from New York by this point, so she hears me saying, "I want to be with my mum." My mum died in November the previous year.

I'm carted off to Mount Sinai Hospital and propelled to my room. There's another burly guy sitting there already. I say, "You can go now. I'm fine."

"Oh no, I'm here for the night."

"What, when I go to the toilet, when I fart, you're here? I don't need you."

But I look on my wrist and see a bracelet: "Dangerous." Might-jump-out-of-a-window dangerous. He's there with his flashlight and his book, to stop me from doing harm to myself, or to anyone else.

The next day I'm ready to get out of there. I have a meeting with the doctor. She says, "I can only let you go if you check yourself into rehab somewhere."

I say, "I don't think I can do that."

I go back to the W Hotel, where somehow I'm still welcome. Dana and Lindsey are both there, and both crying. They can't go on like this. They tell me I can't go on like this. The boys are worried, too.

In Switzerland they had seen me drinking. Once Nicholas had wisely suggested to Lindsey, "I think we have to stop buying drink for Daddy." A gut-wrenching thing for Lindsey to hear from a ten-year-old boy, and an awful image for his dad to process.

They'd also seen me falling over at home in Féchy. Not falling over drunk. It was, again, the lethal combination of Klonopin and alcohol affecting my balance. I got up to give them a hug. *Bang*. My teeth went into the tiles in the living-room floor. There's still a mark there, and my teeth are still chipped. The bloody lip's long healed, but what hasn't healed is the memory of Mathew shouting, "Lindsey! LaLa! LaLa! Daddy's fallen over!"

So by now, in Miami, I'm getting pressure from all sides to go into rehab. But I dig in my heels. I want to do this on my own. I *can* do this on my own.

They keep at it. Tony Smith is now involved. He says he's been in touch with a woman called Claire Clarke, who runs a clinic, Clouds House, in Wiltshire. Will I call her?

I say I will, but I'm not promising anything.

"Hello, Phil," she says. She's a nice lady and an experienced professional well used to addicts and recovering addicts. Eric had been a resident at Clouds, as had Robbie Williams. But it's no "celebrity" rehab. She explains that people tend to view it as a boarding school.

"Can I leave if I want to?"

"Yes, you can."

Lindsey again says, "I can't stand it anymore. I'm not walking in one day and you're lying there, dead." Dana adds, "You're gonna kill yourself."

That persuades me. The next day I call Claire back. "OK."

I fly on a private plane from Miami to Bournemouth, not the most heavily trafficked flight path. On the plane I have a lie-down. But first I say to Dana, "Can I have a last drink?" "Yes." So I have a ceremonial glass of wine. I think we all do, as we finally have something to celebrate. Well, we think we do.

I get off the plane and am driven to Clouds. Our driver, David Lane, who's known me for donkey's years, is surprised. He's never seen me drink at all. "Eh? Where are they taking Phil?" he seems to say to himself. Just another person in my world for whom all this is a sense-scrambling shock.

At Clouds, new arrivals' escorts stay in a holding area while you're shown around. Again, as I meet the inmates, I'm reminded of *One Flew Over the Cuckoo's Nest*.

"And this, Phil, will be your room."

"Haven't I got my own room? I don't want to be with Billy Bib-bit."

"Well, we can work that out."

"I want my own room," I press. "I don't want to be stuck in a room with another loony."

I return to the holding area and say, with a shrug, that I'll stay. Lindsey and Dana breathe out. Everyone is crying. "Are you sure you're gonna be all right, Phil?"

"I guess . . ." But I'm not sure.

The nurse takes my bags and starts going through them. "Don't care who you are. We're searching them."

"Why? You think I've smuggled in booze? I haven't brought any-thing in."

They remove all my prescription pills. They're going to give them to Clouds' clinicians, who will prescribe something "more medically appropriate." Everything else goes in a locked cupboard. My sense of incarceration is mounting.

I'm shown to my room, in which there's another bed.

"Don't put anyone else in that," I growl.

"OK, we'll be OK for a couple of weeks like that."

"Well, how long have I got to be here?"

"Four weeks," they say. "Or six weeks."

I don't know if I can take that.

Because I have medical issues—the pancreatitis, the rib—as well as alcohol issues, they put me next door to the medical bay. Unfor-tunately, in this old house (and boarding school isn't far off it) the medical bay is where everyone queues at 6 a.m. for their morning meds—and queues again at 11 p.m. to get their night meds. So I can never go to sleep before eleven, and am always woken up at six. On top of that, whenever anyone goes outside after dinner for a smoke, they congregate right below my room.

The reasons to hate this place—to hate myself for putting myself in this place—are piling up. But at least I have some smuggled-in help. I've brought some sleeping pills—mild homeopathic ones—and I have a phone. They took the iPhone, but I managed to keep secret my old Sony Ericsson. I have to charge it very discreetly, so I can call the kids every day. Still trying to be a good dad, even from behind bars.

I do the morning prayers, where everyone has to say something revealing/honest/self-lacerating. I don't have any problems with this kind of group-therapy stuff, but it's weird the people you meet, from hard nuts to housewives.

At breakfast, lunch and dinner we tend to sit at the same tables with the same group. There's a lovely lady called Louise, who's a worn late forties. Her husband has sent her here, threatening that if she doesn't stop drinking, she won't see her daughter again. Very sad. And very close. That could be me next.

There's even a journalist from *The Sun* in here. I'm convinced that I'll be all over the front pages of the tabloids again, but he turns out to be very nice. Being here is quite a leveler.

I invite Pud and Danny to come visit. They both say, "This isn't you, is it? You haven't got this kind of problem. You can stop this. You don't need this."

I'm given homework. I have to write a story about myself, then deliver it a month in. Where do I start? "My name is Phil Collins, I've sold zillions of albums . . ." Yeah, we know that. It's a great story. Yet, in spite of being record-shifting, Oscar-winning Phil Collins, here I am in rehab, trying to deal with a drink problem. Just like everybody else.

Tony Smith calls: "Eric is going to come down and see you."

"Please tell him no. I don't want to see anybody."

After a week, I've had enough. I call Danny on my contraband phone. "Get the car and come get me." God bless Danny; he's been staying in the bed and breakfast a few miles down the road. "You'd better book a plane because I'm out of here and I'm going to Switzerland." It's *The Great Escape*.

I say to Claire, "You did say I can leave when I want to."

"Are you sure, Phil?"

"Very sure."

"OK . . . I don't know if it's that easy. But when do you want to leave?"

"Now? Tomorrow?"

As it happens, my leaving has coincided with two other inmates legitimately exiting the building. They've served their time. Me? I'm bailing because I can't stand it, and because I kid myself that I know what has to be done.

After breakfast there's a leaving ceremony for those about to re-enter the free world. Hugs, kisses, singing. I join in, but as I'm cheating, I feel squeamish. They've stuck it for six weeks. Me, only a week. But to my surprise (and comfort) they all insist that just coming in was the big step, and that I should be proud of that. I try hard to be.

The paperwork completed, I'm at the door with my bags and Danny turns up. I say goodbye as nicely as I can muster and get in the car. "Danny. Drive. As fast as you can." Now I feel like Patrick McGoohan in *The Prisoner*. This big bouncing balloon is going to catch up with us and take me back.

We drive for what seems like an age, get to the airport and I climb aboard. I've never been so happy in my life to be flying any-where. To be leaving.

IT'S NOVEMBER 2012 and I'm a week dry. No twitches. No DTs. But I guess I do have a drink, because at home in Féchy on the 15th I find myself at the bottom of my concrete stairs, all eighteen of them. The back of my head is split, there's a pool of blood and, quicker than you can hum "Smoke on the Water," I'm back in the Clinique de Genolier.

Peter Gabriel phones to check on me. Tony Smith, Tony Banks and Mike Rutherford fly in to see me. I'm very touched. I'm also very embarrassed. My bloody head wounds are leaking onto the pillow and we can all see the mess.

With some serious amends to make, I decide to take Nic and Matt away for a break, booking the four of us (lifesaver Lindsey comes too) a holiday in Turks and Caicos. My boys feel further away than ever—an abortive spell in prison-like rehab can make you feel that way—and I'm desperate to keep them as close as possible.

But unfortunately, despite all I've been through—despite all I've put them through—on this holiday I *really* go for it.

Though I need to tell this story, I don't wish to remember it. Neither do my sons. If I bring up Turks and Caicos with Nic or Matt, they say, "Don't mention that place, we're not going there ever again."

We've been there on holiday once before, for Nic's birthday the previous year, and a great time was had by all. But by this trip, my drinking has escalated again. As well as the Klonopin, I'm also on new medication for my hypertension.

We have a lovely beachfront house in Parrot Cay. Keith Richards is in residence in the adjacent property with his family, flying his "Jack Sparrow's father" pirate flag. It takes some going to live next door to Keith Richards and be classed as the rowdy neighbor. No, I'm not proud.

There's no bar on the beach where we're renting our little cottage, but no bother—the kitchen is well stocked. There are bottles of tequila, vodka, whiskey, rum.

The whiskey just disappears. I'll drink it out of sight whenever possible, but I'm not past doing it in front of the boys.

"What's that, Dad?"

"It's Daddy's drink."

I realize that I'm at a crossroads—or, more like, a dead end—as I embark on a lost weekend of catastrophic proportions. These houses have maids, and the maid has seen all these empty bottles ("You *really* like whiskey!") but I plow on, unashamed and unabashed. After the whiskey disappears, I fall asleep. Lindsey wakes me to tell me she's taking the kids out to the beach.

"Do you wanna come?"

"No, I'll stay here."

I go back to catatonic sleep, eventually waking at four. Fuck, we're leaving today! I get up, hurriedly pack my bags and stomp outside. "Hello?" I shout. "Hello, Lindsey, Nic, Matt? We need to go!" But they're nowhere to be seen. The penny drops: it's dawn. It's not four in the afternoon, it's four in the morning. And we've only been here a day.

If Lindsey was worried before, she's now wild with anxiety. She's already long been anticipating finding my lifeless corpse, but this weekend she's seeing the boys witness Daddy not being Daddy. She's frightened for me, and she's terrified for them. So later that morning she gives me an ultimatum: "Enough is enough, Phil. I'm going to have to call a doctor. Because I think you're in real trouble."

"If you really must. I'm feeling fine, though."

Lindsey's also been on the phone to Dana in New York. "He's in a terrible way," she tells Dana. "Possibly even worse than before." Then she calls Dr. Timothy Dutta in New York, who has already been giving advice to both Lindsey and Dana about how to deal with me and my apparent suicide mission.

Dr. Nurzanahwati is the doctor for the island's resort. She comes to check me over and doesn't like what she sees. I'm a danger to myself and, it seems, a liability for the resort—if something goes wrong, we're all in the dock. Or, in my case, the emergency ward. Or worse.

"Mr. Collins, your heart is racing. How were you planning on getting home?"

"We've got a private plane to take us back to Miami."

Danny can organize anything at the drop of a hat. I don't give a fuck about the money. I'll say, do anything to get another quack off my back.

Dr. Nurzanahwati says, "You need to come with me and see another doctor before I can let you leave the island."

I'm thinking, "Well, why? If I've got my own plane."

But I relent. "OK, I'll come with you."

Forty-eight hours into our holiday and it's a bust. Dr. Nurzanahwati's opinion: I am so ill that I need urgent medical attention—attention that is beyond the capabilities of the island hospital.

I tell Lindsey to go to the airport with the boys and I'll meet her there—I first have to get a certificate to allow me to fly. I accompany Dr. Nurzanahwati to this little surgery and it's clear from the tests that I have *a lot* of alcohol in my bloodstream; or, more accurately, a bit of blood in my alcoholstream.

The second doctor says, "I can't let you go."

"What are you talking about? I am gonna leave on my plane! I've got to take my kids to Miami and their mum."

I'm trapped in a catch-22 of my own making: so ill that I need medical help on the mainland, too ill to leave the island.

I see the boys and Lindsey off in a taxi, powerless to hold back my tears. They fly out, headed for Miami. I'm left behind, on my own once again, feeling more than a little fragile, topped with a whole heap of self-loathing. I don't even get a chance to see the boys before they fly, a nauseously familiar feeling.

The disconsolate little party land in Miami and make their way to Customs and Immigration. Lindsey tries to explain to Mr. Rogers, the mercifully kind immigration officer, why she is traveling with two underage boys with another surname, and with her employer's personal belongings—plus the family's pet hamster, Bobby, who has come along for the holiday.

Unbelievably, Mr. Rogers buys Lindsey's story—including the bit about Bobby not being a drug-hamster—and soon nanny, boys and pet are through Customs and Immigration and into the waiting car.

When Orianne sees them and not me, she quite rightly goes apeshit. "You're letting the boys see you this way?" she will later rant over the phone, entirely reasonably.

In the car from the airport, the still-bewildered boys have lots of questions, obviously, but they can be boiled down to this: "Why was Daddy crying, and why isn't he here?"

Meanwhile, back on Fantasy Island, the only way they're going to let me leave is on an ambulance plane or helicopter. So I'm flown straight to New York in an air ambulance. It drops me, at the request of Dr. Dutta, right on the doorstep of the New York Presbyterian Hospital on 68th Street.

Here I am put under the microscope for a couple of weeks. And here I meet Dr. Dutta in the flesh. He's a lovely man, one of the top twenty doctors in the States. I go to him for a complete 10,000 miles' service. He puts it to me straight: "Phil, there is no question, you are going to die if you don't do something about this."

I start seeing a therapist, Dr. Laurie Stevens, and an addiction specialist, Dr. Herbert Kleber—both experts in their fields. I like them and trust them. Maybe they can help me, finally, to start liking and trusting myself again.

It is January 2013. A new year and, I hope, a new me.

I'm put on heavy medication, part of a medically enforced drying-out process. I need to be made to understand how close I am to dying.

After being discharged from New York Presbyterian, I continue to see Dr. Kleber regularly.

"There is something I can give you, Phil, but I can't give it to you yet. Do you want to stop drinking?"

"Well, yeah, now I really do."

He explains how Antabuse—a drug prescribed to people with chronic alcoholism—works: it blocks an enzyme that helps metabolize alcohol, which means *very* unpleasant side effects if you do drink while on it. Basically, have a drink and you suffer an immediate brutal headache and nausea. I'll have to report to him for blood tests and, if there's no alcohol in my blood, Dr. Kleber can give me the Antabuse—but I will have to have a nurse administer it.

"Come on, you can trust me," I say.

"I trust you," he replies, possibly lying. "I don't trust the disease."

But I dig my heels in, again. "I can't." My lifestyle is not such that I can have a nurse come at eight o'clock every morning to give me the pill. I need to be able to take the Antabuse on my own. A compromise is agreed: despite my protests at being babied, Dana gives it to me every day for a month or so.

In the end, close to The End, Dr. Dutta saves my life. He makes me realize how really, actually, truly close I am to dying. My pancreas is not only scarred, it's showing signs of irreparable damage.

That's, finally, a good enough reason for me. I want to see my kids grow up, get married, have their own children. I want to live.

There have been moments of great clarity throughout this rotten period—the Genesis *Turn It On Again* tour, my *Going Back* album and shows. But not enough of them.

And after all the darkness, I do have to thank my kids, all of them. Joely, Simon, Lily, Nicholas and Mathew gave me their huge support throughout this hideous period in my life—in all our lives. For constantly saying, "Good on you, Dad," when maybe they were crying inside. Also Orianne, Dana, Lindsey, Danny, Pud, my sister Carole, my brother Clive and Tony Smith for helping a stubborn bastard to stay alive. The doctors and nurses in Switzerland, America and Britain that I pushed to the limits of their patience—I thank you all.

Telling this story now, it all sounds absolutely horrific. It took me till the age of fifty-five to become an alcoholic. I got through the heady sixties, the trippy seventies, the imperial eighties, the emotional nineties. I was retired, content, and then I fell. Because suddenly, I had too much time on my hands. The huge hole, the void, left by my kids being taken away from me, again, I had to fill somehow. And I filled it with booze. And it nearly killed me.

I'm one of the lucky ones.

22

NOT DEAD YET

*Or: back together—a band of five, a family of
four and one man's life (if not his body)*

IT'S THE MORNING after the hangover before. My lost weekend
became a lost few years, and nearly lost me my life. Now I have to
engage with some sober reflection and wonder: how did I end up like
that, alone and drowning at the bottom of a bottle?

As 2013 becomes 2014 I'm given an opportunity to consider much
of the above. Tony Smith contacts me, Tony Banks, Mike Rutherford, Peter Gabriel and Steve Hackett. The BBC wants to make a
documentary about the entire history of Genesis and all the music
we've spawned. To a man we're pleased. For all the films made about
the band over the years, this is the BBC, and the corporation confers
approval and authority, a stamp of quality that resonates around the
world.

This will be a lovely opportunity to look back on everything
we've achieved, together and apart, and to reconnect with each
other—and with ourselves. Given my recent brush with mortality,
this is perhaps more meaningful to me than to any of the other guys,
so I suggest to the director, John Edginton, that we try to do something that we've never done before. Why doesn't he interview the five
of us together in one room?

Maybe the idea sparks similar emotions in Tony, Mike, Peter and Steve, because it's quickly agreed and swiftly put into action.

In March 2014, in a big white room in a photographer's studio in Notting Hill, west London, the five of us sit down. It's the first time we've been together since our ill-starred Glasgow summit in 2005, and the first time we've ever been filmed in conversation. It's about forty-plus years since I and my fellow new boy Steve joined, and thirty-five years since Peter left, so there's some catching up to do. Yet again, it's eerie how we all revert to type—Steve still the dark one, me the comedian, etc.

With no decisions to be made, no obligations pending, the atmosphere in the studio is relaxed and jovial. Each of us takes the opportunity to say our piece. At one point Peter says, "When we got it right, we had something which none of us could do on our own."

For my part, I tell Peter something that I honestly have never previously had the opportunity to communicate directly: "A lot of people have always thought that I tried to push you out so I could become the singer. I just want you to know that that was not the case."

I don't think Peter ever thought I had been plotting with Machiavellian glee. But this seems a golden opportunity, with the cameras running, to clear up forty years of supposition and gossip about my "taking over" Genesis. Surprisingly, this confession doesn't make the final cut.

The candor goes both ways. As Tony, talking about my solo success, notes in his individual interview in the documentary: "It was great for [Phil]. He was our friend—we wanted him to do well. But you didn't want him to do that well—not initially," he says, half joking. "But . . . it kind of never went away. He was ubiquitous for about fifteen years. You couldn't get away from him. Nightmare," he shrugs, smiling. Just as meaningfully, he adds that Genesis were unique in that we were able to run the band and our individual careers in easy parallels for so long. Hence the documentary's title— *Genesis: Together and Apart.*

During a break in filming, over lunch, Tony Smith, Dana, Steve's wife Jo and the band chew over what's new in our lives, how everyone's kids are growing up, what they're doing. I'm reminded it's great to have friends like these.

There's been talk for a while of a new compilation album, and its conception reflects the lifelong, all-for-one conviviality of this meeting. For the first time ever, the best of the band is gathered alongside the best of the five solo careers. This three-CD, 37-track, near-four-hour career-spanning box set is chronologically assembled and stoutly democratic: three tracks from each of us. I mainly stay out of the conversations about which Genesis tracks will figure—I trust the other guys to carry that torch—but from my albums I pick "In the Air Tonight" (it would be rude not to), "Easy Lover" (partly because it's not on any of my studio albums) and "Wake Up Call" from *Testify* (because it's my favorite song on an overlooked album).

When it comes to what to call this package and how to dress it, it's surprising how easy it is. Although there is a little corner-taking, we've all aged gracefully and it's a process that is mainly diva-free. *The Big Tree and Its Splinters* is a suggestion, but eventually we go with an idea of Peter's, *R-Kive*, the spelling giving a little bit of a nod to "today."

R-Kive is released in September and, just before the BBC broadcast of *Together and Apart* on October 4, 2014, the five of us go to the documentary's premiere in London's Haymarket. It's a lovely, relaxed evening, in the company of a lot of old friends including Hugh Padgham and Richard MacPhail, and many more. At the screening, everyone laughs in the right places and no one takes their ball home in a huff.

At this time I'm considering my legacy in other areas, too. Sixty years since first seeing that Disney Davy Crockett film, and almost two decades after Orianne's first gift to me of an Alamo artifact, I have by now amassed quite a collection of relics and militaria related to the battle. At the suggestion of a Texas publishing house, I have even authored a book, *The Alamo and Beyond: A Collector's Journey* (2012). By some estimates, mine is the world's biggest collection in private hands, with a value somewhere in the region of $10 million.

While the monetary value means nothing to me, the historical value is of huge importance. Now, after my boozy dance-with-death, I'm more concerned than ever with what will happen to my collection after I'm gone.

So, to pre-empt any unseemly squabbling over who gets my rare Crockett musket, and just in case a sibling feud breaks out over my cherished Mexican cannonballs, I decide to donate my 200-piece collection to an appropriate museum or institution in San Antonio.

After talking to friends and experts on the ground in Texas, I agree that the best approach is for this collection to come home: I'll give everything to the Alamo itself, located in downtown San Antonio, and the Lone Star State's largest tourist attraction.

We make the public announcement on June 26, 2014, outside the Alamo, and in October I'm back there again to see the collection arrive from Switzerland. It'll be housed in a museum, the center of a $100 million makeover of the Alamo compound. I'm also granted the title of Honorary Texan on the floor of the Texas House of Representatives. The little Hounslow kid that lives inside me still can't believe that. But if you catch me talking with a Texas twang, feel free to clip me round the ear.

Meanwhile, back in the world of my former day job, all this activity—not to mention the public displays of bonhomie between my former band mates and I—have kick-started another flurry of conversation about a Genesis reunion. As ever, I'm not sure people have entirely thought this through—if the five of us did go back on the road after a forty-year absence, it would necessarily have to be the Peter-era band. This would mean playing the material we made when the five of us were together, and the blunt fact is that that material has a more limited audience. Concert-goers will get "Can-Utility and the Coastliners," and they'll get "Fountain of Salmacis," but they won't get "I Can't Dance" and "Invisible Touch."

All this said, there's a more pressing, more practical problem: I am still not up to the task of drumming. More than that: I'm not even up for the idea of performing.

I know that because, in September 2014, just before the release of R-Kive, at Tony Smith's gentle but insistent urging, I gather together a handful of core musicians in Miami. I'm going to be there anyway, visiting the boys, so I see it very much as no kind of undertaking or commitment. This will be not so much a rehearsal as a friendly thrash around. And it's as much a sop to Nic and Matt, who are desperate to see the old man go out and play some shows. So I agree to a relaxed, three-week rehearsal-room romp through the old stuff.

To bring in a bit of relatively youthful energy, I've asked Jason Bonham to play drums, and we set to working our way through some songs. Initially it all sounds good, Jason kicking some serious butt during the heavy numbers, but I soon find myself, dare I say it, distracted. I think, "Do I really need to sing 'Against All Odds' again, now?"

I'm embarrassed to report that I start to act like a sixty-three-year-old schoolboy. I bunk off early, then the next day I pull a sickie, then I skive off completely. I put keyboard player Brad Cole in charge of the band and they play without me. I'm utterly uninterested.

Unfortunately this flakiness sets off alarm bells around the world. Tony gets to hear of it back in London, and in turn Dana hears about it in New York. Understandably, they fear the worst. Before I know it, Dana is storming into my hotel room in Miami, demanding some answers. Why am I skipping rehearsals? Am I drinking again?

I'm placatory—"No, honestly, I'm not drinking"—but I'm also angry. Alerted by Tony, she's taken a day off work, hopped on a plane from New York, somehow got a key to my room and burst in, ready for confrontation and intervention. Of course she's doing this with my best interests at heart, and of course she's been through a nightmare with me over the last few years. But I don't appreciate being treated like a child.

Our relationship has become a little fractious by this point. I've been spending more and more time in Miami to be with the boys; equally, I believe she has a gnawing feeling that Orianne and I have been drawing closer together again. This certainly doesn't help things.

We're both upset, and upset leads to candor. Dana's expecting to be married by now, while I have no intention of walking down the aisle for a fourth time. Things are said that need to be said, and some tears are shed. She stays over in my hotel room, albeit at arm's length, and when I wake up in the morning, she's gone. After eight years, our relationship is over.

If my behavior, personally and professionally, is showing all the signs of semi-detachment, it could be because other attachments are throwing me off-balance, in an entirely good way. Dana's fears are not unfounded. Orianne and I are becoming close again.

Since she and the boys moved to Miami in July 2012, I've been flying there every other week, taking up regular residence at the Ritz Carlton on South Beach. For sure, some of that early contact may have been clouded with a little booze. But certainly since I've been dry, the connections and the intimacy have been steadily improving. At the same time, Orianne's marriage has been disintegrating. We often tell each other that we shouldn't have divorced, and how much we miss each other, and how much we miss being a family.

Toward the end of December 2014, Orianne flies back to Switzerland for spinal surgery to release trapped nerves. Unfortunately she has a spasm while under the knife. The result: Orianne is left totally paralyzed down her right side. She won't be leaving her bed, far less Switzerland, anytime soon. When she calls to tell me, I think she's joking.

After spending New Year's with the boys in New York as planned, I return them to Miami. Following many conversations with her husband, we agree that I should go and visit Orianne first. Arriving in Switzerland, I'm greeted by the sight of my ex-wife wheelchair-bound and a haunted shadow of her former self. We're both devastated.

I stay a week before flying back to be both mum and dad for the boys. Orianne is stuck in rehab in Switzerland until early March 2015, when she flies home at last. Both she and the kids, to say nothing of me, are relieved and happy.

But this has been a time of healing all round. Over the last few months we have been honest with each other, and spoken our true thoughts and feelings. We have made the decision: Orianne and I will reconcile, if not exactly un-divorce. When we tell Nicholas and Mathew, they're delighted. In fact, Matt says a fantastic thing: "You know, I had a wish on my tenth birthday that this would happen."

The thought that the kids were willing this to happen is very moving.

Together, we start looking at houses in Miami. My criteria are a place where Matt can have a little football pitch and Nic can have a small studio, somewhere he can rehearse with his band and refine his drumming skills.

We find the perfect place, which turns out to be Jennifer Lopez's old house (although I only find that out later when Joely tells me). In June 2015, I sign the papers and we establish a family home in Miami Beach. Now we are four, all over again. Actually, now we are five: Orianne has a son, Andrea, born in 2011, from her second marriage, and he lives with us much of the time. Complicated? With my backstory, nothing's too complicated.

It takes until early 2016 for the news to leak that I am back with my third ex-wife. Cue shock and not a little snark in the giddier corners of the international press.

Whatever, I'm back with my ex-wife and my boys, and we're all very happy campers.

THE COLLINS CLAN is a funny mob. I know how it looks, a fractured, dispersed family, presided over—in the loosest sense of the term—by three-wives Phil. But despite everything, *because of* everything, we laugh about it. Love will find a way.

I carry guilt over each of my kids. I carry guilt for everything, frankly. All the times I was away, all the moments I missed, all the periods when a tour or an album got in the way of a happy home life, or repairs to that home life. Music made me, but it also unmade me.

It won't do that again. Now I'm back being a dad to Nic and Matt, and I give thanks every time I'm on hand for a football match or a school band rehearsal or bit of homework.

But happiness begets more guilt: the happier I am with Nic and Matt, the guiltier I feel for not being there for the older ones. I wasn't there to have those same conversations, enjoy the same domestic bliss, with Joely, Simon and Lily.

We're a work-in-progress—name a family that isn't—but I think we're pretty good, considering. Joely started acting, has won many awards, and is now a producer working in TV and online. She lives in Vancouver, with her Dutch husband, Stefan, and beautiful daughter, Zoe. Born on October 26, 2009, she made me a grandfather at the ripe young age of fifty-eight. They're wonderfully happy, and an example to all.

All respect to Simon: he made it tough for himself by trying to follow the old man's line of work. He's had some trying times, personally and professionally, but he's worked hard at it. He's a fantastic drummer and as a singer he's found his voice. He's won many an accolade in the progressive rock world, and he's done brilliantly to build a fan base and find an audience. To even be able to make records, and to do so on your own terms, in the modern music industry is a huge achievement. He's a strong-headed musician who knows what he wants. Lord knows where he got that from.

Simon and I finally got to drum together in 2008 on his album *U Catastrophe*. He wrote a track for us both to play on, "The Big Bang," and I flew to Las Vegas where he was recording. It's an incredibly fast piece, slightly modeled on the Genesis drum duets, and he really put me through my paces. I barely made it. It's a thrilling track, and I think that collaboration with my oldest son may have been, without my knowing it, my last hurrah as a drummer. Which seems kinda fitting.

Lily's another credit to her parents. A teenage stint modeling became a storming acting career. At the time of writing she's filming the lead role in a new drama series, based on F. Scott Fitzgerald's *The Last Tycoon*, for Amazon. She's been in a couple of heavyweight Hollywood films, including *The Blind Side* (with Sandra Bullock), and *Mirror Mirror* (with Julia Roberts), in which she plays Snow White, and she stars opposite Warren Beatty in his new film *Rules Don't Apply*. Socially conscious and engaged, and a great public speaker, she's also involved with an anti-bullying project in LA.

Brother Clive is still drawing cartoons for a living, and has been honored internationally numerous times. He was awarded the MBE in 2011. I am deliriously proud of him.

Sister Carole is as giggly as she ever was, and has been very happily married to Bob for forty-two years. Following her long stint as a professional ice skater, she carried on Mum's job of being a theatrical agent. She featured in *Buster* as a nosy neighbor, a part she played very well (due to her acting skills, I hasten to add).

Unfortunately, my dear mum couldn't be with us tonight. After suffering her first stroke in April 2009 she'd gone downhill steadily before passing on November 6, 2011, only two years shy of her century.

I was able to spend some time with her before the end. I'd fly in from Switzerland and visit her at Barbara Speake's house in Ealing, sit by the bed, stroking her head as she fell asleep, thinking, "If only I could have done this with my dad."

The one positive thing is that Mum's condition brought Carole, Clive and I much closer together. Because of the geographical distance between us all, we'd become used to not speaking for huge lengths of time. With Mum sick, we were talking all the time and visiting her in hospital.

My mum enjoyed my career, and knew she'd done right by helping and encouraging me. But I still find it hard to deal with the fact that Dad died without seeing any of my success. Where is he, and what does he think of it all? I hope he's forgiven me for avoiding the office job at London Assurance. I hope I've made him proud.

I've been lucky, of that I have no doubt. I've had a long career, and on the whole I think the music has worn well. On the one hand, certain moments from my back catalogue are pinned to a place and time. If a TV show or film wants immediate aural shorthand to evoke the high eighties, it seems they can't go wrong with "In the Air Tonight." On the other hand, it's brilliant to hear younger artists outing themselves as fans. My approval ratings in the hip-hop community are particularly high. Being covered by Lil' Kim, Brandy, and Bone Thugs-N-Harmony is a real thrill, Kanye West called me an inspiration, and there was an entire album, *Urban Renewal* (2001), of hip-hop and R&B covers of my songs. This makes me very happy.

There seems to have been even more of an uptick recently. Pharrell Williams was asked to remix *Face Value*. His response: "Why do you want to do that? I like it the way it is." Lorde is a big fan, and so is songwriter extraordinaire and OneRepublic frontman Ryan Tedder. And then there's Adele.

Such were the depths of my Drinking Years, I managed to miss her rise. In fact, I'd not even heard of her. But when she contacted me in October 2013 with a view to writing together for her third album, I was only too happy to meet. I did a lot of homework and was totally impressed. She's a huge talent, one of the most important of this era.

In November that year, during a visit to London, she comes to see me at the Dorchester Hotel. She calls from the lobby, I tell her the room and she arrives with a security chap. Once he's established she's safe with me, she asks him to wait downstairs.

And there we are, just me and Adele. She's exactly as you'd expect: a friendly, not to mention sweary, north London girl, her down-to-earth personality entirely untouched by her being the pre-eminent artist of the day and the all-conquering savior of the music industry.

I make her a cup of tea and try to hide the shiver of nerves. I feel like I'm being auditioned, but that's my insecurity. For all I know, Adele's thinking, "Blimey, fahkin' Phil Collins is fahkin' older than I thought!" For some people my image is trapped in a particular pop video in a particular year. Let's hope it's not "You Can't Hurry Love."

She pulls out a USB stick, plugs it into my laptop and plays a piece of music, mentioning a Fleetwood Mac type of feel. It's great. And it's quite long. I'm not sure how to respond, or what's being asked of me, so I say, "I'd need to hear it again."

Adele says, "I'll send it to you and you can finish it."

I learn the piece at my piano in New York, then add some parts to it in my little studio down the road in Manhattan. After a while, I email again: "Are you waiting for me, or am I waiting for you?"

"Oh, no," comes Adele's apologetic reply, "I'm moving, I'm changing email addresses, I'm looking after the baby, etc. . . ."

I later read her saying that it was all too early in the writing and recording process for the album that would become the blockbusting 25; that she wasn't ready; that she still thinks I'm awesome. That's cool. It was a lovely little interlude and, for sure, great for my self-esteem.

Unfortunately, before I can start swaggering around town, calling myself Adele's new best mate, it's time for more medical issues.

In October 2015 I wake up in Miami with a horrendous pain down my right side, and I hobble in to see the lovely, not to mention legendary, Dr. Barth Green. You might call him the Adele of the spinal surgery world.

His considered medical opinion is that my back—not to put too fine a point on it—"is totally shot." But not to worry, Dr. Green has the technology and he can rebuild me. He hauls me into the operating theater, installs eight screws into my spine and reassures me that all should now be well.

I hobble home to recuperate, whereupon I promptly take a tumble in the bedroom and fracture my right foot. Back into hospital, back into surgery. During physical therapy, I take another fall and refracture the foot. "Interestingly," in the course of these foot-based traumas, I learn that the "sprain" I suffered after landing heavily at the end of "Domino" on the 1986 Genesis tour of Australia had actually chipped off a piece of bone. Also "interestingly," I learn that it might be the case that all those vocal cords–easing cortisone injections have combined to make my bones somewhat brittle. I could laugh, if I wasn't in so much pain.

All things considered, it seems that bits are falling off me. Am I paying the cost for all those years of drumming? Having started at the age of five, it's sixty years at the time of writing.

Exiting from hospital and recuperating, I'm finally forced to pick up a stick. Unfortunately it's a walking stick.

Ironically, this period coincides with my being required to make myself presentable for the international press. I have to start the long-lead promotion for the 2016 reissues of my solo albums. The year-long campaign is going under the title "Take a Look at Me Now," just at a time when I'd probably rather people didn't take a look at me, this limping, hobbling semi-invalid.

Still, my spirits are up in these media encounters. For the first time in what seems like forever, the interviews and the resulting published stories are garlanded with praise. It's all a bit giddy. So, whether due to my enthusiasm, or the writer's enthusiasm, or a combination of both, a news story breaks in *Rolling Stone*. "Phil Collins Plotting Comeback," runs the headline. "I Am No Longer Retired."

I am on record in the magazine as talking in some detail, viz "I got very involved in these reissues . . . I'm easily flattered. If people rediscover the old stuff and show interest, it would be silly to not make more music . . ." And then: "I don't think I want a very long tour. But I would like to play stadiums in Australia and the Far East, and that's the only way to do that. But there's a part of me that just wants to do theaters, so we'll see."

Did I really say all that? It was probably the medication talking, though it's an interesting suggestion. The man who's declaring this is a chap with a limp who can barely walk, far less rock. Rumors of my comeback may have been exaggerated, not least by me.

At home in the U.K., even BBC Radio 4's very serious current-affairs show *Today* considers my reported emerging from retirement a newsworthy item at breakfast time. A nation chokes on its corn-flakes, then digs out its eighties/nineties party gear.

ACKNOWLEDGMENTS

THIS BOOK, ALTHOUGH called "a memoir," would not have been possible without the help of many people.

Firstly, I need to thank Craig McLean, who listened to me going on and on for months, and then had to transcribe my ramblings into some sort of order, present them to me and stand back while his fine work was decimated by yours truly. Infinite thanks, mate.

Also to my editor, Trevor Dolby, who, just when I thought I'd gotten it right, jumped in with something even better. TD, thank you, sir.

Thanks, too, to Lizzy Gaisford in Trevor's office, who steadied the ship and carried out all the tasks that no one wanted to do. Thanks also to all at Penguin Random House U.K., especially: Susan Sandon, Jason Smith, Charlotte Bush and Celeste Ward-Best.

Thanks, too, to Kevin Doughten, my U.S. editor, who kept an international eye on things. And all at Penguin Random House U.S., especially: David Drake, Molly Stern, Tricia Boczkowski, Christopher Brand and Jesse Aylen. And the lovely Lorenzo Agius, who took the jacket photograph.

Of course, a life is empty without the people who fill it, so I thank, from the bottom of my heart, my children. Joely, Simon, Lily,

Nicholas and Mathew, I have learned from you all. I may be Dad, but you have all taught me.

My partners in life. Andy, Jill, Orianne and Dana. Thank you for putting up with me. You all will always have a place in my heart.

To all the musicians who have put their careers on the line by working with me, tons of love and thanks.

Dear Tony Smith, thanks for your wisdom, love and guidance.

Also thanks to the long-suffering Jo Greenwood at TSPM.

Danny Gillen, and Steve Jones, my "go-to guys," and also my mates.

And to all the fans who have stood by me through fax and thin. Love you.

PC

PHOTO CREDITS

TEXT PHOTO CREDITS

Prologue: Greeting the audience on the First Final Farewell Tour, 2004/5.

Chapter 1: A very young PC on Mum's lap in our swish Zephyr 6. No seat belts! Circa 1956.

Chapter 2: The Mod, taken by Lavinia in our living room at 453 Hanworth Road, circa 1966. (© Genesis Archive)

Chapter 3: At the Converted Cruiser Club HQ on my sixteenth birthday, 1967. (© Genesis Archive)

Chapter 4: Phil Spector and George Harrison at Abbey Road, 1970. (© Bettmann/Contributor/Getty)

Chapter 5: Genesis mean and moody in a field, circa 1973. (© Barry Wentzell)

Chapter 6: Peter Gabriel in his frock and wearing the fox mask, circa 1972. (© Armando Gallo)

Chapter 7: The new Genesis line-up with drummer Bill Bruford at the back, circa 1976. (© Waring Abbott)

Chapter 8: Cutting a rather current "dash" in the days when I could take my shirt off, circa 1976. (© Waring Abbott)

Chapter 9: On an endless tour somewhere reading the newspapers. (© Genesis Archive)

Chapter 10: In the Old Croft studio, circa 1982. (© Armando Gallo)

Chapter 11: With HRH Princess of Wales at the Royal Albert Hall for a Prince's Trust show, circa 1983.

Chapter 12: At Old Croft writing and recording, circa 1983.

Chapter 13: At Live Aid, Wembley, 1985, at the beginning of a long day. (© Popperfoto/Getty)

Chapter 14: The opening scene of *Buster*, 1987. (© Michael Ochs Archives/Handout/Getty)

Chapter 15: Outtake from the "I Can't Dance" video with my pals, circa 1992. (© Henry Diltz)

Chapter 16: Rehearsals for the *Both Sides* tour. This was a great stage to play with, circa 1993/4. (© The Douglas Brothers)

Chapter 17: On my boat to Lac Léman, turning my back on everything, circa 1996.

Chapter 18: Greeting Nelson Mandela and the Queen at the Royal Albert Hall in London, with Hugh Masekela looking on, 1996.

Chapter 19: Party at the Palace, 2002. I played drums in the House Band, but I was persuaded to sing a song. I was much happier at the back, believe me. (© Tim Rooke/REX/Shutterstock)

Chapter 20: One of my proudest moments: a billboard on Broadway for *Tarzan: The Musical*, 2006. It also signaled the beginning of a low point in my life.

Chapter 21: The grim truth. In the Lausanne hospital fighting for survival, 2012.

Chapter 22: Not dead yet, still got things to do. In New York, 2015. (© Patrick Balls)

ABOUT THE AUTHOR

Born in the United Kingdom, Phil Collins rose to fame as the drummer and frontman of Genesis before establishing himself as a solo artist and selling hundreds of millions of records throughout his career.